Past and Present Publi

CW01011270

Horses, Oxen and Technological Innovation

Past and Present Publications

General Editor: PAUL SLACK, *Exeter College, Oxford*

Past and Present Publications comprise books similar in character to the articles in the journal *Past and Present*. Whether the volumes in the series are collections of essays – some previously published, others new studies – or monographs, they encompass a wide variety of scholarly and original works primarily concerned with social, economic and cultural changes, and their causes and consequences. They will appeal to both specialists and non-specialists and will endeavour to communicate the results of historical and allied research in readable and lively form. This series continues and expands in its aims the volumes previously published elsewhere.

For a list of titles in Past and Present Publications, see end of book.

Horses, Oxen and Technological Innovation

The Use of Draught Animals in English Farming from 1066 to 1500

JOHN LANGDON
Assistant Professor, University of Alberta

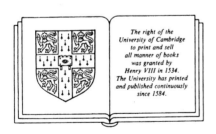

The right of the
University of Cambridge
to print and sell
all manner of books
was granted by
Henry VIII in 1534.
The University has printed
and published continuously
since 1584.

CAMBRIDGE UNIVERSITY PRESS

Cambridge
London   New York   New Rochelle
Melbourne   Sydney

PUBLISHED BY THE PRESS SYNDICATE OF THE UNIVERSITY OF CAMBRIDGE
The Pitt Building, Trumpington Street, Cambridge, United Kingdom

CAMBRIDGE UNIVERSITY PRESS
The Edinburgh Building, Cambridge CB2 2RU, UK
40 West 20th Street, New York NY 10011–4211, USA
477 Williamstown Road, Port Melbourne, VIC 3207, Australia
Ruiz de Alarcón 13, 28014 Madrid, Spain
Dock House, The Waterfront, Cape Town 8001, South Africa

http://www.cambridge.org

First published 1986
First paperback edition 2002

A catalogue record for this book is available from the British Library

Library of Congress Cataloguing in Publication data
Langdon, John.
Horses, oxen, and technological innovation.
(Past and Present publications)
Bibliography: p.
Includes index.
1. Draft horses – England – History. 2. Oxen –
England – History. 3. Animal traction – England – History.
4. Agricultural innovations – England – History.
5. Agriculture – England – History. I. Title.
SF311.3.G7L36 1986 631.3'71 85-31424

ISBN 0 521 26772 2 hardback
ISBN 0 521 52508 X paperback

TO LYNNE

Contents

Figures

Note on maps: The county boundaries shown are those that existed between 1935 and 1974 (Yorkshire being further divided into its three Ridings on the maps), and it is these boundaries that have been used to determine the counties for the various places mentioned in the text and appendix. It is to be noted, however, that there are some discrepancies between these relatively recent boundaries and those that existed in medieval times, although in general these differences are minor and only affect a few of the places mentioned in this study.

Tables

Preface

In a work of this size it is inevitable that the author should accumulate many debts. Chief among these on the academic side is that owed to Dr Christopher Dyer, who supervised this study from its inception and has been a constant source of help and encouragement. He has also read and criticized this work in its entirety in all except the final few drafts and has provided me with much in the way of transcripted material from his own researches. In a similar way, Professor Rodney Hilton, Jean Birrell, Dr Janet Williamson and Gabriele Scardellato have also kindly supplied me with relevant information from their own work, for which I am deeply grateful. Thanks must also go to Professor Ralph Davis, Mr Philip Brooks, Professor Paul Harvey, Dr Bruce Campbell, Dr E. J. T. Collins, Mr Kyle Rae, Dr J. A. Perkins, Dr J. Binns, Mr A. M. A. Woods, Dr David Howlett, and all the members of the Friday Night seminar group at Birmingham, who have allowed me to make use of unpublished material or have offered helpful advice or criticism over the years. I also owe a debt of gratitude to my new colleagues and students at Alberta and especially to Lydia Dugbazah of the secretarial staff, who coped gallantly with the typing of the final draft, and to Marg McIntyre, Marion Johnson and Mary Stares, who helped with the editing out of typographical and other errors. Geoff Lester and Michael Fisher of the Cartographic Division of the Department of Geography here at Alberta did a fine job in preparing the maps and graphs, and the Photography Department of Technical Services dealt very capably with the reproduction of the photographs taken from published works. It scarcely needs saying that without the help of all the above-named this study would be much poorer than it is, although, of course, any errors or imperfections are entirely my own responsibility.

In addition, I am indebted to the Oxford University Press, Editions Gallimard, Editions A. and J. Picard, David and Charles

Ltd, Phaidon Press, *Tools and Tillage*, the Bodleian Library and the British Library for allowing me to reproduce illustrations from their various publications and documents; and to all the personnel in the various record offices and repositories around England, who coped with my enquiries and requests for documents with unfailing patience and courtesy. Special mention must also be made here to Didi, Bill and Peter Mountford, for their warm, generous and entertaining hospitality in providing me with accommodation during all my research trips to London.

Finally, my deepest and most heart-felt gratitude is reserved for my wife Lynne, who has sacrificed much so that I could embark upon my researches in medieval technology. Without her continual support and frequent prodding, this study would not have seen the light of day, and it is to her that this work is dedicated.

Abbreviations

S.R.O.	Somerset Record Office (Taunton)
T.C.L.	Trinity College Library (Cambridge)
W.A.M.	Westminster Abbey Muniments Room
Wa.R.O.	Warwickshire Record Office (Warwick)
W.C.L.	Worcester Cathedral Library
Wi.R.O.	Wiltshire Record Office (Trowbridge)
Wo.R.O.	Worcestershire Record Office (Worcester)
W.Suff.R.O.	West Suffolk Record Office (Bury St Edmunds)
W.Suss.R.O.	West Sussex Record Office (Chichester)

(b) PERIODICALS

Agric. Hist. Rev.	*Agricultural History Review*
Econ. Hist. Rev.	*Economic History Review*
Eng. Hist. Rev.	*English Historical Review*

Introduction

The role of technology in moulding social and economic change is one of the most important – and yet, curiously, often one of the least understood – of historical phenomena. This is particularly the case when dealing with any era before the last two or three centuries, since it is only in the industrial age that a substantial interest in inventions and inventors becomes commonplace in the records and literary tradition of the time. For earlier civilizations references to technological events are relatively rare with a strong emphasis on the eccentric and anecdotal.[1]

However, the lack of readily accessible information concerning technological change in pre-industrial societies does not in any way diminish the importance of the subject. The success (or failure) of technological innovations was as crucial for early civilizations as it is today; and, although the record of these changes is much less prominent for these earlier periods, a progression of notable technological changes from ancient to industrial times can still be discerned.[2] Nevertheless, although the fact that these changes were occurring is not usually denied, the pattern and timing of their dissemination and – more pertinently – their position in the hierarchy of factors promoting social and economic change is often a subject of intense debate.

Accordingly, it is the purpose of this enquiry to examine closely

---

[1] A typical English example being the story of Eilmar of Malmesbury, who, c. 1010, constructed a glider, took off with it from the top of the tower of Malmesbury Abbey and broke both his legs in the resulting crash, after apparently flying for 600 feet. Lynn White, Jr, "The Expansion of Technology 500–1500", in C. M. Cipolla (ed.), *The Middle Ages* (The Fontana Economic History of Europe, i, London, 1972), p. 168.

[2] The most useful compendiums for these changes are C. Singer, E. J. Holmyard, A. R. Hall and T. I. Williams (eds.), *A History of Technology*, esp. vols. i–iii (Oxford, 1954–8) and M. Daumas (ed.), *A History of Technology and Invention*, vols. i–ii (New York, 1962–4).

one of the more well-known of early innovations as it related to medieval English agriculture: that is, the introduction of horses to draught work on English farms as a replacement for oxen. Since horses had theoretical advantages of speed and strength over oxen, their potential for improving traction, both on and off the farm, was substantial, and consequently it is a subject which has already attracted a good deal of important work.[3] It is also a subject upon which historians are very much divided, with some writers seeing the development of horse-power as one of the crucial events in the development of the medieval economy and society, while others claim that it was almost totally irrelevant.[4] Indeed, it is this wide divergence of views over the matter which makes it in many ways an ideal subject to study. It is in order to examine the problem more objectively that a detailed assessment of the introduction of the work-horse to one country over a period of nearly four hundred and fifty years has here been attempted. Particular aims in this study are (1) to determine the proportion of horses versus oxen engaged in English farm work at various stages throughout the medieval and somewhat into the early modern period; (2) to show how these progressive changes in the proportion of horses versus oxen were reflected in changes in practice, particularly regarding ploughing, harrowing and hauling; (3) to investigate the size of the medieval plough-team (with the significance that this had for such matters as the origins of the open-field system); (4) to determine the relationship between plough and vehicle design and the employment of horses and oxen; and (5) to discuss the various considerations influencing demesne[5] and peasant policy as regards the use of horses

---

[3] Particularly among the French, for which see R. Lefebvre des Noëttes' classic study, *L'Attelage et le Cheval de Selle à Travers les Âges* (Paris, 1931) and more latterly J. Spruytte, *Études Expérimentales sur l'Attelage* (Paris, 1977; now published in English as *Early Harness Systems: Experimental Studies*, London, 1983) and R.-H. and A.-M. Bautier, "Contribution à l'Histoire du Cheval au Moyen Âge", *Bulletin Philologique et Historique* (1976 and 1978).

[4] For the view of horse-power as a crucial medieval development, see Lynn White Jr, *Medieval Technology and Social Change* (Oxford, 1962), pp. 57–69; J. Gimpel, *The Medieval Machine* (London, 1977), pp. 32–8. For the opposing view, see R. H. Hilton and P. H. Sawyer, "Technical Determinism: The Stirrup and the Plough", *Past and Present*, no. 24 (1963), pp. 99–100; R. Trow-Smith, *A History of British Livestock Husbandry to 1700* (London, 1957), pp. 92–3; J. Z. Titow, *English Rural Society 1200–1350* (London, 1969), pp. 38–40.

[5] The demesne here being the lord's farm as opposed to those lands held by his tenants.

and oxen. Finally, the diverse strands raised by these issues will be brought together in a concluding chapter during which – among other things – the horse as a technological innovation will be judged against the various social and economic theories currently extant.

The approach followed in undertaking this programme will be based almost purely upon documentary evidence, including Domesday Book, surveys and extents, leases, exchequer pipe roll material, demesne accounts, detailed lay subsidy tax assessments, court rolls, probate wills and inventories, and sundry other records covering the period from the eleventh to the sixteenth century.[6] Iconographic and archaeological sources, which in themselves could provide the basis for viable studies, are also considered, but reference to them has been limited to work or illustrations already published. Finally, it should be mentioned here that only animals involved in farm work are included in this analysis. Thus, except for occasional references, riding animals are excluded, as are horses and oxen used on the transportation network for other than agricultural purposes. Relevant sources relating to road transport do exist, of course, and will be referred to from time to time, but the rural records are the best for obtaining a comprehensive and consistent view of the problem of medieval traction, including comparisons over time.

[6] Discussion of the failings and merits of each of these sources will occur at the proper time in the body of the study.

1. *The work-horse as a technological innovation*

It is possible that a certain difficulty occurs in imagining the introduction of the work-horse as a technological innovation, since, whatever its advantages, the simple substitution of one animal for another might appear to be technologically irrelevant. But in fact this "simple" transition marks the culmination of a series of intricate mechanical and biological changes. These involved not only developments in harnessing, shoeing and breeding, but also refinements in plough and vehicle design. It was, in essence, the substitution of one technological package for another, for which the physical replacement of the ox by the horse in front of the cart or plough was simply the most eye-catching step.

At the outset, however, it should be pointed out that, when we consider horse and ox traction during the period of this study, we are dealing largely with finished technological products, that is, those for which most of the practical problems have already been ironed out. Thus this investigation has at least one important limitation as a technical study, and this is that we are not dealing with the whole of a technological process but only a part of it. Applying a classification worked out by Bertrand Gille, the progression of a technique may be said to fall into five phases: (1) the original idea, (2) testing and perfecting, (3) innovation (that is, the spread of the technique), (4) development (economic consequences of the basic technique and improvements and adaptations upon it) and (5) disappearance.[1] Consequently it is obvious (or soon will be obvious) that, as regards horse traction during the period of this study, we are dealing almost solely with steps three and four and with ox traction mostly step five, although elements of step four are also involved with the latter. This limitation, however, should not be taken too

---

[1] As outlined in M. Daumas, "The History of Technology: its Aims, its Limits, its Methods", *History of Technology*, i (1976), p. 106.

seriously as a criticism of the topic we have chosen to study, since
with almost any aspect of medieval technology we would have been
faced with the same problem: the creative and experimental phases
very seldom come to light in the records.
The stages corresponding to steps one and two in Gille's outline
can at least be sketched in lightly, though. Systems of both ox and
horse traction existed very early in ancient times. Oxen and
donkeys, for instance, were first harnessed at about the dawn of the
historic period (4000–3000 B.C.) and horses perhaps a little later (*c.*
2000 B.C. or after).[2] Then, as now, ox traction was based on a system of yoking, either to the horns or round the neck. The latter
arrangement was made possible by the ox's somewhat bony back
which provided humps between which the neck yoke could comfort-
ably sit,[3] and where, once positioned, it could be secured to the
animal by means of ropes, ox-bows or any other suitable method.[4]
In almost all ancient societies oxen were yoked in single pairs to the
central shaft or rope of the vehicle or plough, as shown in Figure 1.
If more than two animals were required, the tendency was to yoke
abreast rather than in file, a phenomenon noted with much surprise
by R. Lefebvre des Noëttes in his well-known study on the subject,[5]
although more recent research has indicated that ox-yoking in file
may have been more common than he thought.[6]
The system for harnessing equids (that is, horses, donkeys and
mules) was very similar. Donkeys seem to have been yoked in a
fashion identical to oxen (see Figure 2), but for horses and probably
mules a modified version, known as throat-and-girth harness, was
employed, as shown in Figure 3. Here the feature of the yoke was
kept, but adapted to the horse's more upright stance by means of

[2] R. Lefebvre des Noëttes, *L'Attelage et le Cheval de Selle*, p. 25; C. Singer, E. J.
Holmyard, A. R. Hall, and T. I. Williams (eds.), *A History of Technology*, 7 vols.
(Oxford, 1954–78), i, p. 721; A. Burford, "Heavy Transport in Classical
Antiquity", *Econ. Hist. Rev.*, 2nd series, xiii (1960), pp. 7–8·
[3] J. Needham, *Science and Civilisation in China*, 7 vols. (Cambridge, 1954–in
progress), iv, pt 2 (1965), p. 306.
[4] Several examples of yoke types are shown in A. G. Haudricourt and M. J.-B.
Delamarre, *L'Homme et la Charrue à travers le monde* (Paris, 1955), p. 165; see
also G. W. B. Huntingford, "Prehistoric Ox-yoking", *Antiquity*, vii (1934),
p. 457.
[5] Lefebvre des Noëttes, *L'Attelage*, p. 16.
[6] Haudricourt and Delamarre, *L'Homme et la Charrue*, pp. 115–17; Burford,
"Heavy Transport", pp. 5, 13; Needham, *Science and Civilisation*, iv, pt 2, p. 329.

Fig. 1: Etruscan scratch-plough and two-ox team. A bronze figure from Arezzo (as shown in A. G. Haudricourt and M. J.-B. Delamarre, *L'Homme et la Charrue à Travers le Monde* (Paris, 1955), photo 14, opp. p. 97; copyright Editions Gallimard).

Fig. 2: Oxen and donkeys yoked for hauling. From Trajan's Column (R. Lefebvre de Noëttes, *L'Attelage et le Cheval de Selle à Travers les Âges* (Paris, 1931), fig. 84; reproduced by permission of Editions A. and J. Picard).

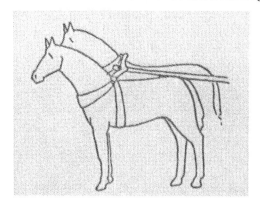

Fig. 3: Diagram of throat-and-girth harness. Drawing after Lefebvre des Noëttes (as taken from Haudricourt and Delamarre, *L'Homme et la Charrue à Travers le Monde*, p. 169; copyright Editions Gallimard).

two supple bands, one encircling the throat and the other the belly.[7] Lefebvre des Noëttes noted that a problem with this method of harnessing was that the throat band tended to slide up the horse's neck to a point where the animal was virtually being strangled.[8] Recent work has indicated that this choking could have been minimized or even avoided altogether by sensible positioning of the straps,[9] but it may always have been a problem to prevent horses from pulling their full weight.

As with oxen, arrangements of more than two horses were made frontally rather than in file, and indeed teams of three or four horses abreast were commonly used for pulling chariots at this time.[10] Lefebvre des Noëttes noted that often only the two inside animals in the team were yoked to the shaft of the vehicle.[11] Horses on the outside were connected by a single rope leading to the top of the throat-and-girth harness, and consequently these animals wasted much of their energy by pulling at an angle to the most effective line of

[7] On occasion, though, only a throat band is evident; e.g. see Singer et al., *History of Technology*, ii, p. 543, fig. 498.
[8] Lefebvre des Noëttes, *L'Attelage*, p. 13.
[9] J. Spruytte, *Études Expérimentales sur l'Attelage*, esp. pp. 9–15, 101–7.
[10] For example, Lefebvre des Noëttes, *L'Attelage*, figs. 21, 54–5, 58–60, 68, 70–1; Singer et al., *History of Technology*, ii, pp. 542–3.
[11] Lefebvre des Noëttes, *L'Attelage*, p. 14.

thrust. An attempt was made to overcome this by employing large frontal yokes, accommodating four rather than just two animals, or by adding extra draught-poles to the front of the vehicle,[12] but even so such systems were manifestly less versatile than a team of horses in single or double file, simply because the number of horses possible abreast was limited by such factors as the width of the road.

Altogether the placing of animals abreast coupled with the potentially disabling effects of the throat-and-girth harness meant that horse traction in particular was likely to be severely limited in ancient times. This is indicated by the Theodosian Code of 438 A.D., which restricted the weights to be drawn by teams to just under 500 kilograms in total, including the vehicles, allegedly to protect the animals from injury.[13] In contrast, by the middle of the nineteenth century, teams of four to eight horses were pulling coach-loads of 6,000 to 9,000 kilograms, well over ten times the Theodosian limits.[14] As a result, horses in ancient times were virtually employed only for pulling light chariots, the aim, apart from their military uses, being "to have a fine show of horses rearing and struggling, and drawing a ridiculously light load as fast as possible".[15] If equid traction were used at all for more practical purposes, it was limited mainly to mules and donkeys;[16] otherwise, oxen carried all the burden for ploughing and hauling in ancient times.[17]

Essentially this pattern did not change until after the collapse of the Roman Empire in the West, although towards the end of the Roman era we do find a quickening in the use of horses for other

---

[12] *Ibid.*, pp. 14–15, 70, 76–7; also figs. 52, 60, 69.

[13] *Ibid.*, pp. 162–4, 157–8; A. C. Leighton, *Transport and Communication in Early Medieval Europe AD 500–1100* (Newton Abbot, 1972), p. 72. Curiously the laws also applied to oxen, although it seems certain they were capable of much heavier loads (e.g., see Burford, "Heavy Transport", pp. 4–5, 9).

[14] Lefebvre des Noëttes, *L'Attelage*, pp. 128–9.

[15] Burford, "Heavy Transport", p. 9.

[16] Mules were employed to haul Alexander the Great's funeral chariot (Lefebvre des Noëttes, *L'Attelage*, pp. 69–71), while donkeys were often used for hauling in Egyptian and Roman times (*ibid.*, pp. 52, 87, fig. 84). Mules and donkeys were also used for ploughing light soils (Columella, *De Re Rustica*, ii, trans. E. S. Forster and E. H. Heffner (London, 1954), Book VI, p. 223; Book VII, p. 231; Singer et al., *History of Technology*, ii, p. 91).

[17] See, for instance, Lefebvre des Noëttes, *L'Attelage*, p. 86 and figs. 84–6; Haudricourt and Delamarre, *L'Homme et la Charrue*, plates V and VI (between pp. 128–9).

purposes than display or sport, primarily for hauling coaches and wagons.[18] It is at this stage that we begin to perceive the first glimmerings of what we might call a new system of traction, one that would dramatically raise the value of the horse as a beast of work. This new system was composed of several technological elements, many of which could be claimed as major innovations in their own right. Treating them roughly in order of their importance, these are: (1) The modern harness. Most of what we know about the development of the modern harness stems from the work of Lefebvre des Noëttes (see above). As he pointed out, the main defect with ancient methods of horse harnessing was that they were likely to choke the animals. In the end, two separate solutions were found: the breast-strap harness and the collar-harness, shown in Figures 4 and 5 respectively. Both worked by removing the point of application of the harness from the throat to a less sensitive area: the breast-strap harness by setting the throat band horizontally so that it bore more against the horse's chest, and the collar by being made large enough so that it rested on the horse's shoulder-blades rather than round its neck. In both cases the yoke was eliminated, to be replaced by traces or lateral shafts attached to one or both sides of the harness (see Figures 4–6 and 8–10).

Although it is not a matter of certainty, it appears from philological evidence that the breast-strap harness arrived in Europe at about the sixth century A.D.[19] From the same evidence the collar-harness did not appear in the West until two or three centuries later,[20] although, once arrived, it soon began to compete successfully with the breast-strap harness, and probably even more so once the technique for padding the collar became common. By the twelfth and thirteenth centuries, according to drawings from illumi-

---

[18] As indicated by various late Roman illustrations: e.g., Singer et al., *History of Technology*, ii, pp. 546, 553 (figs. 494 and 506); Leighton, *Transport and Communication*, pp. 77–81.

[19] Haudricourt and Delamarre, *L'Homme et la Charrue*, p. 178. The first pictorial representation of the breast-strap harness in western Europe appears at the base of an eighth-century Irish cross (Singer et al., *History of Technology*, ii, p. 544, fig. 507). Needham, *Science and Civilisation*, iv, pt 2, pp. 304–28, claims that both the breast-strap and collar-harness originated in China.

[20] Haudricourt and Delamarre, *L'Homme et la Charrue*, p. 178. The first picture of it appears in the ninth century (White, *Medieval Technology and Social Change*, p. 61).

Fig. 4: Breast-strap harness. From a bone carving on a Byzantine casket. Ninth century A.D. (from C. Singer, E. J. Holmyard, A. R. Hall and T. I. Williams (eds.), *A History of Technology*, 5 vols. (Oxford, 1954–8), ii, p. 553; reproduced by permission of the Oxford University Press).

nated manuscripts of the time, the collar-harness was predominant in Western Europe.[21]

(2) Horseshoeing. This markedly improved the endurance of the horse, particularly in the cold, wet climate of northern Europe, where hooves tended to get soft and prone to wear, leading eventually to lameness. Shoeing prevented this premature wearing down of hooves and also allowed the horse to get a better grip on the road surface. Archaeological evidence shows that the horseshoe was known in Roman times, both as a hipposandal and in the more modern version of a bent strip of iron nailed to the horse's hoof.[22] There is, however, a puzzling hiatus from the end of the Roman era, when horseshoes fail to appear in iconographic or literary sources until the ninth century.[23] It is difficult to know whether this is due to the inadequacies of the sources or whether an actual break in the use of horseshoes occurred. In any case, when they reappear in the

[21] See, for instance, the numerous examples provided by Lefebvre des Noëttes, *L'Attelage*, figs. 147–62.

[22] R. E. M. and T. V. Wheeler, *Verulamium: a Belgic and two Roman Cities* (Oxford, 1936), p. 220; R. E. M. Wheeler, *Maiden Castle, Dorset* (Oxford, 1943), pp. 77, 290–1, pl. XXXb; C. F. C. Hawkes and M. R. Hull, *Camulodunum* (Oxford, 1947), pp. 73, 342–3; Leighton, *Transport and Communication*, pp. 104–7; C. Green, "The Purpose of the Early Horseshoe", *Antiquity*, xl (1966), pp. 305–7.

[23] According to the work of Lefebvre des Noëttes, *L'Attelage*, see especially p. 145 and figs. 190–2.

Fig. 5: Collar-harness. From a tenth-century Frankish manuscript (Singer et al., *History of Technology*, ii, p. 554; reproduced by permission of the Oxford University Press).

documents, their adoption seems to have been rapid; by the eleventh century horseshoeing was an almost universal practice.[24]

(3) Harnessing in file. As has been indicated, this was not a noted feature of traction in ancient times, particularly for horses, for which examples of harnessing in file are rare before the end of the Roman era.[25] In contrast, during the medieval period teams arranged in single or double file were the rule almost everywhere, although the first depictions of harnessing in such a fashion do not occur until the tenth or eleventh century.[26] Certainly harnessing in file held great advantages for traction, in that theoretically unlimited power could be added to the team by simply attaching extra units of horses or oxen to the front of the line. In this way some very large teams are recorded for the medieval period; one in France was comprised of twenty-six pairs of oxen.[27]

[24] White, *Medieval Technology and Social Change*, pp. 58–9; Lefebvre des Noëttes, *L'Attelage*, pp. 145–6.

[25] A four-wheeled wagon hauled by four horses in double file is shown on a Gallo-Roman bas-relief found at Langres in 1849. Lefebvre des Noëttes, *L'Attelage*, p. 85; Leighton, *Transport and Communication*, p. 81; Spruytte, *Études Expérimentales sur l'Attelage*, p. 138 (pl. 37).

[26] Perhaps the earliest being the eleventh-century Cottonian MS illustration of an English four-ox plough-team in double file (see Figure 13).

[27] Employed for hauling the capitals and columns for a church at Conques en Rouerges (Lefebvre des Noëttes, *L'Attelage*, p. 132).

(4) Whippletrees, also known in England as whiffletrees, swingle-trees, splinter bars, or swing bars. These are simple bars of wood, attached at their ends to the horses' traces and at their centre to the plough or vehicle, as shown in Figure 6, or else by small lengths of chain or rope to combinations of other whippletrees, which are themselves eventually attached to the vehicle, a typical layout being shown in Figure 7. Whippletrees were an important development for traction. First of all, they allowed much more flexibility in har-nessing arrangements; teams for odd numbers of animals, for instance, could be made up much more easily than under the old sys-tem of yoking (Figure 7). Manoeuvring was made much easier, too, in that the whippletrees equalized the stress on the traces when turn-ing and kept reins and traces apart.[28] Finally, the whippletree pro-vided a cushioning effect for horses in particular as they took up the strain of hauling or ploughing. This last was important because horses tended to pull in jerks, exposing both animals and equipment to injury unless precautions were taken to counter it.[29]

The whippletree may have been an invention dating from the pre-historic era, but the point is one of conjecture.[30] In any case, it seems to have been unknown in medieval Europe until it first turns up in the twelfth-century Herrad of Landsberg illustration shown in Figure 6. Thereafter it becomes a common feature in depictions of medieval traction,[31] although mainly for horse-ploughing. Oxen, with their more deliberate pull, did not need the protection of a whippletree as much; nor did horses hauling in tandem apparently, for in none of the illustrations showing such an arrangement is there a whippletree (see, for example, Figures 8 and 10).

(5) Traces. The use of rope and leather for harnessing animals in

---

[28] Leighton, *Transport and Communication*, pp. 114–17; *The Book of Husbandry by Master Fitzherbert* (1534 edition), ed. W. W. Skeat (London, 1882), p. 25.
[29] Leighton, *Transport and Communication*, p. 115.
[30] A. Steensberg, "The Vebbestrup Plough", *Acta Archaeologica*, xvi (1945), p. 65, feels it was a feature of the Vebbestrup plough (from Jutland in Denmark, *c.* 500–100 B.C.). Haudricourt and Delamarre, *L'Homme et la Charrue*, p. 185, disagree strongly. On the other hand, Needham, *Science and Civilisation*, iv, pt 2, p. 328n., believes that whippletrees were employed in third-century A.D. China at the latest.
[31] E.g. Lefebvre des Noëttes, *L'Attelage*, figs. 150–1; A. Steensberg, "North West European Plough-types of Prehistoric Times and the Middle Ages", *Acta Archaeologica*, vii (1936), pp. 272–3 (figs. 15 and 17); Singer et al., *History of Technology*, ii, p. 94 (fig. 59); Haudricourt and Delamarre, *L'Homme et la Charrue*, pp. 360, 365 (figs. 141 and 147).

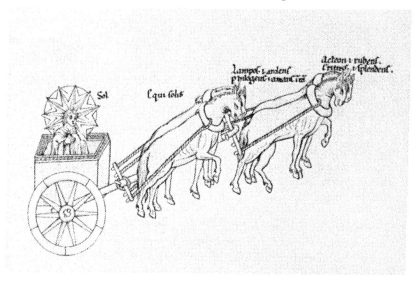

Fig. 6: Padded horse-collars, traces and whippletrees. Herrad of Landsberg, *Hortus Deliciarum*, c. 1170 (as shown in A. C. Leighton, *Transport and Communications in Early Medieval Europe AD 500–1100* (Newton Abbot, 1972), p. 114; reproduced by permission of the author and David and Charles Ltd).

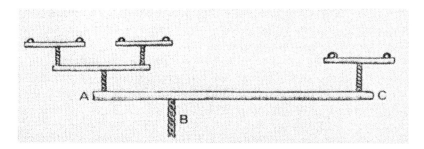

Fig. 7: Nineteenth-century arrangement of whippletrees for a three-horse team (from A. T. Lucas, "Irish Ploughing Practices, Part Three", *Tools and Tillage*, ii, pt 3 (1974), p. 150; reproduced by permission of *Tools and Tillage*).

Fig. 8: Baggage-wagon (with postillion) and wheelbarrow. French manuscript, 1460 (Singer et al., *History of Technology*, ii, p. 547; reproduced by permission of the Oxford University Press).

more complicated fashion than simple yoking became more and more prevalent in the medieval period. Principally, traces formed flexible extensions for the plough and vehicle shafts or draught-pole and so were vital for harnessing in file, either double or tandem (Figures 8, 10, and 11). In combination with whippletrees they provided even greater flexibility, particularly when used with the collar-harness (Figures 6 and 9).

(6) Changes in vehicle design. These took several forms, including the development of lighter, spoked wheels, which offered less resistance to draught, and the substitution of the single vehicle shaft or draught-pole with a double one, in between which a single animal, usually a horse, could be installed. The latter facilitated single file or tandem harnessing, shown in Figure 10, for which the advantages were ease of turning and a more balanced traction. Moreover, because of the horse between the shafts, particularly if it were the only animal in the team, the cart or wagon could easily be reversed as well as pulled forward. The same horse also provided a substantial braking effect against the vehicle when going downhill.[32]

Tandem harnessing was seemingly little known in the ancient European world, although a few examples of single animals harnessed between shafts do exist from the later Roman era.[33] However, it was not until well into the medieval period that double-

[32] Leighton, *Transport and Communication*, p. 112.
[33] Singer et al., *History of Technology*, ii, p. 544 (fig. 489); White, *Medieval Technology and Social Change*, p. 60; Leighton, *Transport and Communication*, pp. 112, 204, and figures on pp. 149, 150.

Fig. 9: Horse-ploughing with padded collar, traces, whippletrees and plough superstructure for reins (presumably attached to the horse's bit, although discontinued in the drawing). From a thirteenth-century Brussels manuscript (drawing after Lefebvre des Noëttes; taken from Haudricourt and Delamarre, *L'Homme et la Charrue*, p. 364; copyright Editions Gallimard).

shafted vehicles and harnessing in tandem became commonplace.[34] Similarly, spoked wheels, although certainly well-known in ancient times,[35] probably did not reach their full potential as load carriers until the later middle ages.[36]

(7) Changes in plough design. The most important development here was the spread of the heavy plough in northern Europe as a replacement for the earlier scratch plough or ard. Unlike the innovations listed above, however, the heavy plough cannot be rated as an improvement for traction, but rather as a change to which the available traction had to adjust. Consequently alterations in plough design that directly improved the effectiveness of animal power were more in the way of minor adjustments, such as – occasionally – the superstructure for the reins shown in Figure 9.[37] This provided better control of the team and to a large extent eliminated the need for a *fugator*, or driver, shown holding a long whip in Figure 11.

---

[34] All medieval illustrations showing harnessing in tandem tend to be twelfth-century or later: e.g., Singer et al., *History of Technology*, ii, pp. 547–9 (figs. 496–7, 499–500).

[35] *Ibid.*, i, pp. 211–14.   [36] *Ibid.*, ii, pp. 548–9.

[37] Similar arrangements for plough-reins were also suitable for small teams of oxen. Haudricourt and Delamarre, *L'Homme et la Charrue*, p. 365 (fig. 147) and photos 52 and 55 (opposite pp. 440 and 441).

Fig. 10: Tandem harnessing, showing padded collars, traces, cart-saddle, double-shafted vehicle and horseshoes. From the Luttrell Psalter, *c.* 1340 (Brit. Lib. Add. MS 42130, fo. 162; reproduced by permission of the British Library).

(8) Miscellaneous developments. These included incidental items, such as improvements in reins, bits and bridles, or relatively new developments, such as cart-saddles and postillions. All of these were designed to enhance the control over the team, or, in the case of the cart-saddles, to distribute the weight of the shafts more evenly over the horse's back (as shown in Figure 10). Such changes are perhaps minor in themselves and were certainly not applicable in every case, but they do show that ingenuity in matters of harnessing was an on-going process in the middle ages. The idea of men riding postillion – see Figure 8 – as an alternative to reins for directing teams in file was a distinctively medieval invention.[38]

When taken together, the innovations and inventions listed above considerably increased the effectiveness of animal power in the middle ages. The point here is not to look at any one development, such as the modern collar-harness, as being crucial. Rather there was a whole series of improvements, some of them known in Roman times and before, which gradually coalesced into a new system or systems of traction. These improvements were especially beneficial to horse traction, where harnessing for all types of work had attained considerable sophistication by the medieval era, as is amply shown in Figures 9 and 10. Ox traction, on the other hand,

[38] Singer et al., *History of Technology*, ii, p. 555.

Fig. 11: Ox-ploughing, showing yokes and double file harnessing. Luttrell Psalter (Brit. Lib. Add. MS 42130, fo. 170; reproduced by permission of the British Library).

was less affected, and even as detailed a representation as that contained in the Luttrell Psalter (Figure 11) indicates that arrangements for harnessing or yoking oxen in the middle ages were still essentially the same as in ancient times, with the possible exception of yoking in file, and even this, as we have seen, may have been known in the earlier period. Some shoeing of oxen was introduced, but it was always less common than in the case of horses.[39] Altogether the improvements to horse traction far outweighed those for ox traction, and as a result this allowed the horse to catch up to and, in many cases, surpass the ox in terms of work efficiency and animal economy.

The same may also have been the case with breeding. This of course applied to horses and oxen alike. The size and strength of one animal versus the other clearly had great importance in the choice of draught animal. Although there is some controversy over the matter, it appears that improvements in the size of both horses

---

[39] For example, see J. Langdon, "The Economics of Horses and Oxen in Medieval England", *Agric. Hist. Rev.*, xxx (1982), p. 35.

and oxen were occurring throughout the medieval period. In the case of cattle, late medieval bone and horn finds from Kirkstall Abbey (Yorkshire) and Baynard's Castle in London show a significant increase in cattle size over that in Anglo-Saxon times and earlier.[40] P. L. Armitage argues that most of this improvement in size dates from the late fourteenth century and after, corresponding to a change in cattle type from a small, short-horned variety to a larger, long-horned animal. Armitage feels that this was not a new breed imported from the Continent, but a result of gradually improving techniques of cattle breeding and keeping.[41] This is supported by documentary evidence, which shows no visible sign of a change in draught breeds; medieval farmers in England at least seem to have employed the same red Devon and black Welsh oxen used by farmers two or three centuries later.[42]

A similar situation existed for horses. The remains of these animals found at the medieval sites of Wharram Percy (Yorkshire) and Petergate in the city of York indicate that they ranged up to 15 hands in height, still of pony size but somewhat larger than Anglo-Saxon horses, which seem to have reached only 13 or 14 hands.[43] This apparently modest increase in the size of the horse during the medieval period may have arisen as a spin-off from the development of the medieval warhorse. It has been claimed that the much vaunted warhorse in the middle ages was never bigger than a cob,[44] but the appearance of the terms *magnus equus* or *grant chival*

[40] Juliet Clutton-Brock, "The Animal Resources", in *The Archaeology of Anglo-Saxon England*, ed. D. M. Wilson (London, 1976), pp. 378–80; P. L. Armitage, "A Preliminary Description of British Cattle from the Late Twelfth to the Early Sixteenth Century", *Ark* (Journal for the Rare Breeds Survival Trust), vii, pt 12 (1980), pp. 405–13; M. L. Ryder, "Livestock", in *The Agrarian History of England and Wales*, i, pt 1, ed. S. Piggott (Cambridge, 1981), p. 387; M. L. Ryder, "Livestock Remains from Four Medieval Sites in Yorkshire", *Agric. Hist. Rev.*, ix (1961), pp. 105–10.
[41] Armitage, "A Preliminary Description of British Cattle", pp. 409–11.
[42] Red and black oxen are mentioned frequently in medieval records, as at Ravenfield (Yorkshire) in 1275: *Court Rolls of the Manor of Wakefield, 1274–1331*, ed. W. P. Baildon, J. Lister and J. W. Walker, 5 vols. (Yorks. Arch. Soc. Rec. Ser., xxix, 1901; xxxvi, 1906; lvii, 1917; lxxviii, 1930; cix, 1946) i, pp. 100, 144; for other examples and their connection with draught breeds of later periods, see J. Langdon, "Horses, Oxen, and Technological Innovation: The Use of Draught Animals in English Farming from 1066 to 1500" (Univ. of Birmingham Ph.D. thesis, 1983, hereafter referred to as "Langdon, thesis"), pp. 27–8, n. 50.
[43] Ryder, "Livestock", pp. 399, 401; Ryder, "Livestock Remains from Four Medieval Sites", pp. 108–9; Clutton-Brock, "The Animal Resources", p. 383.
[44] D. M. Goodall, *A History of Horse Breeding* (London, 1977), pp. 144–6.

in France and England by the beginning of the fourteenth century
when describing such horses indicates that an increase in size was
taking place. At the same time selective breeding programmes to
produce large horses for warfare were evident in Italy,[45] and
perhaps some of this rubbed off onto agricultural horses.

Consequently, it is likely that both horses and oxen were improving in size and presumably power over the medieval period,
although it is not certain which animal was gaining the advantage
over the other. Nevertheless, even if the rate of increase in the
power of horses was no greater than that for oxen, this would still
have favoured the former. Horses were at their worst in heavy,
slow-moving situations, either for ploughing or hauling, and often
broke down completely in such situations.[46] Any increase in power
to help them over this threshold, regardless of how much an
improvement it was compared to that being made by oxen, would
have brought a disproportionate advantage to the horse in its ability
to compete as a draught animal.

In short, from the end of the Roman period onward, it would seem
that the door was increasingly open to the substantial, even massive,
introduction of the horse to general draught work. Outside
England, evidence of this change was already occurring well before
the end of the first millennium A.D. The first uncontested reference
to horse ploughing, for instance, is recorded in King Alfred's
Orosius, written in the late ninth century, in which the Norwegian
chief, Ohthere, when describing his home farm in northern
Norway, stated that "the little that he ploughed he ploughed with
horses".[47] Although this seems to have been exceptional for the
time, references to horses ploughing – whether alone or in mixed

[45] R. H. C. Davis, "The Medieval Warhorse" in *Horses in European Economic History: A Preliminary Canter*, ed. F. M. L. Thompson (Reading, 1983), p. 13.

[46] For example, see *Walter of Henley*, ed. Dorothea Oschinsky (Oxford, 1971),
p. 319, c. 37; J. Langdon, "Horse Hauling: A Revolution in Vehicle Transport in
Twelfth- and Thirteenth-Century England?", *Past and Present*, no. 103 (1984),
p. 49.

[47] *King Alfred's Orosius*, ed. H. Sweet (London, 1883), i, p. 18; a translation of the
pertinent passage is provided by A. S. C. Ross in *The Terfinnas and Beormas of
Ohthere* (Leeds, 1940), p. 21. A possible example of a horse ploughing by the tail
in prehistoric Sweden (i.e., from a rock carving) is shown in P. V. Glob, *Ard og
Plov i Nordens Oldtid* (Ard and Plough in Prehistoric Scandinavia) (Aarhus,
1951), pp. 55, 127–8.

teams with oxen – are frequent enough in the eleventh and twelfth centuries, in parts of Europe at least, to indicate that it was becoming a fairly common occurrence. A pertinent example is that provided by Pope Urban II at the Council of Clermont in 1095, when he extended sanctuary to all oxen, plough-horses (*equi arantes*) and harrowing horses, and to all the men who guided them.[48] This implies a fairly widespread and probably growing distribution of plough-horses at the time, perhaps as the various elements of modern traction were being consolidated and perfected.

Horses for harrowing were also becoming more common, especially as the modern toothed version of the harrow came to be widely used – from at least the tenth or eleventh century onwards – in breaking down the furrow left by the heavy plough.[49] Similarly illuminated manuscripts from about the same time increasingly show horses rather than oxen hauling vehicles.[50]

Altogether it is clear that, with the introduction of the horse to general draught work, a notable metamorphosis in traction was occurring, one that had a double importance because it involved not only agriculture but road transport as well. The domination of horses in medieval traction, however, was by no means a foregone conclusion. As we shall discover, there were several limiting factors to their use, in particular their expense, which meant that oxen continued to be preferred in many circumstances. Indeed the success of the horse (or lack of it) in displacing the ox as a draught animal was to a large extent dependent upon local conditions and inclinations, which encouraged the horse's introduction in some areas but hindered it in others. Nonetheless the potential significance of the change should not be underestimated. For example, it can be calculated that in the late eleventh century over 70 per cent of the power available to English society at the time was supplied by animals, the remaining 30 per cent or so being provided by mill- and manpower together.[51] Thus, any improvement in the nature of this animal

[48] *The Ecclesiastical History of Ordericus Vitalis*, ed. M. Chibnall (Oxford, 1969–80), v, p. 21.
[49] C. Parain, "The Evolution of Agricultural Technique", in *The Cambridge Economic History of Europe*, i, 2nd edn, ed. M. M. Postan (Cambridge, 1966), p. 154; *Histoire de la France Rurale*, ed. G. Duby and A. Wallon (Paris, 1975), i, p. 407; *The Bayeux Tapestry*, ed. F. M. Stenton (London, 1957), plates 11, 12.
[50] For example, see Lefebvre des Noëttes, *L'Attelage*, figs. 140ff.
[51] As calculated using data from the Domesday survey; see Langdon, thesis, appendix A.

power, such as replacing oxen with horses, would clearly have had important ramifications for medieval man's relationship with his physical environment. Practical experiments, for instance, indicate that when pulling equal loads a horse can do so at least 50 per cent faster than an ox.[52] In the middle ages an increase of half again in terms of earth turned or goods transported would have been an event of some moment for medieval farmers. Nor can it be argued that there was little outlet for this extra power. In particular, the upsurge in land clearance that characterized twelfth- and early thirteenth-century Europe would have found this excess traction especially useful. Furthermore, if, as has been claimed, understocking was a problem for much of the middle ages due to the difficulties of maintaining animals in a highly arable farming economy,[53] then using the more efficient horse would make even more sense. The next three chapters of this study will determine how much of this potential motivation to convert from oxen to horses was turned into actual practice in medieval England.

[52] *Rankine's Useful Rules and Tables*, 6th edn (London, 1883), p. 251; see also A. P. Usher, *A History of Mechanical Invention*, 2nd edn (Cambridge, Mass., 1954), p. 156; White, *Medieval Technology and Social Change*, p. 62.

[53] Hilton and Sawyer, "Technical Determinism", pp. 99–100; M. M. Postan, *The Medieval Economy and Society* (Harmondsworth, Middlesex, 1975), pp. 63–7.

2. The initial stages: England from 1066 to 1200

It appears that when the Normans invaded England they found a country in which oxen were, by far, the predominant work animals. The evidence for this state of affairs is fragmentary but nonetheless persuasive. Virtually all Anglo-Saxon references to animals used for traction involve oxen only, particularly in regard to farm work. For example, in the laws of Ine (*c.* 688–94) it is decreed that if a *ceorl* hires another's yoke of oxen he is bound to pay the hire in fodder if he can, or half in fodder and half in other goods.[1] In this case it is not possible to specify the use to which the oxen were being put, but ploughing must certainly be the most likely. The later *Aelfric's Colloquy*, for instance, provides a lively account from about the year 1000 of how the ploughman and his boy drive the oxen to the field, yoke them to the plough, and then proceed to turn over a whole acre a day.[2] The size of the team is not mentioned here, but illustrations from the Caedmon and Cotton MSS show oxen yoked to ploughs in teams of two abreast or of four in double file (see Figures 12 and 13). The tenth-century Cotton MSS also depict oxen being employed for hauling, as shown in Figure 14. Here men are gathering wood and placing it in a cart by which stand two oxen still in their yoke, presumably having a rest before being connected up to the cart again.[3] This apparent Anglo-Saxon preference for oxen

---

[1] *English Historical Documents*, i, *c.* 500–1042, ed. Dorothy Whitelock, 2nd edn (Oxford, 1972), p. 405. The oxen are not specifically mentioned, but the presence of yokes indicates that these were the animals involved.

[2] *Documents in Economic History*, i, ed. H. E. S. Fisher and A. R. J. Juřica (London, 1977), pp. 400–1.

[3] Oxen are also shown hauling two-wheeled carts in Aelfric's translation of the Heptateuch. One of the carts, however, shows a mixed team of what look to be two mules followed by two oxen, all harnessed in yokes. From Brit. Lib. Cott. MS Claud. B. iv, as shown in Lynn White, Jr, "The Origins of the Coach", in his *Medieval Religion and Technology* (Berkeley, 1978), esp. figs. 10–14 (between pp. 216 and 217). See also pp. 24–6 below.

Fig. 12: Anglo-Saxon wheeled plough, probably early eleventh century. From the Caedmon MS (Bodl. Library MS Junius 11, p. 54, middle section; reproduced by permission of the Bodleian Library).

Fig. 13: Anglo-Saxon wheeled plough, from a calendar from the first half of the eleventh century (Brit. Lib. Cott. MS Tib. B. V (pt 1), fo. 3; reproduced by permission of the British Library).

over horses, as far as farm work is concerned, is also reflected in the stock listings found on several estate leases and inventories during the period, as summarized in Table 1. As can be seen, oxen dominate almost totally, the only adult horses being two "stotts" found at Egmere. These listings reflect the arrangements on large agricultural units, probably demesnes of a hundred acres or more, but the same inclination towards oxen also seems to have applied to the farms of lesser men. The *Rectitudines Singularum Personarum* stipulate that the *gebur*, with only seven acres of sown land, was to

Table 1. *Stock listings on some Anglo-Saxon estates*

Estates	Date	Animals
Hatfield, Hertfordshire	prob. 10th cent.	40 oxen, 250 sheep, 47 goats, 15 calves, 190 swine
Yaxley, Huntingdonshire	c. 963	16 oxen, a stalled ox, 305 sheep, 9 one-year-old stallions, 30 swine, 1 fat pig
Beddington, Surrey	899–908	9 full-grown oxen, 114 full-grown pigs, 50 wethers, 110 full-grown sheep, plus assorted sheep and pigs to which the herdsmen were entitled
Egmere, Norfolk	prob. 11th cent.	7 oxen, 8 cows, 4 grazing bullocks, 2 inferior horses or "stotts", 115 sheep and lambs, 1 pig
Luddington, Warwickshire	early 11th cent.	2 teams of oxen, 100 sheep
Norton, Worcestershire	early 11th cent.	6 oxen, 20 sheep

Notes and sources: Anglo-Saxon Charters, ed. A. J. Robertson (Cambridge, 1939), pp. 74–5, 154–5, 156–7, 196–7, 256–7; H. P. R. Finberg (ed.), *The Agrarian History of England and Wales*, i, pt 2 (Cambridge, 1972), p. 498.

have as a normal livestock complement to his land two oxen, one cow and six sheep.[4]

It would not do, though, to suppose that horses were decidedly uncommon in Anglo-Saxon England, since the same *Rectitudines* indicate that the *gebur* was expected to have a horse to fulfil carrying services (probably by pack), although the animal was not listed as essential stock.[5] Horses might also have been used for harrowing, since the technique was obviously performed – and perhaps even introduced – at some stage during the Anglo-Saxon period; for example, the supervision of harrowing is mentioned as part of the reeve's duties in the eleventh-century treatise, *Gerefa*.[6] Some horses may also have been involved in light passenger transport. The clearest sign of this comes from Aelfric's early eleventh-century

[4] *English Historical Documents*, ii, 1042–1189, ed. D. C. Douglas (London, 1961), p. 814.
[5] *Ibid.* Note also the bee-keeper's and swineherd's horses (pp. 814–15).
[6] As printed in W. Cunningham, *The Growth of English Industry and Commerce*, i, 4th edn (Cambridge, 1905), pp. 572, 574.

Fig. 14: Cart and oxen for drawing wood, from a calendar from the first half of the eleventh century (Brit. Lib. Cott. MS Tib. B. V (pt 1), fo. 6; reproduced by permission of the British Library. The same scene is shown in a slightly different form in Brit. Lib. Cott. MS Julius A VI).

Fig. 15: Mule or donkey ploughing, horse harrowing. Bayeux Tapestry, second half of the eleventh century (from F. M. Stenton (ed.), *The Bayeux Tapestry* (London, 1957), pl. 12; reproduced by permission of Phaidon Press, Ltd).

translation of the Heptateuch, where a number of four-wheeled coaches carrying passengers are shown being hauled by teams of two or even four equids. The animals look to be mules, but might have been meant to represent horses. Horses for hauling light chariots and the like were on the Continent and in Ireland at this time and even before, and so their use as such in Anglo-Saxon England is not unlikely, despite the relative lack of evidence for it.[7] Certainly some quite large stud farms for horses are recorded for the Anglo-Saxon period. Burton Abbey, for instance, received 100 wild horses and sixteen tame geldings from a certain Wulfric at the beginning of the eleventh century,[8] and similar bequeathals of studs are also mentioned for Troston in Suffolk and Ongar in Essex.[9] It would appear, however, that the horses from these studs, more often than not, were bound for military use or as riding animals for the privileged.[10]

The indication from all this is that, generally speaking, the horse in Anglo-Saxon times tended to be very much a luxury beast, primarily a riding animal for the well-to-do. At best, as a working beast, the horse was involved as a pack and harrowing animal and perhaps marginally in hauling, particularly in light passenger carrying, much as had been the case in Roman times. In contrast, the ox was tied much more to the menial role as a beast of labour, especially for ploughing and the hauling of goods other than people. It would not do, though, to oversimplify the matter. Although, as has been said, there is no evidence for horses ploughing in Anglo-Saxon England and relatively little evidence for it as a beast of haulage, the Welsh Laws, purportedly referring to conditions in a time as early as the tenth century, mention work-horses and even point to them hauling.[11] Elements of horse harness have also been

---

[7] The Heptateuch illustrations are from Brit. Lib. Cott. MS Claud. B. iv (see note 3 above); for early medieval horse-drawn vehicles on the Continent and Ireland, see Langdon, "Horse Hauling", p. 44n.; White, *Medieval Technology and Social Change*, p. 61; A. C. Leighton, "A Technological Consideration of Early Medieval Vehicles", *Fifth International Conference of Economic History, Leningrad, 1970* (Paris, 1977), pp. 344–5.

[8] *Anglo-Saxon Wills*, ed. D. Whitelock (Cambridge, 1930), pp. 50–1.

[9] That is, *c.* 975–1016 and 1042–3. *Ibid.*, pp. 32–3, 82–3.

[10] The bequeathal of horses, often complete with shields and spears, figures prominently in Anglo-Saxon wills. *Ibid.*, pp. 6–7, 22–3, 26–7, 30–1, etc.

[11] A. W. Wade-Evans, *Welsh Medieval Law* (Oxford, 1909), pp. 68, 215.

found in excavations of Anglo-Saxon village sites,[12] although this again may well be consistent with the use of the horse mainly as a harrowing, pack- or riding animal.

What can be ascertained about the proportions of working horses and oxen on the eve of the Conquest then? Based on the stock listings in Table 1, the preponderance of oxen was very great indeed. Treating the "stalled" ox at Yaxley as a supernumerary and assuming that the teams of oxen at Luddington were comprised of eight oxen apiece, the number of oxen to adult horses works out at ninety-four to two, a great majority for oxen. On the other hand, if the Anglo-Saxon *gebur* did indeed have a horse to go along with his two oxen, then the ratio of oxen to horses in this case would only be two to one, still a majority for oxen, but very much less so. Clearly the true situation was somewhere in between, although at this stage it is impossible to say exactly where. There does seem, however, to have been a distinct division of duties between the two animals. Thus only oxen were employed for ploughing and most likely hauling, while horses were used for riding and probably pack-saddle work. Harrowing is in doubt either way, because of the lack of evidence, but since it is an activity eminently suited to horses we may suspect that horses were in fact performing it.

Beyond this, there is not much to say. The fact that the numbers of oxen in the stock listings of Table 1 are mostly divisible by eight, or thereabouts, indicates that the large plough-teams we will become familiar with in post-Conquest England were already in existence at this earlier period. The small two- and four-animal teams in the Caedmon and Cotton MSS belie this, of course, but more will be said about this later. For the moment we must now turn our attention to the period after the conquest.

a) THE NUMBERS OF HORSES AND OXEN, 1066–1200

i) *At Domesday*

Despite the single mule or donkey drawing a plough and the horse harrowing in the Bayeux Tapestry (see Figure 15),[13] there are

---

[12] D. M. Wilson, *The Anglo-Saxons*, 3rd edn (Harmondsworth, Middlesex, 1981), p. 95.

[13] It is difficult to know how seriously to treat the Bayeux Tapestry as evidence on this point, since a single-animal ploughing team seems very unlikely in the cir-

enough clues in the available documentation to indicate that the ox easily held its position as the dominant draught animal in England for at least a full generation after Hastings. The chief source here is the Domesday survey, for which information about farm animals is given for two separate groups of counties: that is, the East Anglian counties of Norfolk, Suffolk, Essex and Cambridgeshire and the south-western group of Dorset, Somerset, Devon and Cornwall. All these counties are covered by variants of the survey which provide detailed information about manorial livestock otherwise missing from the final exchequer version.[14] Thus, for example, at Great Cressingham in Norfolk the Little Domesday Book recounts that the villeins of the manor had half a plough-team, while the demesne had three, as well as five *runcini* (that is, rounceys; at this time a type of work-horse[15]), twenty-two *animalia* (that is, non-working cattle), seventeen swine and eighty sheep.[16] As can be seen, there are a number of qualifications about this information. First, only the demesne stock is given; peasant stock is never itemized. Second, the plough animals are incorporated in the plough-team figures. This qualification, however, can be got round by simply assuming that each plough-team had eight oxen, an assumption that will be investigated in a short while, but which for the moment can stand as it is. This means, then, that the demesne at Great Cressingham had twenty-four oxen (for its three plough-teams) as well as five horses, and that in this case horses provided 17.2 per cent of the demesne working stock.

Altogether the working stock for some 4,000 demesnes can be extracted in this way for the above-mentioned counties. To speed up matters, a systematic sample of every tenth of these demesnes was taken and the level of horses for each county worked up in the

cumstances (see p. 67 below). It is notable, too, that the ploughing and harrowing scene takes place in that part of the narrative dealing with events in France. Perhaps the scene was meant to reflect agriculture there rather than in England.

[14] That is, the *Domesday Book*, ii, for Norfolk, Suffolk and Essex; the *Inquisitio Comitatus Cantabrigiensis* and the *Inquisitio Eliensis*, ed. N. E. S. A. Hamilton (London, 1876) for Cambridgeshire; and the Exeter Domesday (*Domesday Book*, iv) for Somerset, Devon, Cornwall, and part of Dorset. The *Inquisitio Eliensis* also contains livestock information for a handful of manors in Huntingdonshire and Hertfordshire, but these were not included in the study because it was felt they were too few to be properly representative of the counties involved.

[15] See appendix.

[16] *Domesday Book*, ii, fo. 191; also *Victoria County Histories, Norfolk*, ii, p. 114.

Table 2. *Sampled Domesday data for demesne horses and oxen*

County	(1) No. of demesnes	(2) Demesne plough-teams (A)	(3) No. of oxen (A × 8)	(4) No. of work-horses	(5) Percentage work-horses	(6) Corrected percentage work-horses
Norfolk	69	116.5	932	61	6.1	7.9
Suffolk	62	107.5	861[a]	62	6.7	7.6
Essex	65	129.0	1,032	88	7.9	9.8
Cambridgeshire	18	45.0	360	18	4.8	5.0
Dorset	12	23.5	188	13	6.5	6.5
Somerset	66	126.0	1,008	48	4.5	4.8
Devon	89	135.125	1,081	14	1.3	1.4
Cornwall	25	32.375	259	3	1.1	1.2
Total			5,721	307		
Average					5.1	5.8

[a] Includes an extra ox at Downham.

way shown in Table 2. The number of horses was adjusted for those which were definitely not working animals, namely the large numbers of wild and forest mares which crop up on some estates, particularly in the western counties. These herds of primarily breeding animals, comparable to the Anglo-Saxon studs mentioned above, took no part in the agricultural process and hence are excluded from our analysis. It is presumed that the numbers of adult horses remaining were working animals and these are shown in column 4. Included in these figures are donkeys and mules, which were almost certainly part of the demesne animal work force and, in the case of mules at least, only a little less efficient than horses. In any event, they only amounted to a small fraction of the work-horse total.[17]

Altogether the average level of work-horses for the eight counties (column 5) came to 5.1 per cent, or one horse for every nineteen oxen, a considerable majority for oxen. There is, as well, a significant distinction between those counties in the east, where the proportion of work-horses was 6.7 per cent (or one horse for every fourteen oxen), and those in the west, where the proportion was only 3.0 per cent (or one horse for every thirty-two oxen). We are

[17] Altogether one mule and eleven donkeys are included in the 307 "work-horses" in Table 2, or 3.9 per cent of the total. This is somewhat larger than the proportion of 1.9 per cent indicated by Darby's overall figures (*Domesday England*, p. 164, excluding wild and forest mares and foals) and is due to the chance inclusion in the sample of two demesnes with seven donkeys between them.

fortunate in this respect in having two regions which, based on later experience at least (see, for example, Table 12), were very much on opposite poles as far as the use of work-horses is concerned. As a result, we might expect this range of 3.0 to 6.7 per cent to be fairly representative of demesnes in the country as a whole.

However, there is still the strong possibility that horses were under-enumerated, even in those variants of the survey that normally recorded them. This suspicion is hardened in our sample by the number of demesnes that fail not only to mention horses but all other animals as well, save those included in the plough-teams. This is particularly the case for the eastern group of counties where 24.8 per cent of the demesnes in the sample had no extra animals; in comparison the western group of counties had only 8.3 per cent of such demesnes. In some cases, of course, this may have merely reflected actual conditions, since, as indicated by later sources, it was not unknown for some demesnes to have plough animals only. Even so, it seems probable that the commissioners often simply elected not to record extra animals, particularly those on small demesnes of one plough-team or less. To correct for this possible distortion, the demesnes with no extra animals at all were eliminated from the samples and the results recalculated, as shown in column 6 of Table 2.

In the end, the possibility that some horses may have been purposefully ignored by the Domesday commissioners seems to have had little effect; the exclusion of the suspected demesnes only made a slight change in the overall level of work-horses for the eight counties – a rise from 5.1 to 5.8 per cent, which, given the fact that both regions in the sample are fairly equally represented in Table 2, we can more or less regard as minimum and maximum figures for the average level of work-horses in the country overall. As expected, the correction had rather more effect on the eastern counties, raising the proportion of horses here from 6.7 to 8.0 per cent – in Essex it rose to nearly 10 per cent. The rise in the western counties was much more modest, from 3.0 to 3.1 per cent overall. In both regions, however, oxen still clearly dominated, and this is despite the most optimistic estimate we can make for the overall percentage of work-horses at Domesday; it is unlikely, for instance, that in the remaining demesnes the commissioners would go to the trouble of recording sheep, cattle, goats and pigs without fully recording horses as well.

At this point we must consider an essential question. How sure are we of the assumption that the Domesday plough-team always consisted of eight oxen? The number is not so much in doubt. For most of the country the concept of an eight-animal plough-team was an integral part of the Domesday survey, where it was used more as an accounting aid than as a factual description of plough-team sizes at the time. Reginald Lennard has shown how this intention may have broken down for the south-western counties, where a comparison between the exchequer and Exeter Domesdays reveals that here the commissioners may have elected to deal with actual team sizes rather than a notional one of eight oxen. Thus, for example, when the exchequer Domesday referred to half a plough-team at a certain place, the Exeter version often described the same team as being of three oxen. Lennard, by equating the two, maintained that in cases like these the commissioners were considering a full plough-team as being one of six oxen.[18] On the other hand, H. P. R. Finberg argued that the apparent variability was caused by the clerks rounding up to the nearest half or full team when preparing the final exchequer version.[19] As he put it, "One or two beasts more or less were not allowed to interfere with the standard [of eight oxen]."[20] Therefore three oxen were near enough to half a team of eight oxen to justify them being considered as such. In general, it would seem that, at best, Lennard's argument as to a variable Domesday plough-team only applies to certain parts of the country, particularly the south-west.[21] Even if one accepts his variable plough-teams, they still tend to average out to an eight-animal team, or at worst a seven-animal one, which would not make any significant change to our results.[22]

The composition of the Domesday plough-team presents a much more serious problem. Although we have been assuming that oxen were the only plough animals at Domesday, it is not inconceivable that some of the plough-teams in the country were comprised not

[18] R. Lennard, "Domesday Plough-teams: the South-Western Evidence", *Eng. Hist. Rev.*, lx (1945), pp. 217–33.

[19] H. P. R. Finberg, "The Domesday Plough-Team", *Eng. Hist. Rev.*, lxvi (1951), pp. 67–71.

[20] *Ibid.*, p. 70.

[21] A fact Lennard admits in his rejoinder to Finberg. "The Composition of the Domesday Caruca", *Eng. Hist. Rev.*, lxxxi (1966), pp. 770–5.

[22] The adoption of a seven-ox Domesday plough-team would raise our optimum work-horse level by about a percentage point (i.e. 5.8 to 6.7 per cent).

only of oxen but horses as well, say four of each, or even of horses alone. Fortunately Domesday is full of incidental remarks from which it is possible to infer the normal composition of the plough-team in a particular area. These usually occurred when the number of plough animals available on a manor did not fit neatly into the groups of eight favoured by the commissioners. Thus at Sotterley in Suffolk it was stated that at the time of the Conquest there had been two plough-teams and "now" (1086) there were "three and three oxen"; or it may have been even more explicitly stated, as at Durnford in Wiltshire: "There are six oxen in the demesne plough."[23] Consequently a sample of twelve counties was taken – Norfolk, Suffolk, Kent, Bedfordshire, Buckinghamshire, Oxfordshire, Northamptonshire, Wiltshire, Cornwall, Worcestershire, Cheshire and Yorkshire – and the surveys for these counties examined entry by entry. Altogether there were over 250 references for which the plough animals were specified in a fashion similar to the examples given for Sotterley and Durnford above. *All* the plough animals mentioned were oxen.

These references to oxen in the plough-team were not restricted to demesnes either. In fact the majority of them referred to peasant plough-teams. Take the example of Norfolk. Of nearly a hundred references to oxen in plough-teams, only ten involved demesne ploughs; the rest dealt strictly with the peasantry. Some of these latter references were quite specific, as a small sample of them shows:

(1)   "In Kirby Bedon there are two sokemen and a half with twelve acres. Then as now they plough with three oxen."
(2)   "In Bastwick two freewomen . . . plough now as then with two oxen."
(3)   "In Ashby there are two freemen . . . with nine acres. Now as then they plough with two oxen."
(4)   "In Rockland and Surlingham William de Noers holds two villeins with sixteen acres and two acres of meadow. Then and afterwards they held half a plough; now they plough with two oxen."
(5)   "In Plumstead is one bordar, Godric's man, with nine acres of land. Now as then he ploughs with two oxen."[24]

[23]   *Domesday Book*, ii, fo. 301; *Domesday Book*, i, fo. 67b.
[24]   *Domesday Book*, ii, fos. 143, 174b, 177b, 195, 228b.

Table 3. *Variations in the levels of Domesday work-horses*

County	No. of demesnes with no horses	Less than 5% horses	5.1–10.0%	10.1–15.0%	15.1–20.0%	20.1–25.0%	25.1–30.0%	30.1–35.0%	35.1–40.0%	40.1–45.0%
Norfolk	22	—	10	11	5	—	—	—	—	1
Suffolk	16	1	11	14	2	1	—	1	1	—
Essex	16	3	5	15	7	1	1	1	—	—
Cambridgeshire	8	2	3	1	1	1	—	—	—	—
Dorset	6	—	3	—	3	—	—	—	—	—
Somerset	30	7	11	10	1	1	—	—	—	—
Devon	70	—	5	6	—	—	—	—	—	—
Cornwall	21	—	1	1	—	—	—	—	—	—
Total	189	13	49	58	19	4	1	2	1	1
%	56.1	3.9	14.5	17.2	5.6	1.2	0.3	0.6	0.3	0.3

As can be seen, oxen were employed as plough-beasts by every sort of tenant, and this unanimous preference for the animals at this time is all the more significant when one considers that Norfolk was one of the very first counties to start replacing them with horses, as we shall see later. In short, although such informative references as those above represent only a small fraction of the entries in Domesday, their sheer consistency points to the overwhelming use of oxen as plough animals for all sections of society. The only other interpretation that can be entertained is that the commissioners were so bureaucratic that they blithely ignored all the horses, mules, and donkeys ploughing in front of them and jotted down oxen instead. Had this situation existed, however, it would almost certainly have revealed itself in the variety of the Domesday record. We can only assume, therefore, that oxen were the sole plough animals in use at the time of the survey.[25]

The evidence, then, still swings very much towards the ox as being the pre-eminent draught animal in England at the time. The uniformly low averages for the level of horses, however, does hide a great degree of variation. The contrast from county to county can be seen in Table 2, but even within counties a fair degree of differentiation is encountered. Using our sample again, Table 3 provides a

[25] Despite some speculation to the contrary: e.g. Ryder, "Livestock", p. 400.

county by county breakdown of this variation in work-horse levels, expressed as a percentage of total draught stock – horses and oxen – and excluding those questionable demesnes mentioned above where the presence of horses may simply have gone unrecorded. As is evident from the table, even when the questionable demesnes have been excluded, more than half of the remaining demesnes still had no horses. The majority of these horse-less demesnes came from the west, but even the east had a high proportion of them. Essex, for instance, the county with the greatest proportion of horses, had none of the animals on nearly a third of its demesnes. This seemingly countrywide prevalence of horse-less demesnes goes a long way to explain why the average percentages of work-horses were so low. On the other hand, considered by themselves, the 148 demesnes with horses had an average 11.1 per cent of them in their draught stock totals, and some individual demesnes reached considerably higher levels. Rudham in Norfolk, for instance, with five rounceys and one mule accompanying a single plough-team, consequently had its horses and mule comprising 42.9 per cent of the animal work force.[26] Demesnes with proportions of work-horses at this level, however, were rare, and it could be that these cases included riding horses as well.

An interesting feature of the demesnes that did have horses is that the animals were often found in set proportions to the number of plough-teams on the demesnes. Thus 55 (or 37.2 per cent) of the 148 demesnes with horses had them in proportions of one horse for every plough-team, and another 34 (or 23.0 per cent) had one horse for every two plough-teams. Ratios of this kind are often found in later material, where the single horses are shown to be harrowing animals following after the plough (or ploughs).[27] Presumably the same sort of situation existed at Domesday.

What effect did geographical factors, such as soil or terrain, have on the distribution of Domesday work-horses? Although, as we have seen, some differences in work-horse levels did exist between counties, particularly when comparing the east and west, these geographical factors seemingly had little effect within counties. An

---

[26] Assuming, again, eight oxen per plough-team: *Domesday Book*, ii, 169b.
[27] For example, *Cartularium monasterii de Rameseia*, iii, pp. 257, 274, 279, 307, 311, 313 (for various twelfth-century Ramsey Abbey demesnes).

attempt was made to quantify this by separating the demesnes with work-horses from those without and plotting them statistically to see if there were significant local variations within each county. In view of the time-consuming nature of the exercise, it was limited to the three eastern counties of Norfolk, Suffolk and Essex. The results were inconclusive. Although the distribution of demesnes with horses versus those without did show some differences in trend – for example, in Essex demesnes with work-horses were situated somewhat more northerly than those without – the degree of scatter in the data was enough to rob the results of any great significance.[28] One of the counties, again Essex, was further analysed hundred by hundred. Once more, although there was some grouping of demesnes with work-horses in some hundreds and demesnes without such horses in others, the situation was too mixed to give a clear verdict. We can only surmise that the introduction of the horse into English farming at this time was still too much in its infancy for detailed regional variation to have formed, or that the Domesday data are not accurate enough to support analyses of this type.

Another possible factor affecting the use of horses at Domesday is that of landlordship, in particular whether the demesne was run under lay or ecclesiastic control. Ecclesiastic and especially monastic agriculture during the early medieval period has often been cited as being notably innovative, particularly in such matters as land reclamation and stock raising.[29] Was this supposedly enlightened attitude also reflected in the number of horses found on ecclesiastic estates at Domesday, as churchmen experimented with new modes of traction? To answer this question, the demesnes in our sample – excluding the questionable ones where no extra animals at all were recorded – were separated according to whether they were lay or ecclesiastic and the percentage of horses worked out for each grouping. The results are contained in Table 4.

A particular demesne was considered lay or ecclesiastic according to who was last in the chain of tenure. For example, a demesne held

---

[28] Students' *t* tests performed on the east–west and north–south coordinates showed that in no case were the results significant to more than the $p > 0.05$ level.

[29] E.g., *Cambridge Economic History of Europe*, i, 2nd edn, ed. M. M. Postan (Cambridge, 1966), p. 292; G. Duby, *The Early Growth of the European Economy* (London, 1974), pp. 213–21; C. Platt, *The Monastic Grange in Medieval England* (London, 1969), pp. 13–14; J. Gimpel, *The Medieval Machine* (London, 1977), pp. 46–50.

Table 4. *The level of Domesday work-horses on lay versus ecclesiastic demesnes*

County	Lay demesnes		Ecclesiastic demesnes	
	No. of demesnes	% horses	No. of demesnes	% horses
(a) Eastern counties				
Norfolk	43	7.8	6	8.2
Suffolk	40	7.6	7	7.7
Essex	39	10.4	10	7.5
Cambridgeshire	12	5.4	4	4.1
Average		8.3		7.0
(b)Western counties				
Dorset	9	6.6	3	5.9
Somerset	53	4.5	7	7.1
Devon	76	1.4	5	0.0
Cornwall	20	0.9	3	3.4
Average		3.0		4.6

as tenant-in-chief by a great ecclesiastical lord but given in fee to a lay sub-tenant was considered to be a lay demesne on the grounds that it was the sub-tenant who effectively managed the land.[30] As a result, the proportion of demesnes actively administered by church-men was very small – only 45 (or 13.4 per cent) of the 337 demesnes making up Table 4. In any case, the table indicates that whether a demesne was run by laymen or clerics made very little difference to the number of horses that were employed on it. Seemingly, laymen tended to use more horses than churchmen in the east, but fewer in the west. On the other hand, the proportion of demesnes with horses – as opposed to those without – was greater for church-run than for lay estates, 57.8 per cent (or 25 out of 45 demesnes)

---

[30] The chain of tenure may even have extended beyond this, with the last recorded tenant in Domesday himself letting out his land for a limited term to yet another man. As this limited-term leasing was generally unrecorded, it is impossible to quantify. However, since the stock-and-land lease was probably the most common type of lease in use (R. Lennard, *Rural England 1086–1135* (Oxford, 1959), pp. 195–6), it is felt that the composition of the draught stock given to the tenant would not have changed significantly in his hands. This may not necessarily have been the case, of course, but for the purposes of the analysis it is an assumption we must make.

Table 5. *Percentage work-horses at Domesday and T.R.E.*

County	No. of demesnes	% work-horses	
		T.R.E.	1086
Norfolk	37	7.0	7.9
Suffolk	33	8.8	7.7
Essex	33	6.9	10.0
All 3 counties		7.6	8.6

versus 42.1 per cent (or 123 out of 292 demesnes). The inference here is that, although the overall level of horses was more or less the same on both lay and ecclesiastic demesnes, a rather greater percentage of clerics than laymen was employing the animals. Statistically speaking, though, the significance of this trend is very weak.[31]

In short, it seems for the moment at least that Anglo-Norman landholders, both lay and ecclesiastic, were content to use a heavily ox-dominated system of traction. Was this the one they inherited from the pre-Conquest period? A check on this is furnished by the Little Domesday survey for Norfolk, Suffolk and Essex. Here the livestock was recorded on a considerable number of manors for both 1086 and T.R.E. (that is, the time of Edward the Confessor on the eve of the Conquest). The data from the cases that occurred in our sample are summarized in Table 5.

From the table it seems clear that the percentage of horses in the draught stock of these demesnes differed little in 1086 from that found over twenty years earlier in the time of Edward the Confessor; only Essex demonstrates what could be called a significant shift to horses over the intervening period, although in absolute terms the new levels of horses in the county were still very small in comparison to oxen, at best only one horse to every nine oxen.[32]

If the Domesday survey can be trusted at all, then, the percentage of work-horses engaged on English demesnes remained low for at

[31] The chi-square coefficient was only 0.08 ($\chi^2 = 2.34$).
[32] It is difficult to know how seriously to take this apparent rise in the level of Essex work-horses from T.R.E. to 1086, since, as indicated previously, even at Domesday there was a large proportion of demesnes with no horses at all in the county. The change, if any, would appear to have been a very minor one.

least twenty years after the Conquest.[33] As for peasant draught
animals, we are almost completely in the dark. We do know that
they used only oxen for ploughing, and that consequently most
peasants probably had one or two of the animals and perhaps even
more. As with the Anglo-Saxon *gebur*, however, it is entirely possible that the Domesday peasant also had a horse to go along with his
oxen, and that this would automatically push horse levels among the
peasantry above that on the demesne. That the peasantry probably
did have horses is indicated by an entry for Dean in Bedfordshire,
where it is said that William de Warenne disseised a certain William
Spec of his land there and took away two horses from his men
(*homines*).[34] Beyond this, however, little can be said for the
moment.

ii) *The twelfth century*

Fortunately new and more detailed sources become available in the
twelfth century. First among these are the great estate surveys. The
earliest is the Burton Abbey Survey B, dating from *c*. 1114–18, and
other valuable surveys and extents follow later in the century.
Although the primary purpose of these surveys was to record the
services and dues owed by the various tenants on each manor of the
estate in question, they also included in many cases a short inventory of the demesne livestock. Thus on the Ramsey Abbey manor of
Elton in Huntingdonshire it is stated that, during the reign of
Henry I, the demesne had 5 plough-teams of 8 oxen apiece, 10 cows,
1 bull, 160 sheep, 2 harrowing horses (*equis occatoribus*) and 100
pigs.[35] Such detailed lists are extremely useful for indicating the
labouring horses and oxen, especially at places such as Elton, where
later listings provide interesting comparisons with the earlier ones.

A second source is that provided by stock-and-land leases of the
type already cited for the Anglo-Saxon period. The twelfth century,
particularly the early and middle decades, was a notable time for the
letting out of whole manors, demesne and all, and as a result a

---

[33] This is also supported by two stock-and-land leases contemporaneous within a
decade or so of Domesday. These leases, from Thornley in Durham and
Charlcombe in Somerset, between them listed eighteen oxen but no horses.
Lennard, *Rural England 1086–1135*, p. 195.

[34] Presumably peasants, although not necessarily so. *Domesday Book*, i, fo. 211b.

[35] *Cartularium monasterii de Rameseia*, ed. W. W. Hart and P. A. Lyons (Rolls
Series, 1884–93), iii, p. 257.

number of stock-and-land leases survive for this period. For example, *c.* 1191, two Suffolk manors belonging to the Abbey of St Edmunds, Groton and Semer, were leased to Adam of Cockfield for life. Along with Groton went the stock for one plough-team, namely six oxen and two horses, as well as one harrowing horse; Semer, on the other hand, was supplied with three plough-teams, two of six oxen and two horses apiece and a third of eight horses alone, plus one harrowing horse, six cows, one bull, one hundred sheep and ten pigs.[36] Here, as to a certain extent is the case with the surveys as well, the stock listing may be describing what the lessor thought was suitable for the demesne rather than what the farmer actually used. Still, the leases accurately reflect the practice at the time of leasing (if not afterward), and as such they are statistically grouped with the surveys. Grants of land complete with stock are also included in this category.

A third source is provided by a single set of documents, the *Rotuli de Dominabus et Pueris et Puellis.*[37] This set of rotulets listed all the manors held in wardship or "marriage" by the king or his designates in twelve counties during the period from Whitsuntide to Michaelmas, 1185. The prime concern of the documents was to record the annual monetary return of the manors, but frequently indicated as well is the stock normally appurtenant to the demesne. Thus the demesne of the manor of Dunton Chamberlain in Dunton, Bedfordshire, had twelve oxen, four horses (*averis*), one calf, five pigs and seventy-eight sheep, the manor itself being worth fifteen pounds per year.[38]

A fourth major source is that of the Pipe Rolls, which are continuous in the Pipe Roll Society volumes from 1159 to the end of the century and beyond. Contained in them are numerous references to the restocking of escheated manors. Apparently this restocking often had to be done from scratch, since in a number of cases it is stated that the manor was *sine instauramento.*[39] In cases where the stock purchased was insufficient for even one plough-team, an additional purchase often occurred in the following year which filled out the

---

[36] *The Kalendar of Abbot Samson of Bury St Edmunds and Related Documents*, ed. R. H. C. Davis (Camden Third Series, lxxxiv, 1954), p. 128.

[37] Pipe Roll Society, xxxv (1913).

[38] *Ibid.*, p. 32.

[39] As at Edlesborough, Bledlow, and a number of other Buckinghamshire manors. *Pipe Roll of 7 Richard I* (Pipe Roll Soc., new ser., vi, 1929), p. 35.

working and non-working stock to a more practicable level.[40] In short, it seems reasonable to expect that in the majority of cases the stock bought for the escheated manors does in fact represent complete or nearly complete sets of demesne animals. This is particularly evident in the case of draught oxen, which are continually being bought in multiples of six, eight or ten, corresponding – presumably – to the size of the plough-team on those particular manors. However, since we cannot be certain that the Pipe Rolls are dealing with full sets of demesne stock, it was decided to use them as an independent check rather than combining them with the other sources.

These are not all the sources that can be invoked. Grants involving pasture rights often list work animals, but since it is difficult to know how representative they were of normal demesne or peasant operating levels they have not been employed in this study. In any case, the surveys, leases, *Rotuli de Dominabus* and Pipe Rolls altogether yield demesne draught stock data for over 400 manors or groups of manors. These are summarized by county in Table 6. The surveys, leases, etc., have been divided into those dating from the first half of the century and those dating from the second, while, as indicated, the Pipe Rolls are treated separately.

As in the Domesday material, the only horses considered are adult working animals. Those which were obviously used only for riding or for breeding purposes, as in a stud,[41] are excluded from the analysis, as, too, are young animals. Another point to make here is one of terminology. This particularly applies to horses, which are found under a number of aliases in the documents, where they appear variously as *averi, avri, auri, affri, caballi, stotti, hercarii* and *occatores*, the last two referring to their function as harrowing

---

[40] A good example is provided by the manor of Rotherfield Greys in Oxfordshire, where one ox and four sheep were bought in 1194–5 and a further twelve oxen, one "affer" (that is, a work-horse), five cows, one bull, fifty sheep and six pigs added the following year "to complete the stock of the said land". *Pipe Roll 7 Richard I*, p. 44; *Chancellor's Roll (8 Richard I)* (Pipe Roll Soc., new ser., vii, 1930), p. 203.

[41] Altogether there are four studs mentioned in the twelfth-century sources, amounting to some two hundred animals: that is, at Burton and Whiston, Staffordshire; Glinton, Northamptonshire; and Walton, Somerset. *Burton Abbey Twelfth Century Surveys*, ed. C. G. O. Bridgeman (William Salt Arch. Soc., 1916), pp. 212, 228; "Liber Niger", p. 163; T.C.L. MS R.5.33, fo. 115.

Table 6. *The proportion of work-horses on English demesnes during the twelfth century*

County	Surveys and leases (1101–50)				Surveys, leases and *Rotuli de Dominabus* (1151–1200)				Pipe Rolls (1159–1200)			
	a	b	c	d	a	b	c	d	a[1]	b	c	d
Bedfordshire	3	44	10	18.5	4	88	9	9.3	7	132	8	5.7
Berkshire	1	64	3	4.5	1	30	4	12.1	5	156	7	4.3
Buckinghamshire	—	—	—	—	5	53	15	22.1	8	102	9	8.1
Cambridgeshire	2	28	7	20.0	5	60	21	25.9	2	18	6	25.0
Cheshire	—	—	—	—	—	—	—	—	—	—	—	—
Cornwall	—	—	—	—	—	—	—	—	11	135	12	8.2
Cumberland	—	—	—	—	—	—	—	—	2	70	5	6.7
Derbyshire	2	64	2	3.0	—	—	—	—	1	56	8	12.5
Devon	—	—	—	—	—	—	—	—	6	132	5	3.6
Dorset	3	108	3	2.7	2	50	2	3.8	5	134	6	4.3
Durham	—	—	—	—	1	20	2	9.1	1	8	0	0.0
Essex	2	86	10	10.4	5	70	21	23.1	21	226	78	25.7
Gloucestershire	4	168	14	7.7	1	20	2	9.1	1	8	1	11.1
Hampshire	1	60	5	7.7	1	35	1	2.8	7	182	3	1.6
Herefordshire	5	72	9	11.1	—	—	—	—	2	2	1	33.3
Hertfordshire	1	20	1	4.8	1	54	6	10.0	2	19	5	20.8
Huntingdonshire	8	170	24	12.4	10	238	47	16.5	—	—	—	—
Kent	—	—	—	—	—	—	—	—	9	74	17	18.7
Lancashire	—	—	—	—	—	—	—	—	—	—	—	—
Leicestershire	2	36	1	2.7	—	—	—	—	2	34	3	8.1
Lincolnshire	4	59	2	3.3	4	102	6	5.6	2	17	0	0.0
Middlesex	—	—	—	—	—	—	—	—	1	80	0	0.0
Norfolk	7	91	39	30.0	14	122	59	32.6	2	8	6	42.9
Northamptonshire	17	343	17	4.7	2	24	5	17.2	6	84	13	13.4
Northumberland	—	—	—	—	—	—	—	—	8	171	5	2.8
Nottinghamshire	1	16	0	0.0	—	—	—	—	5	42	0	0.0
Oxfordshire	—	—	—	—	—	—	—	—	20	464	33	6.6
Rutland	1	12	0	0.0	—	—	—	—	—	—	—	—
Shropshire	—	—	—	—	—	—	—	—	—	—	—	—
Somerset	22	446	33	6.6	23	388	31	7.5	11	162	12	6.9
Staffordshire	8	136	11	7.5	—	—	—	—	7	78	5	6.0
Suffolk	—	—	—	—	14	117	59	33.5	2	30	3	9.1
Surrey	—	—	—	—	—	—	—	—	6	65	2	3.0
Sussex	—	—	—	—	—	—	—	—	11	266	25	8.6
Warwickshire	1	16	1	5.9	—	—	—	—	4	93	9	8.8
Westmorland	—	—	—	—	—	—	—	—	—	—	—	—
Wiltshire	8	208	11	5.0	8	127	3	2.3	12	207	9	4.2
Worcestershire	—	—	—	—	—	—	—	—	2	28	2	6.7
Yorkshire	—	—	—	—	2	32	0	0.0	7	154	14	8.3
County unknown[2]	1	22	1	4.3	—	—	—	—	25	903	169	15.8
Total	104	2,289	204		103	1,630	293		223	4,340	481	
Overall %				8.2				15.2				10.0

Key to column headings
a – No. of demesnes   b – No. of oxen   c – No. of work-horses   d – % work-horses

[1]No. of demesnes or groups of demesnes.
[2]Or groups of demesnes covering or likely to cover more than one county.

Notes and sources: Sources as in J. Langdon, "Horses, Oxen and Technological Innovation: The Use of Draught Animals in English Farming from 1066 to 1500" (Univ. of Birmingham Ph.D. thesis, 1983), App. B, pp. 401–15.

animals.[42] Faced with this confusing array of possibilities, doubts may be raised as to whether all of them were horses. In the experience of this study, however, these terms almost invariably referred to horses, and they have been considered as such for the purposes of Table 6. The ones causing the most trouble here are *averus, avrus* and *aurus*; these are often confused with the neuter form, *averium*, which appears to have been a term for livestock in general.[43] When the masculine or feminine forms, *averus, avera, avrus, avra*, etc., are used, the internal evidence always suggests that they are horses. Thus in the *Liber Niger* of Peterborough Abbey, *c.* 1125–8, we find reference being made to an *avra cum pullo* (foal).[44] Similarly, in the *Liber Henrici de Soliaco* of 1189 (for Glastonbury Abbey), *averi* are continually being shoed in a fashion that makes it difficult to consider them as anything but horses.[45] Other examples can be cited, particularly for later material, but for the moment we shall refer the reader to the appendix, where the question is explored more fully. Of mules and donkeys, only three Spanish asses appear in the twelfth-century material (i.e., at Burton upon Trent, *c.* 1114–18). Similarly, the working cattle were virtually all oxen (*boves*), although two cows are mentioned as part of the three plough-teams at Pinbury (Gloucestershire) in the early part of the century.[46] These were considered – statistically at least – as oxen and are included as such in our figures.

The data from Table 6, as regards the percentage of work-horses from period to period, can be quickly summarized as shown in column 1 of Table 7. The figures show a gradual increase in the use of horses (on the demesne at least) from Domesday right through the twelfth century. This is especially the case with the surveys, etc., where the use of horses seems to have tripled by the end of the

---

[42] At Wistow in Huntingdonshire there are also some animals recorded as *crocinis*, which are seemingly horses (*Cartularium monasterii de Rameseia*, iii, p. 273). R. Lennard wondered if this might be a corruption for *runcini*. "The Composition of Demesne Plough-Teams in Twelfth-Century England", *Eng. Hist. Rev.*, lxxv (1960), p. 198n.

[43] For example, in a court case in 1194–5 Avicia de Ocel accused William Basset of unjustly detaining her *averia*, which are later itemized as three cows and nine sheep. *Rolls of the King's Court* (Pipe Roll Soc., xiv, 1891), p. 26.

[44] "Liber Niger", p. 54.

[45] *Liber Henrici de Soliaco abbatis Glastoniae*, ed. J. E. Jackson (Roxburghe Club, 1882), pp. 71, 124, 138, 142.

[46] *Burton Abbey Surveys*, p. 212; *Charters and Custumals of the Abbey of Holy Trinity Caen*, ed. M. Chibnall (British Academy Records of Social and Economic History, new series, v, London, 1982), p. 34.

Table 7. *Percentage work-horses from various sources, 1086–1200*

	(1) % work-horses	(2) Corrected % work-horses
Domesday Book (1086)	5.1–5.8	—
Surveys, etc. (1101–50)	8.2	9.5
Surveys, etc. (1151–1200)	15.2	12.4
Pipe Rolls (1159–1200)	10.0	10.2

twelfth century. The Pipe Roll data show a less obvious rise, but it is still significant when compared to the Domesday figures.

A feature of this rise that becomes clear upon a closer look at Table 6 is the extreme importance of regional variation, as is also readily apparent in Table 8. The figures in brackets refer to the number of demesnes or groups of demesnes upon which each regional percentage is based. Figure 16 shows the same thing in pictorial form for the surveys, leases, etc. only, where the years 1125 and 1175 have been arbitrarily chosen as the midpoints for the pre-1150 and post-1150 periods.

Both Figure 16 and Table 8 show East Anglia taking a clear lead in the use of horses during the twelfth century. It also seems that, towards the end of the century, more horses were beginning to be employed in the Home Counties and the east midlands, although the lower figures from the Pipe Roll data in these areas may cast some doubt on this. All other areas, that is, the south, south-west, west midlands and the north, remained under the 10 per cent level. It seems that in these areas the use of horses on manorial demesnes had not changed substantially since Domesday.

What was the timing in the areas that did change? Figure 16 shows that in East Anglia the shift towards the use of horses was already taking place by the first half of the twelfth century. Such at least was the case on eight Ramsey Abbey demesnes, mostly in East Anglia, which had converted to higher work-horse levels as early as the reign of Henry I.[47] However, it is likely that the change occurred

---

[47] That is, Brancaster with Deepdale, Ringstead, Holme next the Sea, Wimbotsham, and Hilgay with Snorehill (Norfolk); Graveley (Cambridgeshire); Hemingford Abbots (Huntingdonshire); and Pegsdon (Bedfordshire). *Cartularium monasterii de Rameseia*, iii, pp. 261, 266 (*bis*), 285, 287, 278, 277, 307.

Table 8. *Regional variation in demesne work-horse levels, 1086–1200*

Region	Percentage of work-horses			
	Domesday	Surveys, etc. (1101–50)	Surveys, etc. (1151–1200)	Pipe Rolls (1159–1200)
East Anglia	6.7–8.0	21.5(11)	30.2(38)	24.8(27)
Home Counties	—	9.9 (5)	13.1(11)	5.9(49)
The South	—	5.6 (9)	2.4 (9)	6.9(39)
South-west	3.0–3.1	5.9(25)	7.1(22)	5.9(33)
East Midlands	—	6.5(33)	13.7(16)	8.3(15)
West Midlands	—	7.5(20)	9.1 (1)	8.9(17)
The North	—	—	3.7 (3)	5.6(18)

The figures in brackets refer to the number of demesnes or groups of demesnes upon which each regional percentage is based.

Notes and sources: Each region is composed of the following counties: *East Anglia:* Norfolk, Suffolk, Essex, Cambridgeshire; *Home Counties:* Surrey, Middlesex, Hertfordshire, Bedfordshire, Buckinghamshire, Oxfordshire, Berkshire; *The South:* Kent, Sussex, Hampshire, Wiltshire; *South-west:* Dorset, Somerset, Devon, Cornwall; *East Midlands:* Huntingdonshire, Northamptonshire, Rutland, Leicestershire, Nottinghamshire, Lincolnshire; *West Midlands:* Warwickshire, Worcestershire, Gloucestershire, Herefordshire, Shropshire, Staffordshire, Cheshire, Derbyshire; *The North:* Lancashire, Westmorland, Cumberland, Northumberland, Durham, Yorkshire.

Table 9. *The growth in the use of horses as demonstrated on three Ramsey Abbey demesnes*

Demesne	"Tempus H I"			c. 1160		
	a	b	c	a	b	c
Elton, Huntingdonshire	40	2	4.8	24	4	25.0
Houghton with Wyton, Huntingdonshire	24	2	7.7	16	6	27.3
Girton, Cambridgeshire	16	1	5.9	12	5	29.4

Key to column headings

a – No. of oxen
b – No. of work-horses
c – % work-horses

Notes and sources: Cartularium monasterii de Rameseia, iii, pp. 257, 259–60, 279, 313–14.

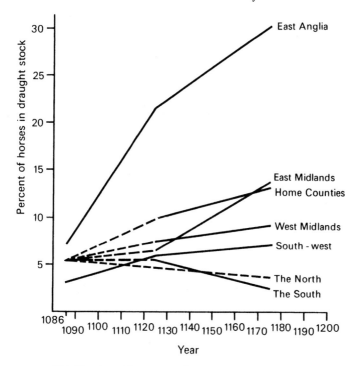

N.B. The dotted lines extrapolate to the midpoint between the minimum and maximum values for the overall Domesday figure.

Fig. 16: Regional trends for the use of horses from Domesday to *c*. 1175 (based on surveys, leases and *Rotuli de Dominabus* only).

towards the end of the reign (1135) rather than earlier, since on three other Ramsey demesnes the alteration did not happen until the middle of the century, as indicated in Table 9.

From the presence of two Huntingdonshire demesnes in Table 9, it would appear that the transition to higher working levels of horses was now moving into the east midlands.[48] Meanwhile, the process

---

[48] The same thing is indicated for the Home Counties, where, for example, the twenty oxen and one horse at Ardeley (Hertfordshire) in 1141 had given way sometime after that to sixteen oxen and eleven horses (according to an undated but probably later lease). *Domesday of St. Paul's of the Year 1222*, pp. 135–8.

was still taking place in East Anglia itself. At "Adulvesnasa", that is, the composite manor of The Sokens in north-east Essex, the arch-deacon, Richard Ruffus, who leased the manor *c.* 1150, was farming land with twenty-nine oxen and thirteen *stotti* that his predecessor had worked with fifty-eight oxen and only six horses.[49] Similarly at Hardley in Norfolk, *c.* 1175–86, the proportion of horses had risen to a third, where as recently as *c.* 1163 the normal complement had seemingly been as many as thirty-two oxen with, at most, two horses.[50] In summary, it appears that the transition to higher levels of working horses was a process taking place throughout the twelfth century, affecting East Anglia first, but gradually moving into the east midlands and the Home Counties.

At this point, it is time to consider in more detail the question of the percentage of work-horses across the country as a whole during the twelfth century. In order to compare this percentage with those of later eras, it is imperative that we obtain as representative a figure as possible, and in this we are faced with at least one major problem: the overall percentage figures as they now stand in Table 6 and column 1 of Table 7 are not based upon data spread evenly across the country. For instance, the post-1150 surveys, etc. produce the relatively high figure of 15.3 per cent for the level of horses among demesne draught animals, but much of this is due to the fact that the sample had an inordinately large proportion of demesnes (over a third) from the distinctly horse-oriented area of East Anglia.

A method by which this distortion can be corrected is to weight the percentages of each of the seven regions in some way such that the unevenness of representation between areas can be eliminated. The difficulty, of course, is to find a suitable means of weighting. In this case it was decided to use the plough-team figures from the Domesday survey, since for each area save the northern-most counties they provide a reasonable indicator of both the amount of arable in cultivation and the number of animals needed to work it. There are of course several reservations about using Domesday materials in a twelfth-century context.[51] Not the least of these is the fact that much land clearance and assarting took place during the

[49] *Ibid.*, pp. 129–32.
[50] *The Register of the Abbey of St. Benet of Holme, 1020–1210*, i, ed. J. R. West (Norfolk Rec. Soc., ii, 1932), pp. 129, 112.
[51] Which I have discussed elsewhere: Langdon, thesis, pp. 60–1.

twelfth century, which added considerably to the cultivated land. It is entirely possible that this clearance altered not only the arable proportion between demesne and peasant but also between region and region, thus tending to render the Domesday data more and more obsolete. Despite this, however, it is to be hoped that the Domesday figures can still provide a reasonable estimate of the *relative* proportions of arable between regions at the end of the twelfth century, even if in absolute terms the figures are somewhat low. In the absence of other suitable material, it is the best we can do.

When corrected in this fashion,[52] the figures undergo some change, as shown by a comparison of columns 1 and 2 in Table 7. The post-1150 survey figure, now corrected, has dropped to 12.4 per cent and is now only 3 per cent or so greater than the level of work-horses in the previous half-century. Only the corrected Pipe Roll figure at 10.2 per cent stays pretty much as it was before.

These figures allow certain conclusions to be made. In short, it seems that the overall percentage of horses in the draught stock of demesnes across the country had risen to about 12½ per cent by the second half of the twelfth century, or one horse to every seven oxen. Relatively this was a considerable advance over the Domesday period when the ratio was more like one horse to every sixteen to nineteen oxen, but in absolute terms oxen were still very much the dominant draught animals. Only in eastern England, and in particular East Anglia, was the heavily ox-dominated system of traction beginning to break up. As for the timing of what change there was, the weighted averages indicate that a good part of it had already occurred by the first half of the century, particularly in counties such as Norfolk. The process was certainly continuing, though, and was spreading outwards from East Anglia right through the twelfth century.

In general, the data were unsatisfactory for determining whether this change in favour of horses was lay- or ecclesiastic-inspired, since no single source provided a suitable mix of lay and ecclesiastic

---

[52] The correction procedure is relatively straightforward and essentially involves the multiplication of each regional percentage of work-horses (as given in the last three columns in Table 8) by the number of Domesday plough-teams for that region. The total of these regional products is then divided by the total number of Domesday plough-teams to yield the overall percentage of horses. The procedure is outlined in more detail in Langdon, thesis, pp. 61–3. Some adjustments were made for the missing Domesday data in the northern counties.

estates with which to compare performance. The first signs of demesne managers suddenly employing greater numbers of horses, however, do occur, as we have already indicated, on the estates of Ramsey Abbey during the reign of Henry I, while similar changes for lay estates are not definitely observed (in the Pipe Rolls and the *Rotuli de Dominabus*) until much later in the century. This, of course, may simply be due to accident, but the lower level of horses on the lay-dominated estates recorded in the Pipe Rolls, even in the latter part of the century, seems to indicate that these estates were slower than their ecclesiastic counterparts to use horses, particularly in the Home Counties and the east midlands.

Finally, it must be noted that any conclusions concerning the level of work-horses in twelfth-century England is severely limited by the fact that, till now, we have only been considering demesne stock. In our discussion of the Domesday material, we questioned whether peasants employed horses at the same level as on the demesne, and the twelfth-century evidence presents us with the same dilemma. A particularly pertinent example occurs in an 1189 survey of the Glastonbury Abbey manor of Kentisford in Dorset, where it is stated that virgate-holders there held of the lord one horse, two oxen and one cow, presumably as a normal livestock complement to the holdings.[53] What is especially interesting here is the ratio of one horse to two oxen, a proportion well above that for demesnes in this part of the country. It is to be noted that this proportion of horses to oxen is identical to that implied for the Anglo-Saxon *gebur* in the *Rectitudines Singularum Personarum* (see pp. 23–4, 27 above) and reinforces the speculation that one horse and two oxen might have been a typical draught stock complement for a peasant holding right through the Anglo-Norman period. Unfortunately there are no more references as clear as the Kentisford case with which to test this intriguing possibility. However, as we shall see, the extensive use of horses by the peasantry is frequently alluded to in twelfth-century documents, particularly in relation to labour services.

b) THE EMPLOYMENT OF HORSES AND OXEN, 1066–1200

Of course, any increase in the proportion of horses engaged in farm work arises directly as a consequence of changes in the way in which

---

[53] *Liber Henrici de Soliaco*, p. 138.

the animals were employed. As we have surmised for Anglo-Saxon times, apart from riding, horses were used mostly for carrying by pack and perhaps harrowing. Oxen performed the major tasks of hauling, particularly of goods, and ploughing. By Domesday, despite the influx of a new ruling hierarchy, the situation had changed little. As we have seen, references to horses in the plough-team are non-existent in the Domesday survey. Nor is there any evidence in the survey as to their use in hauling, where oxen again dominate. Thus, on the demesne at Offenham, Littleton and Bretforton in Worcestershire it is stated that "there are oxen for one plough, but they draw stone to the church".[54] Although there are no other entries in Domesday that so categorically show the ox as both ploughing and hauling beast, oxen for hauling alone are recorded for the Cheshire salt towns of Nantwich, Middlewich and North-wich, where, for instance, "a man who brought a cart with two or more oxen from another shire paid four pence in toll".[55] The Domesday entries for Middlewich and Northwich are also interesting for their references to pack-horses; it was specified that men who loaded up their horses with salt so much as to break their backs paid two shillings if caught within a league of the town.[56] In other words, the Cheshire salt tolls highlight two distinct modes of transport that existed in England at this time, one based on ox-hauled carts or wains, and the other on pack-horses. The scarcity of evidence makes it a matter of conjecture whether this sort of partition existed right across England, but the low level of demesne horses even in East Anglia indicates that it may well have. Presumably, as indicated by the Bayeux Tapestry (see Figure 15), most horses were also employed for harrowing, although there is no direct evidence of this in Domesday save for the *hercerarius* found at Clopton in Cambridgeshire, which was probably a horse.[57] As we have already

---

[54] *Domesday Book*, i, fo. 175b: *Ibi sunt boues ad .I. carucam sed petram trahunt ad aecclesiam.*

[55] *Quisquis ex alia scira carrum ad ducebat cum .ii. bobus aut cum pluribus dabet de theloneo .iiii. denarios* (Northwich). *Domesday Book*, i, fo. 268; see also *English Historical Documents*, ii, p. 871.

[56] *Ibid.* Pack-horses (*sumarii*) are also mentioned in relation to carrying services owed to the queen at Leighton Buzzard, Luton and Houghton Regis, Bedford-shire. *Domesday Book*, i, fo. 209b.

[57] *Inquisitio Comitatus Cantabrigiensis*, ed. N. E. S. A. Hamilton (London, 1876), p. 55. See also appendix under *hercarius*.

indicated, the proportion of one horse to every one or two plough-teams supports this interpretation.

Demesne farms in the Domesday mould can best be seen in the Burton Abbey survey of some thirty years later. Thus, on the home manor of Burton itself there were two ploughs with sixteen oxen, plus four oxen for carting lime and another four for carting wood. On the equid side, there was one harrowing horse (*equa ad herzandum*) and the above-mentioned three Spanish asses, which were probably employed for pack-work. Also present at Burton was a stud of seventy mares and foals, but this was an exceptional feature found on only a few manors in the twelfth century.[58] Excluding these non-working mares and foals, the remaining horse and three asses comprised 14.3 per cent of the working stock. Relatively speaking, this is a much higher proportion than on the eleven other manors in the Burton survey for which the draught stock is adequately recorded.[59] Here the composition of the working stock was just over one horse for every two-and-a-half plough-teams, which, when included with the Burton figures, results in horse levels of 5.9 per cent of the working stock, very close to the Domesday average. On these other eleven manors there were no carting animals *per se*, and it seems that here this duty was performed by the plough oxen. Nor were there any obvious pack-animals on these manors, and it must be presumed that this work was carried out by the one or two horses attending the plough-teams or that such animals were only considered necessary for the home farm at Burton.

As we have already noted, the relative consistency of work-horse levels at Domesday, even between regions as disparate as East Anglia and the south-west, indicates that the sort of draught stock arrangement outlined above was the prevailing mode all across England, and it was to continue so in many areas throughout the twelfth century. In other areas, though, change was clearly occurring. This is first noticed on the Ramsey Abbey demesnes during the reign of Henry I, where for the first time in England horses are recorded as being used for ploughing. For example, at Ringstead in

---

[58] *Burton Abbey Surveys* (*c.* 1114–18), p. 212. See also note 41 above.

[59] That is, Branston, Stretton, Wetmore, Abbots Bromley, Leigh, Stapenhill and Winshill (Staffordshire); Mickleover and Littleover (Derbyshire); Appleby (Leicestershire); Austry (Warwickshire). *Ibid.*, pp. 215, 217, 219, 222, 225–6, 238, 241, 229, 232, 244, 246.

Norfolk, it is stated that in the time of the said king there were three ploughs, "each of four oxen and three horses".[60] As can be seen from this quotation, the horses were not used on their own but in conjunction with oxen, creating what is known as the "mixed team". Here the horses, whether two, three or four, acted as pace-setters for the oxen following behind. Technically the effect was to achieve a greater ploughing speed while retaining the strength of oxen in slow-moving situations, especially when encountering patches of heavy, sticky soil.

However, even a partial replacement of oxen by horses in the plough-team had an immediate effect on the level of work-horses on the demesne, as the three Ramsey manors dealt with in Table 9 amply demonstrate. In time, mixed teams became a dominant feature on the Ramsey Abbey estates, where a possible fifteen out of eighteen demesnes had switched to the new ploughing arrangements by the end of the twelfth century.[61] The mixed team also introduced a new variety into the plough-team structure. Five different types of mixed plough-teams are evident on the Ramsey demesnes, ranging from two horses and eight oxen to four horses and two oxen, and at least three more types can be found on the demesnes of other estates (see Table 10 below for the full range of types). In some cases, plough-teams composed entirely of horses are evident, as, for example, at Semer in Suffolk mentioned above and at Keyston, Huntingdonshire, where the Pipe Roll for 1165–6 records the purchase of three plough-teams of oxen and one of horses.[62] On the other hand, there are no undisputed cases of demesnes using nothing but horses for their draught work.[63]

---

[60] *Et tunc erant in curia de Ringstede tres carrucae. Quaeque de quatuor bobus et tribus equis. Cartularium monasterii de Rameseia*, iii, p. 266.

[61] That is, at Knapwell, Girton, Graveley and Elsworth (Cambridgeshire); Broughton, Hemingford Grey, Warboys, Elton, Wistow, Upwood, and Houghton with Wyton (Huntingdonshire); Wimbotsham, Hilgay with Snorehill and Brancaster (Norfolk); and Lawshall (Suffolk). *Ibid.*, pp. 241, 244, 246, 248, 253, etc.

[62] *Pipe Roll 12 Henry II*, p. 86. The number of animals in each team is not specified, but from the purchase costs it appears the ox-teams consisted of eight animals apiece and the horse-team of only six. See Lennard, "Twelfth-Century Demesne Plough-Teams", p. 202n.

[63] Although two possible instances occur at Great Wratting in Suffolk in 1185 and Olney in Northamptonshire in 1166–7, where only horses were recorded: *Rotuli de Dominabus*, p. 59; *Pipe Roll 13 Henry II*, p. 115. In neither case, however, is it likely that these were the only work animals present; see Langdon, thesis, pp. 67–8.

Since the mixed team was becoming so prevalent in certain parts of the country, it would be instructive to chart its spread throughout the century. The main problem here involves trying to decide whether a demesne had mixed teams or not, since in most cases the plough-team composition can only be inferred from the numbers of draught animals available. Fortunately, this can be simplified statistically. An examination of the Ramsey Abbey demesnes in Table 9 shows the scale of increase in the percentages of work-horses that occurred when there was a transition from all-ox to mixed plough-teams. It appears that a 20 per cent level of horses was the absolute minimum needed to support mixed teams, and indeed all demesnes for which mixed teams were unmistakably present had proportions of work-horses at this level or above. Conversely, where the demesne undoubtedly employed all-ox teams, the level of horses remained below 20 per cent and usually less than 10 per cent. The only possible exception to this rule occurred at Keyston above, where the single horse-plough may have pushed the level of work-horses on this manor up to 20 per cent or above, even though there were no mixed teams. Among the verifiable cases, though, Keyston is very much the exception, and it may be that the single team of horses here was simply the transitory phase of a manorial demesne about to switch to mixed teams.[64] In consequence, it seems reasonable to use the 20 per cent work-horse level as a dividing line in deciding whether a demesne had mixed plough-teams or not. In this case, those demesnes with 20 per cent or more horses are considered as having mixed plough-teams, and those with less than 20 per cent are considered as having all-ox plough-teams. Both types of demesnes have been plotted in Figures 17 to 20 for the first and second halves of the twelfth century.[65]

The maps show definite trends. Reginald Lennard, in his seminal article on twelfth-century demesne plough-teams, stated that mixed teams were generally confined to eastern and east midland England,[66] and certainly this seems to have been the case by the end of the twelfth century (Figure 18). The main concentration of these teams falls within the counties of Norfolk, Suffolk, Essex,

[64] Although later evidence indicates it may have been more permanent than this; see p. 107 below.

[65] These figures have been constructed from the data making up Table 6: details and sources as in Langdon, thesis, pp. 401–15.

[66] "Twelfth-Century Demesne Plough-Teams", *Eng. Hist. Rev.* lxxv (1960), p. 201.

Cambridgeshire and Huntingdonshire. There is also a sprinkling of mixed teams in Kent, and one or two in outlying counties such as Buckinghamshire and Berkshire, although none of these cases is totally verifiable and may in fact be due to faulty data. Even within the mixed team counties, there were still areas – some quite extensive – where all-ox teams continued to predominate, especially in pockets of heavy clay land, such as in south central Essex or west Huntingdonshire (Figure 20). The inference here is that soil or terrain characteristics often prevented or at least delayed the introduction of mixed teams.

Nevertheless, as a comparison of the mixed plough-team distribution from the first to the second half of the century indicates (Figures 17 and 18), the practice of employing mixed teams on medieval demesnes was growing throughout the twelfth century. The striking degree of change over the century as shown on the maps is somewhat illusory, since the relative lack of data for the eastern counties in the first part of the century may hide a greater incidence of mixed teams at that time than is otherwise indicated. However, the practice clearly seems to have been spreading into Huntingdonshire and probably northern Essex from the first to the second half of the century, as we have already seen above from the increase in horse levels.[67] In the early part of the century the incidence of mixed plough-teams was higher for Norfolk than anywhere else, and it seems natural to assume that the practice was first introduced here. This may either have been as a spontaneous innovation or as a technique borrowed from the Continent. The latter would seem more probable, since the use of the horse for ploughing on the Continent clearly predated its employment as such in England;[68] furthermore, East Anglia, with its connections with the Low Countries, would be a natural point of entry for both the idea and the horses needed to implement it.

Did peasants have mixed plough-teams? There is no evidence in the twelfth-century material that they did, and presumably because of their relative lack of animals they might have been tempted to go completely to horses rather than a mixed-team intermediate. Unfortunately there is little evidence that they did this either. Virtually all references to peasant ploughing animals in the twelfth century involve oxen only, such as the ploughing ox (*boue arabili*) owned by

[67] See pp. 45–6 above.   [68] See pp. 19–20 above.

Fig. 17: Distribution of demesnes having or likely to have mixed plough-teams, 1101–50.

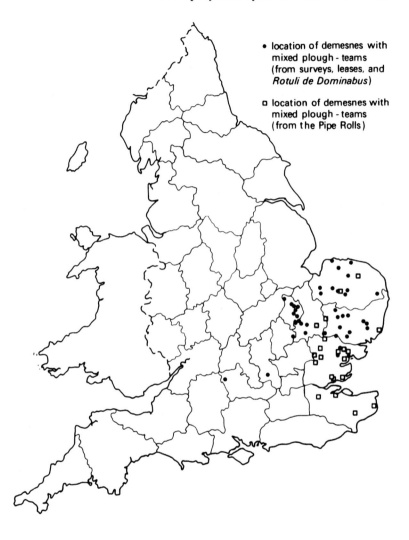

Fig. 18: Distribution of demesnes having or likely to have mixed plough-teams, 1151–1200.

• location of demesnes with
all-ox plough-teams

Fig. 19: Distribution of demesnes having or likely to have all-ox plough-teams, 1101–50.

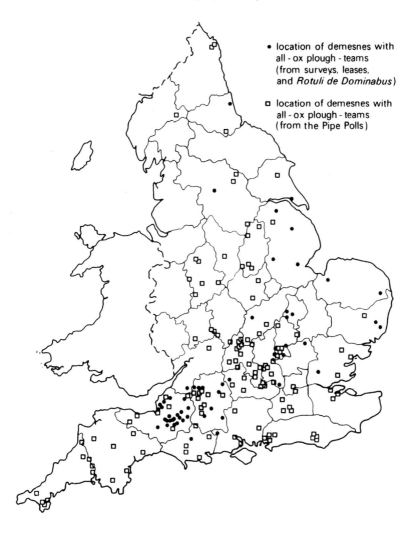

• location of demesnes with
all - ox plough - teams
(from surveys, leases,
and *Rotuli de Dominabus*)

□ location of demesnes with
all - ox plough - teams
(from the Pipe Polls)

Fig. 20: Distribution of demesnes having or likely to have all-ox plough-teams, 1151–1200.

customary tenants at Temple Ewell in Kent in 1185,[69] or those associated with the widow, Gunora de Rode, who, along with other half-virgate holders at Pucklechurch (Gloucestershire) in 1189, had to appear at the lord's plough-boons with as many oxen as she had at the time.[70] Similar references to peasant oxen, usually in relation to ploughing services, occur at a number of other places in the documents.[71] On the other hand, peasant plough-horses are mentioned on the bishop of Worcester's manors of Kempsey (Worcestershire) and Hampton Lucy (Warwickshire), *c.* 1170, where customary tenants were required to harrow with a plough-horse or -horses (*equo arantis* or *equis aratorum*).[72] These are curious references, because they occur in a region which, even in later times, was noted for its loyalty to oxen for ploughing. It is possible that there has been a mistake in transcription – for example, *equis aratrorum* may in fact have been wrongly copied for *equis carectarum* – but since the original document has been lost, there is little that can be done to check this.[73] Otherwise, references to peasant plough-horses are non-existent at this time, and their presence must remain a matter of conjecture.

We have already reviewed the scanty evidence relating to harrowing at Domesday. Fortunately the twelfth century is much more forthcoming in this matter, especially in relation to manorial demesnes, where harrowing horses, appearing as *equi hercatorii*, *equi occatores*, or just *hercarii* and *occatores* in the documents, are a

[69] *Records of the Templars in England in the Twelfth Century*, ed. B. A. Lees (British Academy Records of Social and Economic History, ix, London, 1935), p. 23.

[70] *Cum tot bobus quot habebit. Liber Henrici de Soliaco*, p. 97.

[71] As at Meare, Blackford and Winscombe (Somerset); Nettleton (Wiltshire); Ashbury (Berkshire); Buckland Abbas (Dorset); Fiskerton (Lincolnshire); Ringstead with Holme next the Sea and Walsoken (Norfolk). *Ibid.*, pp. 28, 81, 85–6, 103, 116, 140; "Liber Niger", p. 164; *Cartularium monasterii de Rameseia*, iii, pp. 269, 292. The Walsoken case actually occurs just after the turn of the century in 1200–1.

[72] *Red Book of Worcester*, ed. M. Hollings (Worcs. Hist. Soc., 1934–50), i, p. 84; iii, p. 276. The date of the survey is according to C. C. Dyer, *Lords and Peasants in a Changing Society: The Estates of the Bishopric of Worcester, 680–1540* (Cambridge, 1980), p. 3.

[73] The transcription of the now missing original by the eighteenth-century antiquarian, Dr Thomas, upon which Marjorie Hollings based her published edition of the *Red Book of Worcester*, also refers to "plough-horses". Wo.R.O. Ref. 009:1 BA 2636/10, pp. 50, 163.

common occurrence in all parts of the country.[74] As we have seen with the Burton material, even in areas where oxen seem to have handled every other type of draught work, there were one or two horses to do the harrowing. This use of horses for harrowing even extended to the peasantry. For example, among the services listed for sixteen farmers (*firmarii*) holding twenty-five bovates at Morton (Durham) in 1183, it is stated that every two bovates owed eight days harrowing "with one horse".[75] The same peasant use of horses for harrowing is evident at nearby Warden,[76] and both references are all the more remarkable for occurring so far away from the relatively horse-oriented south and east. In the same way, good references to peasant horses harrowing in the twelfth century are also recorded for Gloucestershire, Kent, Somerset, Warwickshire and Worcestershire.[77] Nowhere in the twelfth-century material examined in this study are oxen mentioned for harrowing.

An activity for which more definite changes were occurring was transportation, especially hauling by vehicle. As we have already indicated (pp. 37–8, 43), the ox was to all appearances the dominant hauling beast in England during the eleventh and early twelfth centuries. During the remainder of the latter century, however, it is evident that a significant change was taking place. Even by the year 1100 it is possible that the horse was beginning to play a more prominent role in English transport, as it is stated that year that the body of William Rufus was brought by peasants to Winchester in a horse-drawn conveyance (*rheda caballaria*), possibly owned by the peasants themselves.[78] Horse hauling for more general goods carry-

[74] E.g., *Bolden Buke: a survey of the possessions of the see of Durham, 1183*, ed. W. Greenwell, (Surtees Soc., xxv, 1852), pp. 3, 5, 6 (*bis*), 8, 10, 18, 19, 20, 21, 29, 34 (*bis*), 35 (*bis*); "Liber Niger", p. 158; *Cartularium monasterii de Rameseia*, iii, pp. 257, 261, 266, 274, 278, 279, 285, 307, 311, 313 (*bis*), 314; *Domesday of St. Paul's of the Year 1222*, pp. 124, 128; *Kalendar of Abbot Samson*, p. 128 (*bis*); *Rotuli de Dominabus*, pp. 20, 56, 61, 62, 63, 66, 68, 69, 74, 77; *Pipe Roll 12 Henry II*, pp. 43, 125 (*bis*); *Pipe Roll 13 Henry II*, p. 30; *Pipe Roll 32 Henry II*, p. 186; *Pipe Roll 33 Henry II*, p. 30; *Pipe Roll 7 Richard I*, pp. 52, 129; *Chanc. Roll (8 Richard I)*, pp. 98, 121. (References are to volumes published by the Pipe Roll Society.)
[75] *Boldon Buke*, p. 8.
[76] *Ibid.*
[77] *Records of the Templars in England in the Twelfth Century*, pp. 23, 51; *Liber Henrici de Soliaco*, p. 85; *Red Book of Worcester*, i, p. 84; ii, p. 169; iii, p. 276.
[78] William of Malmesbury, *De gestis rerum Anglorum* (Rolls Series, London, 1887–9), ii, p. 379.

ing, however, is not definitely recorded until sometime later. Thus, in 1155, a *carectarius equus*, or cart-horse, is listed among the stock on the St Paul's demesne at Sandon in Hertfordshire, and cart-loads (*caretate*) of barley and hay, presumably horse-hauled from the vehicle indicated (see below), are mentioned in 1141 on the demesne at Ardeley in the same county.[79] Towards the end of the twelfth century references to horse hauling are definitely on the increase. Thus, a grant to the nuns at Yedingham in Yorkshire, 1185–95, gave them permission to take a horse and cart every year to fetch plough rods from a wood in Staindale. Similarly, a mixed hauling team of two oxen and two horses was used to cart turves or peat at "Fuelesholme" near Fraisthorpe (Yorkshire), also *c.* 1185–95.[80] Alexander Neckam also mentions horses for hauling and ploughing as a common occurrence in England at this time,[81] while an analysis of peasant vehicle types indicates that peasant horse-hauled vehicles were found on nearly a quarter of manors by the second half of the twelfth century.[82]

Horses, of course, were still employed as pack-animals, especially among the peasantry. Accordingly, *c.* 1114–18, villeins at Burton, Abbots Bromley and Leigh in Staffordshire all owed pack-horse service (*auras ad summagium*) to the abbot of Burton.[83] Later in the century (*c.* 1170) carrying by pack-horse (*cum equis summagia facere*) is specified as a service for tenants of the bishop of Worcester at Tredington (Warwickshire) and similarly at Henbury-in-Salt-Marsh (Gloucestershire).[84] Similarly at Temple Ewell (Kent) in 1185 tenants were given food *ipsi et equi* for bringing two and a half seams (*summas*) of seed from Ospringe or any other appointed place.[85] Here the method of transportation is not indicated definitely, but pack-carrying would seem the most probable.

Nonetheless it is clear that oxen still retained a prominent place in

[79] *Domesday of St. Paul's of the Year 1222*, ed. W. H. Hale (Camden Soc., lxix, London, 1858), pp. 134, 136.
[80] *Early Yorkshire Charters*, i, ed. W. Farrer (Edinburgh, 1914), p. 314; *ibid.*, ii (1915), p. 154.
[81] Alexander Neckam, *De naturis rerum*, ed. T. Wright (Rolls Series, London, 1863), p. 259 (late twelfth century).
[82] J. Langdon, "Horse Hauling", table 3 (p. 56).
[83] *Burton Abbey Surveys*, pp. 212, 222, 226. The same is also implied for Cauldwell, Derbyshire. *Ibid.*, p. 244.
[84] *Red Book of Worcester*, iii, p. 293; iv, p. 409.
[85] *Records of the Templars in England in the Twelfth Century*, p. 23.

the transportation of farm or other goods in the twelfth century, particularly as hauling beasts. This is indicated for both demesne and peasant farms. Thus at Hampton Lucy (Warwickshire), *c* 1170, part of the services owed by the keepers of the oxen (*bovarii*) was to haul material for the demesne ploughs with the lord's *plaustrum* and oxen.[86] Similarly wine-hauling services involving the use of oxen were owed by well-to-do tenants at several Durham villages in 1183, while a certain Godwin, holding a half-hide of land in Nettleton (Wiltshire) in 1189, owed as part of his labour services four oxen to carry a load (*carriatam*) of hay.[87] The same is evident for smaller holdings. Thus Osbert de Bradafeld, holding a half-virgate at Wrington (Somerset), also in 1189, owed carrying services "with that which he has in plough"; given the area, this could only be oxen.[88] Indeed, the aforesaid analysis of peasant vehicle types for the second half of the twelfth century indicates that peasant ox-hauled vehicles were still found on over 80 per cent of manors at this time.[89] The same predilection for using oxen for ploughing and hauling is also seen in twelfth-century Wales, where Giraldus Cambrensis described it as an everyday event.[90]

The general conclusion from all this is that oxen remained the dominant hauling beast virtually throughout the twelfth century, but that horses were starting to challenge this position, especially during the second half of the century when the incidence of horse hauling begins to show a sharp upturn. Horses, too, retained much of their popularity as pack-animals, particularly among peasants, who were often expected to perform pack-carrying services for their lords, a tendency that seems to have been very widespread. Consequently the level of horses owned by the peasantry across the country must have been quite high, if only to satisfy the carrying and

---

[86] *Materium aratrorum adportabunt de bosco cum plaustro et bobus Episcopi. Red Book of Worcester*, iii, p. 277.

[87] *Bolden Buke*, pp. 2 (*bis*), 6, 18, 20, 27 (*bis*), 37 (*bis*), 32, 36; *Liber Henrici de Soliaco*, p. 103.

[88] *Osbertus de Bradafeld tenet unam virgatam pro quinque solidis, et debet . . . carriare cum hoc quod habet in carruca . . . (Liber Henrici de Soliaco*, p. 89). Only oxen are mentioned for ploughing in this survey (for example, at nearby Winscombe, pp. 85–6).

[89] Langdon, "Horse Hauling", p. 56.

[90] *Boves autem ad aratra vel plaustra binos quidem jungunt rarius, sed quaternos frequentius.* Giraldus Cambrensis, *Descriptio Kambriae* in *Opera*, vi, ed. J. F. Dimock (Rolls Series, London, 1863), p. 259.

harrowing services for which they were liable.[91] Indeed, the typical draught stock ratio of two oxen to one horse indicated at Kentisford, Dorset (see above) begins to look quite plausible.

c) THE SIZE OF THE PLOUGH-TEAM, 1066–1200

The argument concerning the size of the medieval plough-team has had a long and distinguished history in England, not only for its importance in interpreting the Domesday survey, but also for its implications concerning the formation of the open- or common-field system. It is over a century since Frederic Seebohm first developed his thesis that the large, eight-ox plough-team held the key to the communal system upon which the open fields were based.[92] Such a large team, Seebohm claimed, was by its very size beyond the means of all but a few cultivators. Consequently the inhabitants of a village had to group together to form communal plough-teams, each villager contributing animals and equipment according to his means. The degree of cooperation thus engendered led to the careful allocation of strips so that, in the words of a later commentator, they "should be ploughed successively for each contributor to the plough team."[93] In its inception, this allocation was very fluid, each peasant annually receiving land according to the size of his contribution. It was only later that the strips became fixed in the possession of individual villagers.[94]

This strict technical interpretation concerning the origins of the open-field system has been much modified and refuted in the years since Seebohm first offered it. Maitland and Vinogradoff maintained that it was the need for the equality of land share-out, rather than any ploughing arrangement, that led to the regular lay-out of strips.[95] Gray, and later Homans, while admitting the importance of

[91] Some peasants even had riding horses, as indicated by the tolls charged for such animals at Bishop's Cleeve and Henbury-in-Salt-Marsh, Gloucestershire. *Red Book of Worcester*, pp. 353, 409 (*c.* 1170).

[92] F. Seebohm, *The English Village Community*, first published in 1883. The fourth edition (London, 1905) was employed for this study. See especially chapter IV, pp. 105–25.

[93] H. L. Gray, *English Field Systems* (Cambridge, Massachusetts, 1915), p. 9.

[94] A process which may have taken centuries, according to Seebohm (*English Village Community*, pp. 123–4, 409–11, 437–8).

[95] F. W. Maitland, *Domesday Book and Beyond* (Cambridge, 1921 edn), pp. 337, 346; P. Vinogradoff, *Villainage in England* (Oxford, 1892), pp. 230–8, 252–4.

co-aration, preferred to see the creation of the various field systems as being imported by successive waves of Germanic tribes, each of which left their cultural imprint on the agriculture of the area where they settled.[96] The Orwins, on the other hand, denied that the open fields were imported but felt that they arose directly out of the pioneering spirit of a people faced with clearing and farming new land, all of which created a nexus of cooperation that was far greater than the simple arranging of communal ploughing that Seebohm postulated.[97] The most radical departure from established theory, however, has been that of Joan Thirsk, who sees the creation of the common- or open-field system as coming from a much later period in English history, primarily the twelfth and thirteenth centuries. Here the problem is not one of original settlement, but of a forced reorganization of agriculture because of population pressure, a reorganization, moreover, in which livestock grazing arrangements played a much more important role than co-aration.[98]

It is not the purpose of this study to delve too deeply into the questions concerning the origins of the open fields,[99] but simply to examine those aspects of the problem that hinge most directly upon the subject of traction, especially ploughing and the related question of co-aration. Here we want to do three things: (1) to look at the average size of the plough-team across England, and thus to show the extent to which co-aration was necessary, (2) to show what effect, if any, the horse had in reducing plough-team size and, hence, the need to practise co-aration, and (3) to resolve certain contradictions concerning plough-team size, in particular the discrepancy noted between the teams indicated in documents and those shown in medieval illustrations.

How do we start? As we have seen, the eight-ox plough-team was an integral part of the Domesday survey, even if only as a computational aid, but there are grave questions as to whether it reflected the actual team size in everyday operation. Fortunately the twelfth-

[96] Gray, *English Field Systems*, esp. ch. X; G. C. Homans, "The Explanation of English Regional Differences", *Past and Present*, no. 42 (1969), esp. pp. 29–31.

[97] Orwin and Orwin, *The Open Fields*, 3rd edn (Oxford, 1967), esp. pp. 12–14, 51–2.

[98] Joan Thirsk, "The Common Fields", in *Peasants, Knights and Heretics*, ed. R. H. Hilton (Cambridge, 1979); also the preface to the third edition of Orwin and Orwin, *The Open Fields*, esp. pp. xiii–xv.

[99] I have not, for instance, dealt with the later theories of, among others, McCloskey, Dahlman and Dodgshon (see bibliography).

Table 10. *Distribution of twelfth-century demesne plough-team sizes*

1. *All-ox teams*

County or area	No. of oxen in team									
	6		7		8		10		12	
	a	*b*	*a*	*b*	*a*	*b*	*a*	*b*	*a*	*b*
Bedfordshire	—	—	—	—	2	5	—	—	—	—
Berkshire	—	—	—	—	1	6½	—	—	—	—
Buckinghamshire	—	—	—	—	1	1	—	—	—	—
Cambridgeshire	—	—	—	—	1	2	—	—	—	—
Cornwall	—	—	—	—	—	—	1	1½	—	—
Derbyshire	—	—	—	—	2	8	—	—	—	—
Devon	—	—	—	—	—	—	2	3	—	—
Dorset	—	—	—	—	1	7	1	8	—	—
Essex	—	—	—	—	1	1	1	5	—	—
Gloucestershire	—	—	—	—	4	21	—	—	—	—
Hampshire	—	—	—	—	—	—	1	4½	—	—
Hertfordshire	—	—	—	—	—	—	1	1	—	—
Huntingdonshire	2	4	—	—	6	22	1	3	—	—
Honour of Lancaster	—	—	—	—	1	15	—	—	—	—
Leicestershire	1	2	—	—	1	3	—	—	—	—
Lincolnshire	1	4	1	1	3	8	—	—	—	—
Middlesex	—	—	—	—	1	10	—	—	—	—
Northamptonshire	1	2	—	—	14	34	—	—	—	—
Nottinghamshire	—	—	—	—	1	2	—	—	—	—
Honour of William Peverill of Nottingham	—	—	—	—	1	7	—	—	—	—
Oxfordshire	1	9	—	—	—	—	—	—	—	—
Rutland	1	2	—	—	—	—	—	—	—	—
Somerset	—	—	—	—	5	15	—	—	—	—
Staffordshire	—	—	—	—	8	16	—	—	—	—
Sussex	—	—	—	—	—	—	—	—	1	7
Warwickshire	—	—	—	—	1	2	—	—	—	—
Yorkshire	—	—	—	—	2	7	—	—	—	—
Total	7	23	1	1	57	192½	8	26	1	7
% (cases)	9.5		1.4		77.0		10.8		1.4	
% (teams)		9.2		0.4		77.2		10.4		2.8

century material is a help here. Many of the surveys, leases and Pipe Rolls are very explicit about plough-team size and composition, for the demesnes at least, and as a result it has been possible to construct in Table 10 a list of all those cases where the demesne plough-team is explicitly given or at least fairly obvious in the documents.

As we can see from the table, there was in fact a wide spectrum of

Table 10. (*cont.*)

2. *Mixed and all-horse teams*

County	5 3H,2O a	b	6 4H,2O a	b	2H,4O a	b	7 3H,4O a	b	8 8H a	b	10 4H,4O a	b	2H,6O a	b	4H,6O a	b	2H,8O a	b
Bedfordshire	—	—	1	2	—	—	—	—	—	—	—	—	—	—	—	—	—	—
Cambridgeshire	—	—	—	—	—	—	—	—	—	—	—	—	1	2	—	—	—	—
Essex	—	—	—	—	—	—	—	—	—	—	—	—	1	1	1	2	1	2
Huntingdonshire	—	—	—	—	—	—	—	—	—	—	1	3	1	4	—	—	1	4
Norfolk	—	—	—	—	1	1	4	8½	—	—	—	—	2	4	—	—	—	—
Suffolk	1	1	—	—	—	—	—	—	1	1	—	—	2	3	—	—	—	—
Total	1	1	1	2	1	1	4	8½	1	1	1	3	7	14	1	2	2	6

	5	6	7	8	10
% (Cases)	5.3	10.5	21.1	47.4	15.8
% (Teams)	2.6	7.8	22.1	46.8	20.8

Key to column headings

a – Number of cases
b – Number of teams
H – Horses
O – Oxen

Notes and sources: For sources, see Langdon, thesis, p. 104, ns. 113a and 113b. Much of this material is also outlined in R. Lennard, "The Composition of Demesne Plough-teams in Twelfth-Century England", *Eng. Hist. Rev.*, lxxv (1960), esp. Table 5 (p. 205)

plough-team sizes on English demesnes in the twelfth century, ranging from five animals in a mixed team in Suffolk (Elveden) to teams of twelve oxen apiece in Sussex (the valley of Singleton). Despite these extremes, the dominant plough-team size was still one of eight animals. Thus over 75 per cent of the all-ox plough-teams contained exactly this number, as well as nearly 50 per cent of the mixed plough-teams. Consequently the decision of the Domesday commissioners to adopt the eight-ox team as a unit of calculation seems quite justified in the circumstances. Nor did switching to mixed teams make any noticeable difference. Although isolated cases of a drop in plough-team size when converting from all-ox to mixed or even all-horse teams appear to have occurred,[100]

---

[100] As at Keyston, Huntingdonshire: see p. 51 above. Also the thirty-two oxen at Hardley, Norfolk, *c.* 1163, implying four plough-teams of eight oxen apiece, had shrunk to a single mixed team of two horses and four oxen by 1175–86. *St. Benet of Holme*, i, pp. 112, 129.

the average size of the mixed and all-horse teams together at 8.0 animals was only slightly less than that for all-ox plough-teams (8.1 animals). It appears that, at this time, the benefit of introducing horses to shorten the plough-team was either not possible or for some reason not acted upon. One must assume that the transition to mixed teams in particular was made almost solely for the technical reason of speeding up the plough.

Not surprisingly the distribution of plough-team sizes displayed a significant degree of regionality. Thus it is noticeable that large plough-teams of ten animals or more tended to be congregated in the south-west (especially Devon and Cornwall), Sussex, and Essex, where the soil was often heavy or the terrain uneven.[101] On the other hand, smaller than average plough-teams of six oxen occurred in the east midlands, particularly in areas of light limestone soils, such as at Great Easton in Leicestershire, Tinwell in Rutland and Cottingham in Northamptonshire.[102] Small mixed teams were also found in Norfolk and Suffolk. In most cases, however, the eight-animal team remained dominant, particularly in the north, which seems to have been a bastion for teams of this size during the twelfth century.[103] In conclusion, it can be said that regionality did play a part in determining plough-team size, but that generally soil and terrain had to be somewhat out of the ordinary to push a particular demesne off the eight-animal standard.

The most basic point to arise from all this is that, with or without horses, the demesne plough-team in the twelfth century was generally a very large one. As such, it tends to give credibility to the idea that co-aration was a powerful force in determining the shape of agriculture in the early medieval period, if we can assume that the peasant plough-team was similar in size to that on the demesne. Here, however, we run up against a major contradiction. Despite this seemingly overwhelming evidence for the large plough-team in the documents, it is seriously – and curiously – at odds with the evi-

---

[101] It is also significant that purchases of oxen recorded in the Pipe Rolls for Devon and Cornwall in the late twelfth century, for instance, are almost always divisible by ten: e.g., *Pipe Roll 15 Henry II*, p. 48; *Pipe Roll 30 Henry II*, p. 88; *Pipe Roll 31 Henry II*, p. 157; *Pipe Roll 7 Richard I*, pp. 132–3; *Chancellor's Roll (8 Richard I)*, pp. 139, 209.

[102] "Liber Niger", pp. 160, 158, 159.

[103] E.g., see the figures for Staffordshire, Derbyshire, Nottinghamshire, Yorkshire and the Honour of Lancaster in Table 10.

dence from medieval iconography, which never shows plough-teams approaching anything like the eight- or ten-animal monsters outlined above. As it happens, the largest plough-teams portrayed in medieval illuminations are found in English manuscripts (for example, see Figures 11 and 13), but in no instance do they portray a team of greater than four animals.[104] This may have been due to an artistic convention of representing large plough-teams by smaller ones, since some of these cases at least show what seem to be impracticably small teams.[105] On the other hand, one is struck by the variety of plough-teams shown – four oxen in double file, two oxen abreast, one horse alone, one mule alone, two oxen led by a donkey, two oxen in tandem, and so on – which would seem unlikely if these illustrations were solely a matter of convention, where the tendency would have been for such representations to have become rapidly stereotyped into, as H. G. Richardson wrote, "a common symbol infinitely repeated".[106] In other words, in some instances at least, it seems likely that the artist drew what he actually saw, especially where the representation was obviously a meticulous one.[107]

One hypothesis reconciling this contradiction between the iconographic and documentary evidence regarding plough-teams was introduced in a persuasive article written by H. G. Richardson during World War II.[108] Richardson suggested that the large plough-team was rather more than it appeared and that in fact it represented two possible types of agricultural organization. The first, which he personally preferred, was that the plough-team recorded in the documents included both ploughing and harrowing animals. As an example, Richardson cited a passage from *Piers Plowman*, where Piers drove a plough of four oxen followed immediately by two harrows drawn by two horses apiece, resulting in the total of eight animals so often seen in the documents.[109]

---

[104] The same applies to a substantial number of medieval illustrations from the Continent which I have examined from various published works.

[105] Such as the small mule or donkey in the Bayeux Tapestry (Figure 15), for which there is very little evidence in English agriculture either before or after.

[106] H. G. Richardson, "The Medieval Plough-team". *History*, xxvi (1942), pp. 288–9.

[107] As in the Luttrell Psalter (Figure 11), where the illustrator also went to the trouble of realistically portraying three- and even five-horse teams, for which we do have substantial documentary evidence: for example, see pp. 152, 224 below.

[108] Richardson, "The Medieval Plough-team", pp. 287–96.

[109] *Ibid.*, pp. 291–2.

Unfortunately, intriguing as this suggestion is, it is not very plausible. For one thing, it is patently obvious that provisions for harrowing were more often than not made outside the recorded plough-team, simply from the number of extra harrowing horses that appear in the documents. In any case, harrowing was seemingly a much quicker chore than ploughing and in fact could be accomplished by one horse alone, as is amply indicated in many medieval illustrations.[110] It would hardly need the four animals indicated in the Piers Plowman example (which in any case were presumably included only for literary symmetry). Some of the "plough" animals may have been used for carting, again theoretically reducing the size of the actual plough-team, but in fact this did not necessarily happen, since much, if not most, of the hauling took place during breaks in the ploughing cycle, particularly at the harvest. In other words, it is most unlikely that the extra duties of harrowing and carting entailed with the operation of one plough-team would have required four or more animals. This becomes even more obvious in the next century, when specialized carting horses begin to appear on the demesne, but without any reduction in plough-team size.

The second possibility in Richardson's theory was that the large plough-team concealed two smaller teams which worked half a day each. Such a system was not unknown in the nineteenth century, but it was reckoned to be very expensive and very much a matter of choice.[111] There is no firm evidence that such an arrangement ever existed in medieval times, and indeed Walter of Henley clearly implies that it did not.[112] Moreover, if a changeover arrangement did exist it would create some curious problems among some of the recorded plough-team sizes. For instance, how would one split up a six-ox plough-team? Oxen are much more conveniently yoked in

---

[110] E.g., Singer et al., *History of Technology*, ii, pp. 91, 94; Millar, *Luttrell Psalter*, fo. 171. See also pp. 113, 221n below.

[111] "Many people who work oxen keep 4, and work each pair only one half of the day. This is a most expensive system, and were a good selection of the oxen to be made is most unnecessary." James Cowie, "An Essay in the Comparative Advantages in the Employment of Horses and Oxen in Farm Work", *Journal Royal Agric. Soc.*, v (1844), pp. 54–5.

[112] Walter expected his oxen to cover six leagues a day while ploughing, equivalent to an acre's cultivation, a good day's work (*Walter of Henley*, p. 315); see also Fitzherbert's reference to oxen ploughing all day (*The Book of Husbandry by Master Fitzherbert*, 1534 edn, p. 15).

pairs (unless one is willing to spend money on the more expensive collar-harness or go to the more cumbersome three-ox yokes), and of course it is more difficult to do this in dividing up a six-ox team without creating a serious imbalance between the two smaller teams – one in fact would have to be double the size of the other. The situation was even more difficult with mixed plough-teams. The division of a team of two horses and six oxen into two equal parts would result in plough-teams of one horse and three oxen, which would look bizarre in almost any arrangement. Finally, if a change-over system did exist, one would expect a bi-modal distribution of plough-team sizes with peaks at the four- and eight-animal levels – as some manors used two teams spelling each other while others tried to make do with only one – instead of the uni-modal distribution which in fact was the case.[113]

Another explanation for the discrepancy in the size of the plough-team between the documents and the illustrations is that they may well have been describing two different things, the documents being concerned only with demesne plough-teams and the illustrations with peasant plough-teams. The idea is not new,[114] but it does run counter to one long-held assumption. When large plough-teams are mentioned it is usually presumed that their large size was necessary to pull the heavy plough of the time through the soil. In other words, it was a strictly technical limitation that applied to lords and peasants alike.

But did this technical limitation necessarily apply? If it did, the most obvious consequence was that peasants would have to practise co-aration or cooperative ploughing, since a large plough-team was patently beyond the resources of the average peasant. For example, it has been calculated that the more well-to-do peasants at Domesday had only about three oxen apiece at Domesday.[115] Consequently, *if* the normal working plough-team was of eight or so animals, then at least two and probably three of these peasants

[113] See especially Figure 29 below.
[114] E.g., E. Miller and J. Hatcher, *Medieval England: Rural Society and Economic Change 1086–1348* (London, 1978), p. 13. The idea of small peasant plough-teams was in fact first postulated by Seebohm (*English Village Community*, pp. 84–5), who saw it as a result of the natural decay of co-aration throughout the middle ages. See also Vinogradoff, *Villainage in England*, pp. 252–3.
[115] That is, for villeins and sokemen: Lennard, *Rural England*, pp. 352–3.

would have to club together to make it up.[116] Were peasants in fact forced to group together to this extent? Or, as Vinogradoff suggested, was the four- or even two-animal team, despite the contradiction between them and the larger demesne plough-team, still the more likely complement for the peasant plough, such that most peasants did not have to practise co-aration at all?[117] The answers to these questions are not easy to find. Although some cases of co-aration must be assumed for Domesday,[118] it is never explicitly mentioned. However, cases specifying or at least hinting at co-aration are sometimes found in the twelfth-century material, especially in relation to ploughing services which tenants performed on the lord's demesne. A number of these cases are found in the Glastonbury Abbey survey of 1189 contained in the *Liber Henrici de Soliaco*. Thus at Meare in Somerset John Bulbulcus, holding a messuage and three acres, owed two days ploughing to his lord in winter, which he performed by joining his one or two oxen with those of his friends to make up a plough (. . . *si habet unum bovem ut duos junget illos cum sociis et perficient carrucam*).[119] The same thing is implied for more substantial tenants. For instance, Godwin, the half-hide holder at Nettleton already mentioned above, owed three-quarters of an acre's ploughing to the lord each week; but if he only had one or two oxen, he still had to find a whole plough or plough-team (*carruca integra*) with which to fulfil his services.[120] Where he obtained the oxen from is not mentioned, but presumably there is a good chance that he entered into a ploughing arrangement with other tenants. On the other hand, he may simply have borrowed or hired them.

The "whole plough" in the passage above may have referred to the large demesne plough-team rather than any smaller peasant one, and it has been suggested that peasants cooperated to plough the lord's demesne but did so to a much lesser extent on their own

---

[116] The situation would be even worse for peasants of lesser means – cottars, bordars and many free-men – where, if the Domesday survey is to be believed, as many as eight (or even more) men had to join together to make up a single team: e.g., *ibid.*, pp. 353–4. See also note 118 below.

[117] Vinogradoff, *Villainage in England*, p. 253.

[118] The sheer number of tenants given for a single plough often presupposes some degree of co-aration, as at Bradenham in Norfolk, where eight sokemen held half a plough-land and had between them one plough. *Domesday Book*, ii, fo. 235.

[119] *Liber Henrici de Soliaco*, p. 28.

[120] *Ibid.*, p. 103.

lands.[121] The Glastonbury material gives some indirect support for this. Thus at Winscombe in Somerset each half-virgate holder was required to plough three times during Lent with a "whole" team, while at the more flexible plough-boon (that is, the occasional ploughing service theoretically performed for the "love" of the lord) he could plough "with as many oxen as he has".[122] The implication here is that the monks of Glastonbury preferred their tenants to use a full eight-ox team to do their ploughing services, perhaps to accomplish a deeper ploughing that might not otherwise have been possible with the peasants' smaller teams, but were willing on occasion to allow them to do it with less. Similarly at Buckland Abbas in Dorset, Walter de Hennelea, a virgate holder, is cited as owing nine ploughing services during the year, which he ploughed "with a whole plough if he has one, with half a plough if he only has that, (or) with two oxen if he has no more."[123] The same thing is observed on other estates. Thus on the bishop of Worcester's manor at Withington (Gloucestershire), *c.* 1170, virgate holders were allowed to do their weekly ploughing for the demesne "with as many animals as they have", while at "Bulney" in Suffolk, *c.* 1198–1200, Galant Blund and his heirs, holding some twenty to thirty acres from the abbot of St Edmunds, owed ploughing services "with as many animals of his as he will have in his plough".[124] It is possible that when peasants arrived at ploughing services with their animals and ploughs, the lord's bailiff or reeve recombined their animals into larger teams, but often it seems they were used as is. At Northwick (Worcestershire), for instance, again *c.* 1170, it is specified that each virgate holder should perform his ploughing services with his own plough (*quaeque virgata . . . arare debet proprio aratro*).[125] It should also be pointed out that the above cases are generally the exception as far as ploughing service formulae are concerned. Most simply state that so-and-so owes so many ploughing services, without qualifying how large the plough-team should be or whether the person involved should plough with others. In this case, we must presume that the practice of peasants clubbing together to

[121] H. S. Bennett, *Life on the English Manor* (Cambridge, 1937), p. 46.
[122] *Liber Henrici de Soliaco*, p. 86: *Et in quadragesime debet ter arare cum integra carruca. et semel ad preces cum tot bobus quot habet.*
[123] *Ibid.*, p. 141.
[124] *Red Book of Worcester*, iv, p. 367; *Kalendar of Abbot Samson*, p. 130.
[125] *Red Book of Worcester*, i, p. 34.

form a full-size demesne plough-team was so prevalent that it did
not need mentioning, or that, more likely, lords were not so fussy
and let the peasant get on with his demesne ploughing as he saw fit.

In short, the evidence seems to imply that the peasant very often
managed to get away with ploughing with much smaller teams than
the eight-animal standard, with all the advantages that had for cost
and convenience. Giraldus Cambrensis indicated that the normal
plough-team size among Welsh farmers in his time (late twelfth century) was most often one of four oxen and sometimes even two.[126]
What prevented these smaller teams from being employed on
English demesnes? Perhaps they were. It has been suggested (without invoking Richardson's theories) that the large plough-teams
described in the surveys were in fact only employed on special
occasions during the year, that is, when virgin land was being
broken up or in the spring planting season, when stock was weakest
after the long winter layover.[127] On almost all other occasions, it is
claimed, smaller teams were used. Such a theory, however, seems
improbable. Apart from the obvious waste of keeping a large team
available all year for use on only a few occasions, it is not supported
by the operating costs for the animals recorded in the thirteenth and
fourteenth centuries, which generally show the operation of a full
demesne team throughout the winter and spring at least.[128]

Also suggested to explain the probable difference between
peasant and demesne plough-teams is that the peasants used lighter
ploughs to save on team strength,[129] and the apparent attempts of
the Glastonbury monks to keep their tenants' ploughing services up
to the demesne mark tends to support this. Nevertheless, more
direct evidence as to the nature of peasant ploughs, scanty as it is
(see below), shows no sign that these ploughs would be considerably
easier to draw than those on the demesne. Nor should we assume

---

[126] See note 90 above.
[127] B. H. Slicher van Bath, *The Agrarian History of Western Europe A.D. 500–1850*
(London, 1963), p. 69; M. M. Postan, "The Economic Foundations of Medieval
Society", in his *Essays on Medieval Agriculture and General Problems of the
Medieval Economy* (Cambridge, 1973), p. 17; S. R. Eyre, "The Curving Plough-
strip and its Historical Implications", *Agric. Hist. Rev.*, iii (1955), p. 93.
[128] Almost any number of demesne accounts from the thirteenth and fourteenth centuries will verify this, where fodder costs remain constant right through the winter
and early spring months.
[129] Miller and Hatcher, *Medieval England: Rural Society and Economic Change*,
p. 13.

that light ploughs must necessarily be the explanation for small peasant plough-teams. Another plausible factor is the organization of demesne versus peasant ploughing. Demesne ploughing was a very long-winded affair. A conservative estimate would be 180 full days' ploughing per team dispersed over the year, and in many cases it was likely to be much more.[130] Under these conditions it was mandatory to have a large team simply so the plough animals were never over-taxed at any point. The variability of team size – whether six, eight, ten, or even twelve animals – reflected the different cost optimums for different types of ground. Any reduction in team size below these optimums, which were presumably arrived at through centuries of experience, would lead to excessive animal losses, while any beasts above would be wasted.

On the other hand, such high work-levels per team did not normally apply to the peasantry, simply because they ploughed very much less than on the demesne. It is difficult to cite a typical example, since the amount of ploughing required for a peasant holding could vary considerably according to circumstances, not least in the amount of ploughing services owed. Nevertheless it can be calculated that only in exceptional cases would peasant ploughing requirements have exceeded 100 days per year,[131] and in most cases it would have been considerably less.[132] On Russian peasant farms at the beginning of the present century the actual number of days spent ploughing was seldom greater than sixty to seventy days,[133] and an upper limit of this sort would not seem out of line for

---

[130] Walter of Henley, for instance, suggested a total of 240 to 264 days' ploughing per year as a likely work-load for the average plough-team. *Walter of Henley*, p. 157.

[131] For example, see Langdon, thesis, p. 88 and pp. 107–8 (ns. 146–7), where this calculation was performed for thirty-acre virgate-holders. Only when ploughing services were very substantial and some degree of co-aration was needed did the number of days' ploughing exceed 100.

[132] For example, at Cuxham in Oxfordshire, twelve-acre half-virgate tenants in the thirteenth century, with virtually nothing in the way of ploughing services to perform, seemingly ploughed little more than 30 days per year, even assuming that each tenant had to co-operate with a friend (Langdon, "Economics of Horses and Oxen", p. 38). This was probably a fairly typical case, judging from the average size of peasant holdings noted elsewhere in England – the majority had a half-virgate or less – and the fact that labour services were as often as not apt to be very light. E. A. Kosminsky, *Studies in the Agrarian History of England in the Thirteenth Century* (Oxford 1956), pp. 214–17; Miller and Hatcher, *Medieval England: Rural Society and Economic Change*, pp. 121–6.

[133] A. V. Chayanov, *The Theory of Peasant Economy*, ed. D. Thorner, B. Kerblay and R. E. F. Smith (Illinois, 1966), p. 156 (table 4-24).

most medieval peasant holdings. In consequence, peasant draught animals tended to have a much easier life than their counterparts on the demesne, even including the additional hauling and harrowing that these animals may have been expected to do. As a result, it was possible to keep fodder costs for peasant draught animals down,[134] while still allowing their peasant owners to work them very hard when needed. Chayanov, when considering the Russian case, commented: "The fact that the Russian peasant horse is not used much explains why, although it is fed on hay, it endures much, serves long, and, in general, is little subject to disease."[135]

The difference between the peasant and demesne plough-teams can thus be reconciled on economic grounds as much as technical ones, the demesne manager preferring large teams in order to cut down on his animal losses through overwork. Nor does a difference in the weight of plough need to be postulated. Working his animals in short bursts, it is entirely possible that the peasant could have had as heavy a plough as on the demesne. After all, some of the ploughs being hauled by small teams in medieval illustrations are decidedly heavy affairs (see Figure 11). There were limits, of course, as to how long these "short" bursts could be maintained, but for most peasants they were probably sufficient to see them through the ploughing year.

This rather lengthy exposition of the plough-team problem has been set out to provide a basis for discussion in this and later chapters. It is apparent from what we have discussed here, however, that the demesne plough-team in the twelfth century was a large one centring around eight animals and one which the introduction of the horse had little effect in reducing, at least at this time. Consequently we are really only left with two possibilities for explaining the smaller teams of no more than four animals shown in medieval illustrations: one, that these smaller teams were the product of artistic convention, or, two, that they were a notable feature of peasant farming. The evidence we have presented in this chapter suggests that the latter premise is the correct one. Beyond this, we must leave the question for a later chapter, where more abundant evidence provides a clearer picture.[136]

---

[134] Langdon, "Economics of Horses and Oxen", pp. 38–40.
[135] Chayanov, *The Theory of Peasant Economy*, p. 155.
[136] See especially pp. 241–4 below.

d) PLOUGHS, HARROWS AND VEHICLES, 1066–1200

The relationship between the larger farm implements and the use of horses and oxen is often a very precise one. The early dichotomy between horses for harrowing and oxen for ploughing and hauling has already been remarked upon, but even where horses do begin to plough and haul in the twelfth century, there are some areas where they patently perform better than in others. Much of this is connected with soil and terrain, but the type of plough and vehicle used in a certain area can often have a bearing as well.

Dealing with ploughs first, the vital distinction to consider here is between the scratch plough (or ard) and the heavy mould-board plough. Unfortunately the post-Conquest documentation is unhelpful in this regard. Linguistic evidence in particular is disappointing. The distinction between the light scratch plough and the heavier mould-board plough is thought to have been reflected at one time in the Latin terms *aratrum* (for the scratch plough) and *carruca* (for the heavy mould-board plough).[137] Both terms occur frequently in the twelfth-century documents, but so interchangeably that the distinction seems obviously to have become blurred in the minds of the clerks.[138] Certainly on demesnes both *aratrum* and *carruca* are recorded in connection with the large plough-team, indicating that any difference represented by the two terms must have been largely superficial; it would seem by this time that they were virtually synonymous.

The only certifiable plough illustration from the period of a likely English origin is that of the Bayeux Tapestry.[139] The plough in this case is wheeled, although, as with the Anglo-Saxon examples in Figures 12 and 13, the function of turning a furrow is not clearly evident. As a result, we may be seeing a wheeled ard here rather than,

---

[137] E.g., R. C. Collingwood and J. N. L. Myers, *Roman Britain and the English Settlements* (Oxford, 1936), p. 211, as quoted in Orwin and Orwin, *The Open Fields*, pp. 10–11. The same distinction exists between the French *araire* and *charrue*, which are seemingly derived from the Latin terms, although Georges Duby in particular has some reservations about the connection. *Rural Economy and Country Life in the Medieval West* (London, 1968), pp. 18–19; see also Haudricourt and Delamarre, *L'Homme et la Charrue*, p. 47.

[138] As on the Ramsey Abbey manors in the twelfth century, where the use of both terms is split about evenly when the demesne ploughs or plough-teams are mentioned: e.g., *Cartularium monasterii de Rameseia*, iii, pp. 241, 257, 259, 261, 265, 266, 273, 274, etc.

[139] See Figure 15.

as some people have assumed, a heavy, wheeled mould-board plough.[140] The presence of large plough-teams on the demesne does argue strongly for the existence of heavy ploughs here, but the same cannot be said of the peasant case. As long as small peasant plough-teams remain a possibility, so too must small ard-like ploughs (although, as we have seen, the connection between small plough-teams and light ploughs was by no means inevitable). Unfortunately the documentary evidence is almost totally inadequate here; the only useful piece of information comes from the 1185 Templar inquest, where, at Temple Ewell in Kent, a carrying service is detailed in which plough-wheels, plough-tails and yokes are to be transported from Canterbury.[141] This implies that wheeled ploughs were prevalent in this part of the country at least.

The information about harrows at this time is even less. That the practice of harrowing was country-wide has already been discussed, but only the Bayeux Tapestry shows what a harrow might have been like, in this case, rectangular and seemingly of the modern toothed variety.

Fortunately there is rather more information about vehicles used in this period. Altogether four types are mentioned frequently in the documents: carts (*carectae*), *carrae*, *quadrigae* and *plaustra*. (The Latin is retained for the last three of these because of the great variety of interpretation, often wrong, that these terms undergo.) By the late thirteenth century it appears that carts were becoming an important vehicle for road transport. For example, in the Pipe Rolls we read of carts being employed to haul various items for the king to all parts of England.[142] Carts, although here they faced strong competition from the other types of vehicles, were also found on the farm, where they turned up in connection with labour services.[143]

---

[140] A. Steensberg, "North West European Plough-types of Prehistoric Times and the Middle Ages", *Acta Archaeologica*, xvi (1945), pp. 264–6, feels this.

[141] *Records of the Templars in England in the Twelfth Century*, p. 23.

[142] *Pipe Roll 18 Henry II*, p. 53; *Pipe Roll 24 Henry II*, p. 97; *Pipe Roll 30 Henry II*, pp. 80, 85, 92; *Pipe Roll 31 Henry II*, pp. 78, 127; *Pipe Roll 34 Henry II*, p. 13; *Pipe Roll 6 Richard I*, pp. 113, 211. (References are to volumes published by the Pipe Roll Society.)

[143] In the twelfth-century records examined in this study carts or cart-loads were found on manors in Cambridgeshire (2), Hertfordshire (1), Huntingdonshire (3), Somerset (1) and Yorkshire (2). The figures in brackets refer to the number of manors in each county. Sources for these references and for others to *carrae* and *plaustra* can be found in Langdon, "Horse Hauling", table 3 (p. 56), or Langdon, thesis, ch. 2, ns. 159, 163, 176 (pp. 109–10).

Presumably these carts were two-wheeled, although there is no twelfth-century evidence to prove this. The Yedingham example and the *carectarius equus* at Sandon (see above) indicate that even at this early date they were hauled by horses. A more popular vehicle on demesne and peasant farms at this time was the *carra* (or sometimes *carrus*), which outnumbered carts by about three to one in the twelfth-century manorial documents. They were most common in the southern part of the country, from Essex in the east to Somerset and Gloucestershire in the west.[144] The *carra* may have been related to the cart, but later evidence indicates that it was a larger, heavier vehicle.[145] The same is indicated by some of the twelfth-century surveys, where carrying services are measured in terms of *dimidiae carrae* rather than whole vehicles as is always the way with carts.[146] It appears that these *carrae* were hauled by oxen, as indicated, for example, by the four oxen required to carry the *carriatam* (or *carra*-load) of hay at Nettleton (see above).

The third type of vehicle was the *quadriga*, which, in the twelfth century, was commonly recorded in carrying services for manors in the north and north-west.[147] They were also cited for road hauling in Yorkshire and Lincolnshire.[148] Concerning the vehicle itself, the term *quadriga* has been taken as meaning a wagon, although strictly speaking it refers to a vehicle drawn by four animals. The latter interpretation is supported by the wine-hauling services in *Boldon Buke*, which indicate that *quadrigae* were most often hauled by four

---

[144] Altogether they were found on manors in Cambridgeshire (2), Dorset (2), Essex (4), Gloucestershire (1), Hertfordshire (2), Huntingdonshire (2), Lincolnshire (2), Northamptonshire (7), Nottinghamshire (1), Somerset (3), Warwickshire (1), Wiltshire (1) and Worcestershire (2). For sources, see note 143 above.

[145] In a few cases even a four-wheeled one, although these were not used for farm work; see p. 152 below.

[146] *Liber Henrici de Soliaco*, pp. 95, 141, 195. The masculine form, *carrus*, was used in this survey.

[147] Altogether they were found in relation to carrying services for hay, wood and corn on manors in Durham (3), Staffordshire (2), Warwickshire (1) and Worcestershire (1). *Boldon Buke*, pp. 6, 12–13, 23; *Burton Abbey Surveys*, pp. 212–13, 215, 246; *Red Book of Worcester*, ii, p. 187. Wine-hauling services involving *quadrigae* also appear in *Boldon Buke*, pp. 2 (*bis*), 6, 18, 20, 27 (*bis*), 31 (*bis*), 32, 36.

[148] *Early Yorkshire Charters*, i, p. 465; *Records of the Templars in England in the Twelfth Century*, p. 257.

oxen.[149] According to Alexander Neckam, they could also be hauled by horses.[150]

The fourth type of vehicle was the *plaustrum*, which first shows up at Domesday in a reference to five *plaustratas*, or *plaustrum*-loads, of lead sheets paid as part of the pre-1066 render for the manors of Bakewell, Ashford and Hope in Derbyshire.[151] Again the *plaustrum* is often interpreted as being a wagon, but, as we shall see in the next chapter, it should be more properly referred to as a two-wheeled wain. Like the *carra*, it was apparently ox-hauled, although its geographical distribution was more to the west and south-west.[152]

This, of course, does not exhaust the total variety of vehicles that could be found in post-Conquest England. We have already referred to the *rheda* in relation to the death of William Rufus, and nearly a century later Alexander Neckam produced a long passage describing its virtues as a travelling carriage, possibly four-wheeled.[153] Although the earlier reference indicates that it may have been a peasant vehicle on occasion, it is not found in any of the twelfth-century manorial documents. On the other hand, another vehicle mentioned by Neckam, the *biga*,[154] is recorded for the manors of Grittleton (Wiltshire) and Fladbury (Worcestershire).[155] As with the *quadriga*, this probably indicates a vehicle hauled by two animals rather than one with two wheels (although it was undoubtedly the latter as well). It was a small vehicle, at least smaller than the *plaustrum*, since the Grittleton passage refers to a carrying service that had to be done *cum dimidio plaustro vel cum biga*. Finally there is an interesting reference at Old Weston in Huntingdonshire to various carrying services being performed using a sled (*traham*).[156]

Consequently by the end of the twelfth century the medieval farmer had a variety of vehicles from which to choose, both wheeled

---

[149] Sources as in note 147 above. *Quadrigae* with three and six oxen, however, are indicated in at least two instances (*Boldon Buke*, pp. 6, 36).

[150] *De naturis rerum*, p. 259.

[151] *Domesday Book*, i, fo. 273.

[152] Altogether they were found on manors in Bedfordshire (1), Cambridgeshire (2), Dorset (2), Gloucestershire (3), Somerset (1), Warwickshire (2), Wiltshire (2) and Worcestershire (2). For sources, see note 143 above.

[153] *De naturis rerum*, pp. 279–80.

[154] *Ibid.*, p. 259. Neckam indicates that it was hauled by horses.

[155] *Liber Henrici de Soliaco*, p. 107; *Red Book of Worcester*, ii, p. 148.

[156] *Cartularium monasterii de Rameseia*, iii, p. 312.

and unwheeled. Admittedly some of the terms on the documents may have been describing the same vehicle – later evidence, for example, indicates that the *carra* and *plaustrum* were often identical vehicles – but certainly there were enough distinct types to establish some sort of pattern. Thus, although carts (*carectae*) were employed extensively for road transport, their use in farm work was more circumscribed, where heavier and larger vehicles, probably ox-hauled, tended to dominate. Regionally it seems that carts and *carrae* were to be found more to the south and east, *quadrigae* and *plaustra* to the north and west. It would appear that ox-hauling still dominated in most of the regions and that horses, whenever they did manage to penetrate farm hauling, only did so at the light end of the vehicle range.

Summarizing the chapter, the situation as regards the level of work-horses on manorial demesnes throughout the period is fairly clear. At Domesday it was on average little more than 5 per cent of the total animal draught force on the demesne and no greater than 10 per cent in any of the regions for which we have figures. The twelfth century saw a gradual rise as the horse began to penetrate demesne ploughing and hauling, although most of this rise was restricted to eastern areas, notably East Anglia. By the end of the century the level of work-horses on English demesnes had reached 10–15 per cent on average, with some of the East Anglian counties reaching 30 per cent or more.

On the peasant side it is impossible to say with certainty what the level of horses was among their draught stock, but most signs indicate that it was always higher than on the demesne. Even at Domesday it may have been as high as a third (or 33 per cent) right across the country, if only to satisfy the harrowing and carrying services (particularly by pack-animal) to which the peasants were liable. However, it is impossible to tell how much of the change towards horses shown on the demesne was also occurring on a peasant level,[157] and for this we must wait for the greater abundance of later material.

---

[157] Although some at least was undoubtedly happening, as indicated by the increase in the use of horses for peasant hauling; see p. 60 above.

3. The demesne: 1200–1500

By the beginning of the thirteenth century medieval agriculture had entered a distinctly new phase. This was the era of direct demesne farming,[1] when rising grain and livestock prices persuaded even the greatest lords to farm their demesne land directly under a manager rather than rent it out (as had often been the case in the twelfth century). As leases on demesnes expired, lords simply took the land and any appurtenant stock back into their own hands. This was a policy already evident in the closing decades of the twelfth century,[2] and it continued to gain in strength during the next hundred years or so. As a trend, however, it was relatively short-lived, effectively reaching its zenith – at the latest – in the last quarter of the thirteenth century, when faltering grain prices began to make the renting out of demesnes or at least portions of them attractive again to demesne owners.[3] Nevertheless, the decline of interest in direct demesne farming was not immediate. Leasing of demesnes did not become wholesale until the beginning of the fifteenth century, and some remnants of direct demesne farming lingered on into the late fifteenth and even the sixteenth century. Thus we have a period of about two hundred years, from the beginning of the thirteenth century to the beginning of the fifteenth when demesne farming – as often as not – tended to find itself under the effective control of landlords rather than lessees.

In short, the demesne became again the lord's farm, that is, those lands on the manor which were farmed directly for his own profit

---

[1] Throughout this chapter and the book in general, the words "farm" and "farming" are used in the modern context of practising cultivation and husbandry rather than – as is often the case in historical writing – to indicate leasing.

[2] P. D. A. Harvey, "The English Inflation of 1180–1220", in *Peasants, Knights and Heretics*, ed. R. H. Hilton (Cambridge, 1976), pp. 58–9.

[3] Miller and Hatcher, *Medieval England: Rural Society and Economic Change*, p. 59.

and provisions, as opposed to those let or held by his various free and customary tenants. As before, these demesnes remained as rather large affairs, normally encompassing well over a hundred acres and sometimes over a thousand. This acreage included wood, pasture, meadow and waste, but most of it was usually arable, either scattered in strips among those of the peasantry or gathered together in one large compact holding.[4] The labour requirement for these demesnes was largely provided for by a permanent staff of *famuli*, or demesne servants, particularly for those jobs which required a relatively constant labour demand – primarily ploughing, carting, dairying and animal-herding. The remaining labour needs were met by labour services owed by tenants – to which we have already alluded in the previous chapter – or by casual hired labour, both of which were particularly important during periods of exceptional activity, such as the harvest or hay-making. Overall management of the farming operations was carried out by some form of manorial official, sometimes a bailiff or sergeant, but most often a reeve appointed or elected from among the village tenantry.

In the period under discussion, demesne farming tended to have a strong market orientation. Although much of the demesne produce was admittedly destined for household consumption, substantial amounts were sold. The location of a manor often determined the emphasis of its demesne's production, whether for the market or for home consumption. This was particularly the case for large estates consisting of several manors, which were often split into "farm" manors (that is, for home consumption) and "revenue" manors.[5]

Finally, a crucial point as far as our analysis of draught animals is concerned, a much greater emphasis on documentation was introduced as lords reclaimed their demesnes. Three main classes of manorial records were involved here: court rolls, surveys and extents, and accounts. Court rolls in general are more illuminating for peasant farming than for that of the demesne, for which we must

---

[4] For examples of each type of demesne layout, see Orwin and Orwin, *The Open Fields*, p. 76, and P. D. A. Harvey, *A Medieval Oxfordshire Village: Cuxham 1240–1400* (Oxford, 1965), pp. 20–2.

[5] "Farm" manors tended to be near the administrative headquarters of the estates; "revenue" manors were more outlying. See R. A. L. Smith, *Canterbury Cathedral Priory* (Cambridge, 1943), pp. 132–3; E. Miller, *The Abbey and Bishopric of Ely* (Cambridge, 1951), p. 76; Miller and Hatcher, *Medieval England: Rural Society and Economic Change*, p. 183.

turn to the other two classes of documents. First of all, the surveys and extents, which were so valuable in analysing the situation in the twelfth century, continue in substantial number for the thirteenth and early fourteenth centuries. Unfortunately proportionally fewer of them comment on the demesne draught animals during the latter centuries, and so they become progressively less valuable for the purposes of this study. On the other hand, this deficiency is more than amply compensated for by the third class of document: the manorial account. The first surviving series of these dates from 1208–9 in the Winchester pipe rolls, which form a remarkably complete run for the bishopric until the sixteenth century. Accounts for other manors and estates exist only sporadically before 1250, but they become increasingly abundant afterwards. The accounts describing manors where direct demesne farming was still being carried on are especially detailed and informative, each one containing a more or less complete record of yearly[6] receipts and expenditures incurred in running the demesne, plus – usually – a detailed accounting of the grain and livestock on the back of the account. It is from these accounts that the bulk of information for this chapter is derived, and from now on they will be referred to as "demesne" accounts, in order to distinguish them from the generally much shorter accounts which describe manors where the demesne was already leased out.

In preparation for the various analyses performed in this chapter, the relevant account material was gathered into two large samples, one covering the period 1250 to 1320, henceforward called Sample A, and the other the period from 1350 to 1420, henceforward called Sample B. The two samples roughly cover the period when this account material is most abundant. Before 1250, with the notable exception of the Winchester pipe rolls, accounts in general are scarce, while after 1420 demesne leasing substantially reduces the number of demesne accounts available. The thirty-year gap from 1320 to 1350 was to allow for a sharper differentiation between the two samples and also to eliminate as much as possible the effect of the serious animal murrains or diseases, particularly for cattle, that affected draught stock proportions during the 1320s. Thus Sample A represents a period of peak population levels and of "high"

---

[6] Most accounts covered the period from Michaelmas (29 September) of one year to Michaelmas of the next.

demesne farming. Sample B, on the other hand, represents an era of sharp population decline and of increasing difficulties for direct demesne farming. The seventy-year period for each sample was chosen as a compromise between having a sample time-span large enough to allow a geographical representation across the country and yet small enough so that variations through time within the samples would not seriously affect the reliability of the overall results.

Altogether the demesnes of 637 manors were surveyed for Sample A (based on 956 accounts) and the demesnes of 399 manors for Sample B (based on 609 accounts).[7] The difference in size between the two samples reflects the greater difficulty in obtaining information for the later period. Unavoidably the spread of data through time within each sample is somewhat uneven. Thus the bulk of information for Sample A is found towards the end of the sample period (the median year being 1293), while that for Sample B is found more towards the beginning (median year, 1381). The geographical spread of data is also uneven. Figures 21 and 22 show the distribution of demesne accounts for both samples.[8] As can be seen, the south and east of the country, with the notable exception of the Weald (particularly in Sample A), are much more fully represented than the north and west, essentially reflecting the relative scarcity of suitable accounts in these latter areas.[9] As we shall see, these distortions in data distribution may only have marginal effects but they should be kept in mind.

---

[7] A minimum of 162 demesnes was common to both samples. It should also be pointed out that, although we have indicated that only accounts have been included in the samples, there are a small number of cases (about thirty) which are based on documents that should strictly be called inventories. Since these inventories often supplied as much relevant information as the accounts, however, they have been included in the samples.

[8] Not included on the maps are twenty-six manors (seventeen in Sample A and nine in Sample B), which could not be identified with absolute certainty, although in all but seven of these cases the county could be ascertained.

[9] Which, in turn, was probably due to (1) a lack of good farming land in the north and west; (2) a less developed tradition of record keeping in these areas; and (3) the continued leasing of demesnes in these outlying areas, even during the high farming period of the thirteenth century. All these are discussed in Langdon, thesis, pp. 115–17.

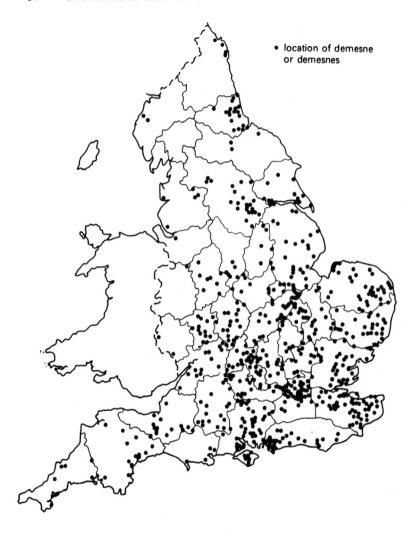

Fig. 21: Distribution of demesnes for Sample A (1250–1320).

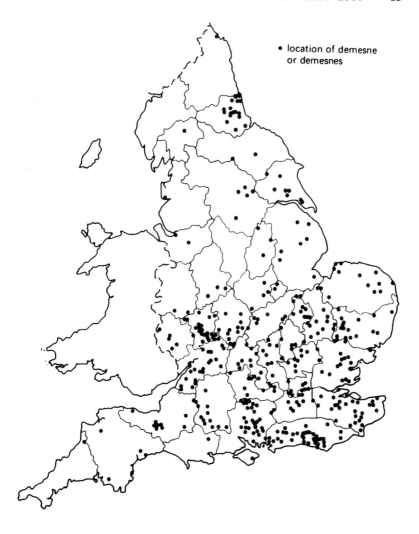

Fig. 22: Distribution of demesnes for Sample B (1350–1420).

a) THE NUMBERS OF HORSES AND OXEN ON MEDIEVAL
DEMESNES, 1200–1500

Altogether Sample A contains 625 demesnes for which draught
animal numbers are given and Sample B 393 demesnes. In both
cases only adult horses and oxen (including the odd bull[10]) are considered and – with few exceptions – only those remaining at the end
of each account year. As in Chapter 2, horses for riding or patently
for stud are not included,[11] although mares serving as combination
working–breeding stock are, as well as a small number of pack- and
mill-animals.

The same proliferation of terms for horses occurs in the accounts
just as they did in the twelfth-century surveys. Five terms are most
commonly encountered: *affrus*, *stottus*, *jumentum*, *equus
carectarius* and just *equus* (or *equa*). The first three represent low-
grade animals. These were generally used for ploughing in those
regions where horses were employed for this, but often for harrowing and hauling as well. The higher-priced *equus carectarius*, as the
name implies, was used mainly for hauling, as was – usually – the
equus. Less often, but still occasionally encountered are the older
terms of *runcinus* and *aver'* (see appendix), and the occupational
terms of *hercatorius* (harrowing horse), *summarius* (sumpter or
pack-horse) and *equus molendinarius* (mill-horse).[12] As with the
Domesday and twelfth-century material, mules and donkeys are
also found in the accounts and, as before, have been considered as
horses for the purposes of the following analyses. Their proportion

---

[10] That is, when these bulls were included in the "Oxen" section and not in a group
by themselves. Cows were also occasionally used for draught on demesnes (e.g.,
see David Postles, "Problems in the Administration of Small Manors: Three
Oxfordshire Glebe-demesnes, 1278–1345", *Midland History*, iv (1977), p. 9).
None, however, is listed as being employed for such in the accounts used for
Samples A and B. It has also been assumed that all the oxen (*boves*) recorded in
the account samples were draught animals, although it is perhaps possible that
some were "fat" oxen, that is, intended solely for meat rather than work. However, the continual references to ox-yokes, bows, ox-shoeing and so on in the
accounts indicate that the vast majority of them were used for work.

[11] As in the twelfth-century material, horse studs are evident, but they are
infrequent. Altogether only six demesnes had studs in Sample A and only four in
Sample B, containing a total of 124 adult animals with followers in Sample A and
58 adult animals with followers in Sample B.

[12] Or some form of these.

in the totals, however, is very small, being well less than 1 per cent in both samples.[13]

When finally collated, the numbers of horses and oxen found in Samples A and B appear county by county as in Table 11. The overall proportion of work-horses came to 26.7 per cent for the 1250–1320 period and 29.4 per cent for the 1350–1420 period. In both cases the level of horses represents a significant rise over that evident in the twelfth century, although oxen were still easily dominant at a ratio of between two and three of the animals to every horse. This, however, does hide the performance of some individual counties, which were beginning to employ quite high levels of demesne horses (e.g., Hertfordshire, Essex, and Norfolk). On the other hand, other counties, particularly those in the far west and north, continued to use horses at levels little changed from those at Domesday, although in general almost all counties showed some increase. Table 12 shows the figures arranged by region. Again East Anglia tops the list with nearly 50 per cent horses during the period before the Black Death, rising to nearly 60 per cent afterwards. The Home Counties and the east midlands followed with 25–40 per cent, in both cases rising after the Black Death. The south came in at about 25 per cent, while the remaining regions – the south-west, west midlands and the north – were all less than 20 per cent, confirming the trend noted for the twelfth century that the use of horses tailed off markedly towards the north and west.

Notwithstanding the degree of regional variation, if Samples A and B had conformed strictly to the precepts of random sampling we might have been fairly confident in saying that the figures for the country as a whole were accurate to within a few percentage points.[14] However, even allowing for the fact that true random sampling is seldom possible within the confines of the various record offices across the country, the uneven distribution of the accounts over time and geography makes the creation of truly representative samples highly unlikely. As a result, we are again faced with the

---

[13] Altogether fourteen mules and five donkeys are included in the draught animal totals for Sample A and only one mule in Sample B.

[14] When the percentage of work-horses is calculated for each individual demesne, we obtain 95 per cent confidence levels of ± 1.9 per cent around the mean percentage horse level for Sample A and ± 2.7 per cent around the mean percentage horse level for Sample B. For the method of calculation, see R. Floud, *An Introduction to Quantitative Methods for Historians* (London, 1975), pp. 167–8.

Table 11. *The proportion of work-horses on English demesnes, 1250–1320 and 1350–1420*

County	Sample A (1250–1320)				Sample B (1350–1420)			
	a	*b*	*c*	*d*	*a*	*b*	*c*	*d*
Bedfordshire	9	135	59	30.4	5	75	47	38.5
Berkshire	17	379	113	23.0	11	142	77	35.2
Buckinghamshire	15	238	118	33.1	10	199	92	31.6
Cambridgeshire	13	173	100	36.6	11	119	91	43.3
Cheshire	1	34	5	12.8	2	62	14	18.4
Cornwall	8	194	43	18.1	2	28	14	33.3
Cumberland	2	27	4	12.9	—	—	—	—
Derbyshire	4	40	8	16.7	—	—	—	—
Devon	14	402	53	11.6	5	72	14	16.3
Dorset	4	131	18	12.1	1	18	2	10.0
Durham	19	614	87	12.4	17	325	58	15.1
Essex	30	287	370	56.3	19	110	235	68.1
Gloucestershire	12	330	51	13.4	20	279	54	16.2
Hampshire	45	1,381	451	24.6	31	631	176	21.8
Herefordshire	2	83	12	12.6	6	81	15	15.6
Hertfordshire	14	107	231	68.3	11	48	98	67.1
Huntingdonshire	11	207	126	37.8	8	122	78	39.0
Kent	49	520	494	48.7	28	213	210	49.6
Lancashire	6	101	8	7.3	1	29	4	12.1
Leicestershire	8	155	39	20.1	5	96	52	35.1
Lincolnshire	29	654	184	22.0	7	103	67	39.4
Middlesex	15	185	136	42.4	5	51	31	37.8
Norfolk	37	252	266	51.4	13	26	70	72.9
Northamptonshire	25	511	233	31.3	9	119	59	33.1
Northumberland	3	50	13	20.6	1	26	5	16.1
Nottinghamshire	5	129	31	19.4	3	42	11	20.8
Oxfordshire	30	507	195	27.8	11	152	69	31.2
Rutland	3	26	15	36.6	2	12	13	52.0
Shropshire	1	18	2	10.0	2	27	2	6.9
Somerset	16	409	34	7.7	11	204	14	6.4
Staffordshire	10	246	31	11.2	2	46	8	14.8
Suffolk	29	271	222	45.0	17	152	163	51.7
Surrey	19	225	121	35.0	13	151	65	30.1
Sussex	28	661	84	11.3	36	681	154	18.4
Warwickshire	19	357	63	15.0	14	217	64	22.8
Westmorland	—	—	—	—	1	11	1	8.3
Wiltshire	19	569	81	12.5	10	219	39	15.1
Worcestershire	11	275	30	9.8	25	398	94	19.1
Yorkshire	38	804	143	15.1	16	333	74	18.2
County unknown	5	74	20	21.3	2	12	6	33.3
Total	625	11,761	4,294		393	5,631	2,340	
Overall %				26.7				29.4

problem of determining how seriously our results are affected by these difficulties.

Fluctuations over time do not appear to be much of a problem. In most cases the level of work-horses on a demesne changed little unless events of an exceptional nature occurred, and these in general happened infrequently in our samples.[15] Geographical distortions, however, are much more of a problem. For example, is the rise in the percentage of work-horses after the Black Death a real trend, or is it due to the type of uneven distribution from region to region that complicated the comparison of our twelfth-century material? The problem, as before, is to find a suitable method of correction for this uneven geographical distribution. One method is to use the Domesday plough-team figures again, although the same reservations about using them for the twelfth-century material apply with even more force now. Land reclamation and assarting continued to make their mark on the English landscape well into the thirteenth century, and this process must surely have altered the proportion of demesne arable between regions. Demesne leasing, especially those let out piecemeal to peasants, would also upset these proportions. Unfortunately we have no adequate method of measuring the total effect of these changes and must assume for the

Notes to Table 11

Key to column headings
a – Number of demesnes
b – Number of oxen
c – Number of work-horses
d – % work-horses

Notes and sources: For reasons of space, a full list of sources cannot be provided, although several of them are referred to in the footnotes of this chapter. A complete listing of sources, including an abbreviated summary of the data taken from them, is given in Langdon, thesis, Appendix C, pp. 416–56.

[15] Only on demesnes where a policy change was effected, such as the decision to go from all-ox to mixed plough-teams, to use horses for hauling rather than oxen, or even to go to all-horse farming, did the level of work-horses change permanently. In the event, such policy changes were relatively rare during our two sample periods. For instance, most of the transition to all-horse farming appears to have occurred either before our two sample periods, between them, or even after them. The same seems to have held true for the transition from all-ox to mixed plough-teams and the development of horse hauling, which appear to have reached their medieval limits by the 1250–1320 period at least and probably earlier (see pp. 106–7 below; also Langdon, "Horse Hauling", p. 58).

Table 12. *Regional variation in demesne work-horse levels,*
1250–1320 and 1350–1420

Region	Sample A (1250–1320)				Sample B (1350–1420)			
	a	b	c	d	a	b	c	d
East Anglia	109	983	958	49.4	60	407	559	57.9
Home Counties	119	1,776	973	35.4	66	818	479	36.9
The South	141	3,131	1,110	26.2	105	1,744	579	24.9
South-west	42	1,136	148	11.5	19	322	44	12.0
East Midlands	81	1,682	628	27.2	34	494	280	36.2
West Midlands	60	1,383	202	12.7	71	1,110	251	18.4
The North	68	1,596	255	13.8	36	724	142	16.4

Key to column headings
a – Number of demesnes
b – Number of oxen
c – Number of work-horses
d – % work-horses

Notes: For the counties making up each region see Table 8.

moment that the demesne arable proportion between regions had
not altered sufficiently to invalidate the use of the Domesday figures
as a correction factor.

A second method of correction can be attempted by using the
1377 poll tax returns, although again a number of somewhat questionable assumptions must be made. The first is that the population
in a particular region is directly related to the amount of arable land
in production there and hence, to a large degree, the draught stock
population. The second is that the relative differences in population
levels among regions remained fairly constant, despite fluctuations
in the absolute level of that population, especially over the Black
Death period. Thirdly, it is assumed that the proportion of demesne
to peasant arable land – and hence the proportion of draught
animals in each sector – also remained constant. All of these
assumptions, of course, are open to question, although generally
speaking they are not totally unreasonable and suggest that the 1377
poll tax figures are as suitable a weighting parameter as can be found
for the period.[16] In any case, the poll tax method of correction provides a useful alternative to that of the Domesday plough-team, as

[16] As discussed in Langdon, thesis, pp. 122–3.

Table 13. *Overall percentage of demesne work-horses corrected by the Domesday plough-team and 1377 Poll Tax methods*

	Uncorrected from Table 11	Corrected by Domesday plough-team method	Corrected by 1377 Poll Tax method
Sample A (1250–1320)	26.7	26.3	25.9
Sample B (1350–1420)	29.4	30.5	30.1

it should give more weight to those areas where the effect of such things as land reclamation and assarting – and hence population growth – was likely to have been the greatest. The results for each method of correction are contained in Table 13 above.[17]

The agreement between the uncorrected and the two corrected values is surprisingly good for both samples. There is a slight widening between the corrected figures, for Samples A and B, but in absolute terms the difference is small. It seems that the overall figures in Table 11 were relatively unaffected by an uneven geographical distribution in the accounts, unless both corrected methods curiously fail to point it out.

There is, however, another factor that we would do well to consider. This is the question of landlordship. We have up till now been ignoring the differences between demesne landlords, major or minor, lay or ecclesiastic. There is a strong possibility that these differences in types of lords might have had an important bearing on the level of horses found on a particular demesne, and so would add yet another distorting factor to our figures in Table 11. This is a worrisome problem, because our samples are biased, through the survival of records, towards major, mainly ecclesiastic, landlords with many manors under their control. Minor landlords, both lay and ecclesiastic, tend to be severely under-represented, particularly during the earlier period covered by Sample A. It is difficult to assess how much effect this under-representation, if corrected, would have on the levels of horses and oxen as recorded in Table 11. From our analysis of lay subsidy material in the next chapter, however, it appears that the draught animal holdings of minor landlords

---

[17] The method of calculation is indicated in Chapter 2, note 52.

(and indeed the more substantial peasants) did not differ markedly from that of more powerful and wealthy lords and thus their absence is unlikely to have affected the figures substantially.[18]

Fortunately it is much easier to make the basic distinction between lay and ecclesiastic lords in our samples, and this is of some use. As we have already indicated, farming management by churchmen in the middle ages has often been considered more progressive than that by laymen. The ecclesiastic and particularly the monastic contribution to the development of agriculture in undeveloped areas of marsh and waste is well-known,[19] and even on land with a long history of cultivation the ecclesiastic performance was often superior.[20] We should not assume, however, that lay estate management was automatically substandard, particularly in its ability to adjust to new circumstances; some lay estates displayed a keen awareness of changing conditions and reacted to them with commendable speed.[21]

How did these possible differences between lay and ecclesiastic management affect the demesne use of horses and oxen? To answer this question, the demesnes in Samples A and B were classified, where possible, according to whether they were lay or ecclesiastic, and the level of work-horses for each group was calculated. The results by region are shown in Table 14.

Altogether ecclesiastic demesnes used rather more horses than lay demesnes, although the difference was more pronounced in Sample A (28.2 vs 23.0 per cent) than in Sample B (30.0 vs 27.2 per

[18] See Chapter 4; also the similar conclusions of R. H. Britnell, "Minor Landlords in England and Medieval Agrarian Capitalism", *Past and Present*, no. 89 (1980), especially pp. 21–2.

[19] E.g., B. Waites, *Moorland and Vale-land Farming in North-east Yorkshire*. Borthwick Papers, no. 32 (York, 1967), especially pp. 33–5; R. A. L. Smith, *Canterbury Cathedral Priory*, ch. xi; C. Platt, *The Monastic Grange in Medieval England*, pp. 13–14.

[20] B. M. S. Campbell, for instance, has shown how poorly the grain yields of the lay estates of Roger Bigod showed up against the much better yields on the nearby lands of Norwich Cathedral Priory on almost identical types of soils. "Field Systems in Eastern Norfolk during the Middle Ages: A Study with Particular Reference to the Demographic and Agrarian Changes of the Fourteenth Century" (University of Cambridge Ph.D. thesis, 1975), pp. 352–3. More recently, however, Campbell has demonstrated that *on average* the cultivating performance of ecclesiastic estates was probably no better than their lay counterparts: "Agricultural Productivity in Medieval England: Some Evidence from Norfolk", *Journal of Economic History*, xlviii (1983), pp. 397–8.

[21] E.g., see M. Mate, "Profit and Productivity on the Estates of Isabella de Forz (1260–92)", *Econ. Hist. Rev.*, 2nd series, xxxiii (1980), pp. 327–33.

Table 14. *Regional variation in work-horse levels on lay and ecclesiastic demesnes, 1250–1320 and 1350–1420*

| | Sample A (1250–1320) | | | | Sample B (1350–1420) | | | |
| | Lay Demesnes | | Ecclesiastic Demesnes | | Lay Demesnes | | Ecclesiastic Demesnes | |
Region	*a*	*b*	*a*	*b*	*a*	*b*	*a*	*b*
East Anglia	47	44.4	59	52.8	17	59.3	39	57.6
Home Counties	32	35.7	84	34.7	19	36.1	44	37.5
The South	27	14.0	111	28.3	32	16.4	70	28.7
South-west	20	10.9	22	12.0	9	12.7	8	5.7
East Midlands	39	23.3	41	30.5	15	36.2	16	34.9
West Midlands	18	11.1	41	13.3	22	17.6	48	19.1
The North	42	14.2	25	13.0	8	16.1	27	16.0
Overall	228	23.0	385	28.2	122	27.2	253	30.0

Key to column headings
a – Number of demesnes
b – % work-horses

Notes and sources: For the counties making up each region see Table 8. The "overall" figures also include demesnes where the region was unknown.

cent). Part of this difference, however, seems to have arisen from there being a somewhat greater concentration of lay demesnes in the more ox-oriented parts of the country. As a result, when corrected for this geographical distortion (by either the Domesday plough-team or 1377 poll tax methods) the difference between the percentages of work-horses on ecclesiastic versus lay demesnes remains at about 5 per cent for Sample A, but closes to within 1 per cent for Sample B. From these figures it appears that there was some difference between the percentages of horses used by ecclesiastic and lay demesnes during the 1250–1320 period but little or none for the 1350–1420 period.

It is difficult to assess the significance of all this. For one thing, it is certain that lay demesnes are significantly under-represented in the samples. Altogether they comprise only 37.2 per cent of the demesnes in Sample A for which the lords are known and 32.5 per cent in Sample B, or roughly two ecclesiastic demesnes for every lay demesne. The true proportions are likely to have been the other way around, that is, two (or more) lay demesnes to every ecclesiastic one.[22]

This lop-sidedness in representation makes it very difficult to treat the problem of lay versus ecclesiastic demesnes in a statistical manner, since it is obvious that true random samples are almost impossible to obtain. The discrepancy in the percentages of horses for lay and ecclesiastic demesnes in Sample A, however, is marked enough for us to speculate that it is based on some real differences occurring at the time.[23] If such a situation were the case, then the inflated ecclesiastic presence in Sample A would distort the overall percentage of work-horses in the direction of a higher figure. When corrected, this would result in a level of work-horses some one of two per cent lower than that given in Table 11. After 1350, when the difference between the percentages of work-horses on lay and ecclesiastic demesnes closes, this sort of distortion is no longer a problem.

It appears, then, that the overall figures given at the bottom of Table 11 are plausible. The marked ecclesiastic presence in both samples may have inflated the overall percentage of horses in Sample A, but it would have been by no more than a per cent or two. In general the figures tell us that the level of working horses on English demesnes climbed to 25 per cent or so during the high farming period 1250–1320, and that after the Black Death it continued to rise to about 30 per cent. Altogether the proportion of demesne work-horses seems to have doubled or better since the twelfth century.

When did the bulk of this rise occur? The survival of pre-1250 accounts has generally not been great enough to allow an adequate answer to this question. The single exception occurs with the bishopric of Winchester pipe rolls, which provide a very good run of

[22] Kosminsky's work on the Hundred Rolls shows that the proportion of lay to ecclesiastic manors in the six counties he studied was about three to one. Even allowing for the possibility that churchmen may have indulged to a greater degree than laymen in direct demesne cultivation, it would almost certainly still leave a heavy preponderance of demesne lands in lay possession. Kosminsky, *Studies in the Agrarian History of England*, pp. 108–9.

[23] Certainly *if* the lay and ecclesiastic components of Sample A were true random samples of the country as a whole, then the difference noted would be very significant indeed, being equal to about two and a half standard errors. This is equivalent to a probability of well over 95 per cent that the observed difference was not due simply to chances of sampling.

accounts from the first decade of the thirteenth century. Here, an interesting analysis can be made by taking one of the early pipe rolls and comparing it with some that follow. For this purpose, the rolls for 1210–11, 1286–7 and 1381–2 have been chosen.[24]

Altogether thirty-four demesnes are common to all three rolls,[25] and the percentage of work-horses for these thirty-four demesnes works out to 12.6 per cent for the 1210–11 roll, 18.1 per cent for the 1286–7 roll, and 22.5 per cent for the 1381–2 roll. The low levels for the 1286–7 and 1381–2 rolls compared to the overall percentages for Samples A and B highlight the fact that the bulk of the Winchester demesnes comes from relatively ox-oriented regions of the country, primarily the south and south-west. Of most interest here is the horse level in the 1210–11 roll, which is considerably lower than that later in the century, but at the same time quite a bit higher, considering the region it covers, than that in the twelfth century. Clearly the position in the 1210–11 roll is an intermediate one,[26] and suggests that the first half of the thirteenth century and probably the last decade or so of the twelfth were optimum periods for increasing the involvement of horses in demesne agriculture.

What are the reasons for this rise in demesne work-horse levels? Two stand out. The first is a greater participation of horses in ploughing, which will be discussed later. The second is a sudden popularity in the use of horses for hauling. For example, of the 4,294 horses recorded in Sample A, 591 (or 13.8 per cent) are specifically referred to as *equi carectarii*, while of the 2,340 horses in Sample B, 513 (or 21.9 per cent) are similarly referred to as cart-horses. Compared to the twelfth century, when only one such demesne animal is recorded in all the material examined (see p. 60 above), this represents a considerable advance, and to this must be added a great

---

[24] Sources as follows: *The Pipe Roll of the Bishopric of Winchester, 1210–1211*, ed. N. R. Holt (Manchester, 1964); H.R.O. Eccles. 2 159308 (1286–7); H.R.O. Eccles. 2 159388 (1381–2).

[25] Twyford, Marwell, Crawley, Mardon, Bishopstoke, Bentley, Overton, North Waltham, High Clere, Burghclere, Fareham, Bishop's Waltham, East Meon Manor, East Meon Church, Hambledon, Cheriton, Beauworth, Old Alresford and Wield (Hampshire); Downton, Bishopstone, Knoyle and Upton Knoyle (Wiltshire); Brightwell, Harwell, Wargrave, Waltham St Lawrence and Culham (Berkshire); Witney and Adderbury (Oxfordshire); West Wycombe (Buckinghamshire); Farnham (Surrey); Taunton and Rimpton (Somerset). Although they are recorded separately in the 1286–7 and 1381–2 rolls, the various demesnes in the Taunton group of manors – Poundsford, Holway, Staplegrove, etc. – are counted as one here.

[26] See also p. 87 above.

number of *equi, affri, stotti* and *jumenta*, which, although not referred to specifically as "cart-horses", are often unmistakably connected with hauling.[27] This increase in hauling horses was perhaps natural in the context of the expanding economy that characterized the latter part of the twelfth century and most of the thirteenth. Once any technical limitations were overcome, the attractions of quick transport for hauling grain and other goods to market must have become very tempting to demesne managers and administrators.[28]

More difficult to explain is the continued rise in the level of demesne work-horses after the Black Death. This is a period which, although not without its spells of recovery, has been characterized as one of economic decline.[29] Despite this atmosphere of decline, the level of horses, and particularly those named as "cart-horses", continued to increase. What makes it all the harder to account for is that, seen in economic terms, the level of horses should have dropped. One of the characteristics of horses is that, compared to oxen, they are grain rather than grass consumers. This made them more expensive animals to feed,[30] but when meadow and pasture were in short supply this consideration became less important. On the other hand, when grass and hay were in plentiful supply, then for economic reasons the ox became, in theory at least, the more sensible animal to keep, as Fitzherbert indicated in the early six-teenth century.[31] Consequently, with much more pasture land being freed upon the shrinkage of arable after the Black Death, it would seem natural to expect a shift back to oxen, but in fact, as we have seen, the proportion of horses on demesnes still continued to rise. Much of this seems to have been due to an increase in all-horse farms (to be discussed later), and consequently when these farms are excluded, the percentages of work-horses in Samples A and B close to within a percentage and a half of each other (25.4 and 26.7 per cent respectively). There was, as well, a tendency for demesne

---

[27] As at Bosham (Sussex) in 1368–9: *Et in prebenda vj affrorum euntium ad carectas carucas & ad hercias* (W.Suss.R.O. Bosham Manor Collection Acc. 939 II/A/II).
[28] For which see Langdon, "Horse Hauling", especially pp. 49–54, 60–6.
[29] E.g., J. Hatcher, *Plague, Population and the English Economy 1348–1530* (London, 1977), pp. 11–20, 31–6.
[30] See Langdon, "Economics of Horses and Oxen", table 5 (p. 37).
[31] *Fitzherbert*, p. 15.

farms, or at least the arable component of these farms, to become smaller after 1350.[32] This in turn may have led to a greater proportion of horses, since – seemingly – these animals were less economical on smaller farms.[33]

In short, it does appear that the period after the Black Death continued to experience an increase in the level of work-horses employed on demesnes, and that this increase was probably significant.[34] The rise in the number of all-horse farms and the decline in demesne arable would both seem to have played a part. Added to this would be the continued buoyancy of grain prices and farming for the market in general in the late fourteenth century, which would have maintained the need for hauling horses in particular.

What happened after 1420? The buoyancy of grain prices in the late fourteenth century meant that direct demesne farming was slow to die off, but by the early fifteenth century most demesnes were now being leased. As a result, details about farming on these lands were now lost to documentation, and consequently we have records of only a handful of demesnes remaining in direct exploitation during the remainder of the century. Table 15 lists the results from some twenty-four demesnes, based on fifty accounts and inventories.

Only ten counties are represented and half of these by only one demesne apiece. The overall percentage of work-horses is lower than that for both Samples A and B, but this is hardly surprising given the bias towards northern and western counties. Altogether the post-1420 sample is too small to draw any firm conclusions, but movement in both directions is clearly evident. Thus, for example,

---

[32] Two samples of 100 demesnes each taken from Samples A and B show that the average sown acreage per demesne for the 1250–1320 period was 218.4 acres compared to 147.0 acres for the period 1350–1420.

[33] An analysis of the demesnes in Samples A and B (excluding those farms with horses only) shows that the proportion of horses among the draught stock tended to decrease from 30 per cent or more on those demesnes with 20 or less draught animals to 25 per cent or less on those demesnes with 40 or more draught animals (see Langdon, thesis, p. 130). This trend still exists when the figures are analysed by region, but it is weaker.

[34] For instance, if the percentage of work-horses is calculated for each demesne, the means for Samples A and B are 3.3 percentage points apart. This is equivalent to almost exactly two standard errors, which signifies that there is a 95 per cent probability that the 3.3 per cent difference is due to more than just sampling error. For the method of calculation, see Floud, *An Introduction to Quantitative Methods for Historians*, pp. 168–71.

Table 15. *The percentage of work-horses on English demesnes,*
1420–1500

County	No. of demesnes	No. of oxen	No. of horses	% horses
Dorset	1	0	7	100.0
Durham	9	171	27	13.6
Essex	1	7	4	36.4
Norfolk	3	0	17	100.0
Northumberland	1	15	4	21.1
Somerset	1	20	2	9.1
Warwickshire	2	35	7	16.7
Wiltshire	1	17	4	19.0
Worcestershire	3	64	13	16.9
Yorkshire	2	35	7	16.9
Total	24	364	92	
Overall percentage				20.2

Notes and sources: Demesnes, account-years and sources as follows: Waterston (in
Puddletown), Dorset, 1434–5 and 1446–7, P.R.O. S.C.6 835/24, 36; Finchale,
Durham, 1439–41 and 1441–2, *The Priory of Finchale*, ed. J. Raine (Surtees Soc., vi,
1837), pp. ccxxxiii, ccxxxvi; Jarrow, Durham, 1424–5, 1436–7 and 1491, *The Inven-*
tories and Account Rolls . . . of Jarrow and Monk-Wearmouth, ed. J. Raine (Surtees
Soc., xxix, 1854), pp. 96, 105, 127; Monkwearmouth, Durham, 1427–8, 1428–9,
1446–7 and 1448–9, *ibid.*, 197 (*bis*), 203, 220; Elvethall (near Durham), 1422–3,
1424–5, 1461–2 and 1472–3; D.C.D. Hostillar's Accounts; Pittington, Durham,
1446, 1450–1, *Wills and Inventories . . . of the Northern Counties of England*, ed. J.
Raine (Surtees Soc., ii, 1835), pp. 95–6, D.C.D. Bursar's Accounts; Ferryhill,
Durham, 1446–7, D.C.D. Bursar's Accounts; Westoe, Durham, 1446, *Wills and*
Inventories . . . of the Northern Counties of England, p. 95; Fulwell, Durham, 1446,
ibid., p. 95; Bewley, Durham, 1446, *ibid.*, p. 96; Wivenhoe, Essex, 1425–6, E.R.O.
T/B 122 (Wivenhoe Records); Taverham, Norfolk, 1420–1, N.R.O. Ref. No.
R232A; Hindringham, Norfolk, 1422–3, N.R.O. Ref. No. R233C; Sedgeford,
Norfolk, 1423–4, N.R.O. Ref. No. R233D; Holy Island, Northumberland, 1421–2,
1429–30, 1437, 1480–1 and 1493–4, D.C.D. Cell Accounts; Porlock, Somerset,
1424–5, P.R.O. S.C.6 973/26; Budbrooke, Warwickshire, 1421–2, 1422–3, 1424–5
and 1428–9, Wa.R.O. CR 895 8/11, 12, 13, 16; Snitterfield, Warwickshire, 1430–1,
Brit. Lib. Egerton Roll 8624; Chippenham, Wiltshire, 1428–9, t. Hen. VI and
1460–1, Wi.R.O. 192/29B, 29C, 29D; Overbury Manor, Worcestershire, 1422–3,
W.C.L. C721; Leigh, Worcestershire, 1423–4, P.R.O. S.C.6 1089/11; Hewell
Grange, Worcestershire, 1424–5, 1426–7, 1432–3, 1434–5, 1442–3, 1449–50 and
1458–9, P.R.O. S.C.6 1068/11, 12, 14, 15, 16, 18, 19; York, Yorkshire, 1423,
Testamenta Eboracensia, ed. J. Raine, Jr (Surtees Soc., xlv, 1864), pp. 80–1;
Methley, Yorkshire, 1435–6, S.L. MX Archives, no. 10. I am indebted to Dr C. Dyer
for supplying me with a microfilm and transcripts of the Wivenhoe, Budbrooke,
Snitterfield and Overbury material.

the demesne at Waterston in Dorset is an all-horse farm in an area where such farms were not apparent before, while in other parts of the country a partial reversion to oxen is noticeable, especially in the north.[35] This limited evidence suggests that there was a growing polarization in the use of horses and oxen, with some demesnes in some areas going completely to horses while others took up the option of reverting to oxen and the economic advantages that that held.

As has been said, once demesnes were leased, details of agricultural practice are no longer available. In some cases, however, the accounts for the period after the demesne is leased continue to list the draught stock normally appurtenant to the demesne. Here the lord is handing on the draught stock to the lessee as part of a stock-and-land lease, probably with the intention of having the draught stock immediately available should the demesne revert to direct cultivation. Generally the draught stock recorded in these "lease" accounts are at the same level as when the lord farmed the demesne himself. On the other hand, there are one or two cases where the level of horses in the leased accounts is significantly higher than when the demesne was farmed directly, indicating, perhaps, that the levels of draught animals on the demesne were changing to fit the actual levels preferred by the lessee. For example, at Knowle (Warwickshire) in 1398–9 and 1400–1 the nine oxen and six *jumenta* supposedly present on the demesne gave a level of horses of 40 per cent, which was much higher than the 20 per cent or so when the demesne was farmed directly.[36] It is of course difficult to project how accurately these levels of leased stock represent the actual levels employed by the lessee, but it does seem that the trend in many areas may have been towards using more horses. This conclusion, however, can only be a very tentative one.

In concluding this section, then, we can say that there was a marked increase in the use of demesne work-horses from 1200 to 1500. Although most of this increase occurred in the very early stages of our period, there was a continued progression in the use of the animals right through to the beginning of the fifteenth century at least and possibly beyond. We have already indicated that some of this was due to the rise and continued buoyancy of the market

---

[35] See pp. 156, 210–12.
[36] W.A.M. 27719, 27720. Cf. W.A.M. 27705 (1362–3) and others when the demesne was under direct cultivation.

economy, but we must also consider how much of it was due simply to changes in practice, a topic we shall discuss in the next section.

b) THE EMPLOYMENT OF DEMESNE HORSES AND OXEN, 1200–1500

The most dramatic manifestation of changes in practice regarding demesne draught oxen and horses occurred with the creation of all-horse farms, in which the use of oxen as draught animals was completely eliminated. Although these demesnes were always in a minority, their numbers grew steadily throughout the period.

Considering the 1250–1320 sample (A) first, there were altogether twenty-eight demesnes (or 4.5 per cent of the 625 demesnes in Table 11) which were employing nothing but horses for their farm work.[37] The geographical distribution of these demesnes is shown in Figure 23. Most of them are clustered in three areas: Norfolk, the Chiltern Hills, and parts of eastern Kent. Norfolk is a county with a large area of light, easily worked soils, especially in the sandy regions of the north-west, where most of the Norfolk all-horse demesnes in Figure 23 are found. As noted by Fitzherbert, ploughing with horses is more suited to light soils, since here they are much quicker than oxen and will not become bogged down as they are prone to do on heavier soils.[38] Similarly, soils undoubtedly accounted for the presence of all-horse farms on or very close to the Chiltern Hills, represented on Figure 23 by a string of demesnes from Wheathampstead and Kingsbourne in Hertfordshire to

[37] That is, West Wycombe and Beamond (in Little Missenden), Buckinghamshire; Soberton and East Meon Church, Hampshire; Wheathampstead, Berkhamsted, Ashwell and Kingsbourne (in Harpenden), Hertfordshire; Agney with Orgarswick, Appledore, Ebony, Copton (in Preston), Bishopsbourne, Westgate and Petham, Kent; Catton, Thornham, Sedgeford, Hindringham, North Elmham, Gnatingdon (in Sedgeford), Deopham, Brancaster and Bircham, Norfolk; Kirtlington, Watlington and Checkendon, Oxfordshire; Farleigh, Surrey. The sources for these demesnes are in Langdon, thesis, Appendix C, pt 1.
    Four of these demesnes – Beamond, Soberton, Kingsbourne and Bishopsbourne – did display small numbers of oxen, but these were mostly supernumerary beasts which arose naturally from the breeding cattle on the demesne and were sent or sold off as working stock elsewhere. There were as well four other demesnes – West Wycombe, Ebony, Catton and Hindringham – that were in transition during the period, three proceeding towards the status of all-horse farms (see the example of West Wycombe below, pp. 164–8) and one – Ebony – reverting from an all-horse state to using oxen again.
[38] *Fitzherbert*, pp. 15–16.

Checkendon in Oxfordshire. The soils here were not only thin but often stony, precisely of the type that Walter of Henley conceded were poor for oxen, since the animals tended to slip on the stones.[39]

Kent provides a more variable experience. While some of the demesnes, such as Petham and Bishopsbourne fringing on the North Downs, conformed to the upland pattern typified by the Chiltern manors, others are less easy to categorize. This is particularly the case with the Romney Marsh demesnes of Agney with Orgarswick, Appledore and Ebony, all belonging to Canterbury Cathedral Priory. These demesnes contained much newly reclaimed land and the high percentages of oats grown upon it indicates that it was wet and poorly drained and of a type seemingly ill-suited to horses.[40] It may, however, have had a high sand content, making it easier to work than other alluvial soils.

During the fourteenth century the number of all-horse demesnes increased markedly. Alftogether in Sample B, despite its smaller size, there are thirty-seven all-horse demesnes (or 9.4 per cent of the total of 393).[41] The area of most notable increase was Norfolk, although the smaller number of demesnes in Sample B disguises this somewhat in Figure 24. Almost all the county, with the exception of the fen districts, now had all-horse demesnes.[42] All-horse demesnes also began to appear in Suffolk, Essex and Cambridge-

---

[39] *Walter of Henley*, p. 319, c. 36.

[40] A. Smith, "Regional Differences in Crop Production in Medieval Kent", *Archaeologia Cantiana*, lxxviii (1963), p. 151; R. A. L. Smith, *Canterbury Cathedral Priory*, pp. 177–8.

[41] Upper Culham and Didcot, Berkshire; West Wycombe, Buckinghamshire; Burwell and Uphall with Hinton, Cambridgeshire; Milton Hall, Eastwood and Lawling, Essex; East Meon Church, Hampshire; Wheathampstead, Great Gaddesden, Knebworth, Ashwell and Kingsbourne, Hertfordshire; Agney with Orgarswick, Elverton (in Stone, near Faversham), Peckham, Copton, Dengemarsh and Bekesbourne, Kent; Thornham, Sedgeford, Plumstead, Hindolveston, Taverham, Scratby, Trowse Newton, Tunstead, Gimingham and Bircham, Norfolk; Oakham, Rutland; Exning, Lakenheath and Lackford, Suffolk; Farleigh, Surrey; Wetwang and Market Weighton ("Wighton"), Yorkshire. References as in Langdon, thesis, Appendix C, part 2.

Of these thirty-seven demesnes, two record oxen at one time or another but did not use them for draught, while two other demesnes were in a state of transition. One of these – Knebworth in Hertfordshire – became an all-horse farm during the period, while Farleigh (Surrey) seemingly reverted to using oxen sometime in the 1360s.

[42] Recent work by Dr Bruce Campbell has indicated that some areas on the southern fringe of the county also continued to use oxen into the second half of the fourteenth century. Personal communication.

Fig. 23: All-horse demesnes (Sample A: 1250–1320).

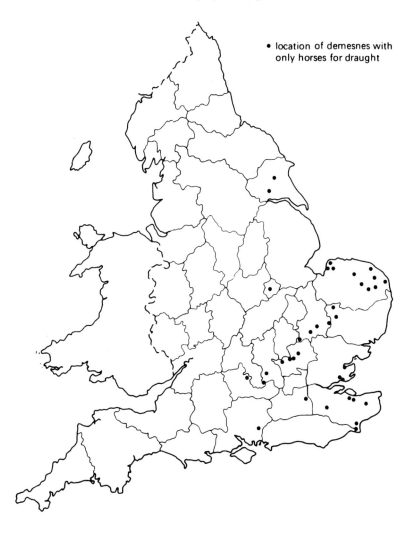

Fig. 24: All-horse demesnes (Sample B: 1350–1420).

shire. There was also a scattering of such demesnes well outside the previous area of concentration, notably at Oakham in Rutland and Wetwang and Market Weighton in the Yorkshire Wolds.[43] In Kent and the Chilterns, on the other hand, the spread of all-horse demesnes did not proceed much beyond that in the previous century. In fact, in the Romney marshlands the trend was markedly in the opposite direction, where at least two previously all-horse demesnes – Ebony and Appledore – were employing as many oxen as horses by the latter part of the fourteenth century. It may be that the land here was gradually stiffening, perhaps because of the use of marl and other dressings, which were employed in considerable quantities here.[44]

Despite these instances of reversion, the prevailing trend was solidly in the other direction. Of the all-horse demesnes in Sample B, twelve are definitely found to have been employing oxen in Sample A.[45] Examination of the accounts for several of these demesnes indicates that in many cases the turnover to horses seems to have taken place in the 1340s, either before or immediately after the plague. Why this decade is so popular is not clear, but in a number of cases the transition seems to have been a prelude to the final leasing of the demesnes, as at Oakham in Rutland, which existed as an all-horse demesne for barely ten years before it was leased out in the 1350s. Here it seems that the switch to horses was a failed attempt to revive the fortunes of the demesne. On the other hand, demesnes such as that at Plumstead in Norfolk, once they had been converted to all-horse draught, continued to be farmed in that way until well into the fifteenth century.

In summary, it appears that the trend towards all-horse demesne farming was a very real one, although admittedly on a minor scale. Only in Norfolk and probably the Chilterns could all-horse demesne

---

[43] M. L. Ryder, in his analysis of bone finds at the deserted medieval village of Wharram Percy, only a few miles from Wetwang, has commented on the high proportion of horse bones found there. "Livestock Remains from Four Medieval Sites in Yorkshire", *Agric. Hist. Rev.*, ix (1961), pp. 106, 109.

[44] R. A. L. Smith, *Canterbury Cathedral Priory*, pp. 136–7; M. Mate, "Medieval Agrarian Practices: The Determining Factors", *Agric. Hist. Rev.*, xxxiii (1985), p. 23. For the soil stiffening characteristics of marl, see G. E. Mingay, *The Agricultural Revolution* (London, 1977), p. 35.

[45] West Wycombe, Buckinghamshire; Milton Hall and Lawling, Essex; Peckham and Elverton, Kent; Plumstead, Hindolveston, Taverham, Scratby and Trowse Newton, Norfolk; Oakham, Rutland; Lakenheath, Suffolk.

farming be said to be consolidating itself into a definite regional characteristic. Outside these areas, all-horse demesnes were very scattered and generally surrounded by demesnes that used oxen. This indicates that the choice to go completely to horses was seldom easy to make, but was a finely balanced decision that could go either way.

Demesnes that did go to all-horse farming were generally employing large proportions of horses already, not only for harrowing and hauling but also for ploughing in conjunction with oxen, especially in mixed plough-teams. It is these in-between cases where horses were heavily involved in ploughing without, however, monopolizing it that contributed most to the increase in numbers of demesne horses. In the previous chapter we have shown how the phenomenon of mixed plough-teams spread through eastern England during the twelfth century. As to be expected, it continued to spread. Over the next three centuries references to mixed teams or at least to horses ploughing are found all over England. Thus, at Fareham, Cheriton and Beauworth (Hampshire) in 1286–7, among the ploughing expenses listed were charges for shoeing affers "drawing before the oxen".[46] The most northerly indication of mixed plough-teams occurred at Westoe (Durham) in 1446, where a fairly obvious reference to two teams of two horses and six oxen apiece is given.[47] Horses used for ploughing, probably in mixed teams, are also recorded at Portbury and Bedminster (Somerset) in 1323–4, where three and two affers respectively were shoed "for drawing the lord's plough".[48]

It is, therefore, easy to obtain likely examples of mixed plough-teams from almost anywhere in England. As in Chapter 2, the problem is to determine whether these cases were typical or exceptional in the counties in which they are found – a difficult proposition, since in most cases the only real clue lies in the numbers of draught animals listed. Fortunately, an indication of this can again be

---

[46] E.g., at Beauworth: *In ij affris ferrandis trahentis ante boues, iiijd.* H.R.O. Eccles. 2 159308, fo. 31v; see also fos. 18, 30v for Fareham and Cheriton.

[47] *ij Aratra cum toto apparatu tam ligneo quam ferreo pro xij bobus et iiij equis. Wills and Inventories . . . of the Northern Counties of England*, ed. J. Raine (Surtees Soc., ii, 1835), p. 95.

[48] *Et in ferrura iij affrorum trahentorum ad caruc' domini xijd.* (Portbury; similar for Bedminster; P.R.O. S.C. 6 974/1).

obtained statistically, since, as we have seen in Chapter 2, demesnes without mixed plough-teams generally fail to top the 20 per cent horse level. This, however, is complicated by the rise of cart-horses in the post-1200 material, which may have pushed even demesnes with no plough-horses above the 20 per cent mark. Fortunately this can be corrected. For example, if a demesne has horses which are specified as being carting animals, these can simply be subtracted. If the level of horses in the remaining draught stock is still 20 per cent or more, we can be fairly sure that mixed plough-teams, or at least horses for ploughing, were present on the demesne. The correction applied to those demesnes where horses for hauling are not openly specified presents a more difficult problem. An examination of the demesnes with cart-horses, however, indicates that there is usually one such animal to about every ten draught animals total. Thus, a demesne having ten or less draught oxen and horses is likely to have an equivalent of one of them engaged in hauling work, even though none of the animals is specified as such. Similarly those demesnes with eleven to twenty draught animals on them can be assumed to have two cart-horses, those with twenty-one to thirty draught animals, three cart-horses, and so on. In each case, if the level of horses in the animals remaining after these notional cart-horses have been subtracted still comprises 20 per cent or more, we can assume that we are dealing with mixed plough-teams. Using this criterion, we can separate all the demesnes in Samples A and B into those with all-ox plough-teams and those with mixed plough-teams (excluding, of course, all-horse demesnes). We are admittedly dealing with probabilities rather than certainties here, but, as in Chapter 2, the model does fit the experience of those cases where we are certain of the plough-team composition.

Altogether 274 demesnes in Sample A exhibited mixed plough-teams and 328 demesnes exhibited all-ox teams. In comparison Sample B had proportionally fewer mixed-team demesnes (132) as against all-ox team demesnes (226), but much of this was due to the greater proportion of all-horse demesnes in Sample B, with great gaps beginning to appear in Norfolk in particular, where all-horse plough-teams were taking over. The distribution maps for each type of demesne are shown in Figures 25 to 28 for both samples. Comparing the distribution of mixed teams in Figures 25 and 26 with that for the late twelfth century in Figure 18, it is obvious that the area employing mixed teams clearly expanded during the intervening period, such that the frontiers of the mixed team had been pushed out to a curving line stretching from the Solent to the Wash. Outside this boundary sprinklings of mixed teams were spreading into Lincolnshire and Leicestershire and even beyond. Inside it, only Sussex remained a haven for all-ox plough-teams, although occasional all-ox teams were found in other south-eastern counties. Equally obvious, as indicated by the similarity in the distribution of Samples A and B for both mixed and all-ox teams, is that by the end of the thirteenth century this situation had effectively stabilized, so that there was little change afterwards.

It would be mistaken to think, however, that all these cases we have labelled as "mixed teams" were necessarily so. We have already indicated in the twelfth-century example of Keyston, Huntingdonshire, how a demesne employing separate all-horse and all-ox plough-teams would show up as a mixed-team demesne in our analysis without actually having such teams. It appears that in several instances this happened in Samples A and B as well. Thus the 1286–7 bishopric of Winchester pipe roll records a number of Hampshire and Wiltshire demesnes where all-ox plough-teams operated in parallel with all-horse teams, often throughout the year.[49] It is tempting to surmise, as we did for Keyston, that these arrangements were of a passing nature, the stage before proceeding to mixed teams, but in fact the use of separate horse- and ox-teams in this fashion often lasted for a considerable time. At East Meon Manor (Hampshire), for instance, separate horse- and ox-teams are mentioned not only in 1286–7 but again in 1381–2.[50] In any case,

---

[49] E.g., at Ashmansworth (Hampshire): *In ferramento ij carucarum bouum & j caruce affrorum per totum annum*; H.R.O. Eccles. 2 159308. fo. 11. Similar references segregating ox- and horse-ploughs are also recorded at Mardon, Overton, Twyford with Marwell, and East Meon Manor (Hampshire), as well as at Downton (Wiltshire). *Ibid.*, fos. 8v, 10, 14, 27v, 7. For other examples in Bedfordshire, Northamptonshire and Gloucestershire, see Langdon, thesis, p. 142.

[50] Six ox-ploughs and five horse-ploughs were in operation in 1286–7 and five ox-ploughs and three horse-ploughs in 1381–2. H.R.O. Eccles. 2 159308, fo. 27v; *ibid.*, 159388, fo. 29v. It is difficult to guess at the reasoning behind such an arrangement, since two different systems of draught performing the same duty would seem an unnecessary complication. It is not inconceivable, however, that a demesne may have had some areas suitable for ox-teams and others suitable for horse-teams. Demesnes having a mixture of vale and uplands, such as at East Meon, would fit this pattern, with all-ox plough-teams being employed on the heavier land in the valleys and all-horse plough-teams on the lighter, high-ground soils. Quick ploughing by horses may also have been needed when there was a

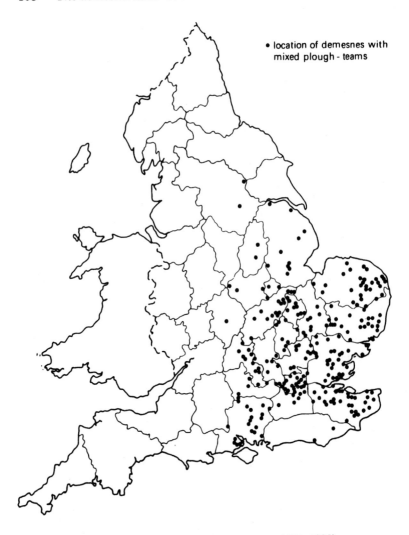

Fig. 25: Demesne mixed plough-teams (Sample A: 1250–1320).

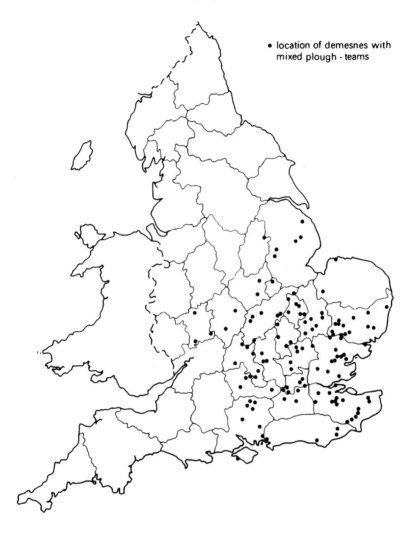

Fig. 26: Demesne mixed plough-teams (Sample B: 1350–1420).

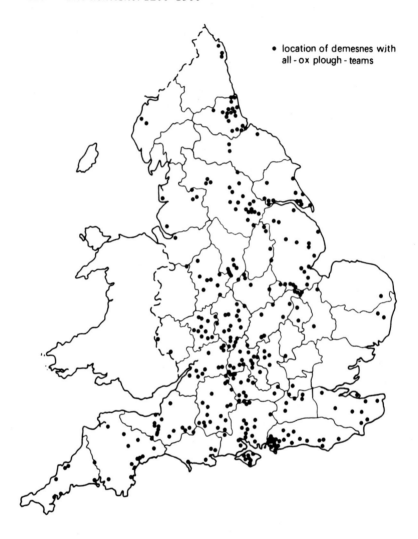

Fig. 27: Demesne all-ox plough-teams (Sample A: 1250–1320).

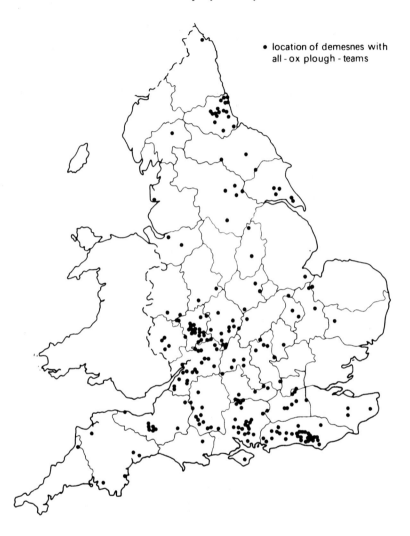

Fig. 28: Demesne all-ox plough-teams (Sample B: 1350–1420).

these demesnes with separate horse- and ox-teams seem to have been restricted to the outlying areas of our "mixed-team" region, particularly in Hampshire, as indicated by the bishopric of Winchester material. Further inside the region true mixed teams clearly predominated. A 1251 survey for the lands of the bishop of Ely, for instance, provides detailed plough-team information for thirty-nine demesnes in the counties of Cambridgeshire, Huntingdonshire, Hertfordshire, Norfolk, Suffolk and Essex. Thirty-four of these demesnes had mixed plough-teams, with compositions ranging from six horses and four oxen at Rattenden (Essex) to three horses and two oxen at Feltwell (Norfolk) and Brandon (Suffolk). The remaining five demesnes, all in the fenlands, employed ox-teams. Only two demésnes had separate horse-teams: Ely (Cambridgeshire) and Somerham (Huntingdonshire), both in combination with mixed teams.[51]

In summary, the extent of our "mixed-team" area as indicated on Figures 25 and 26 would seem to represent with reasonable accuracy the geographical limits that the mixed plough-team actually achieved in the thirteenth and fourteenth centuries. The maps do include some demesnes where the practice was to have separate horse- and ox-teams rather than the mixed variety, but these are unlikely to have constituted more than a small minority of cases and were in any event limited to the fringes of the mixed-team area. By the end of the thirteenth century the change to mixed plough-teams seems to have been more or less complete, since there was little expansion and perhaps even a reduction in mixed plough-team demesnes in the following century, as they were increasingly replaced by all-horse farms.

Compared to ploughing, the story for harrowing is easier to tell. Harrowing, of course, is considered to have remained a preserve of the horse all through this period, and there is little in this study to revise this picture. Occasionally it was a very specialized activity, as

heavy spring planting, perhaps because of the sowing of catch-crops or *inhokes* on the fallow. Extra ploughs for this or for emergencies were often raised on a temporary basis from the cart- or other horses on the demesne, as at Cuxham (Oxfordshire) in 1309, where a third plough comprised of two cart-horses, two horses belonging to the reeve, and an unspecified number of affers was into action because the spring planting had been delayed by frost (Harvey, *Medieval Oxfordshire Village*, pp. 58–9). For other examples of these "occasional" horse-ploughs, see Langdon, thesis, pp. 143–4. .

[51] Brit. Lib. Cott. MS Claud. C. XI.

at Belper (Derbyshire) in 1256–7, when an affer was bought specifically for the harrow and where the level of horses and the lack of carts indicates that this was all the animal did.[52] On several other occasions demesne horses are referred to as *hercatorii, equi hercatorii, affri herciantori* etc.,[53] again indicating that this was their main, if not sole, function. It was much more common, however, for harrowing to be only one of a number of duties that a horse might be asked to perform, particularly as harrowing involved only the winter and spring seedings, which left much time that could be filled in with other chores. Very early on we find horses doing a multitude of tasks, as at Bitterne, Hampshire, in 1210–11, where the "avers" not only harrowed, but ploughed and hauled marl as well.[54] Even more common was for the harrowing to be done by the cart-horses, as many references in the oats sections of the accounts indicate.[55] Even where it is not specifically stated that the cart-horses did harrowing, it is often implied by the extra rations fed to these animals during the planting seasons. The overwhelming impression one gets from all this is that although horses are often grouped as to whether they were ploughing, harrowing, or hauling beasts, in practice the lines of demarcation were not that rigid, allowing for much overlapping of function.

Concerning the size of the harrowing team, all medieval illustrations pertaining to England show it to have consisted of a single horse, and the odd reference in the accounts confirms this.[56] Two-horse harrowing teams should not be ruled out, however, as at least

---

[52] *In j affro masculo empto ad herciandum, viijs.* P.R.O. S.C. 6 1094/11, fo. 14v.

[53] As at Great Chart (Kent) in 1273–4; Croydon with Cheam (Surrey) in 1273–4; West Derby (Lancashire) in 1256–7; Hemyock (Devon) in 1286–7; Horton (Gloucestershire) in 1386–7; and so on. Sources as in Langdon, thesis, Appendix C.

[54] *In prebenda 2 avrorum, qui araverunt, et hericiaverunt, et marlaverunt per annum, 10 quarteria* (of oats). *Pipe Roll of the Bishopric of Winchester, 1210–1211*, p. 7. Many more examples could be cited.

[55] E.g.: *Et in prebenda ij equorum carettariorum euntium in herciis per xiiij septimanas tempore utrusque seminis, vj qr. j b.* (Holywell (in Caresby), Lincolnshire, 1294–5; P.R.O. S.C. 6 1090/3). Similar references are given for Exminster, Devon (1286–7); Bishop's Sutton, Hampshire (1286–7); Stretton, Rutland (1294–5); Long Bennington, Lincolnshire (1294–5); Boreham, Essex (1378–9); Bibury, Gloucestershire (1388–9); Blockley, Gloucestershire (1383–4); and Malden, Surrey (1379–80). Sources as in Langdon, thesis, Appendix C. Many other examples can be cited.

[56] As at Newport (Essex) in 1296–7: *In prebenda 1 equi euntis ad herciam ad semen quadragesimale. Earldom of Cornwall*, i, pp. 51–2.

one early sixteenth-century European illustration shows such an arrangement.[57] Certainly harrowing could be an onerous job, as at Cuxham (Oxfordshire) in 1327–8, where extra rations of oats were issued to the cart-horses and affers *pro suo magno labore* at harrowing.[58] Sometimes the ground to be harrowed was so obdurate that oxen had to be used, and Fitzherbert indicates that in many parts of the country in the early sixteenth century the practice was to use ox-harrows to break down the big clods first before using horse-harrows.[59] The same practice was evident on a number of English demesnes in medieval times, particularly in the west and north, where ox-harrows were often found.[60] But even when demesnes did have ox-harrows, it is clear that most of the harrowing on these farms was still done by horses. Thus at Monkwearmouth, Durham, where ox-harrowing seems to have been a regular practice, only one out of the seven harrows on the demesne in 1362 was actually an ox-harrow, only one out of the ten harrows in 1370, and only two out of the twelve harrows in 1378–9.[61]

If harrowing changed little in England during this time, the face of hauling was altered dramatically as horses increasingly replaced oxen in front of vehicles. As we have already indicated, this was a trend that had its origins in the twelfth century. By the end of the thirteenth century the sight of horses hauling vehicles must have been a common occurrence in all counties, particularly for road transport. Journeys involving carts and horses are recorded on the road systems to all parts of England.[62] Even on demesnes, where

[57] *Histoire de la France Rurale*, ii, p. 153. Two-horse harrows are also implied in the story of Piers the Plowman, where Piers's four horses harrowed "Wyth two harwes that thei hadde. an olde and a newe". *The Vision of William concerning Piers the Plowman*, ed. W. W. Skeat (London, 1869), p. 356.

[58] *Manorial Records of Cuxham*, p. 362. Fitzherbert also emphasized how important it was to keep harrowing horses "well kepte and shodde, or elles they wyll soone be tyred". (*Fitzherbert*, p. 25).

[59] *Fitzherbert*, p. 24.

[60] As at Newport, Essex (1296–7); Berkeley, Gloucestershire (1305–6); Beverley, Yorkshire (1373–4); Ham, Gloucestershire (1375–6); Sutton-under-Brailes, Warwickshire (1379–80); Monkwearmouth, Durham (1362, 1370, 1378–9); etc. Sources as in Langdon, thesis, Appendix C.

[61] *Inventories and Account Rolls of the Benedictine Houses or Cells of Jarrow and Monk-Wearmouth*, ed. J. Raine (Surtees Soc., xxix, 1854), pp. 159, 164, 172.

[62] For example, see J. F. Willard, "The Use of Carts in the Fourteenth Century", *History*, xvii (1932), p. 247; *idem*, "Inland Transportation in England during the Fourteenth Century", *Speculum*, i (1926), p. 367.

speed of hauling was perhaps not so urgent, the shift to horse hauling is still readily apparent, simply from the number of "cart-horses"
(*equi carectarii*) found in the records.[63]
However, we should not think that horses totally monopolized
hauling in England from the thirteenth century onwards, since ox
hauling still remained prevalent in some parts of the country. Thus
at Huntington, Herefordshire, in 1371–2 the reeve recorded that
more ploughing services than usual were required "because the
lord's oxen were occupied in hauling wood and stone for work at the
castle". The dual nature of oxen for ploughing and hauling implied
in this reference is indicated at several other places. Thus at
Wingate (Durham) in 1360 the demesne stock included seventeen
oxen for "two ploughs and *plaustra*". Demesne oxen for ploughs
and *plaustra* are also listed on the manors of Burstwick and
Keyingham (Yorkshire) in 1353–4 and Maidwell (Northamptonshire) in 1383–4. Even when oxen are not specifically mentioned for
hauling, it is often clear from other references that they did. For
instance, among the livestock and equipment listed for the demesne
at Finchale (Durham) in 1411 were "ten yokes for the plough and
plaustra".[64] It appears that oxen were particularly desired for hauling heavy materials, such as stone, wood, or coal (as indicated by
the Huntington case above).
An estimation of the extent of horse versus ox hauling can be
obtained by noting the frequency with which the various vehicles
associated with each animal occurs, in particular the horse-hauled
carecta versus the ox-hauled *plaustrum* and *carrus*. When an
analysis of this sort is carried out and some correction made for
uneven data distribution, it appears that at least 75 per cent of
demesne hauling across the country was performed by horses by the
end of the thirteenth century, although this dipped to 65–70 per cent
by the end of the fourteenth, thanks to a modest recovery by ox-
hauled vehicles.[65]

* * *

[63] See pp. 95–6 above.
[64] P.R.O. S.C. 6 861/1; *Priory of Finchale*, p. liii; P.R.O. S.C. 6 1083/4; No.R.O.
F.H. 482; *Priory of Finchale*, p. clviii.
[65] Langdon, "Horse Hauling", pp. 46–54, 58n.; also p. 157 below. For the
geographical distribution of (horse-hauled) *carecta* versus the (ox-hauled)
plaustrum and *carrus* see Figures 36–41 below; see also Langdon, "Horse Hauling", maps 1 and 2 (pp. 52–3).

Although our study is concerned mainly with draught- rather than pack-horses, some examination of the latter is desirable in order to assess their impact as work animals on the demesne relative to that of the hauling beasts. J. F. Willard, in his article on fourteenth-century hauling by carts,[66] assigned a minor role to pack-animals in the transportation of the time, and the work here on demesne draught stock does little to contradict this view. Nor should this be especially surprising. On the basis of the weight of goods transported per animal, the pack-horse was patently inferior to the cart-horse. The maximum load for the former is thought to have been just over 400 lbs.[67] On the other hand, a good cart-horse in the fourteenth century was seemingly capable of hauling over a ton on his own,[68] and at least one reference from the surveys indicates that carrying by pack-horse was only half as efficient as carrying by cart.[69] Therefore, whenever the transportation of large amounts of goods was required, such as bringing in the harvest or taking grain to market, carting or some other form of vehicle-hauling was preferable. On the other hand, for small amounts of goods, especially perishables or those needed in a hurry over a long distance or in difficult winter conditions, carriage by pack-horse was best.[70] In the material examined in this study, most of the pack-horses were found

[66] J. F. Willard, "The Use of Carts in the Fourteenth Century", *History*, xvii (1932), pp. 246–50.

[67] M. E. Seebohm, *The Evolution of the English Farm* (London, 1927), p. 220. In fact, 200–240 lb was more likely (David Hey, *Packmen, Carriers and Packhorse Roads* (Leicester, 1980), pp. 90–1; A. C. Leighton, *Transport and Communication*, p. 104, quoting Clive Day's *A History of Commerce*, puts it at 220–330 lb).

[68] An illuminating example is provided by a late fourteenth-century court roll for Writtle in Essex (E.R.O. D/DP M 189), in which one tenant of the manor sued another over the sale of a horse which the vendor had allegedly claimed could pull a cart and five quarters of wheat. At the modern conversion of about 63 lb per bushel of wheat, this works out to a load of 2,520 lb excluding the cart. Even allowing for the inflated claim of the man selling the horse (Hey, *Packmen, Carriers and Packhorse Roads*, p. 90, indicates that at least two horses would have been needed to haul such a load in early modern times), this still represents a considerable improvement over the amount that could be carried by a pack-horse. I am greatly indebted to Dr C. Dyer for providing me with a photocopy of the relevant passage; the 63 lb conversion rate for a bushel of wheat was supplied by Mr A. M. A. Woods, agricultural correspondent for the *Stratford-upon-Avon Herald*.

[69] See p. 226 below.

[70] E.g., see J. Crofts, *Packhorse, Waggon and Post* (London, 1967), pp. 5–6, dealing with early modern experience.

on demesnes which adjoined large, usually monastic, households.[71]
Here it seems the animals were used for day-to-day provisioning, a
state of affairs also observed on demesnes without any obvious
household connection; thus, two *summarii* at Henley-in-Salt-Marsh
(Gloucestershire) in 1378 are mentioned in relation to a journey to
fetch fish from Bristol.[72] Otherwise, unless terrain made them
essential, as appears to have been the case at Yealmpton (Devon) in
1395–6,[73] it was not worth having any of these specialized pack-
animals on the demesne, and altogether there are only a very small
number of them mentioned in the account material looked at in this
study.[74] This does not mean that some of the other horses on the
demesne could not at times have performed some pack-saddle
carrying, but that it was seldom their primary function. In any case,
judging by entries in surveys and extents, such carrying was more
often done by the peasantry as part of their labour services than by
demesne animals.[75]

Finally, an interesting feature of the demesne material is the light
it throws on the question of horse-milling. Mill-horses (*equi
molendinarii*, *equi pro molario*, or *equi ad molendinum*) or horse
mills (*molendini equini*) appear a number of times in the material
examined in this study.[76] It is difficult to say whether this was a rela-

---

[71] Particularly in the north, as in the case of Finchale and Harrow in Durham. *Priory
of Finchale*, pp. ii, lxii, lxxviii, cxviii; *Inventories and Account Rolls . . . of Jarrow
and Monk-Wearmouth*, pp. 27, 36, 71.

[72] Wo.R.O. Ref. 009:1 BA 2636 165 92226 2/7.

[73] Where the carrying of gravel and dung seems to have been done by pack-affers
rather than by carts. P.R.O. S.C. 6 830/29.

[74] Less than 0.1 per cent of the demesne work-horses in Samples A and B were
specifically designated as pack-animals (*summarii*).

[75] See pp. 225–7 below.

[76] As at Wells, Wisbech and Horningsea (Cambridgeshire) in 1251; Westgate
(Kent) in 1273–4; Wick Episcopi (Worcestershire), *c.* 1290; Riccall (Yorkshire),
c. 1295; Widnes (Lancashire) in 1295–6; Stepney (Middlesex) in 1303; Old
Alresford and Brockhampton (Hampshire) in 1381–2; Bromsgrove (Worcester-
shire) in 1385–6; and Pershore (Worcestershire) in 1386–7. Brit. Lib. Cott. MS
Claud. C. XI, fos. 24v, 73, 113v; Brit. Lib. Add. MS 29794; *Red Book of
Worcester*, i, p. 57; *Extents of the Prebends of York*, ed. T. A. M. Bishop
(Miscellanea, iv, Yorks. Arch. Soc. Rec. Ser., xciv, 1937), pp. 1–2; *Two
"Compoti" of the Lancashire and Cheshire Manors of Henry de Lacy, Earl of
Lincoln, xxiv and xxxiii Edward I*, ed. P. A. Lyons (Chetham Soc., cxii, 1884),
pp. 94–6; H.R.O. Eccles. 2 159388, fos. 26–7, 31v–32; W.C.L. C554; W.A.M.
22127.
    Not all the specified "mill-horses" actually drove mills, though, since in at least
one instance – Wick Episcopi – the horses probably carried grain to and from an
already established water-mill.

tively new trend or not, since horse mills are found in England as early as 1183.[77] Marc Bloch, however, cites a thirteenth-century case where the Abbot of St Albans replaced a water-mill, for which the feed channel had dried up, with a mill driven by horses,[78] and there are signs that this sort of phasing out of water-mills was happening elsewhere.[79] It is likely, though, that horse mills in general were much smaller than mills driven by water – perhaps little more than large handmills – since they do not seem to have been beyond the means of peasants.[80] The smaller and probably less expensive scale of their construction may thus have appealed to demesne managers, although the horses they employed amounted to only a tiny proportion of all the horses involved in draught work.[81]

c) THE SIZE OF THE DEMESNE PLOUGH-TEAM, 1200–1500

We have already discussed in Chapter 2 the importance that plough-team size has had in discussions of the origins of the open-field system and of the contradiction that arises when comparing the small plough-team shown in medieval illustrations with the much larger ones indicated in the documents. The purpose of this section is to carry this discussion further by considering the demesne plough-team from 1200 to 1500. In particular we want to determine if there were any deviations from the large plough-team noted in the twelfth century, and what effect the further introduction of the horse had on the size of this team. As we have already indicated, the documentation for much of this period is very rich. Surveys and extents, which provided the bulk of material for determining demesne plough-team size in the twelfth century, continue to grow in abundance after 1200, although there was an increasing tendency to omit the information about demesne plough-teams given in the earlier

---

[77] The Bishop of Durham had a *molendinum equorum* at Oxenhall (Durham) in that year. *Bolden Buke*, p. 17.

[78] "The Advent and Triumph of the Watermill", in *Land and Work in Medieval Europe* (London, 1967). p. 149.

[79] For example, the horse mill at Riccall (note 76 above), along with a windmill, seems to have replaced a water-mill that was previously there.

[80] For example, "full-land" customary tenants at Wisbech (Cambridgeshire) in 1251, each holding thirty-four acres, were excused suit of mill if they had their own horse mills: *Et debet sectam molendini nisi habeat molendinum equorum proprium* (Brit. Lib. Cott. MS Claud. C. XI, fo. 80v).

[81] Less than 0.2 per cent of the demesne work-horses in Samples A and B.

documents. Nevertheless there is still a significant amount of evidence to be gained, especially for the period before 1350. Most of this evidence is very explicit, as at Downham in Cambridgeshire in 1251, where it was stated that there was enough land to require three ploughs or plough-teams, "each of six oxen and two stotts [or horses]".[82] Altogether specific data of this sort have been gathered for eighty-three demesnes over the period 1200–1350. These are itemized in Table 16 under four categories: (1) all-ox teams, (2) mixed teams, (3) all-horse teams, and (4) teams of known size but unknown composition.

The mean plough-team size for each group is summarized below:

	No. of animals in team
All-ox teams	7.8
Mixed teams	7.7
All-horse teams	5.7
Teams of unspecified composition	9.5
Altogether	8.0
Altogether, excluding all-horse teams	8.1

Again, as in the twelfth century, the dominant plough-team size was one of eight animals. Of the 253¼ teams detailed in Table 16, 139¼ (or 54.9 per cent) were of this size. Only the all-horse teams and those of unspecified composition differed markedly. In the latter case this is probably due to coincidence, but the substantial reduction in the all-horse team size does seem to be a true reflection of the actual situation existing at the time, as we shall see from account material. Otherwise the presence of horses in the plough-team made little difference to its size. Despite the more varied experience of mixed teams, for instance, the overall similarity in

[82] *Quelibet de sex bobus et duobus stottis* (Brit. Lib. Cott. MS Claud. C. XI, fo. 34). While most of the references were of this very clear nature, some of the cases for the all-ox teams simply stated that so many animals were available for so many ploughs (e.g., as at Northwick and Whitstones, Worcestershire, where it was stated that there were *xl boves ad quinque carucas*; *Red Book of Worcester*, i, p. 30). To obtain the number of animals in a team, the oxen were simply divided by the number of ploughs, the assumption being that all the ploughs were of the same size. Cases which did not yield a practicable number were excluded, as at Hanbury, Worcestershire (*xliiii boves ad iiii carucas*; *Red Book of Worcester*, ii, p. 185). In the case of Hanbury it is likely that extra animals had been included in the figure – for example, compare it with the case of Buckland, Gloucestershire, where there were also forty-four oxen for four ploughs, but the entry made it clear that four of these oxen were extras and that each plough was in fact of ten animals (*Historia et cartularium monasterii Sancti Petri Gloucestriae*, iii, p. 64).

Table 16. *Distribution of demesne plough-team sizes, 1200–1350*

1. All-ox teams

County	No. of oxen in team					
	6		8		10	
	a	b	a	b	a	b
Cambridgeshire	1	5	1	3	—	—
Durham	—	—	1	5	—	—
Gloucestershire	2	9	4	10¼	4	12
Norfolk	3	8	—	—	—	—
Warwickshire	—	—	3	9	—	—
Worcestershire	—	—	8	24	1	2
Total	6	22	17	51¼	5	14
% (cases)	21.4		60.7		17.9	
% (teams)		25.2		58.7		16.0

2. Mixed teams

County	No. of horses and oxen in team																	
	4		5		6				7		8				10			
	2H,2O		3H,2O		4H,2O		2H,4O		3H,4O		4H,4O		2H,6O		6H,4O		2H,8O	
	a	b	a	b	a	b	a	b	a	b	a	b	a	b	a	b	a	b
Cambridgeshire	—	—	—	—	1	2	2	5	—	—	—	—	9	23	—	—	—	—
Essex	—	—	—	—	—	—	—	—	—	—	5	14	—	—	2	4	1	3
Gloucestershire	—	—	—	—	—	—	—	—	—	—	—	—	1	2	—	—	—	—
Hertfordshire	—	—	—	—	—	—	—	—	—	—	4	9	1	2	—	—	—	—
Huntingdonshire	—	—	—	—	—	—	—	—	—	—	—	—	1	5	—	—	—	—
Norfolk	1	1	1	3	—	—	3	6	1	2	—	—	1	4	—	—	—	—
Suffolk	—	—	1	3	—	—	—	—	—	—	5	13	2	4	—	—	—	—
Surrey	—	—	—	—	—	—	—	—	—	—	—	—	—	—	—	—	1	2
Total	1	1	2	6	1	2	5	11	1	2	14	36	15	40	2	4	2	5
% (cases)	2.3		4.7		14.0				2.3		67.4				9.3			
% (teams)		0.9		5.6			12.1			1.9			71.0					8.4

Table 16 (*cont.*)

3. *All-horse teams*

| | No. of horses in team | | | | | |
| | 4 | | 5 | | 6 | |
County	a	b	a	b	a	b
Cambridgeshire	—	—	—	—	1	6
Gloucestershire	1	1	1	1	—	—
Hampshire	—	—	1	1	—	—
Hertfordshire	—	—	—	—	1	2
Huntingdonshire	—	—	—	—	1	1
Total	1	1	2	2	3	9
% (cases)	16.7		33.3		50.0	
% (teams)		8.3		16.7		75.0

4. *Teams of known size but unknown composition*

| | No. of animals in team | | | |
| | 8 | | 10 | |
County	a	b	a	b
Berkshire	1	6	—	—
Dorset	1	2	—	—
Essex	2	3	3	7
Gloucestershire	—	—	4	20
Kent	—	—	1	2
Middlesex	1	1	—	—
Wiltshire	—	—	1	6
Total	5	12	9	35
% (cases)	35.7		64.3	
% (teams)		25.5		74.5

Key to column headings
a – Number of cases
b – Number of teams
H – Horses
O – Oxen

Notes and sources:

All-ox teams
Cambridgeshire: Brit. Lib. Cott. MS Claud. C. XI, fos. 61, 72v (date: 1251); *Durham: The Priory of Finchale,* ed. J. Raine (Surtees Soc., vi, 1837), p. xvi (date: 1335); *Gloucestershire: Historia et cartularium monasterii Sancti Petri Gloucestriae,* ed. W. W. Hart, 3 vols. (Rolls Series, London, 1863–7), iii, pp. 183, 187, 55 (*c.* 1266–7); *The Red Book of Worcester,* ed. M. Hollings, 4 vols. (Worcs. Hist. Soc., 1934–50), iii, pp. 313, 322 (*c.* 1290; for the date of these extents see note 168 below); *Historia et cartularium monasterii Sancti Petri Gloucestriae,* iii, pp. 183, 61, 64

(*c.* 1266–7; the quarter plough (from Northleach) was designated as such because it was only used from Christmas to Easter); *Red Book of Worcester*, iv, 403 (*bis*) (*c.* 1290); *Norfolk:* Brit. Lib. Cott. MS Claud. C. XI. fos. 182, 192v, 199v (1251); *Warwickshire: Red Book of Worcester*, iii, pp. 258, 275, 292 (*c.* 1290); *Worcestershire: Red Book of Worcester*, i, pp. 30, 57, 82, 90; ii, pp. 142, 166, 231, 237, 144 (*c.* 1290).

Mixed teams
Cambridgeshire: Brit. Lib. Cott. MS Claud. C. XI, fos. 127v, 115v, 132, 24, 34, 38v, 43v, 49, 53, 111, 145–145v, 149 (1251); *Essex: ibid.*, fos. 168, 171 (1251); *Domesday of St. Paul's of the Year 1222*, ed. W. H. Hale (Camden Soc., old series, lxix, London, 1858), pp. 64–5, 69 (1222); G. F. Beaumont, "The Manor of Borley, A.D. 1308", *Trans. of the Essex Arch. Soc.*, new series, xviii (1928), pp. 262–3 (1308; although the number of ploughs was not given here, two have been estimated from the demesne acreages); Brit. Lib. Cott. MS Claud. C. XI, fo. 176v (1251); *Domesday of St. Paul's of the Year 1222*, iv, pp. 48, 85–6 (1222); *Gloucestershire: Red Book of Worcester*, iv, p. 376 (Bibury; *c.* 1290); *Hertfordshire:* Brit. Lib. Cott. MS Claud. C. XI, fos. 152, 155v, 163v (1251); *Domesday of St. Paul's of the Year 1222*, i, pp. 13 (1222); Brit. Lib. Cott. MS Claud. C. XI, fo. 162 (1251); *Huntingdonshire: ibid.*, fo. 97 (1251); *Norfolk:* B. M. S. Campbell, "Agricultural Progress in Medieval England: Some Evidence from Eastern Norfolk", *Econ. Hist. Rev.*, 2nd ser., xxxvi (1983), p. 37n. (Reedham, 1291; Dr Campbell indicates that there was at least one other plough-team of this size and composition at nearby Lound in Suffolk); Brit. Lib. Cott. MS Claud. C. XI, fos, 254, 221v, 234v–235, 258v, 209v (1251); *Suffolk:* Brit. Lib. Cott. MS Claud. C. XI, fos. 307v–308, 263, 276v, 284, 292, 314, 270v, 299v (1251); *Surrey: Domesday of St. Paul's of the Year 1222*, pp. 103–4.

All-horse teams
Cambridgeshire: Brit. Lib. Cott. MS Claud. C. XI, fo. 24 (1251); *Gloucestershire: Historia et cartularium monasterii Sancti Petri Gloucestriae*, iii, pp. 183, 187 (*c.* 1266–7; the five affers at Aldsworth are assumed to be in the demesne's fifth plough, although the entry is slightly ambiguous); *Hampshire:* H.R.O. Eccles. 2 159308, fo. 31 (Cheriton; 1286–7); *Hertfordshire: Domesday of St. Paul's of the Year 1222*, p. 13 (1222); *Huntingdonshire:* Brit. Lib. Cott. MS Claud. C. XI, fo. 97 (1251).

Teams of known size but unknown composition
Berkshire: P.R.O. S.C. 12, Portfolio 18/22 (late 13th c.); *Dorset: ibid.*; *Essex: Domesday of St. Paul's of the Year 1222*, pp. 33, 73, 28, 38, 74–5 (1222); *Gloucestershire:* P.R.O. S.C. 12, Portfolio 18/22 (*quater*) (late 13th c.); *Kent:* F. R. H. Du Boulay, *The Lordship of Canterbury* (London, 1966), p. 213 (Bexley; 1285); *Middlesex: Domesday of St. Paul's of the Year 1222*, p. 99 (1222); *Wiltshire:* P.R.O. S.C. 12, Portfolio 18/22 (late 13th c.)

size between them and all-ox teams persisted. It seems that the combination of horses and oxen in plough-teams continued to be done for reasons of speed rather than to enable a reduction in the number of animals per plough. As a result, the average plough-team size for all teams during the period 1200–1350 was virtually identical to that in the twelfth century (see pp. 65–6 above), particularly if all-horse teams are excluded.

After 1350 only a handful of reliable references exists concerning the size of the demesne plough-team, mostly in accounts and inventories from the county of Durham. Thus eight-ox teams are evident at Finchale in 1363, Bewley and Ferryhill in 1446, and Elvethall in 1405–6 and 1422–3. Six-ox teams appear at Monkwearmouth in 1416–17, ten-ox teams at Jarrow in 1362, 1370, 1371, and 1373, and what looks to be a twelve-ox team at Pittington in 1446. Two mixed teams of two horses and six oxen apiece appear at Westoe in 1446, while all-horse teams of five and six horses each are found at Durham in 1446 and at Market Weighton (Yorkshire) in 1403.[83] In general, these scattered references indicate that large demesne plough-teams, either mixed or wholly of oxen, remained in evidence well after the advent of the plague, with teams of horses alone being somewhat smaller. This evidence is sufficient only as a vague indication, however, and must be supported by much other evidence before we can say that the state of affairs evident before 1350 continued after that date as well.

Fortunately the account data help in this regard, since a rough indication of plough-team size can often be worked out from the draught stock listings on the dorse of the accounts, particularly if the accounts also indicate the number of demesne ploughs in normal operation. The latter are intimated either directly by the number of ploughs that needed regular maintenance during the year, particularly with iron, or indirectly by the number of ploughmen hired during the same period. For instance, concerning the latter, with all but the smallest of plough-teams two men per plough were required, one to hold the plough (the *tentor*) and the other to drive the team (the *fugator*); the number of ploughs can thus be deduced by simply dividing the number of ploughmen by two. When the number of working ploughs is thus known for a particular demesne, it is a simple matter to divide it into the number of ploughing animals present – presumed for convenience in this study to be that remaining at the end of the account year – in order to obtain a rough estimate of plough-team size, all calculations being rounded off to the nearest whole number. The ploughing stock here is assumed to be the total draught stock less hauling stock; harrowing and other animals are presumed to be included with either the hauling or ploughing beasts.[84] For those demesnes where the hauling stock was

[83] *Priory of Finchale*, p. lxii; *Wills and Inventories . . . of the Northern Counties of England*, p. 96 (*bis*); D.C.D. Hostillar's Accounts (*bis*); *Inventories and Account Rolls . . . of Jarrow and Monk-Wearmouth*, p. 91; *ibid.*, pp. 44, 53, 58, 63; *Wills and Inventories . . . of the Northern Counties of England*, p. 95 (*ter*); *Testamenta Eboracensia*, ed. J. Raine, Jr (Surtees Soc., xlv, 1864), p. 24.

[84] For example, at Islip (Oxfordshire) in 1357–8 there were four ploughs in operation, for which there were thirty-four oxen and five cart-horses available as draught animals. Omitting the cart-horses, this leaves thirty-four oxen as the ploughing stock, which when divided by four results in a notional plough-team size of 8.5, or – rounding off – nine animals. W.A.M. 14799.

Table 17. *The frequency of plough-team sizes on English demesnes as indicated by accounts, 1250–1320 and 1350–1420*

Plough-team size (animals/plough)[1]	Sample A (1250–1320)		Sample B (1350–1420)	
	a	b	a	b
2	1	1	0	0
3	1	4	4	8⅓
4	9	20	10	19
5	15	29½	11	20
6	32	92	22	44½
7	52	150	27	54⅖
8	76	202	53	114
9	93	232½	68	143⅔
10	48	137	48	97⅚
11	28	74½	20	44
12	26	65	9	16

Key to column headings
a – No. of demesnes
b – No. of plough-teams (where there was more than one account available for a particular demesne, averaging the number of ploughs in these accounts sometimes resulted in fractions)
[1] Rounded off to the nearest whole number.
Notes and sources: Sources as in Table 11.

not directly indicated, one draught animal out of ten was subtracted, as in our previous calculation for determining the extent of mixed teams, with the exception that the subtraction was not made on demesnes with less than five animals. Here it was assumed that any hauling needing to be done would be performed by the ploughing stock, especially as these very small demesnes invariably had a high proportion of horses.

Altogether, using these methods, the notional plough-team sizes for 381 demesnes in Sample A and 272 demesnes in Sample B were calculated. The frequency of each plough-team size is shown in Table 17 and pictorially in Figure 29. All demesnes giving results of thirteen or more animals were excluded, as it was felt that these high numbers probably resulted from an underestimation of the number of ploughs or hauling animals on the demesne. In any case, these demesnes represented less than 10 per cent of the total data. The frequency distributions for both samples are strikingly uni-modal, although the mode value here is nine rather than eight as in the sur-

Table 18. *Average plough-team size as indicated by the accounts,*
1250–1320 and 1350–1420

	Sample A (1250–1320)		Sample B (1350–1420)	
	a	b	a	b
All demesnes	381	8.5	273	8.4
All, except all-horse demesnes	363	8.6	248	8.6
All-horse demesnes	18	5.4	25	5.0

Key to column headings
a – Number of demesnes
b – Average plough-team size (animals/plough)

vey and extent material. Presumably this reflects the tendency of
most demesnes to have one or two animals per plough as spares or
perhaps as harrowing animals. There is also a greater spread across
the whole range of plough-team values, reflecting the relative weak-
ness of the account material as a measure of plough-team size. Most
important, the frequency profiles for the two samples are remarkably similar, and it appears that plough-team size after 1350
followed much the same pattern as it had before. This is also
revealed in the average plough-team sizes for the samples (see
Table 18), which are virtually identical, particularly if all-horse
demesnes are excluded. Also evident is the much reduced plough-
team size on these same all-horse demesnes, which again verifies the
survey and extent material. Teams having only two or three horses
are indicated on some demesnes.[85]
    Small regional differences can be detected in the figures, as
shown in Table 19. Excepting the result for the north in Sample B,
the smallest plough-teams on average are those for East Anglia,
reflecting the presence of all-horse farms there, although this is
offset to some degree by large teams in Essex.[86] On the other hand,

[85] As at Thornham (Norfolk), where only two horses were kept for the demesne
plough (N.R.O. Ref. No. R232B; e.g., the 1265–6, 1277–8, 1309–10 and 1351–2
accounts).
[86] The average plough-team size from the Essex accounts was 9.5 animals for
Sample A and 9.2 animals for Sample B. In contrast, the average plough-team
size from the Norfolk accounts was 6.6 animals for Sample A and – when all-horse
demesnes began to dominate after the Black Death – 4.9 animals in Sample B.

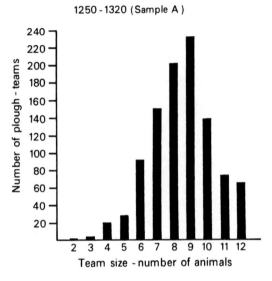

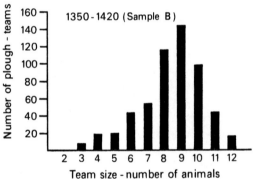

Fig. 29: Plough-team size frequency as indicated by accounts.

as expected from Chapter 2, larger plough-teams are observed in the south and south-west. Beyond this, the striking feature is the uniformity of the average plough-team figure right across the country. Even East Anglia, with its relatively high proportion of all-horse demesnes (30 per cent in Sample B), used on average a number of animals per plough not far behind that in the rest of the country.

Table 19. *Average plough-team size by region as indicated by the accounts, 1250–1320 and 1350–1420*

	Sample A (1250–1320)		Sample B (1350–1420)	
Region	*a*	*b*	*a*	*b*
East Anglia	74	7.8	46	7.9
Home Counties	67	8.4	53	8.3
The South	74	8.8	72	8.7
South-west	24	9.4	12	9.0
East Midlands	61	8.4	21	8.2
West Midlands	33	8.0	46	8.6
The North	45	8.8	21	7.9

Key to column headings
a – No. of demesnes (including all-horse demesnes)
b – Average plough-team size (animals/plough)
Notes and sources: Sources as in Table 11. For the counties making up each region, see Table 8.

What conclusions can be drawn from this information? From the surveys and extents it is obvious that the large demesne plough-team of eight animals or so, abundantly evident in the twelfth century, continued with equal popularity into the thirteenth and probably the fourteenth and fifteenth centuries as well, and this is strongly supported by the information in the accounts. It seemingly made little difference whether these teams were comprised of oxen alone or of horses and oxen combined. Only all-horse teams showed a substantial reduction in size, but as they were in such a minority they had little impact on demesne plough-team size as a whole across the country.

d) PLOUGHS, HARROWS AND VEHICLES ON THE DEMESNE, 1200–1500

As would be expected from the increase in documentation, information about farming equipment on the demesne is much more forthcoming during this period. This is particularly true for ploughs, about which a great deal more is known than in the twelfth century. Demesne accounts are especially useful because they generally have a section dealing with plough costs. It is from these costs that many valuable clues concerning plough design and construction can be gleaned. Unfortunately the accounts tend to record only those costs dealing with iron and steel, the most expensive items for the plough in terms of materials and workmanship. The various wooden parts of the ploughs, because of their cheapness, are usually omitted or referred to only in the most general of terms. This is disappointing for at least one important aspect of plough typology. It would be most instructive, for example, to know if demesne ploughs were definitely of the heavy mould-board type capable of turning a furrow or whether they were of the ard or scratch-plough variety. References to mould-boards do occur from time to time,[87] but it is difficult to tell whether these are typical. The widespread presence of large demesne plough-teams makes us think they must have been, but it would be nice to have more extensive documentary proof of this. Mould-boards are often seen on medieval illustrations of ploughs, but they are also occasionally missing.

Linguistic evidence is equally ambivalent. In the accounts, as in the twelfth-century survey material, the terms *aratrum* and *carruca* often occur interchangeably. This is particularly the case in the north, where it appears that *aratrum* was a fifteenth-century term which gradually replaced the word *carruca*. Both terms would seem to be describing essentially the same plough, since they were both drawn by large plough-teams of eight or more animals.[88] Whether or not the *aratrum* and *carruca* represented the same type of plough, Fitzherbert in the early sixteenth century talks about the "sheld-" or mould-board plough as if it were a normal occurrence, suggesting the presence of such ploughs, on demesnes and elsewhere, for a considerable time before that.[89]

Even though the accounts fail to establish the complete domination of the heavy mould-board plough on the demesnes, they are very useful for another type of classification: that is, whether the ploughs were of the wheeled, foot, or swing variety. Although there were some important sub-groups,[90] these were the three main kinds

[87] Such as the three "moldebredes" bought at Pittington, Durham, in 1376–7. D.C.D. Bursar's Accounts.
[88] E.g., see especially *Wills and Inventories... of the Northern Counties of England*, pp. 95–6, where *carucae* of eight oxen at Bewley and Ferryhill (Durham) in 1446 are listed alongside *aratra* of eight and twelve oxen at Westoe and Pittington.
[89] *Fitzherbert*, pp. 9–11.
[90] In particular, the turn-wrest plough of Kent. Despite their distinctive feature of turning furrows all in the same direction, however, they were still wheeled ploughs (or at least they tended to be in England).

of plough in medieval England.[91] The differentiation amongst them is based on the degree of regulation in the depth of ploughing. Wheeled ploughs provided the greatest control in this respect. They could be set up to plough at any given depth by adjusting the wheels in relation to the plough body. If more modern experience is applicable, they were also quicker, easier to handle, and, despite the weight of the wheels, easier to pull.[92] Altogether they were ideal for light, well-drained soils. But once the ground became heavier and stickier, the wheels tended to clog up, such that in extreme conditions they "resembled two large balls of earth".[93] In such situations, it was often better to have a foot plough instead. Here the wheels were replaced by an adjustable piece of wood or iron, called a "foot", one end of which was inserted in the plough-beam before the coulter while the other rested on the ground. As the foot slid along it kept the plough-beam at a constant height above the soil and assisted the plough-holder in maintaining the share tip at a constant depth. Finally, we have swing ploughs, where virtually all the depth regulation was in the hands of the ploughman. The handling of these ploughs needed considerable skill, and differences in abilities among ploughmen could make considerable differences in ploughing efficiency.[94] Swing ploughs were most useful on stiff, heavy soils or upon ground of extreme unevenness, where the regulation provided by wheeled or foot ploughs was rendered ineffective.[95]

It is the purpose of this study to analyse the distribution of these three basic types of plough on medieval demesnes through the use of Samples A and B. The method is a simple one. Whenever plough wheels or plough feet are mentioned in an account, it is presumed that the demesne concerned has wheeled or foot ploughs. When neither is mentioned, it is presumed that the demesne has only swing ploughs.

[91] See, for instance, F. G. Payne, "The British Plough: Some Stages in its Development", *Agric. Hist. Rev.*, v (1957), p. 83.

[92] Such at least were the results of dynamometer trials in the nineteenth century (P. Pusey, "Experimental Inquiry on Draught in Ploughing", *Journal Royal Agric. Soc.*, i (1840), p. 224; H. Handley, "On Wheel and Swing Ploughs", *Journal Royal Agric. Soc.*, i (1840), p. 144).

[93] Pusey, "Experimental Inquiry on Draught", p. 226.

[94] For example, see H. Handley, "On Wheel and Swing Ploughs", pp. 144–6.

[95] E. Kerridge, *The Agricultural Revolution* (New York, 1968), p. 33; *The Agrarian History of England and Wales*, iv, ed. J. Thirsk (Cambridge, 1967), p. 164.

This "simple" method, however, presents several problems. The first is that of under-recording. Just because an account does not mention plough wheels or plough feet does not necessarily mean there were no ploughs of either type on the demesne. It may be that these items were simply not bought that year, perhaps because some were already in stock, or that they were caught up in some more general entry (e.g., *In ferramento carucarum*, etc.). In this sense, under-recording is bound to be an unavoidable and largely unmeasured factor. Nevertheless plough wheels and plough feet were normally expensive enough objects to merit individual attention in the accounts, plough wheels because they required a degree of carpentry beyond that of the run-of-the-mill manorial servant and plough feet because – in most cases at least – they required some iron. Consequently the recording of them on demesnes where they were used was generally very consistent. Thus at Cuxham (Oxfordshire), where both wheeled and foot ploughs were apparently the norm, the purchase of plough wheels and *ferra pedalia* occurred virtually every year.[96]

The second problem concerns terminology. In general this causes little trouble. Plough wheels are usually referred to as *rote ad carucam* (or some variation), or occasionally just as *rote*, but in such a situation, such as being in the plough costs, that it is obvious they are for the ploughs. In a few cases *rote* are mentioned in contexts where it is not possible to say whether they are for the ploughs or for the carts or other vehicles. These cases have been excluded from the analysis. Plough feet are generally indicated by references to a *ferrum pedale* or occasionally just a *pedale*.[97] In few instances the

[96] P. D. A. Harvey (ed.), *Manorial Records of Cuxham* (Oxfordshire Rec. Soc., 1, 1976), pp. 163–606.
[97] There is some confusion as to what exactly was meant by the *ferrum pedale* or just *pedale*. Most authorities have felt that they were indeed plough feet (for example, J. E. Thorold Rogers, *A History of Agriculture and Prices in England*, i (Oxford, 1866), pp. 537–8; Canon J. L. Fisher, *A Medieval Farming Glossary of Latin and English Words* (London, 1968), p. 26). On the other hand, Colonel J. S. Drew, drawing upon a wealth of account material from the south of the country, eventually came to the conclusion that the *ferrum pedale* was a plough-iron or sole-plate to protect the bottom of the plough (from unpublished notes in the care of the committee for the *Dictionary of Medieval Latin from British Sources* at the Bodleian Library in Oxford; I am indebted to the editor, Dr David Howlett, for allowing me to consult these notes), and it is this interpretation that has been adopted by the *Revised Medieval Latin Word-list*, ed. R. E. Latham (London, 1965), pp. 189, 338. Drew's main argument to this effect was that there are often

anglicized *footeyre* (foot-iron) is found.   Other terms, such as *plowsho* or *longum ferrum*, may or may not indicate plough feet,[98] but it has been decided to err on the side of caution, and so the demesnes displaying them have been excluded.[99] In summary, only definite references to plough wheels and plough feet have been included in the analysis. This has probably led to some underestimation of the extent of wheeled and foot ploughs, but this underestimation is thought preferable to including false or confusing information. In those cases where a series of accounts has been consulted for the same demesne, that demesne is considered to have had wheeled or foot ploughs if definite reference to them is made in half or more of the accounts.

In the end, the accounts for 508 demesnes in Sample A and 332 demesnes in Sample B have been considered suitable enough to determine whether the particular demesnes had wheeled, foot, or swing ploughs. The frequency with which each plough type occurs is indicated for both samples in Table 20.

Anyone adding up the number of demesnes for each sample in Table 20 will quickly realize that they come to more than the 508 and

signs that the *ferrum pedale* was fixed with nails to the plough, instead of being adjustable as in a "true" plough foot.

Nevertheless, it is very unlikely that this interpretation is the correct one, since, whatever it was, the characteristic of a *pedale* was important enough for it to be classified as a type of plough. Thus at Aldenham (Hertfordshire) in 1352 it is stated that four ploughs were made from the lord's wood, *unde ij caruce pedales et ij caruce rotabiles* (as quoted in the *Dictionary of Medieval Latin from British Sources*, fascicule II, ed. R. E. Latham (London, 1981), p. 289, under *2 carruca*). In this case the reference to foot ploughs would seem to be unmistakable, particularly as it parallels so closely the references to "foot ploughs" in later documents (e.g.: "Item j fote plow & one whele plowe *with* theire furnyture" from the 1573 inventory of the goods of John Wyghte of Isleworth, Middlesex; P.R.O. Probate 2, no. 396). Foot ploughs are also indicated by the words themselves, which would seem to point conclusively to the plough foot or at least some part of it. It may be that the *ferrum pedale* was a piece of iron attached to the bottom of the plough foot rather than the foot itself, which would reconcile Drew's point about it being fixed to the plough. On balance, despite Drew's *caveat*, the evidence does suggest quite strongly that whenever a *pedale* or *ferrum pedale* is mentioned it signifies the presence of a foot plough, and we have considered it as such in this study. The striking regional pattern of demesnes displaying these terms, as we shall see, would appear to bear this out.

[98] Drew, notes, gives evidence that suggests that the *ferrum longum* at least was identical to the *ferrum pedale*.

[99] In any case, they only amount to a small number of references (ten or less) in Samples A and B. For the difficulties involving these and other terms, see Langdon, thesis, pp. 162–3.

Table 20. *Frequency of demesne plough types, 1250–1320 and 1350–1420*

Type of plough	Sample A (1250–1320)		Sample B (1350–1420)	
	a	*b*	*a*	*b*
Wheeled	136	26.8	93	28.0
Foot	119	23.4	140	42.2
Swing	280	55.1	141	42.5

Key to column headings
a – No. of demesnes
b – % of all demesnes in sample for which the plough type was determined
Notes and sources: Sources as in Table 11.

332 demesne totals. This is because some demesnes – twenty-seven in Sample A and forty-two in Sample B – had both foot and wheeled ploughs and so are counted twice. Comparing the results for the two samples, the domination of swing ploughs is evident in both cases, although much less so in Sample B. It should be remembered, though, that this is not based on positive proof of the existence of swing ploughs, but rather on the absence of evidence for the other two types. In this regard, it is interesting to note the rise of foot ploughs in the later sample, mostly at the expense of swing ploughs. Does this reflect a real change in the type of plough used on many demesnes? Or is it simply because manorial officials were now more careful in recording the existence of foot ploughs (or, more accurately, the need to purchase extra iron for these ploughs) than they were before? The same uncertainty applies to the much smaller rise in wheeled ploughs.

To a certain extent, a look at the plough type distributions across the country, as shown in Figures 30 to 35, helps to clarify matters. The situation as regards wheeled ploughs is simplest to deal with, since for both samples these ploughs are narrowly concentrated in two main areas: south-east England (mainly below the Thames) and eastern Norfolk. Comparing Figures 30 and 31 shows the situation to have been a fairly static one for wheeled ploughs. There was virtually no expansion from one sample period to the next; what little there was seems to have been in the direction of Hertfordshire and across the southern reaches of Sussex, although in the latter case this may be due to the relative lack of information for this area in the earlier sample. In the south-eastern region the predilection for wheeled ploughs for upland areas is clear, particularly in the earlier period, where the distribution closely follows the curve of the Hampshire Chalklands and the North Downs, presumably because the well-drained soils found here were ideal for such ploughs. It is more difficult to explain the concentration of wheeled ploughs in low-lying eastern Norfolk in the same way, but it is known from later times that depth regulation was considered crucial here because of the desire not to bring up the "pan" or subsoil, which was thought to be detrimental to crop yield.[100] Outside these areas references to wheeled ploughs are extremely scattered. The wheeled ploughs at Adderley (Shropshire) stand out alone in the 1250–1320 sample, but occasional wheeled ploughs are also seen at Jarrow, Durham, in 1381–2 and probably at Finchale in the same county in 1397, 1408–9, and 1410–11.[101] These last are not included on Figure 31, however, because they occur in less than half of the accounts consulted for these particular demesnes.

The main concentration of foot ploughs occurs in a region running from London in the east to the Bristol Channel in the west and from the Solent northwards to the west midlands (see Figures 32 and 33). Outside this area foot ploughs can be seen extending in scattered frequency towards the north. In comparing the two samples, there seems to have been a withdrawal of foot ploughs from Hertfordshire, Bedfordshire and Middlesex after the Black Death, perhaps because of the spread of wheeled ploughs into these areas, but advances in Hampshire, western Sussex, and probably the north, although in geographical terms these changes are marginal. Most of the increase in the proportion of foot ploughs, in fact, seems to have come in areas where they were already present in the first sample, raising the suspicion that they were better recorded in the second sample.

This is confirmed by the swing plough distributions. In the first sample (Figure 34) no definite regional pattern is discernible. Our presumed swing ploughs are found virtually everywhere, and it seems probable that in many cases our instances of swing ploughs are simply cases of unrecorded wheeled and especially foot ploughs.

---

[100]   William Marshall, *The Rural Economy of Norfolk*, 2nd edn (London, 1795), i, pp. 11–13.
[101]   *Inventories and Account Rolls . . . of Jarrow and Monk-Wearmouth*, p. 70; *Priory of Finchale*, pp. cxix, cxliii, clix.

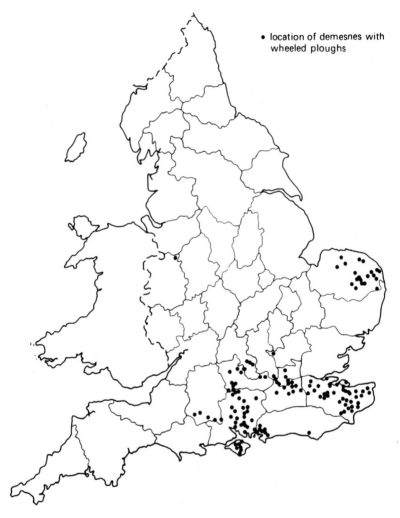

Fig. 30: Demesne wheeled ploughs (Sample A: 1250–1320).

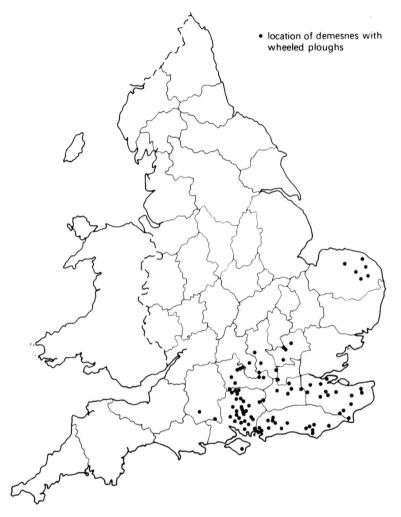

Fig. 31: Demesne wheeled ploughs (Sample B: 1350–1420).

Fig. 32: Demesne foot ploughs (Sample A: 1250–1320).

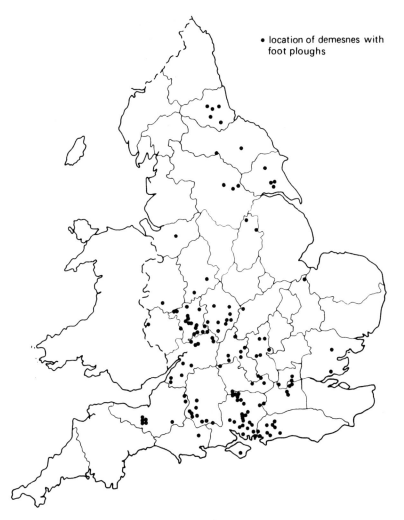

Fig. 33: Demesne foot ploughs (Sample B: 1350–1420).

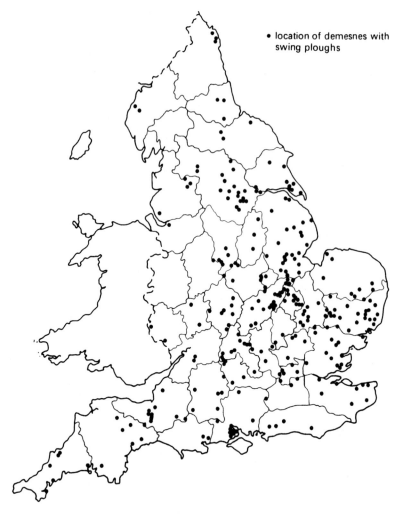

Fig. 34: Demesne swing ploughs (Sample A: 1250–1320).

Fig. 35: Demesne swing ploughs (Sample B: 1350–1420).

In the second sample (Figure 35) the situation is much clearer. The distribution of swing ploughs has shrunk away from areas dominated by foot and wheeled ploughs, indicating that the recording of plough wheels and feet is much more consistent now. From what remains, it appears that swing ploughs dominated in East Anglia and the east midlands, particularly in that gap between the concentration of wheeled ploughs in Norfolk and south-east England. The swing plough also seems to have competed with wheeled ploughs in Kent and east Sussex and with foot ploughs in the south-west and the north.

As has already been mentioned, some demesnes had more than one type of plough. This is particularly the case with wheeled and foot ploughs, which seem to have been employed simultaneously on many demesnes, especially in the counties of Berkshire, Hampshire, Surrey and Sussex, where this combination of plough types was steadily increasing. It would seem the practice was to use the foot or unwheeled plough in the damper conditions of the winter and to use wheeled ploughs during the drier ploughings in the summer;[102] indeed, ploughs specifically designated for the summer or winter are recorded on some demesnes.[103] A similar relationship may have existed between swing and wheeled ploughs or even swing and foot ploughs. For example, Kent, with its mixture of wheeled and swing plough demesnes, even in the late fourteenth century, would indicate that both types of ploughs were being used simultaneously on some manors at least. In this case, the incidence of swing ploughs would be *underestimated*, since we are not counting them on demesnes where wheeled and foot ploughs already exist.

Nevertheless, although some non-recording of wheeled, foot, and even swing ploughs has undoubtedly occurred in our samples, the situation by the end of the fourteenth century is still relatively clear, with definite regional patterns appearing for all three types of

---

[102] As in nineteenth-century Buckinghamshire: "In working the land it is found necessary to use two different descriptions of ploughs; one an old-fashioned wooden plough for winter, and the other a more modern iron-wheel plough for summer. The wheel plough comes into use 'with the cuckoo', the ground being so soft in winter that the wheels will not then work." James Caird, *English Agriculture in 1850–1* (London, 1852), p. 10.

[103] E.g.: ... *in caruca yemali et alia estivali reparandis de maeremio domini* ... ; from a 1325 Pershore (Worcestershire) account, as quoted in the *Dictionary of Medieval Latin from British Sources*, fascicule II, p. 289.

plough: namely, that wheeled ploughs were prevalent in the south-east and eastern Norfolk, foot ploughs mainly in the south-west from Hampshire to the west midlands, swing ploughs in East Anglia and the east midlands, and swing and foot ploughs together in the north. Of these, wheeled ploughs seem to have been the least popular overall, and their use expanded very little during the period covered by the two samples. If any plough were gaining in popularity it was the foot plough, and this is consistent with the view that it was a fairly recent development.[104] This conclusion, however, is clouded by the suspicion that much of the apparent growth in the popularity of foot ploughs observed in Table 20 is based on the under-recording of the evidence for these ploughs in the earlier sample.

Harrows are mentioned frequently in the accounts, but it is difficult to discern much about their construction and appearance. English medieval illustrations generally show them to be rectangular in shape. Triangular and trapezoidal harrows became popular on the Continent during this period,[105] but it is difficult to say how prevalent they were in England, since there is no definite sign of them in the material, documentary or iconographic, examined in this study.[106] Wood was the universal material of construction for the body of the harrow, and the construction of the implement must have generally followed that shown in the Luttrell Psalter and described by Fitzherbert, with four, five, or six wooden "bulls" set with iron or wooden teeth and joined by a series of wooden cross-members.[107]

Sizes of harrows varied considerably, particularly between the horse and ox varieties. Thus an ox-harrow containing thirty iron teeth at Berkeley (Gloucestershire) in 1305–6 appears alongside a horse-harrow containing only twelve teeth. Similarly, the horse-

---

[104] Foot ploughs only begin to appear in medieval illustrations in the thirteenth century. Haudricourt and Delamarre, *L'Homme et la Charrue*, p. 363.

[105] Singer et al., *History of Technology*, ii, p. 94; *Histoire de la France Rurale*, ii, p. 98; E. Blum and P. Laver, *La Miniature Française aux xve et xvie Siècles* (Paris and Brussels, 1930), plate 6.

[106] There is, however, a curious reference to "French" and "English" harrows (*herciam gallicam* and *herciam anglicam*) among the labour services for two tenants of Avening (Gloucestershire), *c*. 1200: *Charters and Custumals of the Abbey of Holy Trinity Caen*, pp. 83–4. Unfortunately, what the distinction was between these two types of harrow is not indicated.

[107] Millar, *The Luttrell Psalter*, fo. 171; *Fitzherbert*, p. 24.

harrow in the Luttrell Psalter has sixteen teeth, while the ox-harrow described by Fitzherbert had thirty-six.[108]

As indicated by a recent study, the use of iron in harrows may have been a late thirteenth-century development.[109] Certainly by the fourteenth century some estates were employing almost nothing but harrows with iron teeth.[110] On the other hand, Fitzherbert has indicated that harrows with wooden teeth were preferable on stony ground, where iron wore away too quickly to be economical.[111]

The variety of vehicle types observed on English demesnes in the twelfth century has already been discussed, and this variety continued to be evident on English demesnes for the next three hundred years. Again the accounts are very useful in naming the various vehicle types and in supplying clues as to what they actually looked like, since, in addition to a section for plough costs, each account generally has one for vehicle costs as well. By using these sections, vehicle type information has been obtained for 509 demesnes in Sample A and 340 demesnes in Sample B. The frequency with which each vehicle appears is given in Table 21, while distribution maps for the three most common types – carts (*carectae*), *plaustra* and *carrae* – are shown in Figures 36 to 41.

It was a fairly common practice to have more than one type of vehicle on a demesne, and so the total number of vehicle references in Table 21 exceeds the number of demesnes for both samples (and hence the percentages add up to more than 100). Without doubt, the most popular type of vehicle was the *carecta*[112] or cart, being found on nearly 90 per cent of demesnes with definite vehicle references in Sample A and nearly 80 per cent of demesnes with vehicle references in Sample B. Figures 36 and 37 show their distribution to have been virtually countrywide for both samples. There was a tendency for them to become less frequent towards the north and

---

[108] P.R.O. S.C. 6 850/12; Millar, *Luttrell Psalter*, fo. 171; *Fitzherbert*, p. 24.

[109] Mate, "Profit and Productivity on the Estates of Isabella de Forz", pp. 329–30.

[110] Thus a series of inventories for the east Sussex manors of the Earl of Arundel in 1397 lists sixteen harrows with iron teeth against only one with wooden teeth; there were also five harrows where the type of teeth was not specified. L. F. Salzman, "The Property of the Earl of Arundel, 1397", *Sussex Arch. Coll.*, xci (1953), pp. 41–2.

[111] *Fitzherbert*, p. 25.

[112] The most common spelling, although sometimes found in other variants, such as *carrecta, caretta, careta*, etc.

west, as they were supplemented or replaced by other vehicles, especially the *plaustrum*, although this is exaggerated on Figures 36 and 37 because of the relative scarcity of data in these areas. As we have already indicated, carts appear to have been solely horse-hauled, as evidenced by the numerous references to halters and traces in cart costs sections, the ubiquitous "cart-horse", and so on. They were invariably two-wheeled,[113] although this does not mean they were uniform in size, since both long and short varieties were evident.[114] In general, though, we should see carts as small vehicles, often of simple construction, as at Glatton (Huntingdonshire) in 1313–14, where the body of a cart could be bought for 18d. and wheels of two felloes and four spokes made for 8d. each.[115]

The second most popular vehicle was the *plaustrum*. As seen in Figures 38 and 39, it had a much more northerly and westerly distribution, with the exception of a notable concentration of the vehicles in Sussex and southern Kent, especially in the post-1350 sample. Up till now, it has been most commonly interpreted by historians as being a four-wheeled wagon,[116] although in fact the accounts strongly suggest that it was a two-wheeled vehicle, as indicated by the following selection of references:

(1) *Et in j pare rotarum & j corpore ad plaustrum cum toto atillio* (Little Humber, Yorkshire, 1285–6)

(2) *In uno plaustro novo et in j pare rotarum pro plaustro* (Jarrow, Durham, 1364)

(3) *In j pare rotarum empto pro j novo plaustro* (Wellow, Somerset, 1365–6)

(4) *In j pare rotarum empto pro plaustro* (Barnhorn Manor, Bexhill, Sussex, 1385–6)[117]

---

[113] As, for example, at Sevenhampton (Wiltshire) in 1281–2: *In j pari rotarum j sella ad carectam* (*Accounts and Surveys of the Wiltshire Lands of Adam de Stratton*, ed. M. W. Farr (Wilts. Arch. Soc. Rec. Ser., xiv, 1959), p. 129).

[114] Thus a "long cart" and a "short cart" are found among the household effects of both the abbot of Westminster in 1289–90 and the bishop of London in 1303 (*Documents Illustrating the Rule of Walter of Wenlok, Abbot of Westminster, 1283–1307*, ed. B. F. Harvey (Camden Fourth Series, ii, 1965), p. 185; *Accounts of the Executors of Richard Bishop of London 1303 and of the Executors of Thomas Bishop of Exeter 1310*, ed. W. H. Hale and H. T. Ellacombe (Camden New Series, x, 1874), p. 59).

[115] P.R.O. S.C. 6 876/14.

[116] E.g., *Revised Medieval Latin Word-list*, p. 355.

[117] P.R.O. S.C. 6 1079/4; *Inventories and Account Rolls . . . of Jarrow and Monk-Wearmouth*, p. 48; P.R.O. S.C. 6 974/25; E.Suss.R.O. Add. MS 4930.

Fig. 36: Demesne carts (Sample A: 1250–1320).

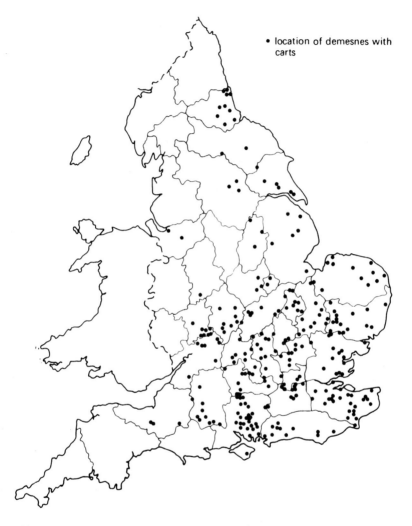

Fig. 37: Demesne carts (Sample B: 1350–1420).

Fig. 38: Demesne *plaustra* (Sample A: 1250–1320).

Fig. 39: Demesne *plaustra* (Sample B: 1350–1420).

Fig. 40: Demesne *carrae*, *carri*, or *curri* (Sample A: 1250–1320).

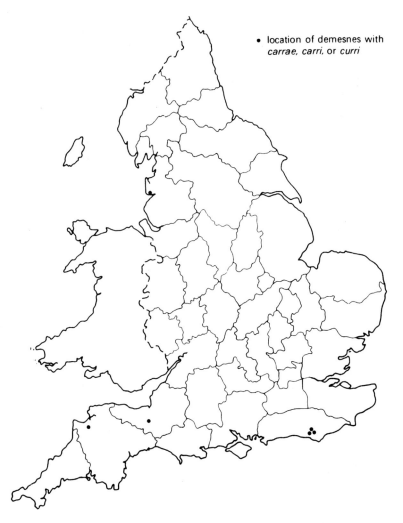

Fig. 41: Demesne *carrae*, *carri*, or *curri* (Sample B: 1350–1420).

Table 21. *The frequency of vehicle types on English demesnes,
1250–1320 and 1350–1420*

Type of vehicle	Sample A (1250–1320)		Sample B (1350–1420)	
	a	*b*	*a*	*b*
Cart (*carecta*)	453	89.0	269	79.1
Plaustrum	102	20.0	113	33.2
Carra, carrus, or *currus*	43	8.4	6	1.8
Curtena or *cortena*	8	1.6	12	3.5
Tumbrel (*tumberellus*)	7	1.4	6	1.8
Biga	6	1.2	2	0.6
Quadriga	2	0.4	0	0.0
Curta, courta, or *corta*	2	0.4	3	0.9
"Courtpot"	0	0.0	12	3.5
"Dungpot"	0	0.0	1	0.3
"Coupwayn"	0	0.0	2	0.6
"Coup"	0	0.0	1	0.3
"Draght"	0	0.0	1	0.3

Key to column headings
a – Number of demesnes
b – Percentage of all demesnes in sample with vehicle references (see p. 142)

Notes and sources: Sources as in Table 11. As with plough type, only those vehicles mentioned in half or more of the accounts for a particular demesne have been included. Similarly, section headings (e.g., *Custus Carectarum, Custus Plaustrorum* or *Custus Carrorum*) have not been used as indicators, since these headings could become stereotyped from year to year. Only definite references to vehicles *within* sections were considered acceptable.

There are numerous other references of a similar sort, but none of the type, *ij pares rotarum pro j plaustro*, which one would expect had the *plaustrum* been a four-wheeled vehicle. It has been suggested that the word "pair" should be interpreted here as meaning "set",[118] but this interpretation is contradicted by several other references where the actual number of wheels is given.[119] Axle costs bear out the same contention. For example, at Porlock (Somerset) in 1424–5 a cost is recorded for *j axtre de novo facto pro j plaustro*.[120] Even more significant is a comparison of costs for fitting axles to both carts and *plaustra* at Pittington (Durham) in 1376–7. Here two carts were "axled" (*axacione*) for 6d. and four *plaustra* for 12d., an

[118] Salzman, "Property of the Earl of Arundel", p. 43.
[119] For example, at Knowle (Warwickshire) in 1293–4: *In factura ij novarum rotarum ad plaustrum*. W.A.M. 27693; for other examples, see Langdon, thesis, p. 176.
[120] P.R.O. S.C. 6 973/26.

Ploughs, harrows and vehicles 151

identical cost of 3d. per vehicle for both carts and *plaustra*.[121] Presumably such an equality of cost would be impossible unless both vehicles had the same number of axles and wheels (i.e., one axle and two wheels apiece).

Nevertheless, although *plaustra* were two-wheeled, they were not the same vehicles as carts. First, as we have already discussed, they were ox-hauled. Second, they were considerably larger. Thus, for example, seventy-one *plaustrum*-loads of hay bought for the archbishopric of York manors of Sherburn, "Couhous", Cawood, Skidby and South Burton (Yorkshire) in 1373–4 cost an average of just over 35d. per load, while thirty-two cart-loads of hay bought for Beverley (Yorkshire) and Scrooby (Nottinghamshire) on the same estate in the same year were only 18d. per load.[122] This two-to-one ratio between *plaustrum*-loads and cart-loads is also evident from survey material, where, for the purposes of carrying services, one *plaustrum* was considered equal to two carts.[123] To maintain stability with these heavier loads, *plaustra* were probably wider than carts, with heavy solidly-built wheels. Thus, at Knowle (Warwickshire) in 1293–4 a pair of wheels made for a *plaustrum* cost 20d. to make, while a pair for a cart cost only 8d.[124]

If the *plaustrum* were neither wagon nor cart, what was it then? It seems, in fact, that it was the medieval equivalent of the sixteenth-century wain, which was also a two-wheeled, ox-drawn vehicle.[125] This shows up most clearly in later accounts. Thus at Elvethall (Durham) in 1446–7 it is stated that there are four *plaustra, vnde ij long' & ij cowpwaynes*. Similarly at Hewell Grange (Worcestershire) in 1432–3 there is recorded among the expenses: *xj Waynneclowtes emptis pro plaustris*.[126] The inclusion of pieces of equipment with some connection to wains occurs in the *plaustra* costs of various other accounts as well.[127]

[121] D.C.D. Bursar's Accounts.
[122] P.R.O. S.C. 6 1144/10.
[123] Thus at Tillingham (Essex) in 1222 customary tenants had to haul between hundreds *unum plaustrum vel duas carectas de busco. Domesday of St. Paul's of the Year 1222*, p. 62. For further examples, see chapter 4, n. 235, below.
[124] *In factura ij novarum rotarum ad plaustrum de meremio domini ad tascham xxd. . . . Et in factura iiij parum rotarum ad carectas de meremio domini ad tascham ijs.*; W.A.M. 27693.
[125] Kerridge, *Agricultural Revolution*, pp. 35–6; *Probate Inventories and Manorial Excepts of Chetnole, Leigh and Yetminster*, ed. R. Machin (Bristol, 1976), p. 13.
[126] D.C.D. Hostillar's Accounts; P.R.O. S.C. 6 1068/14.
[127] As at Pittington (Durham) in 1376–7: D.C.D. Bursar's Accounts.

The third most common type of demesne vehicle was the *carra*, *carrus*, or *currus*. It appears most frequently in Sample A and tails off considerably in Sample B. Its distribution, as indicated by Figures 40 and 41, is similar to that of the *plaustrum*, although with a more southerly emphasis. Altogether it is the most difficult vehicle to categorize, mainly because the term *carra* or *carrus* may have covered two distinctly different classes of vehicle. The first of these seems to have been a four-wheeled wagon for household use. For example, among the effects of the recently deceased Bishop of Exeter in 1310 was found *j carro cum iiij rotis* worth ten pounds. Seven years previously, among the effects of the Bishop of London, there appears *uno carro cum apparatu pro quinque equis*.[128] The conjunction of these two references indicates a four-wheeled, five-horse-hauled ceremonial wagon of the type seen in the Luttrell Psalter.[129] Even better in this regard is a reference taken from a 1452/3 inventory of William Druffield, canon residentiary of York, Southwell and Beverley, who at his death owned a four-wheeled, covered *currus*, worth over six pounds, which was drawn by five horses decked in black trappings.[130]

These *carri* or *curri* are clearly not farm vehicles but showy household conveyances. On the other hand, when *carrae*, *carri*, or *curri* are found in a farm setting, as they are in all the cases given in Samples A and B, the impression of them changes substantially. Thus, at Stogursey (Somerset) in 1300–1, we have a purchase of *vno pari rotarum ad vnum carrum* for 4s. 10d.[131] Here we have what appears to be a two-wheeled vehicle, and one which could be ox-hauled, since yokes relating to the equipping of *carrae* are also found at West Hatch (Somerset) in 1356–7,[132] not to mention the numerous references to ox-hauled peasant *carri* given in the surveys.[133] These *carrae* or *carri* also seem to have had double the carrying capacity of a cart, as at Northwick with Whitstones and Hartlebury (Worcestershire) in 1299, where again one *carra*-load

---

[128] *Accounts of the Executors of Richard Bishop of London . . . and Thomas Bishop of Exeter 1310*, pp. 12, 59. The bishop of London's *carrus*, however, was worth only 53s. 4d.

[129] Millar, *The Luttrell Psalter*, fos. 181b–182.

[130] *j karr cum iiij rotis et v fallaris de nigro, pro v equis, ad trahendum hujusmodi currum, et j seredclothe ad cooperiendum eundum currum vjli. xiiijs. iiijd.* (*Testamenta Eboracensia*, p. 137.)

[131] P.R.O. S.C. 6 1090/6, fos. 5 and 5v.

[132] S.R.O. DD/CC 112826 13/18.   [133] See p. 247n below.

was considered equal to two cart-loads in the performance of carrying services.[134] This similarity to *plaustra* is probably more than just a coincidence, since in many cases the terms *carra* and *plaustrum* are used interchangeably, seemingly to describe the same vehicle.[135] In this case, the rise in *plaustra* and fall in *carrae* noted in the transition from Samples A to B may simply be the result of a change in terminology.

Bigae and *quadrigae* figure in the accounts as well, although the number of *quadrigae*, in particular, is well down from the twelfth century. It would appear that this latter was an antiquated term, gradually fading from use. The term *biga*, on the other hand, survived for a longer period, and it appears from the accounts that the vehicle it represented was a close relative of the cart.[136]

The other types of vehicles listed in Table 21 will be dealt with briefly, since in general they are found on no more than a few demesnes. The *curtena* (or occasionally *cortena*) is a vehicle found almost solely in Kent, although isolated cases occur in Sussex, Essex and Lincolnshire. There is virtually no indication in the accounts as to its use, but survey material indicates that it was ox-hauled and perhaps specifically used for hauling dung.[137] The *curta*, *courta*, or *corta* found elsewhere may have been the same vehicle or perhaps a small cart.[138] Tumbrels were another class of small vehicle. Although found only occasionally, their distribution was very scattered.[139] There is little in the accounts to describe them, beyond the mention of their existence, but presumably they were the ances-

---

[134] *Red Book of Worcester*, i, p. 14; ii, p. 194; see also chapter 4, note 235.

[135] For instance, it is not uncommon to find *carrae* or *carri* mentioned in the heading of a vehicle costs section, yet with nothing but *plaustra* recorded within the section itself. See also p. 247 below.

[136] As at Farleigh (Surrey) in 1278–9, where two types of vehicle, *biga* and *carecta*, appear to have been virtually synonomous and both seemingly horse-hauled, since only horses were used for draught here. *Surrey Manorial Accounts*, ed. H. M. Briggs (Surrey Rec. Soc., no. 37, 1935), p. 18. On occasion, though, *bigae* may have been ox-hauled: e.g., see *Dictionary of Medieval Latin from British Sources*, fascicule I, p. 198 (where, among other references to horse-hauled *bigae*, two show the vehicles being hauled by oxen).

[137] See pp. 247–9 below.

[138] *Curtae*, etc., were found in Lincolnshire, Northamptonshire, Rutland, Sussex and Yorkshire.

[139] In this study they were found in Berkshire, Hampshire, Hertfordshire, Kent, Oxfordshire, Suffolk, Warwickshire, Wiltshire, Worcestershire and Yorkshire. They also occurred in occasional accounts for demesnes in Buckinghamshire and Durham.

tors of latter-day tumbrels, that is, small tip-carts.[140] "Courtpots" in this study were found exclusively on the Sussex estates of the Earl of Arundel in 1397 and were possibly also small tip-carts.[141] "Dungpots" were probably very similar and perhaps even connected in some fashion to the back of a larger vehicle.[142] All these were probably horse-hauled vehicles, but smaller ox-hauled vehicles also existed, as indicated by the "coupwanes" and possibly also the "coups".[143] Finally, a "draght" was mentioned at Cleobury Barnes (Shropshire) in 1372–3; presumably this was a sled or perhaps even a "drag" (that is, a harrow).[144]

The variety of farm vehicles on medieval English demesnes is impressive, yet it seems that two main types dominated. Both were two-wheeled. The first, the cart or *carecta*, was light and horse-hauled. The second, the *plaustrum* (and perhaps the *carra* or *carrus*) was heavy and seemingly pulled by oxen. Often both types operated side by side in the field.[145] The necessity of using oxen to pull two-wheeled *plaustra* may seem paradoxical when horses have shown themselves perfectly capable of hauling potentially heavier four-wheeled vehicles,[146] but there is a very logical reason for it. Two-wheeled vehicles have all their load resting on two points only, whereas wagons and the like have it distributed over four. As a result, the wheels of the latter are normally lighter and more finely made than those of their two-wheeled counterparts,[147] and hence

---

[140] See, for example, J. Arnold, *Farm Waggons and Carts* (Newton Abbot, 1977), pp. 118ff.

[141] Salzman, "Property of the Earl of Arundel", pp. 43–4, however, surmised that they were wheelbarrows.

[142] For example, there is a mention in the 1385–6 Henbury (Gloucestershire) account to the making of *j Dongpot pro plaustro pro fimis*, indicating that the dungpot was perhaps connected to the *plaustrum* in some fashion. Wo.R.O. Ref. 009:1 BA 2636 166 92251.

[143] Ox-hauled "coops" were a feature of eighteenth-century Yorkshire. W. Marshall, *The Rural Economy of Yorkshire*, i, p. 252.

[144] P.R.O. S.C. 6 965/12.

[145] As at Little Humber (Yorkshire) in 1285–6: *In stipendiis homini onerant* [sic] *plaustra & carectas in campis cum bladis tassandis in grangia* (P.R.O. S.C. 6 1079/4).

[146] E.g., see p. 152 above.

[147] P. Deffontaines, "Sur la Répartition géographique des Voitures à deux Roues et à quatre Roues', *Travaux du Ier Congrès International de Folklore, Paris, 1937* (Tours, 1938), p. 118.

much less bothered by obstructions to the wheels, such as stones or mud. On the other hand, the heavy wheels of the *plaustrum*, with the positioning of the load directly over them, meant that these vehicles were that much more susceptible to bogging down in muddy or obstacle-ridden ground. It seems likely that medieval horses were incapable of pulling the vehicle through in such cases, much in the same way as they often had difficulties with ploughs.

The seemingly obvious solution, of course, when heavier loads were desirable, was to use four-wheeled vehicles, but the fixed nature of the front wheels made this impossible, as some measure of manoeuvrability was essential in field work. Recent research has indicated that the moveable forecarriage or pivoted front axle for wagons was introduced to western Europe during the fourteenth century and possibly earlier.[148] However, even with moveable forecarriages, several additional design features of some sophistication, such as dished, outward-slanting wheels or small front wheels cutting under the bodies of the vehicles, were needed before wagons had sufficient locks or turning arcs to be practicable for normal farm work.[149] These conditions were not to be fulfilled for some time.[150] Meanwhile medieval farmers, both demesne and peasant, were limited to using two-wheeled vehicles. With oxen being the only animals able to pull the larger varieties of these vehicles, it provided a considerable incentive for continuing to use them for such duties. Despite this, horses still became the much preferred hauling animal during the later middle ages, even though they were physically limited to the lighter vehicles. Many demesne managers did employ oxen for hauling, as indicated by the number of *plaustra* about, but generally only by using the existing oxen in the plough-team. Thus levels of oxen in the accounts seem to have been only those necessary to pull the existing ploughs, seldom more. And when references

---

[148] M. N. Boyer, "Medieval Pivoted Axles", *Technology and Culture*, i (1959–60), pp. 128–38; A. R. Hall, "More on Medieval Pivoted Axles", *Technology and Culture*, ii (1961), pp. 17–22; C. A. McNeill, "Technological Developments in Wheeled Vehicles in Europe, from Prehistory to the Sixteenth Century" (Univ. of Edinburgh Ph.D. thesis, 1979), pp. 83–7.

[149] For some of the problems involving the design of moveable forecarriages, see James Arnold, "Waggons of Mystery", *Countryman*, lxxxiv (1979), p. 186.

[150] Wagons, in fact, were virtually non-existent on farms until at least the seventeenth century: e.g., S. Porter, "Farm Transport in Huntingdonshire, 1610–1749", *Journal of Transport History*, iii (1983), pp. 35–45; J. G. Jenkins, *The English Farm Wagon* (Reading, 1961), p. 10.

to oxen hauling do arise, more often than not it is specified that the animals did ploughing as well.[151]

It would be wrong, though, to suggest that the only reason *plaustra* were found on demesnes was to provide effective employment for the oxen in between ploughing sessions. Indeed, in some cases, local conditions made the *plaustrum* almost essential. This is particularly the case in the north-east, where the mining of coal began to give the region a marked industrial character. The need for vehicles capable of holding large, heavy loads must have been of prime importance, and consequently hauling with oxen seems to have quickened markedly in the area during the fifteenth century. Thus at Finchale (Durham) there is a dramatic increase in the number of references to oxen in relation to *plaustra* from the late 1440s to the late 1470s.[152] At the same time references to horses carting drop away completely. It seems that on this demesne oxen were valued as much, if not more, for their hauling as for their ploughing abilities. At Finchale this may well have had a lot to do with coal mining, since it is notable that the era of the greatest concentration of references to oxen hauling coincides with a sustained period of high coal production from the priory mines.[153] The larger capacity of the *plaustrum* must have been very valuable here, if only to carry the coal needed by the priory itself. Eighty chaldrons (about eighty-eight tons) were apparently consumed by the household in 1457–8.[154] The accounts of other Durham demesnes – for example, Jarrow, Monkwearmouth, and Elvethall – show that the experience at Finchale was not an untypical one, since they all demonstrate a striking lack of carts and horses for carting in the later fifteenth century, in contrast to the horses and carts evident on these demesnes a half-century or so earlier.[155]

[151] E.g., see p. 115 above.
[152] *Priory of Finchale*, pp. ccxlix, ccliii, cclxviii, cclxxii, cclxxvi, cclxxxi, ccxcvii, ccciii, cccvii, cccxiv, cccxviii, cccxxviii, and cccxxxviii. The references sometimes take the form of so many oxen *pro plaustro* (or *plaustris*) *et aratro*, but most often simply *pro plaustro*.
[153] Coal production from the priory mines, as evidenced by cash receipts, began as early as the 1350s at Softley. After some ups and downs it eventually reached a peak in the 1470s and then slowly declined afterwards. *Ibid.*, pp. xliff.
[154] *Sed respondet de x¹. receptis de minera carbonum de Morehouseclose, ultra iiij^{xx} celdras liberatas ad expensas hospicii hoc anno. Ibid.*, p. cclxvi. J. U. Nef estimates that a chaldron of Newcastle coal weighed 22 cwt in the late 1450s. *The Rise of the British Coal Industry* (London, 1932), ii, p. 369.
[155] For example, the last (horse-hauled) carts appear at Jarrow in 1416–17 and at

*   *   *

The purpose of the above discussion has been to show how intimately the use of horses and oxen dovetailed with the types of farm vehicles available, and how the technical backwardness of four-wheeled vehicles could provide an impetus for a reversion to oxen. It is difficult to assess how important this reversion was, since most of it took place after the periods covered by the data in Samples A and B, but we must presume that it contributed to the growing polarization in the use of horses and oxen evident during the fifteenth century.[156] Certainly, considering the distribution of vehicles in Samples A and B, it does seem that the spread of carts reached its peak at the end of the thirteenth century. The increase in carts, especially when compared to the twelfth century, when the vehicles were very much in a minority, gives testimony not only to the spread of carts, but also to the spread of horse hauling. After the Black Death, however, there seems to have been a definite switch from carts to *plaustra*, with the proportion of the latter increasing by over a half. This, however, assumes that the *plaustra* and *carrae* in the accounts are different vehicles. If in fact they were the same, then the rise is a much more modest one, the two vehicles together being found on 27.1 per cent of demesnes with vehicles in Sample A, increasing to 34.1 per cent of demesnes with vehicles in Sample B.[157] It would seem from this that we must be careful in postulating a significant reversion to ox-hauled vehicles. The drop in carts from Samples A to B of about 10 per cent of all demesnes with vehicles suggests that some of this reversion was happening, but that it was marginal, at least to the beginning of the fifteenth century. Certainly, in terms of the average demesne horse level across the country, it was not enough to offset changes in the other direction, such as the creation of all-horse farms.

Monkwearmouth in 1408–9. *Inventories and Account Rolls . . . of Jarrow and Monk-Wearmouth*, pp. 91, 190. After that, apparently only oxen were used for hauling, as indicated at Monkwearmouth in 1446–7: *Et in ix bobus emptis pro plaustris et carucis* (*ibid.*, p. 203).
[156] See pp. 97–9 above.
[157] Demesnes having both *plaustra* and *carrae* have only been counted once.

e) THE ROLE OF HORSES AND OXEN IN DEMESNE
MANAGEMENT, 1200–1500

So far in this study we have shown that the introduction of the work-
horse to medieval demesnes could not be called a spectacular one.
By the end of the fourteenth century the overall level of demesne
horses had barely reached 30 per cent of all demesne draught
animals, and it is debatable how much this increased during the
fifteenth century. The purpose of this section is to investigate why
this advance was so slow on medieval demesnes and to examine
some of the problems affecting demesne decision making as a whole
regarding the use of draught horses and oxen.

The employment of horses versus oxen was a subject much discussed among medieval contemporaries. Walter of Henley, for
instance, devoted several passages of his thirteenth-century
treatise, *Husbandry*, to a discussion of the problem. Walter was an
ardent advocate for the use of oxen, particularly for ploughing. Like
Fitzherbert after him, he made the point that horses were susceptible to breaking down when ploughing on hard or heavy soils and
were really only useful – he claimed – when ploughing stony land
where oxen had trouble with their footing.[158]

The main force of Walter's argument, however, was that horses
were simply more expensive to keep than oxen, four times or more
according to his figures.[159] To some extent, cost data taken directly
from accounts back him up, where oats in particular comprised a
large portion of the expenses for horses. Cart-horses, especially,
were extremely expensive to feed and maintain, on average nearly
25s. per year each compared to a little over 7s. per year for an ox.
However, the more modest plough-horses, to which the costs of
oxen are more realistically compared, required an average of just
over 10s. each per year, an increase of only about 40 per cent or so
over oxen.[160] The key discrepancy between these figures and
Walter's concerns the cost of hay and straw, which oxen mainly consumed and which Walter ignored. When these expenses for hay and

---

[158] *Walter of Henley*, p. 319, c. 37; see also *Fitzherbert*, p. 15.

[159] Walter estimated that a horse for the plough cost 13s. 6d. per year to feed and
maintain compared to only 3s. 4d. per year for an ox. *Walter of Henley*, p. 319,
cc. 38–40; see also Langdon, "Economics of Horses and Oxen", pp. 31–2.

[160] As calculated in Langdon, "Economics of Horses and Oxen", see especially table
5 (p. 37).

straw are omitted from the account figures, the difference in costs between plough-horses and oxen does approach that four-to-one ratio postulated by Walter.[161]

This selectiveness in estimating costs was not a piece of deception on Walter's part. He and his colleagues simply felt that some costs could be legitimately ignored. This was particularly the case for hay and straw, where the market for these fodders was seemingly so weak, due to transportation costs, that there was a tendency among manorial officials to think of them as being virtually without value and so suitable as a "free" source of food for the demesne draught animals.[162] In real terms, however, the situation was very different, and we must presume that in many cases manorial and demesne officials must have been aware of these "ignored" costs, such as those for hay and straw, the omission of which gave such a bias towards the use of oxen. Demesnes where there was little recourse to labour services, for instance, either because these services were already commuted for cash or because they had never been available in any great amount to begin with, must have seemed very expensive to farm from the point of view of such activities as hay-making, and consequently the transition to horses may have been easier to make here.

Regional variation in fodder availability was also very important. Oxen, for instance, had a reputation for faring better on rough pasture than horses,[163] and where this was usually in plentiful supply, as in the north and west, the ox was in a very advantageous position. It was here, too, that the physical limitations of the horse tended to weigh most heavily, as the combination of obdurate soils (such as the strong clays of the midlands) and a wetter climate conspired to create conditions where, in ploughing especially, the horse repeatedly broke down. On the other hand, in areas where relatively little pasture was available, particularly in the east, draught animals inevitably received a greater proportion of grains in their feed.[164] This suited horses better, as they benefited more from a

---

[161] Ignoring hay and straw lowers the cost for plough-horses to just over 8s. per year each, while the cost for oxen shows a much more dramatic fall to just over 2½s. per year each. *Ibid.*

[162] As discussed in Langdon, *ibid.*, p. 37.

[163] *Fitzherbert*, p. 15.

[164] See, for example, the oats consumption table in Langdon, "Economics of Horses and Oxen", p. 33, where the highest consumptions per animal occur in East Anglia and the Home Counties.

high grain diet than oxen.[165] Similarly, it was these areas in the east
that often had the conditions of lighter soils, more even terrain and
drier climate, in which horses performed best.

Altogether these environmental considerations make attempts to
judge the relative merits of horses and oxen on a strict economic
basis somewhat hypothetical. Nonetheless the question of expenses
was undoubtedly uppermost in the minds of officials, and there is no
doubt that horses cost more to keep than oxen, even with the most
unbiased of calculations. Against this disadvantage of cost, what did
the horse have to offer? The two advantages most quoted for the
animal are those of speed and stamina.[166] The most obvious of these
is speed, and it has been widely asserted that, when exerting the
same pull, the horse can do so 50 per cent faster than the ox,[167]
although this is a claim that ignores not only the variation from task
to task but also from region to region.

In fact, it is very difficult to assess how much speed advantage the
horse gave over oxen during the middle ages. Dealing with ploughing first, the best set of demesne ploughing speed figures comes
from a series of extents, dated *c.* 1290, for the lands of the bishop of
Worcester.[168] Ploughing speeds here ranged from a third of an acre
at Hanbury (Worcestershire) in the summer to one acre a day at
Fladbury in the same county,[169] the average ploughing speed over
the whole estate being a little over half an acre per day. All these

[165] E.g., see White, *Medieval Technology and Social Change*, pp. 72–3; J. A.
Perkins, "The Ox, the Horse, and English Farming, 1750–1850" (unpublished
working paper in economic history, University of New South Wales, 1975), p. 8;
The Complete Grazier, 13th edn, by William Fream (London, 1893), p. 1053;
A. L. Anderson, *Introductory Animal Husbandry* (New York, 1943), pp. 714–17.

[166] E.g., see White, *Medieval Technology and Social Change*, p. 62; R. J. Forbes,
Studies in Ancient Technology, ii (Leiden, 1955), pp. 83–5; N. Harvey, "Walter
of Henley and the Old Farming", *Agriculture*, lix (1953), p. 491.

[167] E.g., White, *Medieval Technology and Social Change*, p. 62. Most historians
have obtained this figure from *Rankine's Useful Rules and Tables* (e.g., see the
sixth edition (London, 1883), p. 251), which is purported to have derived from
trials using dynamometers (A. P. Usher, *History of Mechanical Invention*, 2nd
edn (Cambridge, Mass., 1954), p. 156).

[168] For twenty-two demesnes altogether: *Red Book of Worcester*, i, pp. 30, 57, 82,
90, 108; ii, pp. 142, 144, 166, 185, 205, 231, 237; iii, 259, 275, 292, 313, 322; iv,
350, 366, 376, 403, 405; most of these are also summarized in Lloyd, "Ploughing
Services on the Demesnes of the Bishop of Worcester", p. 196. For the dating of
these extents, see Dyer, *Lords and Peasants in a Changing Society*, pp. 3–4.

[169] *Red Book of Worcester*, ii, pp. 142, 185. The Fladbury case may be inaccurate,
since the high number of demesne ploughs for the amount of land under cultivation suggests a much slower ploughing speed than that given.

demesnes had all-ox plough-teams with the exception of Bibury (Gloucestershire), where mixed teams were indicated.[170] Significantly the ploughing speed at Bibury, at three-quarters of an acre per day, was one of the highest on the bishop's estate. Certainly mixed plough-teams in the east ploughed much faster than the majority of those on the bishopric of Worcester manors. Thus at Bocking, Essex, in 1309, it is recorded that a mixed team of four horses and two oxen could plough an acre a day, while at Borley in the same county in 1308 another mixed team of four horses and four oxen was supposedly able to plough an acre a day and sometimes more.[171] Unfortunately no direct evidence about the ploughing speeds of all-horse teams in the middle ages has been found in this study,[172] but the presence of the animal in mixed teams does seem to have provided a definite improvement in ploughing speed over those teams comprised solely of oxen. Not knowing the type of acre, the ploughing depth, or furrow width[173] in each of the examples

[170] The teams at Bibury were described as *iiii affri et xii boves ad ii carucas*, with two cart-horses also being mentioned (*ibid.*, iv, p. 376). This apparently uncontroversial reference to mixed plough-teams, presumably of two affers and six oxen apiece, is at odds with a series of late fourteenth-century accounts for Bibury, however, which refer to the horses on the demesne solely as "cart-horses" (Wo.R.O. Ref. 009:1 BA 2636 160 92050, 159 92049 4/7, 160 92053, etc.). Nevertheless, the fact that some of these latter horses were occasionally shod on the front feet only (as was common for plough-horses, cart-horses generally being shod on all four feet) indicates that they were probably used for ploughing as well.

[171] Vinogradoff, *Villainage in England*, p. 315; G. F. Beaumont, "The Manor of Borley, A.D. 1308", *Trans. of the Essex Arch. Soc.*, new series, xviii (1928), pp. 262–3.

[172] Later evidence suggests that the horse on its own could in fact plough up to 50 per cent faster than oxen. Thus in Cornwall during the last century a pair of horses could plough a customary acre a day while four oxen could barely manage three-quarters of this; W. F. Karkeek, "On the Farming of Cornwall", *Journal Royal Agric. Soc.*, vi (1845), p. 457. Similarly Gervase Markham stated that oxen in his time (the seventeenth century) could only plough an acre a day while horses could manage 1¼–1½ acres (*Farewell to Husbandry* (London, 1631 edn), p. 147). On some occasions, however, it was not unknown for oxen to plough every bit as fast as horses: e.g. Caird, *English Agriculture in 1850–1*, p. 168; B. Almack, "On the Agriculture of Norfolk", *Journal Royal Agric. Soc.*, v (1844), p. 381; J. Cowie, "An Essay in the Comparative Advantages in the Employment of Horses and Oxen in Farm Work", *Journal Royal Agric. Soc.*, v (1844), p. 55.

[173] All of these could have a dramatic effect upon ploughing speed as measured in acres per day. For instance, a man ploughing a foot-wide furrow will plough an acre significantly faster than one who used, say, a nine-inch furrow. Ploughing depth has a similar effect in speeding up or slowing down the cultivation of an acre. Finally we have the problem of deciding what kind of acre is being employed

given, however, makes it difficult for us to be precise about this, but the difference would seem large enough to be significant.

The improvement in medieval hauling speeds upon the introduction of horses is equally difficult to determine. The best medieval evidence that allows some comparison to be made applies not to Europe but to Asia. Here a Florentine manual giving instructions on the route to China in the first half of the fourteenth century records that it took twenty-five days to travel from Tana (*now* Azov) to Astrakhan by ox wagon but only ten to twelve days by horse wagon. Significantly the normal loads for these wagons are also specified, the ox wagon containing 2,500 Genoese pounds and the horse wagon 1,625 Genoese pounds. In both cases the wagons were to be hauled by one animal apiece.[174] The indication here is that, although horse hauling was patently quicker, it did not have much advantage over ox-transport in terms of hauling efficiency, the ox being able to make up for much of its slow speed by its ability to carry a heavier load. A similar situation seems to have existed in medieval England, as indicated by the two-to-one load ratio already noted between the ox-hauled *plaustra* and *carri* and the horse-hauled *carectae*. Nevertheless, for small loads, the introduction of horse hauling must have been a boon, and it is likely that in these cases a hauling speed for horses of at least twice that for oxen was the normal occurrence.[175] In view of the large amounts of money demesne managers were willing to spend on cart-horses, anything less would seem a poor return.

There is virtually no information with which to make an estimate of harrowing speeds. A reference to labour services at Hutton (Essex) in 1388–9 seems to indicate that tenants there were responsible for harrowing two acres a day with "one man and one horse".[176] It is impossible, however, to say how this compared to

– measured (or standard), conventional (or customary), fiscal, or local (for a discussion of all these, see A. Jones, "Land Measurement in England, 1150–1350", *Agric. Hist. Rev.*, xxvii (1979), pp. 10–18). Apparent changes in ploughing speed or the acreage cultivated per year could occur simply by the clerks changing from one type of acre to another when entering their figures.

[174] R. S. Lopez and J. W. Raymond, *Medieval Trade in the Mediterranean World: Illustrative Documents* (London, 1955), pp. 355–8.

[175] The same thing is also indicated by peasant carrying services: see Langdon, "Horse Hauling", p. 61.

[176] *Et de herciatura ix acrarum terre domini ad semen quadragesimale proventa de consuetudine xvj customariis quorum ij utrique inveniet [sic] j hominem & j equum ad terram domini herciandam per j diem ad semen quadragesimale a mane vsque*

harrowing with oxen, although later evidence suggests that a horse could harrow over twice as much as an ox in a day.[177] We can only surmise that, whatever the speed advantage was in medieval times, it was enough to ensure that harrowing with horses was the much preferred practice.

The other major advantage claimed for the horse is that of stamina. As Lynn White, Jr, writes, "a horse has more endurance than an ox, and can work one or two hours longer a day".[178] In most cases, though, this endurance or stamina was not reflected in longer working hours for the horse, but rather in its use in smaller teams, particularly for ploughing or hauling. This may seem to cast doubt on the premise that oxen can exert the same pull as horses, but in fact a single ox can draw a load equal to that drawn by a horse, but for a much shorter distance or period of time. Thus it was noted of East African farming during the first part of this century that "the common single-row horse-hoe is pulled by one horse, but requires two oxen; one ox can pull it, but does less than half an acre a day, as against 2½ acres with two oxen . . . "[179] Consequently more oxen than horses were needed to fulfil a task over the whole day, a phenomenon seen repeatedly in post-medieval England.[180]

The same occurred in medieval times. The consistently smaller all-horse plough-teams when compared to mixed or all-ox teams have already been observed, and this reduction in team size is also encountered on individual demesnes, as we shall see shortly. The switch to horses exclusively not only had the effect of reducing the number of animals in the plough-team, but also the number of men needed to run the plough, if the reduction in team size were severe

ad horam nonam . . . & estimatur opus eorum ij acras: P.R.O. S.C. 6 844/30. In Ireland, however, an extent for the manor of Cloncurry (co. Kildare) in 1304 states that a one-horse harrow would only be able to cover half an acre a day: J. Bell, "Harrows Used in Ireland", *Tools and Tillage*, iv, pt 4 (1983), pp. 195–6.

[177] As in nineteenth-century Cornwall, where a pair of horses could harrow eight acres per day (i.e., four acres per animal), while four oxen could only manage six (i.e., an acre and a half per animal). Karkeek, "On the Farming of Cornwall", p. 457.

[178] White, *Medieval Technology and Social Change*, p. 62.

[179] Huntingford, "Prehistoric Ox-Yoking", p. 458.

[180] Thus Arthur Young noted in 1776 that both teams of six oxen and teams of four horses could do an acre a day at Benthall in Shropshire, while a few years later at Bowood, near Calne (Wiltshire), he found of the farmers there that "6 oxen they find to do as much work as 4 horses." Arthur Young, *Tours of England and Wales*, London School of Economics and Political Science, Reprint No. 14 (London, 1932), pp. 147, 34.

enough.[181] In this regard, it is interesting to note again that there was virtually no drop in team size when proceeding from all-ox to mixed plough-teams. We must presume that the partial introduction of the horse in this case was done solely for reasons of speed, as in fact the limited data for medieval ploughing speeds given above seem to indicate. Only in the second stage of switching from mixed to all-horse plough-teams did demesne managers capitalize on the stamina of the horse in allowing the use of smaller teams.

As we can see, then, speed and stamina were the two vital factors favouring the use of horses. Against these were ranged the disadvantages that horses tended to break down in certain hauling and ploughing conditions and, more importantly, that they cost more to keep. In the main, it was the balance between these opposing sets of factors that determined whether horses or oxen were used for a certain type of work. For harrowing and hauling the horse obviously came out on top, as reflected by the animal's overwhelming adoption for both these tasks. But for ploughing the situation was less clear, and in fact most demesne managers were reluctant to employ horses for ploughing, except perhaps in a mixed team.

   When demesne officials did decide to go completely to horses for all jobs, including ploughing, it was clearly a decision that needed some thought, as Walter of Henley's reflections on the subject indicate. To form some idea as to the considerations that might have gone into such a decision and the mechanisms by which it occurred, it would be instructive to consider the case of a demesne that did make the change. One such demesne was that for the manor of West Wycombe (Buckinghamshire), held by the bishop of Winchester. The incomparable series of accounts held in the bishopric's pipe rolls makes it an ideal demesne to study. Table 22 contains a summary of the data taken from a selection of these accounts, concentrating especially on the years 1315–21, when the switch to all-horse farming was made. What stands out immediately is that the change coincides with the agrarian crisis of these years, and this suggests a direct connection between the two. In fact, the situation

---

[181] For example, on the Norfolk manor of Thornham, where two-horse demesne ploughs seem to have been the norm, it appears (in the 1309–10 and 1351–2 accounts at least; N.R.O. Ref. No. R232B) that only one *tenator caruc'* was hired; seemingly no *fugator* or driver of the plough-team was required, as was the case with teams of over two animals.

Table 22. *Pipe roll account data for West Wycombe, Buckinghamshire*

Account year	No. of draught animals at end of account year			No. of ploughs in use	Equipment bought for ploughs	
	Cart-horses	Affers	Oxen		Wheels	*Ferra Pedalia*
1210–11	—	9	31	4	yes	no sign
1231–2	—	15	32	4	no sign	no sign
1256–7	2	12	12	3[a]	no sign	no sign
1286–7	2	12	10	3	no sign	no sign
1300–1	2	12	14	3	no sign	no sign
1309–10	2	12	10	3	no sign	no sign
1313–14	2	13	12	3	no sign	yes
1315–16	2	12	1[b]	3/2[c]	yes	yes
1316–17	2	12	4	2	no sign	yes
1317–18	2	13	1	2	no sign	yes
1318–19	2	13	5	2	no sign	yes
1319–20	2	12	–	2	no sign	yes
1320–1	2	18	–	2[d]	yes	yes
1325–6	2	18	–	3	yes	yes
1340–1	2	20	–	3	yes	yes
1360–1	4	18	–	3	yes	yes
1381–2	6	17	–	3	yes	no sign
1406–7	4	13	–	2	yes	no sign

[a] Plus one plough *per j terminium*.
[b] There were thirteen oxen at the start of the account, to which one was added from young stock. Of these, one died and twelve were sold.
[c] Three ploughs were in operation from Michaelmas (29 September) to the Saturday before the feast of St Gregory (6 March) and two ploughs from then to the feast of Sts Peter and Paul (29 June).
[d] A third plough was mentioned in the plough costs section and three were mentioned among the *Utensilia* at the bottom of the account. It appears that this third plough was gradually being brought back into permanent operation.

Notes and sources: Sources in order as in table: *The Pipe Roll of the Bishopric of Winchester, 1210–1211*, ed. N. R. Holt (Manchester, 1964), pp. 78–82; H.R.O. Eccles. 2 159282, 159292, 159308, 159319, 159325, 159328, 159330–3, 159335, 159334, 159338, 159351, 159371, 159388, 159410.

is rather more complicated than this and involves two events totally unconnected with the crisis, that is, the deaths of Bishops Henry of Marwell and John of Sandale. The sequence of events seems to have been as follows. First, the famine years of 1315–17, beginning with the disastrous harvest of 1315, affected West Wycombe as much as any other place. It appears that the manor was so badly struck that there was difficulty finding enough seed to sow the following year's crop, a condition probably aggravated by the temptation on the part of manorial officials to sell as much grain as they could at high famine prices. Consequently the sown acreage dropped from 255¾ acres in 1313–14 to 171½ acres in 1316–17.[182] This reduced the number of ploughs in operation from three to two. It was at this juncture that Henry of Marwell died on 28 or 29 June 1316. The first thing his executors seem to have done was to sell off much of the demesne stock, including most of the oxen. Presumably the oxen were no longer essential because of the reduced ploughing and hence were considered fair game for the depredations of executors or escheators. As a result, the demesne managers were forced to carry on with horses only. The small numbers of oxen evident in the 1316–17, 1317–18 and 1318–19 accounts may indicate that they were trying to rebuild the level of the animals up to the pre-1315 mark, but in fact these new oxen, added from young stock, were – as often as not – quickly sold again. In any event, any ideas of returning to a situation where oxen once again played a key role in performing draught work on the demesne at West Wycombe were quickly dashed by two almost concurrent events. The first was the death of another bishop, John of Sandale, in November 1319, with yet another purge of the demesne livestock; it seems that only the cart-horses, affers or plough-horses, and a few pigs were left behind. The second was the great cattle plague of 1319–21, which, for a few years at least, made the obtaining of oxen difficult, as well as a risky investment. By 1320–1 the bishop's officials had accepted the situation at West Wycombe as being permanent, and from then on only horses were used for draught on the demesne there. Presumably the experience of the previous five years, as a somewhat enforced trial period, had convinced them that horses alone were a viable alternative to a mixture of horses and oxen. It has been suggested elsewhere that the cattle plague was the primary cause for the conversion to all-horse farming at West Wycombe,[183] but in fact, as we can see, it only set the seal on a train of events which had begun

---

[182] The sown acreage continued to drop, reaching a low of 141 acres in 1317–18 and only climbing to 164 acres in 1318–19 (all acreages are standard). Small amounts of peas, vetches and dredge, unmeasured in acres, were also sown in some of the accounts.

[183] I. Kershaw, "The Great Famine and Agrarian Crisis in England 1315–22", in *Peasants, Knights and Heretics*, ed. R. H. Hilton (Cambridge, 1976), p. 108.

some years earlier and which had a combination of natural and man-made causes.

Interesting as these initial causes are, however, they do not answer the vital question of what made the bishop's officials *persist* in the practice of all-horse farming at West Wycombe. Unless the exclusive use of horses offered real advantages, it seems inevitable that they would have drifted back to using oxen at previous levels once the cattle plague had eased, as, in fact, many other demesnes did in similar circumstances.[184] That this did not happen at West Wycombe suggests that all-horse farming was perceived as a definite improvement here. In what way though? As we have already indicated, the two main attractions of employing the horse instead of the ox were the former animal's speed and endurance. Hauling and harrowing at West Wycombe were already catered for by horses before the change occurred, so only ploughing was affected. Improvements to the speed of ploughing, however, seem to have entered little into the calculations of the demesne officials. The primary advantage of increasing ploughing speed is that fewer ploughs are needed to cultivate a given area of land, and it is true that the number of ploughing teams at West Wycombe were reduced by a third during the period 1315–20; but then again so was the area under cultivation. More significantly, when the area under crops returned to "normal" – the sown acreages in the 1325–6 and 1340–1 accounts, for instance, were 238½ and 233½ acres respect-ively – the number of ploughs rose again to three, despite the fact that the total (sown) acreage was still less than it had been in the pre-1315 era. Obviously any increase in speed attributable to the all-horse teams had little effect on the number of ploughs.

On the other hand, there was a definite reduction in team size. To go back a little to the early thirteenth century, it appears that each plough at West Wycombe then consisted of eight oxen, or even possibly of eight oxen with two horses. By the middle of the century, however, mixed teams definitely prevailed, as in 1256–7, when twelve affers and twelve oxen were all specified as being "at the plough" (*ad caruc'*). The most likely combination here is that each of the demesne's three ploughs was made up of four horses and four oxen. After 1315, with the oxen gone or going, the level of affers to

---

[184] E.g., Kershaw, "Great Famine", p. 108; also I. Kershaw, *Bolton Priory* (Oxford, 1973), pp. 96–7.

ploughs indicates that the team composition had shifted to six horses. In other words, the four oxen previously in each plough had been replaced by a further two horses, resulting in a net reduction of two animals per plough.

What does this mean in terms of cost? The same two ploughmen per year were still in use at West Wycombe after the transition to all-horse teams, but the reduction in animals was a definite saving. An estimation of the costs involved suggests that the changeover from the mixed to the smaller all-horse teams would result in a reduction of costs in the order of 10–15 per cent (that is, a saving of 8–9s. out of a total expense of 60–70s. per team).[185] Seen against total manorial expenditure, this is a marginal, perhaps even unnoticeable, saving; but, since manorial officials were very cost conscious, they may have detected it. On the other hand, this calculation assumes that the demesne officials were aware of the true cost of hay and straw (not to mention depreciation). If, however, they followed what seems to have been the common policy of ignoring hay and straw as real costs, then the cost per team *increases* by 10–15 per cent when using only horses. A certain amount of confusion on the part of the manorial officials as to what was saved and what was not is therefore understandable. In any case, the range of benefit or loss was fairly narrow and must have favoured the existing state of affairs. It is to be noted that the change to all-horse farming at West Wycombe depended to a large degree on accident, and that the decision to follow the practice unreservedly only came after several years of what was probably an unintentional test run. In this regard, any planning was clearly retrospective. Significantly West Wycombe, being a Chiltern manor, lay in a region which already had a reputation for all-horse farming (see pp. 100–1 above), and the influence of local experience more than anything else may have swayed the demesne managers to their final decision.

In the case of West Wycombe, then, we can see how finely balanced the choice often was to employ more horses on demesne farms, depending, among other things, on how demesne officials viewed the various costs that affected the problem. In other cases, the decision was more clear-cut. This was particularly true of some of

---

[185] These calculations, given in more detail in Langdon, thesis, pp. 194–5, take into account the whole range of expenses, including depreciation.

the Norfolk demesnes, where the change to all-horse farming was made by simply dropping off the oxen from the existing mixed plough-teams and continuing on without adding any extra horses at all![186] It is difficult to understand why this was not done earlier, since the reduction in costs must have been of the order of 30 per cent or more in real terms.[187] Perhaps some sort of technical adjustment was necessary first, which may have added an additional cost. It is interesting to note from Table 22 that the West Wycombe transition to all-horse farming was accompanied by a marked increase in expenditure for plough wheels and *ferra pedalia*. Possibly a similar sort of thing occurred on the Norfolk demesnes, although most of them seem to have been using wheeled ploughs at least already. In general, demesne decision making was a difficult and complex matter, as indeed are business decisions of any age. What seems to have characterized the medieval demesne manager, whether he be reeve, bailiff, steward, or even the lord and his advisors[188] was the degree played by accident rather than assessment in his decision making.[189] The awareness of the possible benefits of change, such as

[186] As at Plumstead, Taverham, Scratby, Trowse Newton, Martham and Eaton, where the elimination of the demesne oxen mostly occurred in the decades immediately before or after the Black Death. N.R.O. Ref. Nos. R233D, R232A, R233A.

[187] For example, as at Plumstead during the 1340s, where the transition to all-horse farming resulted in a reduction in costs of nearly 35 per cent (based on the same figures as employed in the West Wycombe case above and including hay and straw costs). N.R.O. Ref. No. R233D.

[188] It is perhaps most natural to think of the demesne manager as the reeve, bailiff or sergeant who actually supervised the running of the demesne on site; but, in terms of decision making, the concept of demesne management should be broadened to include members of the central administration, particularly the steward. In fact, it is difficult to say at what level most of the decisions regarding changes to the operation of the demesne were made. Smaller matters, such as the decision to use the cart-horses for ploughing in the spring or to shoe oxen, were obviously undertaken at the demesne level by the reeve or bailiff, as indicated by the occasional statement justifying their actions to those above them in the hierarchy. But these justifications imply that even minor changes ought ideally to have been approved beforehand, and thus we should see most decisions, especially those involving long-term changes, as inevitably being done in consultation with the steward and perhaps even the lord and his advisors. The agricultural treatises do not always provide help in this matter, their emphasis being on the continuity of practice rather than its improvement, but some idea of the various decision-making relationships between lords, stewards, bailiffs, reeves, etc., can be gained from, particularly in *Seneschaucy* and Bishop Grosseteste's *Rules* (*Walter of Henley*, pp. 265ff, 389ff).

[189] Although this is not to say that some hard-headed assessment could not be made at times, particularly in the calculation of whether to continue farming a demesne

replacing oxen by horses, was obviously there, but the accounting equipment with which to analyse the situation accurately was often lacking. The omission of hay and straw as a fodder cost is only one symptom of the unclear thinking that made it difficult for demesne managers to commit themselves to new techniques. The advent of more progressive, profit-and-loss type accounting, as at Norwich Cathedral Priory, was a considerable improvement here, where such things as labour services, meadow, and pasture began to be considered as valuable assets not to be expended freely without some sort of accountability.[190] Perhaps the reason why the Priory monks dropped their demesne oxen from so many of their Norfolk manors during the 1340s was because they were beginning to realize how much in real terms the animals were costing them.[191]

In conclusion, then, we have shown that the trend to using horses continued on English demesnes throughout the later middle ages, such that by the beginning of the fifteenth century some 30 per cent of the demesne draught force in England was comprised of horses. As in the twelfth century, the south and east of the country led the way, such that many counties were now employing more horses than oxen. Even so, over England as a whole, oxen still dominated on English demesnes at a ratio of two to three of the animals to every horse.

Of all the tasks assumed by demesne horses, hauling was the one in which they created the greatest change, easily pushing ox-hauling into a secondary role. The horse's adoption into demesne ploughing was less spectacular. Mixed teams continued to gain in popularity and some all-horse farms surfaced, particularly in East Anglia and the Home Counties; but in general the all-ox plough-team was still the dominant form for most of the country's demesnes. It was the oxen contained in these all-ox and mixed teams that gave the

directly or to lease it out. E.g., see R. A. L. Smith, *Canterbury Cathedral Priory*, pp. 191–4.
[190] E. Stone, "Profit-and-Loss Accountancy at Norwich Cathedral Priory", *Trans. of the Royal Hist. Soc.*, 5th series, xii (1962), pp. 34–5.
[191] Profit-and-loss accountancy on the priory estates, however, had already been in existence for nearly fifty years by this time, and in fact had just been discontinued when the switch to all-horse farming was made on their eastern Norfolk demesnes; so the connection between the two is not as direct as it could be! *Ibid.*, p. 39.

animals their numerical superiority over horses among the draught stock on demesne farms.

Despite smaller all-horse teams, demesne plough-team size in general remained high at eight animals or so per plough and demonstrated a surprising consistency right across the country. On the other hand, plough and vehicle types on the demesne had developed definite regional patterns, and some of these displayed an intimate connection with the use of horses and oxen. This was particularly the case with the horse-hauled *carecta* or cart and the ox-hauled *plaustrum* and *carra* (or *carrus*).

As in the twelfth century, most of the technological innovations regarding traction on demesnes spread from the east to the west of the country. Little arose spontaneously elsewhere, indicating that demesne innovation in England was imitative rather than inventive and that most of it originated in the east, perhaps because of the special conditions existing there or because of its proximity to the Continent.

By modern standards, of course, the pace of this innovation was slow. Even relatively successful developments – such as horse hauling and the introduction of mixed teams – took a century or more to attain broad acceptance. Change when it came, however, could be rapid on demesnes, as the West Wycombe example has shown, although it would seem there was often a large element of accident to it. The cold-blooded planning of technological change was possible, but it was always held back by faulty conceptions about cost and profitability. This must have encouraged indecision and the passing up of otherwise quite acceptable innovations. On the other hand, it should not be thought that the failure to follow up a promising innovation was always a result of faulty decision making. Demesne officials often had sound reasons for failing to react to a given technological change, reasons which are not always obvious to our eyes today, such as a reluctance to use plough-horses where soils were difficult and where there was plenty of lush grass suitable for oxen. To obtain a balanced picture of this particular aspect of demesne management, many more West Wycombe-like analyses of the process of technological change on demesnes should be undertaken. Unfortunately, because of the broad nature of this study, it was only possible to scratch the surface of this interesting and promising line of investigation.

4. The peasantry: 1200–1500

During the interval covered by this chapter peasant farmers found themselves subject to much the same forces that had influenced demesne farming. Here the advent of the plague in 1348–9 neatly divided the period into two phases. The first was a period of population growth and pressure that lasted effectively until the middle of the fourteenth century (although there are signs that the rate of demographic increase slowed drastically and perhaps even went into reverse sometime before this, particularly during the famine years of 1315–17).[1] This phase of relatively high population was intimately connected with a number of economic and social conditions that had a marked effect upon the peasantry and peasant farming. Some of the more obvious of these were high food prices (especially for grains); falling real wages; a state of relative land shortage and perhaps even land abuse, as some soils were farmed more intensively than they should have been; high rents and entry fines to land; an emphasis on arable rather than pastoral farming; increasing levels of landlessness and deprivation among the peasantry; and, finally, the fragmentation of holdings into smaller agricultural units, particularly through inheritance. Although these conditions conspired to make this a time of increasing hardship for most of the peasantry, for the economy as a whole the period was one of expansion. The remaining 150 years after the middle of the fourteenth century, however, saw a dramatic decline in population, with all the above trends set firmly in reverse. Thus grain prices stabilized and even fell; real wages rose; land became more available and could be obtained for lower rents and entry fines; there was a strong swing to

---

[1] For this and what follows in this paragraph, many works can be cited. For recent and useful summaries, however, see Miller and Hatcher, *Medieval England: Rural Society and Economic Change*; Hatcher, *Plague, Population and the English Economy*; J. L. Bolton, *The Medieval English Economy 1150–1500* (London, 1980).

pastoral farming; the proportion of landless and smallholding
peasants declined; and the average size of the peasant holding
increased markedly, including the creation of a class of wealthy
peasant farmers, whom we might almost classify as "capitalist".
Also, although definite improvements in peasant living standards
can be discerned, the economy in general seems to have been in
retraction.

Changes in the peasant use of horses and oxen, then, must be seen
against the background of these two contrasting periods, one of
population increase and general market expansion, and the other of
population decline and (it appears on balance) of economic
recession. Nonetheless, although peasant farming was to see many
changes over the period in response to these varying economic and
demographic conditions, many of its basic characteristics tended to
remain the same, particularly when compared to demesne farming.
First of all, in contrast to demesne farming, peasant farming was on
a much smaller scale. Whereas a farm of fifty acres was a tiny operation for a demesne, it would rank as an unusually large farm by
peasant standards, even in the late fourteenth and fifteenth centuries. Indeed, before the Black Death, the median peasant holding
was unlikely to have been much more than fifteen acres,[2] and even
this would be large in some parts of the country.[3]

A second characteristic that distinguished peasant from demesne
farms was that they were largely family-run enterprises, with relatively low levels of hired help.[4] This may seem to lend a certain
homogeneity to peasant farming, but this would be misleading. Not
only were peasants socially and economically differentiated, but
also technically. Thus, the extents and surveys in particular show a

[2] Most studies show the median group of peasant farmers holding half- or even
quarter-virgates at this time (e.g. Kosminsky, *Studies in the Agrarian History of
England in the Thirteenth Century*, pp. 216, 223; Postan, *Medieval Economy and
Society*, pp. 143–5).
[3] Peasant holdings in East Anglia, for instance, were very much smaller, in many
cases averaging no more than five acres apiece. B. M. S. Campbell, "Population
Change and the Genesis of Commonfields on a Norfolk Manor", *Econ. Hist.
Rev.*, 2nd series, xxxiii (1980), p. 177; see also Miller and Hatcher, *Medieval
England: Rural Society and Economic Change*, p. 144.
[4] The family run nature of peasant farming has been cited as a defining character-
istic of the medieval peasantry by R. H. Hilton (*The English Peasantry in the
Later Middle Ages* (Oxford, 1975), p. 13), although the level of hired servants on
these farms could sometimes be quite high (e.g., Dyer, *Lords and Peasants in a
Changing Society*, pp. 314–15).

sharp division between those holdings that were expected to perform all the agricultural processes and those that were not. In other words, a certain size of holding was thought necessary before the purchase and maintenance of a full set of cultivating tools and animals was feasible. Judging from the surveys, it would appear a minimum of ten acres was needed. Peasants with holdings smaller than this seem to have done much of their cultivation by hand or to have relied upon equipment and animals borrowed or hired from others.[5] In practice, however, this division was less sharp than the surveys would indicate, and there was in fact an in-between group which had animals for some of the lighter chores, such as harrowing, but not for the heavier ones, such as ploughing. As we shall see, it was this group that often had a marked effect on the number of horses found in a village.

Because of the family-oriented nature of the peasant holding, labour arrangements were of necessity different from those evident on the demesne (see p. 81 above). Very seldom did a tenant command sufficient labour so that he could carry out several chores at once. Rather, when such things as ploughing needed to be done, everything else was dropped. This was particularly the case for young families, where a man and his wife would often be the only source of labour for a holding.[6] As a result, most activities – ploughing, harrowing, going to market, threshing, hay-making, harvesting and so on – had to be done in sequence, rather than doing some at the same time, as happened on the demesne. This led to certain inefficiencies. Draught animals in particular were often without work. For instance, unless it was being used for harrowing, a man's cart-horse would be idle while his plough-beasts worked. Similarly the plough-beasts would be idle when he went to market. Sometimes both would be idle, for example when the man was threshing. It obviously helped if a peasant combined his ploughing and carting beast in one animal, but even here there must have been long periods when the animal was not used. This was not entirely a bad thing for the peasant. It is true that long spells of idleness for the

[5] G. C. Homans, *English Villagers of the Thirteenth Century* (Cambridge, Mass., 1942), pp. 79–81.

[6] As graphically portrayed in *Pierce the Ploughmans Crede*, ed. W. W. Skeat (London, 1867), pp. 16–17, where a man and his wife are found struggling with a plough in winter.

draught animal were wasteful, but at the same time he could put the animals on a low cost feed of hay, straw or pasture. As we shall see, this approach to the use of draught animals had a marked effect on the decision whether to employ horses or oxen on peasant farms. Finally, although it is difficult to be categorical about this, it seems that most peasant farms were geared for subsistence rather than for the market. For smallholders in particular, most of the grain produced by the peasant must have been consumed by him and his family.[7] On the other hand, payments that the peasant had to make to the lord in rents and other dues almost certainly forced him into some involvement with the market at least, an involvement that heightened as labour services began to be commuted for money payments over the course of the middle ages. Cash payments of this type could in some cases equal as much as half the cash value of a peasant's crop.[8] Despite the depression in the rural economy in the later fourteenth century and into the fifteenth, cash outlays by peasants to pay for labour services more and more frequently commuted to money payments must have meant an increasing involvement of these peasants in the market in order to raise this cash. Trips to the market must have been frequent, making carting or carrying animals a virtual necessity.

Because of this and other features of peasant farming, there are strong reasons why peasants might have been attracted to using horses rather than oxen for draught. Not only was the speed of the horse useful for ploughing and hauling to market or to some far-flung strip in the open fields, it was also the more versatile animal, able to do a much greater range of tasks than the ox, from ploughing through to harrowing, carting, carrying by pack and riding. Just how much this was reflected in the number of horses found on peasant farms will be considered next.

---

[7] E.g., Postan, *Medieval Economy and Society*, pp. 144–5.
[8] As, for example, for half-virgate tenants at Churcham (Gloucestershire), *c.* 1266–7, where, depending on the type of course rotation in effect, cash payments to the lord, king and church could total from a third to a half of the value of a peasant's annual crop after tithes (estimated from data given in *Historia et cartularium monasterii Sancti Petri Gloucestriae*, iii, pp. 137–8, and assuming normal crop yields and prices and that all labour services are commuted to cash payments; the calculation also includes an estimate for irregular payments such as merchets, court fines, etc.).

a) THE NUMBERS OF HORSES AND OXEN ON PEASANT
FARMS, 1200–1500

The main difficulty here is obtaining suitable sources for statistical
analysis. Unlike the accounts, which provide a comprehensive and
accurate source for the numbers of demesne draught animals, there
is no one source as appropriate for the peasant case. The most
promising from the standpoint of accuracy are peasant inventories.
These crop up occasionally in court rolls, inquisitions, and even
accounts, often in relation to cases where a peasant's goods have
been confiscated for some reason. For example, at Earnwood (in
Kinlet), Shropshire, in 1388–9, the goods of three tenants were confiscated because they were alleged to be felons. The most substantial of these men was Walter de Morhall, whose goods included one
horse (*equus*), six oxen, one cow, two heifers, one bullock, six
sheep, two pigs, a wain (*plaustrum*) and various other goods. His
colleague and perhaps partner in crime, John Bulkere, was less
well-off, having only one horse (*equus*), one cow and one sow with
followers. The third man, John Turnor, had no stock at all and left
only two blankets and two linen sheets.[9] We have in this set of three
inventories a useful indication of livestock holdings right across a
village society, from a wealthy tenant (Walter de Morhall) through
to perhaps a smallholder in the case of John Bulkere and possibly a
landless labourer in the case of John Turnor. Such inventories, were
they available in large number, would seem more than sufficient for
the purposes of this study. However, apart from the fact that they
are relatively few in number, inventories are not always reliable.
This is particularly the case for those inventories taken upon the
death of a tenant, where the heriot or mortuary animals may already
have been removed by the lord or rector.[10] Even those inventories
involving convicted felons, outwardly the most trustworthy since
the goods often seem to have been transferred *in toto* into the lord's
or king's possession, must often be treated with caution; for

---

[9] P.R.O. S.C. 6 967/9.

[10] Thus, in a court roll entry listing the goods and chattels of the recently deceased
Thomas Page of Harton (Durham) in 1379, it is noted at the bottom of the entry
that the Master of Jarrow had already taken a horse worth 18s. as mortuary.
Halmota Prioratus Dunelmensis, ed. W. H. D. Longstaffe and J. Booth (Surtees
Soc., lxxxii, 1886), p. 151.

instance, there must have been a great temptation on the part of the man's relatives and neighbours to take as much of his goods as they could before the bailiff or escheator seized them, and such an occurrence is indicated in several cases.[11]

With these qualifications in mind, a sample of 52 inventories has been collected and is summarized in Table 23. Only the adult draught animals from each inventory are listed, and altogether these totalled 56 horses[12] and 116 oxen, a proportion of horses of 32.6 per cent. Taken by themselves, these inventories indicate a level of horses only marginally higher than that on demesnes over-all, and this must also be qualified by the fact that some of the horses noted may have been riding rather than work animals. There are, however, three important points to be made. First, there is a decided bias in the sample towards the western and northern counties. Forty-four of the 52 inventories came from the south-west, west midlands and the north, all areas where, as we have seen from the demesne material, oxen tended to be found much more readily than elsewhere.[13] Second, there is a marked over-representation of substantial tenants. Smallholders, that is, those with, say, less than ten acres of land overall, are poorly represented. This may be because they had no draught animals, but it does also seem that the peasants for whom it was thought worthwhile to make up an inventory were large- rather than smallholding tenants. As a result, 31 of the 52 inventories had three draught animals or more, a group which is in a substantial minority in the lay subsidy returns (as we shall see), but is in a definite majority here. It is also this group that, as we shall see, tended to use more oxen than those who had smaller draught stock holdings, a feature that can easily be seen in these inventories by simply comparing the draught stock holding of Walter de Morhall of Earnwood with that of his fellow villager,

[11] For example, it is recorded in an inquisition held at Nottingham in 1292 that Thomas le Pynder and Robert le Vacher of Newbo (Lincolnshire) and William, groom to the cellarer of Newbo Abbey, drove an ox and other stock belonging to the fugitive, James de Casthorp, to the house of John le Grant in Hawksworth (Nottinghamshire). The detailed nature of the entry suggests that this was done without permission. *Calendar of Inquisitions Miscellaneous* (London, 1916–68), i, p. 458.

[12] Including *equi, jumenta, affri, stotti*, etc.

[13] Although the inventorial material shown in Table 23 does have some anomalies, as in Staffordshire where – surprisingly – only horses were found.

178   *The peasantry: 1200–1500*

Table 23. *Peasant inventories, 1200–1500*

County	No. of inventories	Range of dates	No. of oxen	No. of horses	Percentage of horses
Berkshire	1	1403	0	6	100.0
Cornwall	4	1342–1404	14	1	6.7
Devon	5	1397–1417	15	3	16.7
Durham	17	1296–1383	35	17	32.7
Essex	1	1359	0	1	100.0
Hertfordshire	1	1348	2	1	33.3
Kent	2	1372–82	0	6	100.0
Norfolk	1	1384	0	2	100.0
Shropshire	2	1388–9	6	2	25.0
Staffordshire	6	1338–1414	0	8	100.0
Surrey	2	1332–40	10[a]	2	16.7
Worcestershire	7	1271–1462	31	5	13.9
Yorkshire	3	1286–96	3	2	40.0
Total	52		116	56	
Overall %					32.6

[a] Six of these were given as "bulls" in Elsie Tom's translation of the Chertsey court records, but they were almost certainly oxen.

Notes and sources: Sources as they appear in the table: *Calendar of Inquisitions Miscellaneous*, 7 vols. (London, 1916–68), vii, p. 128; J. Hatcher, *Rural Economy and Society in the Duchy of Cornwall, 1300–1530* (Cambridge, 1970), p. 255 (*quater*); *Calendar of Inquisitions Miscellaneous*, vi, p. 94; vii, pp. 330, 332, 334 (*bis*); *Halmota Prioratus Dunelmensis*, ed. W. H. D. Longstaffe and J. Booth (Surtees Soc., lxxxii, 1886), pp. 1, 8, 9, 55, 79, 95, 97, 144, 145, 151 (*bis*), 154, 159, 165, 167, 168, 178; *Calendar of Inquisitions Miscellaneous*, iii, p. 109; A. E. Levett, *Studies in Manorial History* (Oxford, 1938), p. 189; *Calendar of Inquisitions Miscellaneous*, iii, p. 314; iv, p. 103; B. M. S. Campbell, "Field Systems in Eastern Norfolk during the Middle Ages: A Study with Particular Reference to the Demographic and Agrarian Changes of the Fourteenth Century" (Univ. of Cambridge Ph.D. thesis, 1975), p. 238; P.R.O. S.C. 6 967/9 (*bis*); J. R. Birrell, "Medieval Agriculture", *Victoria County Histories, Staffordshire*, vi (Oxford, 1979), p. 31; *Calendar of Inquisitions Miscellaneous*, vii, p. 277 (*quinquiens*); *Chertsey Abbey Court Roll Abstracts*, ed. E. Toms, 2 pts (Surrey Rec. Soc., nos. 38 and 48, 1937 and 1954), i, p. 38; ii, pp. 112–13; *Court Rolls of the Manor of Hales, 1272–1307*, ed. J. Amphlett, S. G. Hamilton and R. A. Wilson, 3 pts (Worcs. Hist. Soc., 1910–1933), i, p. 32 (*bis*); W.A.M. 21020; R. H. Hilton, *The English Peasantry in the Later Middle Ages* (Oxford, 1975), p. 42; Wo.R.O. Ref. 009:1 BA 2636/167, Ref. 705:4 BA 54, Ref. 009:1 BA 2636/175; *Court Rolls of the Manor of Wakefield, 1274–1331*, ed. W. P. Baildon, J. Lister and J. W. Walker, 5 vols. (Yorks. Arch. Soc. Rec. Ser., xxix, xxxvi, lvii, lxxviii, cix, 1901–45), iii, p. 171; i, pp. 232, 243. I am indebted to Dr C. Dyer for supplying me with transcripts of the Worcestershire Record Office (Wo.R.O.) inventories.

John Bulkere.[14] Third, the inventories cover a span of almost two hundred years. While not necessarily distorting the proportion of peasant work-horses in either direction, it does mean that some inventories, particularly those in the fifteenth century, were taken in markedly different social and economic conditions than others. It becomes questionable, then, whether they can be meaningfully grouped together as in Table 23.

To obtain a more representative picture of peasant draught stock holdings, we obviously need more information. The most promising body of documents in this regard is lay subsidy returns. Subsidies, lay and clerical, were the traditional royal tax in the middle ages, the first known example of the type occurring in 1188.[15] Subsidies were levied on moveables, that is, those goods that a man could move from place to place. Strictly speaking, this only exempted land, buildings, and fixed appurtenances such as wells, fences, etc. There were, however, other exemptions, particularly those thought necessary for the well-being of the realm. Thus it was officially recorded that the armour and war-horses of the gentry were exempt, as well as their jewels, clothes and other valuables.[16] Unlike the goods belonging to the aristocracy, the exemptions for peasants seem to have been guided more by customary principles than by formally recorded ones.[17] Thus essential farming equipment, such as ploughs, harrows, forks and spades, were almost totally exempt, perhaps in regard to the principle of "wainage" (i.e. the inviolability of a man's right to his means of cultivation); only carts were occasionally taxed. Also exempt (less understandably) were household goods, such as bedding, clothes, cooking vessels, eating utensils, and so on.[18] Some corn was taxed, but the amounts

---

[14] Altogether those inventories with only one or two draught animals (21 out of the total 52 inventories) had 51.6 per cent horses; the rest, with three or more draught animals, had only 28.4 per cent horses.

[15] *The Taxation of 1297*, ed. A. T. Gaydon (Beds. Hist. Rec. Soc., xxxix, 1959), p. vii.

[16] J. F. Willard, *Parliamentary Taxes on Personal Property 1290 to 1334* (Cambridge, Mass., 1934), pp. 77–8.

[17] *Ibid.*, pp. 79–80.

[18] "Utensils" and "vessels", however, were taxed in the 1327 and 1332 Buckinghamshire lay subsidies. *Early Taxation Returns*, ed. A. C. Chibnall (Bucks. Rec. Soc., xiv, 1966), pp. 2ff.

were usually so small as to suggest that only corn for sale was actually assessed.[19]

The item most comprehensively taxed was livestock, including the draught animals, despite their being essential to cultivation. Only smaller animals, such as poultry, were consistently exempt. There were some variations, however. For example, the collectors for the 1225 lay subsidy were instructed to exempt the work-horses of freemen and nobles.[20] This exemption, however, was not allowed in the 1232 subsidy, and these more rigorous conditions seem to have been followed thereafter, such that there were no obvious exemptions in the working animals of either peasant or demesne farmers.

In the middle ages the collection of the tax fell into two main phases. In the first phase, from 1188 to 1334, the goods of each tax-payer were individually recorded and their value assessed, from which the tax owed was then calculated. Because of the growing problem of evasion, however, a new system was devised in 1334, whereby the community was assessed rather than the individual. The amount of tax levied was arrived at through a process of bargaining between each community and the royal tax collectors. Once it was agreed, the community's new levy acquired the status of a rateable value, which quickly became standardized and remained unchanged from subsidy to subsidy.[21]

It is only the first phase of individual assessment that we are concerned with in this study, since after 1334, with very few exceptions, only the community and the tax owed appears in the records. Up to 1334, however, the levying of tax upon individuals is clearly recorded in the documents. The general procedure followed by the local tax collectors was this. First, they would draw up a list of each taxpayer's relevant moveables. Sometimes, if the total value of a peasant's goods failed to reach a certain minimum, usually about

---

[19] Willard, *Parliamentary Taxes*, pp. 84–5; *The Taxation of 1297*, pp. xix–xxii.

[20] *Calendar of Patent Rolls* (London, 1891–in progress), Henry III, 1216–25, p. 560. The exemption, however, applied only fitfully, as in south Wiltshire (see Table 24 below, where, for instance, no horses were assessed on the demesnes). Other counties in the same subsidy, such as Lincolnshire, fared less well, with horses being taxed even on demesnes.

[21] At least into the sixteenth century. For a summary of this evolution in tax, see *Surrey Taxation Returns*, ed. H. Jenkinson, with an introduction by J. F. Willard (Surrey Rec. Soc., no. 18, 1922), pp. v–vi.

ten shillings,[22] he would be excused the tax altogether and in fact would not appear in the assessment; but otherwise he and his animals would be entered on a document called, historically, a local assessment roll,[23] which resembled a series of inventories.[24] If these local assessment rolls had been the only documents used in the taxation process, then we would likely have had a veritable mountain of information dealing with peasant goods and livestock. Unfortunately the rolls only proceeded as far as the chief taxor for the county. Here a new roll was made up, listing the names of the villagers and the tax that they owed, but expunging all the detailed information about livestock and goods contained in the local rolls. This new county roll, summarizing all the information from the local rolls, was made in duplicate.[25] One of the duplicate rolls was sent to the exchequer, and it is these rolls and the final enrolled accounts of the exchequer that have largely survived instead of the local rolls.[26] Occasionally, though, local rolls were also sent to the exchequer, probably as a check on the county roll,[27] and thus have survived. A few local assessment rolls have also turned up in manorial collections.[28] As a result, local rolls for at least fifteen counties are in existence, most of which have been used in this study.[29] These rolls cover a period from 1225 to 1332, although they are most frequent after 1280. Altogether the taxpayers covered by the rolls come to a

---

[22] These minima varied from nothing in 1225 and presumably before to 15s. in 1307. Willard, *Parliamentary Taxes*, p. 88; M. M. Postan, "Village Livestock in the Thirteenth Century", *Econ. Hist. Rev.*, 2nd series, xv (1962), p. 220.

[23] E.g., see Willard, *Parliamentary Taxes*, pp. 64–8.

[24] For example, the first name appearing on a roll for Barford Hundred in Bedfordshire in 1297 is that of William Joye of Chawston with Colesden. William had one mare, one calf, one piglet, one quarter of wheat, a half-quarter of rye, a half-quarter of dredge, one quarter of oats, and 8d. worth of hay and forage. The total value of his goods came to 12s., and, being taxed at a ninth, he ended up owing 16d. After William there were listed 34 other taxpayers for the community, including the local lords, William de Kyrkeby and the prior of Caldwell. Each had their goods listed, valued and taxed, as in the case of the first William. *The Taxation of 1297*, pp. 1–3.

[25] Willard, *Parliamentary Taxes*, p. 68.

[26] J. F. Hadwin, "The Medieval Lay Subsidies and Economic History", *Econ. Hist. Rev.*, 2nd series, xxxvi (1983), esp. pp. 202–5.

[27] Willard, *Parliamentary Taxes*, p. 67; *Surrey Taxation Returns*, p. xii.

[28] As at Cuxham, Oxfordshire; see *Manorial Records of Cuxham, Oxfordshire*, ed. P. D. A. Harvey (Oxfordshire Rec. Soc., 1, 1976), pp. 712–14.

[29] See Table 24 below. A few rolls for urban communities, such as Colchester, Dartford and Shrewsbury, were omitted.

considerable number, some 7,000 in the rolls examined in this study (see below).

Thus, despite the problems of document survival, the amount of information supplied by the local assessment rolls is fairly abundant. Indeed, if these 7,000 taxpayers were spread uniformly over the country they would form a very reasonably sized sample. Unfortunately, as with the inventories, they are crowded into a few select areas, the best represented being the south and east. Relatively few rolls survive for the north and west, and regions like the west midlands and the south-west have hardly any at all. Even counties fortunate enough to have local assessment rolls may not be adequately represented by them. Leicestershire and Oxfordshire, for instance, are only represented by rolls covering single villages, hardly an adequate sample from which to assess the performance of an entire county.[30]

Even more serious is the question as to just how reliably the local rolls reflect the amount of a peasant's goods, particularly – as regards this study – his draught livestock. The problem of under-assessment immediately comes to mind here. Peasant and demesne taxpayers had every incentive to try to have their assessments pitched as low as possible. This could be done in several ways,[31] but the most destructive from our point of view is the tendency to devalue the *numbers* of livestock. Young animals seem, in many cases, to have been especially under-represented,[32] and doubts must also be raised about the adult animals. A. T. Gaydon, in comparing the numbers of livestock recorded on demesnes in the 1297 Bedfordshire lay subsidy with those given in contemporary account material, found a significant level of evasion, the underassessment in draught animals often being of the order of 20 per cent or more.[33] These underassessments were obviously arranged in collusion with the tax collectors, and indeed the accounts for Cuxham (Oxfordshire) record bribes to the collectors of up to 10s., "so that they

---

[30] Even where counties have local rolls covering several communities, they are often crowded into a single hundred, as, for example, in the 1283 roll for the hundred of Blackbourne in Suffolk. E. Powell, *A Suffolk Hundred in the Year 1283* (Cambridge, 1910).

[31] For example, by setting the assessed values of the goods taxed as low as possible. The recorded values of these goods in the lay subsidy returns, especially livestock, were generally well below the prevailing market prices.

[32] *The Taxation of 1297*, pp. xxiii–xxiv.

[33] *Ibid.*, pp. xviii–xix.

might be lenient in their assessment".[34] Not having the financial
resources of the demesne, we might expect that the peasantry were
less successful in escaping the tax, but in fact they may even have
fared better. Thus Cuxham tenants were only assesed one affer
apiece in 1304, as far as draught animals went, even though trespasses recorded in the court rolls for the manor indicate they had at
least two apiece.[35] It may be that here each peasant was allowed one
horse as a riding animal.

In addition to this deliberate underassessment in numbers, there
are other problems as well. We have already indicated that the value
of a peasant's goods had to reach a certain level before he was taxed.
These taxable minima were generally set at amounts that would
allow the purchase of one or even two draught animals at the values
given in the subsidies, and we must wonder how many draught
animals escaped the tax net in this way. We must also consider
richer peasants and lords who managed to use their influence to
avoid the tax net altogether. In this regard it is to be noted that
jurors and collectors themselves were often exempt or at least able
to have their taxes set at nominal levels, presumably without
recourse to a formal assessment.[36] These cases of total exemption,
whether for reasons of poverty, influence, or services rendered,
may have added up to a half or more of the peasants in any given
village.[37] While not necessarily affecting the value of the results
obtained from examining the goods and livestock of their tax-paying
neighbours, these cases of omission may seriously distort any
analysis that tries to relate assessed livestock to the economic or
social cross-section of the community.

It was difficulties like these that made one commentator despair
of ever being able to use this sort of taxation document in a mean-
ingful way.[38] Such a verdict would seem unnecessarily gloomy. The
degree of reliability in the local assessment rolls varied tremendously from subsidy to subsidy. As a general rule, the earliest rolls

[34] Harvey, *Medieval Oxfordshire Village*, p. 105. The whole range of corrupt
practices undertaken by the taxors and sub-taxors, including bribery and the
concealment of funds, is considered by Willard, *Parliamentary Taxes*, pp.
210–19.
[35] Harvey, *Medieval Oxfordshire Village*, pp. 131, 174–5.
[36] E.g., Willard, *Parliamentary Taxes*, pp. 207–10.
[37] E.g., as at Caddington below.
[38] L. F. Salzman, "Early Taxation of Sussex, Part II", *Sussex Arch. Coll.*, xcix
(1961), pp. 18–19.

were the best, probably because subsidies then were relatively infrequent.[39] The pattern changed in the 1290s with the outbreak of war with Wales, Scotland and France. Urgent demands for cash to cover the expenses of these wars meant that the subsidies became more frequent; between the years 1294 and 1297 they were levied annually. The revenues from them, however, immediately began to decline, and soon were only a half or a third of what they used to be.[40] The causes behind this steady diminution of tax are not absolutely clear. Besides evasion, there may have been a gradual depletion of capital in the country because of the war demands. Evasion, however, remains the most likely answer, since, although there was a modest increase in the level of revenues collected from the subsidies in the early fourteenth century, they in no way recovered to the levels of the early 1290s and before. It would seem, as J. F. Willard has commented, that methods of evasion, once learned and carried out successfully, continued to be practised thereafter.[41]

As a rough rule, then, the subsidies before 1294 – the point at which the tax revenues started to drop – are likely to have had a much lower scale of evasion than those after. M. M. Postan, for instance, examined three of these early local assessment rolls and concluded that almost all the eligible taxpayers in the villages concerned were in fact recorded in the rolls and that the numbers of livestock listed for them also seem to have been accurate.[42] In some cases, however, Postan would appear to have been overly optimistic in his assessment. The 1283 subsidy roll for Blackbourne Hundred in Suffolk, for example, seems to have underassessed the number of draught animals on peasant farms, in particular horses, by as much as 15 per cent or even more; and the number of taxpayers in some villages at least may have been up to 30–35 per cent short of the number of heads of households actually living there.[43] Some of

[39] There were, for instance, only four taxes levied on moveables during the reign of Henry III and only three during the early years of Edward I.

[40] Willard, *Parliamentary Taxes*, pp. 343–5.

[41] *Ibid.*, p. 345. A certain amount may also have been lost through simple concealment of funds, with the taxors handing in to the exchequer less than they had actually received. *Ibid.*, pp. 214–17.

[42] Postan, "Village Livestock", pp. 220–8. The rolls examined were those for south Wiltshire in 1225, Blackbourne Hundred (Suffolk) in 1283 and the Ramsey Abbey *banlieu* in Huntingdonshire in 1290.

[43] This evaluation of the accuracy of the 1283 subsidy roll was made on the basis of

these last may have been exempt because of poverty or some other reasons, but even so the discrepancy would seem suspiciously large. It should be pointed out, however, that the Blackbourne Hundred tax list is probably the worst of the early assessments in regard to reliability. On the other hand, within their terms of reference, other early subsidies, such as those for south Wiltshire and the Ramsey Abbey *banlieu*, seem to have been very accurate.[44]

Altogether it is unlikely that the under-representation in draught animals was much greater than 25 per cent in any of the early assessments. This would seem an acceptable level of accuracy in the circumstances. In contrast, the assessments after 1294 deteriorated quickly in reliability, as indicated by the loss of revenues. Thus at Caddington (Bedfordshire) in 1297 only twelve people were taxed, despite the fact that a survey for the same year indicated that 104 free and villein tenants lived in the village.[45] Examples like this could be cited *ad nauseam*,[46] but it is sufficient to note here that the later assessments contain only a fraction of the potential taxpayers, probably a half or less in most cases. It seems, too, that a similar situation occurred with the number of animals listed for those taxpayers who did appear. We have already considered the case of Cuxham (p. 183), where one horse per tenant was the norm according to the tax assessment there in 1304, but where in fact, according to other records, two horses per tenant were more likely. The scarcity of sources with which to compare such animal listings makes it difficult to judge the reliability of any other of these later assessments, but suspicion as to their accuracy is often raised by the stereotyped nature of the entries, with the same number of animals being

comparing the assessment with a number of contemporary records. For a full discussion, see Langdon, thesis, ch. 4, n. 54 (pp. 318–20).

[44] The main point of difference arises over the south Wiltshire roll, where the exemption for horses granted to lords and freemen noted above appears to have operated in full. Otherwise, when compared to other contemporary documents, the early rolls do seem to have included most, if not all, of the eligible taxpayers, and, where checks against animals can be made, the correlation between taxed animals and those actually present also seems good: for example, see Postan, "Village Livestock", pp. 225–8, 234–5; also Langdon, thesis, ch. 4, n. 55 (pp. 320–1).

[45] *The Taxation of 1297*, p. xxxiii.

[46] For example, L. F. Salzman, "Early Taxation in Sussex, Part I", *Sussex Arch. Coll.*, xcviii (1960), pp. 42–3, estimated that only two out of five potential taxpayers were actually taxed in the 1327 and 1332 Sussex assessments; see also Willard, *Parliamentary Taxes*, pp. 174–5, 179; Postan, "Village Livestock", p. 220.

repeated from taxpayer to taxpayer. The danger here is that the taxors omitted so many animals from their count that the actual detailed assessment became little more than a convenient fiction (and often a poorly contrived one) to present to their superiors.[47]

To sum up, we have two main periods to consider. The first, up to about 1294, was one where the local tax assessment rolls reflected the number of taxpayers and draught animals in villages reasonably well. After 1294, however, massive underassessment in both the number of taxpayers and in the goods of those who did pay seriously impairs these later subsidies as evidence. Nevertheless, even for these later assessments, the situation is not irretrievable. We have at least one good period where the evidence is sound, and if we have sizeable doubts about the later evidence, we can at least compare it with the earlier material before we cast it away as totally useless. There is, as well, one further reason to take an optimistic view. Because of the nature of this study, we are more interested in the relative proportions of horses and oxen than in their absolute numbers. Thus even massive underassessment in the subsidy stock listings need not be fatal. For example, at Cuxham, where we know that the peasant draught animals were underassessed by at least a half in the 1304 subsidy when compared to the evidence from the Cuxham court rolls, the level of horses in both cases was still 100 per cent.[48] Thus, if we assume that the horses and oxen are underassessed to the same degree, then even the later assessments have some value in determining the proportion of horses in peasant draught stock. We must wait until we see the evidence that actually derives from the subsidies before we make our final judgement.

This rather involved discussion has attempted to outline some of the problems associated with handling lay subsidy data. The data themselves are contained in Table 24. The format for the table has been to divide the assessments into two groups: those before 1294, representing the more reliable assessments, and those after, representing the less reliable ones. Besides listing the totals of horses and oxen for each assessment, the data are further broken down into

---

[47] Salzman, "Early Taxation, II", pp. 18–19; Hadwin, "Medieval Lay Subsidies", p. 211.

[48] See above. According to the trespasses, one of the freemen residing at Cuxham did have some oxen, but he is not listed in the 1304 assessment. Harvey, *Medieval Oxfordshire Village*, pp. 174–5.

their peasant and demesne constituents. Altogether the five assessments before 1294 covered 72 villages and 2,744 taxpayers, while those after 1294 covered at least 263 villages and 4,288 taxpayers, a total of over 7,000 individual assessments for all the subsidies, early and late, of which 344 were for demesne lands.[49] As with the accounts, there were a great number of terms used to signify horses: *affri, stotti, jumenta,* and so on. The same criteria as given in the appendix were used for determining whether a certain term meant a horse or not. Similarly donkeys were considered as horses for the compilation of the statistics, but in fact only five were found, all in the village of South Kirkby, Yorkshire. No mules were listed anywhere.

The most obvious conclusion to be drawn from Table 24 is that the level of horses on peasant farms was much higher than on demesnes. In fact, only in the three 1225 assessments and the later ones for Minety (Wiltshire) and the West Riding of Yorkshire did the levels of horses on peasant farms come to less than 50 per cent of the total draught stock. It is notable, too, that the three 1225 assessments were in a period when the transition to the use of horses was still taking place in a major way.[50] It is also significant that the two later assessments with relatively low levels of horses were found in the west and north of the country, confirming the trend noted for the demesne.[51] In other counties, however, such as Bedfordshire and Suffolk, horses dominated almost completely among the peasantry. It was in these counties that the dichotomy between demesne and peasant farms in the use of horses was at its most extreme, but all counties showed it to some degree. In general, the incidence in the use of horses on peasant farms was almost double that on demesnes.

[49] Determining whether a particular taxpayer was a demesne-holding lord or just a peasant was not always easy to do. In the end, it was decided to accept a list of animals and goods as belonging to a demesne only in those cases where the taxpayer could definitely be established as a lord or at least as a tenant holding a knight's fee or some portion of one. (This was accomplished using the various *Victoria County Histories,* the *Book of Fees* and *Feudal Aids,* and assorted antiquarian histories.) Inevitably some demesnes will have slipped through the net and thus have been counted as peasant farms, but the number of cases where this actually happened is seemingly very small – for example, all but one of the farms having over ten draught animals were proven to be demesnes – and should have little effect upon the results.
[50] See pp. 94–5 above and pp. 202–3 below.
[51] See p. 87 above.

Table 24. *The proportion of work-horses on demesne and peasant farms according to lay subsidy local assessment rolls*

Place (Year of Subsidy)	No. of villages	Demesnes				Peasant farms				All farms			
		a	b	c	d	a	b	c	d	a	b	c	d
1. Subsidies before 1294													
Stathern, Leicestershire (1225)	1	1	0	0	—	23	31	24	43.6	24	.31	24	43.6
Ten Lincolnshire Villages (1225)	10^f	12	129	35	21.3	164	147	124	45.8	176	276	159	36.6
South Wiltshire (1225)	23	19	353	0	0.0	954	1117	505	31.1	973	1470	505	25.6
Blackbourne Hundred, Suffolk (1283)	33	45	183	200	52.2	1345	204	1020	83.3	1390	387	1220	75.9
Ramsey Abbey Banlieu, Huntingdonshire (1290)	5^u	4	58	36	38.3	177	138	195	58.6	181	196	231	54.1
2. Subsidies after 1294													
Three Bedfordshire^v Hundreds (1297)	44	77	331	212	39.0	1048	102	777	88.4	1125	433	989	69.5
Spelhoe Hundred, Northamptonshire (1297)	10	—	—	—	—	25	3	17	85.0	25	3	17	85.0
West Riding, Yorkshire (1297)^w	121	74	317	96	23.2	951	760	638	45.6	1025	1077	734	40.5
Shillington, Bedfordshire (1301)	1	1	8	4	33.3	49	2	20	90.9	50	10	24	70.6
Ruxley Hundred, Kent (1301)	18	26	94	106	53.0	503	116	302	64.5	529	260	408	61.1
Somerden Hundred, Kent (1301)	?^x	5	16	6	27.3	100	63	71	53.0	105	79	77	49.4
Cuxham, Oxfordshire (1304)	1	1	12	4	25.0	16	0	13	100.0	17	12	17	58.6
Wendon, Essex (1307)	1	2	2	8	80.0	22	0	5	100.0	24	2	13	86.7
Nazeing, Essex (1309)	1	—	—	—	—	26	9	19	67.9	26	9	19	67.9

188

		a	b	c	d	a	b	c	d	a	b	c	d
Minety, Wiltshire (1312)	1	—	—	—	—	44	56	41	42.3	44	56	41	42.3
Buckinghamshire (1327)[y]	11	10	17	22	56.4	217	81	182	69.2	227	98	204	67.5
Buckinghamshire (1332)[y]	38	51	120	130	52.0	805	236	703	74.9	856	356	833	70.1
Three Sussex Hundreds (1332)[z]	16	16	83	27	24.5	219	84	93	52.3	235	167	120	41.8

Key to column headings   a – Number of taxpayers   b – Number of oxen   c – Number of adult horses   d – % horses

[t] Evedon, Scredington, "Bortona" (Burton, near Lincoln?), Mumby, "Torp" (Thorpe, near Mabelthorpe?), "Kirkeby" (Kirkby, near Market Rasen?), Ingoldsby, Kelby, Heckington and Authorpe (P.R.O. E179 242/127, ms. 2, 3, 5, 8, 9, 10, 12, 16, 18 and 22). This entire document was very fragmented and torn. As a result, only ten of the membranes were thought worth transcribing. Even these ten were in very poor condition with, in many cases, several entries missing from the bottom of the membranes. A recent transcription of these assessments has been published by the Pipe Roll Society (1983).

[u] Wistow, Great Raveley, Upwood, Bury next to Ramsey cum Heighmongrove, and Heighmongrove. The assessment for Ramsey, also included in the same roll, was omitted because of its urban status.

[v] Barford, Biggleswade and Flitt Hundreds.

[w] Includes Ewcross, Strafford and Agbrigg Wapentakes and the Liberty of Ripon.

[x] The taxpayers for this hundred were listed on the document without separating them into communities; several villages were obviously represented, however.

[y] Includes a scattering of villages, covering more or less the whole county.

[z] Rotherbridge, Holmstrow and Henhurst Hundreds.

Notes and sources

Subsidies before 1294
P.R.O. S.C. 11, Roll 531; P.R.O. E179 242/127; P.R.O. E179 242/47; *A Suffolk Hundred in the Year 1283*, ed. E. Powell (Cambridge, 1910); *Early Huntingdonshire Lay Subsidy Rolls*, ed. J. A. Raftis and M. P. Hogan (Toronto, 1976).

Subsidies after 1294
The Taxation of 1297, ed. A. T. Gaydon (Beds. Hist. Rec. Soc., xxxix, 1959), pp. 1–73; P.R.O. E179 238/119a; *The Yorkshire Lay Subsidy, 25 Edward I*, ed. W. Brown (Yorks Arch. Soc. Rec. Ser., xvi, 1894); P.R.O. E179 123/5 (Ruxley and Somerden Hundreds); *Manorial Records of Cuxham, Oxfordshire*, ed. P. D. A. Harvey (Oxfordshire Rec. Soc., I, 1976), pp. 712–14; P.R.O. E179 242/12 and 13; R. A. Fuller, "The Tallage of 6 Edward II (Dec. 16, 1312) and the Bristol Rebellion", *Trans. of the Bristol and Gloucestershire Arch. Soc.*, xix (1894–5), pp. 196–8; *Early Taxation Returns*, ed. A. C. Chibnall (Bucks. Rec. Soc., xiv, 1966); L. F. Salzman, "Early Taxation in Sussex, Part II", *Sussex Arch. Coll.*, xcix (1961), pp. 10–17.

Although some of the assessments are far from trustworthy, the results for the demesnes from the lay subsidy data often compare favourably with those from the accounts, as shown in Table 25 for the larger assessment rolls. As might be expected, the agreement between the lay subsidy assessments and the accounts is best for those assessments before 1294. Only that for Wiltshire is patently out of step, because of the 1225 exemption for the horses of nobles and freemen already noted, which seems to have been in effect here. For some of the assessments, however, the agreement is somewhat illusory. For example, the percentage of horses on the demesne in the 1225 Lincolnshire assessment does agree very closely with that given for the county in the Sample A accounts, but there is something like a half-century gap between the two. As we have seen in the case of the bishopric of Winchester, we should then have expected the level of horses in the 1225 assessment to be somewhat lower than that indicated for the county in Sample A. Similarly the level of horses in the 1283 Blackbourne Hundred (Suffolk) assessment also agrees more with the account levels of a century later than those contemporary with the subsidy. Part of this is probably due to the inclusion in the assessments of small demesnes, or even of cases where the demesne was leased out and the lord was left with only one or two animals, usually horses. Thus, for example, the average number of draught animals per demesne in the 1283 Blackbourne Hundred assessment was 8.5 compared to 17.0 draught animals per demesne for Suffolk in the Sample A accounts and 18.5 animals per demesne in Sample B. Since these small demesnes tended to use a higher proportion of horses than the larger demesnes did,[52] it is not surprising that relatively more horses turn up in the lay subsidy material than in the accounts, although it is unlikely that it explains all the difference.[53] This bias towards horses is even more marked in the post-1294 subsidies, particularly those for Buckinghamshire in 1327 and 1332, where the levels of horses in the assessments are a full 20 per cent above those indicated by the accounts. Again, some of this discrepancy may be due to the greater incidence of smaller demesnes in the subsidies, but it is more

[52] See Chapter 3, note 33.
[53] Thus in the Blackbourne Hundred assessment, even when demesnes having less than five animals are subtracted, the proportion of horses in the draught stock of the remaining demesnes is still higher (at 51.2 per cent) than that for Suffolk in the Sample A accounts.

Table 25. *Demesne horse levels from lay subsidies and accounts*

Lay subsidy	% horses on demesnes according to subsidy	% horses on demesnes according to the accounts	
		Sample A (1250–1320)	Sample B (1350–1420)
Lincolnshire (1225)	21.3	22.0	39.4
South Wiltshire (1225)	0.0	12.5	15.1
Blackbourne Hd. (1283)	52.2	45.0	51.7
Ramsey Banlieu (1290)	38.3	37.8	39.0
Bedfordshire Hundreds (1297)	39.0	30.4	38.5
Yorkshire West Riding (1297)	23.2	15.1	18.2
Ruxley Hd., Kent (1301)	53.0	48.7	49.6
Somerden Hd., Kent (1301)	27.3	48.7	49.6
Buckinghamshire (1327)	56.4	33.1	31.6
Buckinghamshire (1332)	52.0	33.1	31.6
Sussex Hundreds (1332)	24.5	11.3	18.4

Notes: The subsidy figures are from Table 24 (under "Demesnes"). The account figures (taken from Table 11) are those for the county in which the subsidy concerned is found.

likely that the severe underassessment in animals that obviously occurred in the Buckinghamshire subsidies[54] also had a decidedly distorting effect on the level of horses indicated there. In other cases, though, the discrepancy can be accounted for by the fact that surviving assessments only covered small parts of counties. Thus, it is interesting to compare the subsidy results of Ruxley Hundred in Kent, which agrees quite well with the results for the county in our two account samples, with those for Somerdon Hundred, which do not. Clearly regional variation is significant here and consequently makes comparison with the account material that much more difficult. In general, however, although the discrepancy between the lay subsidy and account material is perhaps no greater than might be expected in the circumstances, there does seem to be some bias towards horses in the former as far as demesnes are concerned. We may suspect the same applied to the peasant draught animals, but just how much this bias affects our overall estimate as to the level of

[54] The average number of draught animals per demesne in the 1327 assessment was 3.9, and for the 1332 assessment it was 4.9. This compares with 23.7 draught animals per demesne in the Sample A accounts and 29.1 draught animals per demesne in the Sample B accounts.

Table 26. *Lay subsidy assessments arranged by number of draught animals*

Place (year of subsidy)		No. of taxpayers with no draught animals	Taxpayers with 1 or 2 draught animals		Taxpayers with 3–5 draught animals		Taxpayers with 6–10 draught animals		Taxpayers with over 10 draught animals	
		a	a	b	a	b	a	b	a	b
South Wiltshire (1225)	1. All	315	367	56.0	225	25.1	50	6.9	16	0.0
	2. Demesne	—	—	—	—	—	4	0.0	15	0.0
	3. Peasant	315	367	56.0	225	25.1	46	7.7	1	0.0
Blackbourne Hundred, Suffolk (1283)	1. All	587	673	96.1	91	57.5	25	48.6	14	52.8
	2. Demesne	4	6	81.8	7	53.3	15	47.2	13	53.0
	3. Peasant	583	667	96.3	84	57.9	10	50.1	1	50.0
Ramsey Abbey Banlieu, Huntingdonshire (1290)	1. All	77	33	84.9	55	56.4	13	45.1	3	38.6
	2. Demesne	—	—	—	—	—	1	33.3	3	38.6
	3. Peasant	77	33	84.9	55	56.4	12	46.1	—	—
Three Bedfordshire Hundreds (1297)	1. All	311	730	92.7	42	46.5	26	35.9	16	35.8
	2. Demesne	4	11	80.0	22	44.7	24	36.5	16	35.8
	3. Peasant	307	719	93.1	20	48.6	2	28.6	—	—
West Riding, Yorkshire (1297)	1. All	232	566	51.9	184	34.0	38	25.9	5	14.3
	2. Demesne	5	3	40.0	30	23.4	31	25.7	5	14.3
	3. Peasant	227	563	51.9	154	36.7	7	26.7	—	—

Key to column headings
a – Number of taxpayers
b – % horses in draught stock

Notes and sources: For sources, see Table 24.

horses among these same peasant draught animals is difficult to tell without recourse to other data, such as heriots (discussed below). For now, it is enough to note that horses were used substantially more by the peasantry than by demesnes.

The distinction between "peasant" and "demesne" farms is, in a way, very artificial and misleading. In fact, it would be better to analyse the use of horses on an economic basis rather than on a social or legal one: that is, to judge the use of horses on the basis of the size of farms rather than on the status of their owners or proprietors. The difficulty here, however, is that we have relatively little information as to the farm acreages held by each taxpayer in the subsidies, especially for the peasantry, while to find a suitable parameter as a substitute is far from easy.[55] In the end, it was felt that the best method was simply to classify each taxpayer by the number of draught animals he had. Table 26 contains the results of such an analysis for a selection of five of the lay subsidies. In each, the taxpayers were divided into five categories: those with no draught animals, those with 1 or 2 draught animals, those with 3–5, those with 6–10 and those with over 10. The classification might be seen as corresponding roughly with the economic stratification in a village, the first two categories corresponding with the landless, smallholding, or even middling tenants; the third category (3–5 draught animals) corresponding with more substantial tenants holding, say, a virgate apiece; the 6–10 draught animals category equating to small demesnes and that select group of free and customary tenants with, say, two virgates or more each; and finally the last category equating to large demesnes and perhaps the very wealthiest of peasants (although, in fact, almost all the cases with over 10 draught animals were known demesnes).

Examining the results, the proportion of tenants having no draught animals varied from subsidy to subsidy, ranging from 22.6

---

[55] One such parameter is wealth, since most of the individual assessments also give the total value of the man's taxed goods. However, the connection between a taxpayer's arable land holding and the total value of his moveables is not direct. Some tenants, for instance, had considerable holdings in sheep and not much else (for example, Hervicus Bude and others at Livermere Parva, Suffolk, in 1283: *A Suffolk Hundred in the Year 1283*, table 21), indicating that arable farming and hence the use of draught animals formed only a small part of their activities.

per cent in the West Riding of Yorkshire[56] to just over 42 per cent for Blackbourne Hundred in Suffolk and the Ramsey Abbey *banlieu* in Huntingdonshire. It is difficult to be precise about this, partly because of the complicating factor of each subsidy having its own exemption limit, but broadly speaking, eastern counties, such as Suffolk and Huntingdonshire, tended to have a higher percentage of taxpayers with no draught animals than those in the west and north,[57] not unexpected given the greater degree of holding fragmentation in the former counties. For those taxpayers that did have draught animals, the situation is clearer. The fewer draught animals a farm had, the more likely it was that those beasts would be horses.[58] This was a rule that applied both to peasant holdings and demesnes. Oxen by and large were the preserve of larger farms. But here "larger" must be used advisedly, since it appears it was only on the very smallest of farms – that is, those having only one or two draught animals – that horses were used to a markedly greater degree than elsewhere. In contrast, the proportion of horses employed in the 3–5 draught animal grouping was much reduced, even in supposedly horse-oriented country, such as Blackbourne Hundred in Suffolk. The indication is that, at the time of the subsidies, the farm size threshold for the substantial use of oxen was low, perhaps equivalent to a virgate or even half a virgate. On the other hand, the decline in the proportion of horses from the 3–5 level to the 6–10 and over 10 draught animal levels was much more moderate, and indeed the 6–10 grouping often had fewer horses proportionally than the over 10 grouping.

The conclusions to be drawn from this set of observations are these. First, horses were especially favoured on smallholdings. A typical situation for this type of farmer would be one where the peasant (or even lord) had enough land to justify the use of some draught animals for hauling and harrowing, but not enough to justify the possession of his own plough and team; rather he either

---

[56] That is, 232 taxpayers over a total of 1,025 (as given in Table 24) times 100. The percentages for the other subsidies were worked out in an identical fashion.

[57] The same trend is evident for the thirteen other subsidies so analysed (see Langdon, thesis, table 4.4). Some anomalies do exist, however; the 1297 Bedfordshire lay subsidy, for instance, only had 27.6 per cent of taxpayers with no draught animals.

[58] Again, a trend not only evident in these five subsidies, but also in the other subsidies when so analysed (*ibid.*, table 4.4.).

borrowed or hired a plough-team from someone else, or he dug up his plot by hand. That such an arrangement existed is indicated by the occasional reference in surveys and extents to tenants who were required to do harrowing and carrying services, but not ploughing, as their more substantial neighbours were obliged to do.[59] As carrying and harrowing were very much horse-oriented activities, we would naturally expect this group of tenants to have more horses proportionally than their more affluent neighbours. It may be that these same tenants also ploughed with their horses, since we have seen that two-horse ploughing teams were by no means unknown to the demesne at this time,[60] and the same was probably true of peasant farms.[61]

Since this group holding only one or two draught animals was most often the largest from the point of view of draught-animal-owning taxpayers and very often from the number of animals involved, it is hardly surprising that it raised the level of horses among the peasantry as a whole significantly. However, this horse-oriented experience was only typical of this particular group. From then on, the experience of those taxpayers holding more than two draught animals rapidly approached that of the demesne. In some communities the substantial use of horses by the peasantry did go beyond the smallholding level, but this tended to happen only in areas where the demesnes were also using horses alone for draught, such as in the Chilterns.[62] In this regard, it is noticeable how similar demesne and peasant experience was, when compared solely in terms of the number of draught animals each had. The fundamental difference between peasant and demesne farms thus dissolves when looked at in this light, the demesne simply being a large farm that would be cultivated in the same way, at least in terms of the proportion of horses involved, whether it was managed by lord or peasant. From the lay subsidy assessments, it seems that this was a phenomenon that occurred regardless of region, since the tendency of small farms to employ proportionally more horses than large ones

---

[59] See pp. 220–1, 227 below.
[60] See p. 125 above.
[61] As at Cuxham: Langdon, "Economics of Horses and Oxen", p. 38.
[62] For example, see the assessments for Medmenham and High Wycombe, Buckinghamshire, in 1332 (*Early Taxation Returns*, pp. 47–50; the editor translates *affrus* as "beast", but it is almost certain that these animals were horses; see appendix).

was as evident for Yorkshire and Wiltshire as it was for Bedfordshire and Suffolk, even though the former areas may have used far
fewer horses overall than the latter.

So far, the evidence cited as to the number of horses employed as
draught animals by the peasantry has been contradictory. The
inventories show a much lower level of horses among the peasantry
than do the lay subsidy assessments. Some of this can be reconciled
by the fact that the inventories are dealing mostly with substantial
tenants in the more ox-oriented north and west, while the subsidies
deal much more with smallholders in the horse-oriented south and
east; but there is still enough of a difference to create doubt. A third
source of information is thus very useful. One such source involves
those numerous references in accounts and court rolls to animals
given to the lord as heriots (or, occasionally, mortuaries) upon the
death of a tenant. These heriots are often useful as an indication of
the work animals a peasant had. Their use, however, does present
several problems. For example, a heriot, or even a heriot and a mortuary together, hardly represents all the stock a peasant had. It is
therefore difficult to draw conclusions about a peasant's total stock,
or even just his draught stock, on the basis of these one or two animals. Nevertheless some inferences can be made. Heriots were generally chosen on the basis of value. Sometimes it was specified what
this animal should be, whether horse, ox, or otherwise,[63] but such
provisions were rare, and generally any animal would do provided it
was the best beast in terms of value that the peasant had (or second-
best in the case of mortuary). As a result, animal heriots from
peasants ranged from poultry and pigs to cattle and horses, although
in most cases the heriot was a major animal, either an ox, horse or
cow. Consequently draught animals figured frequently as heriots
and thus provide a potentially valuable source for the study of working beasts. Heriots, however, were not distributed evenly across the
country, but tended to be more common in some areas than in
others; East Anglia, for instance, is a region where the exaction of

---

[63]   As on the bishop of Chichester's manor of Selsey (Sussex), where in the latter half
of the thirteenth century it was specified that the heriot should be an ox or 2s. 6d.
Similarly at Aldingbourne in the same county in 1256/7 tenants owed a horse and
gear as heriot, while at Preston, again in Sussex, in the latter half of the thirteenth
century, the stipulated heriot was the peasant's best beast, *save his horse.*
Thirteen Custumals . . . of the Bishop of Chichester, pp. 15, 38. 85.

heriots was much less frequent than, say, in the west midlands and the south. Heriots also tended to occur only in dribs and drabs. A court roll or yearly account will often have only one heriot recorded, if any, and often this is not an ox or horse, but a cow, sheep or some other animal. As a result, a great number of accounts and court rolls are needed before a modest number of draught animal heriots can be found. Nonetheless, there are some exceptions. As the number of heriots is directly linked to the rate of mortality, years of plague and famine yielded rich harvests of heriots. In particular, the Black Death year of 1348–9 provided heriots in substantial number. Accordingly, a number of accounts and court rolls for that year, involving eighty-one manors, plus an account for Whaddon (Buckinghamshire) in the plague year of 1360–1, were examined. Altogether they provided draught animal heriots for fifteen counties, as shown in Table 27. As before, the horses have been divided into "cart-horses" (*equi carectarii* or just *equi*) and the inferior *affri*, *stotti* and *jumenta*.

These Black Death heriots show horses in a slight majority over oxen.[64] Indeed, the percentage of horses from county to county was generally very consistent, with ten of the fifteen counties being found in the 50–70 per cent range. This degree of consistency, however, is somewhat illusory, since the variation in the level of horses within counties was often very great. For instance, the proportion of horses found among the draught stock heriots of the six Buckinghamshire manors during the plague years fluctuated from 100 per cent at West Wycombe to only 16.7 per cent at Whaddon. In a county such as Buckinghamshire, with its widely differing types of soil and terrain, such variation is perhaps not surprising; but the degree of change found in other counties is not so easily explained in these terms.[65] Across the country as a whole some trends are evident, with counties in the south-west and the west midlands having more oxen as heriots than, say, those in East Anglia or the Home Counties, but there are some curious anomalies. For example,

---

[64] The same is evident in heriots and mortuaries taken from a series of accounts or court rolls over long periods of time. For example, the proportion of horses in the draught animal heriots and mortuaries for thirteen manors or groups of manors spread over the country and covering the period from 1269 to 1453 came to 52.5 per cent. Langdon, thesis, table 4.6 (p. 260).

[65] Particularly in Hampshire, where many of the manors giving widely differing results were on distinctly similar types of soil and terrain.

198   The peasantry: 1200–1500

Table 27. *Black Death draught animal heriots (1348–9 and 1360–1)*

County	No. of manors	No. of cart-horses	No. of affers, stotts or *jumenta*	No. of oxen	% horses
Berkshire	6	3	46	32	60.5
Buckinghamshire	6	0	32	50	39.0
Cambridgeshire	1	0	2	1	66.7
Essex	3	0	12	7	63.2
Hampshire	29	57	275	323½	50.6
Hertfordshire	4	4	24	16	63.6
Kent	4	4	59	33	65.6
Leicestershire	1	2	7	5	64.3
Middlesex	6	2	28	19	61.2
Oxfordshire	4	8	35	35½	54.8
Somerset	7	0	68	121	36.0
Suffolk	2	0	19	2	90.5
Surrey	2	2	18	56	26.3
Wiltshire	5	0	55	37	59.8
Worcestershire	2	22	4	28	48.1
Total	82	104	684	766	
Overall %					50.7

Sources: H.R.O. Eccles. 2 159358 (Wargrave, Waltham St Lawrence, Culham, Warfield, Brightwell and Harwell, Berkshire); *ibid.*, W.A.M. 7796 & 27744, P.R.O. S.C. 6 764/3 (Ivinghoe, West Wycombe, Morton, Turweston, Thornborough and Whaddon, Buckinghamshire); P.R.O. D.L. 29 4717/288 (Soham, Cambridgeshire); W.A.M. 25444 & 25665, C.C.L. Bedels Rolls (Birdbrook, Feering and Bocking, Essex); H.R.O. Eccles. 2 159358, P.R.O. S.C. 6 986/14 and 16 (Twyford, Marwell, Bishopstoke, Crawley, Mardon, East Meon Manor, East Meon Church, Hambledon, Fareham, Brockhampton, Bishop's Sutton, Old Alresford, Avington, Wield, Beauworth, Bentley, "Erbere" (?; presumed to be in Hampshire from position in roll), Bishop's Waltham, Droxford, Bitterne, High Clere, Burghclere, Ecchinswell, East Woodhay, Ashmansworth, North Waltham, Overton, Bowcombe (Isle of Wight) and Whitefield (Isle of Wight), Hampshire); W.A.M. 26090–1 & 8923, P.R.O. S.C. 6 867/7 & 869/9 (Aldenham, Wheathampstead, Meesdon and Standon, Hertfordshire); W.A.M. 26436, C.C.L. Bedels Rolls (Westerham, Hollingbourne, Meopham and Orpington, Kent); P.R.O. S.C. 6 908/35 (Nailstone, Leicestershire); W.A.M. 26733–4, 26904, 32562–3, 16430, 27136, 16872 (Ashford, Eye, Hendon, Knightsbridge, Laleham and Yeoveney with Staines, Middlesex); H.R.O. Eccles. 2 159358, W.A.M. 14796–7, P. D. A. Harvey, *A Medieval Oxfordshire Village: Cuxham 1240–1400* (Oxford, 1965), p. 174 (Witney, Adderbury, Islip and Cuxham, Oxfordshire); H.R.O. Eccles. 2 159358, P.R.O. S.C. 6 974/22 (Bishop's Hull, Poundsford, Nailsbourne, Holway, Staplegrove, Rimpton and Wellow, Somerset); P.R.O. S.C. 6 966/6, Brit. Lib. Add. Ch. 32934 (Erbury and Palgrave, Suffolk); H.R.O. Eccles. 2 159358, W.A.M. 27322 (Farnham and Morden, Surrey); H.R.O. Eccles. 2 159358 (Downton, (East) Knoyle, Bishopstone ("Ebblesbourne"), Bishop's Fonthill and Upton Knoyle, Wiltshire); W.A.M. 21019–20, B.R.L. 346320–2 (Longdon and Halesowen, Worcestershire).

Wiltshire holds a much greater percentage of horses in its Black Death heriots than the account and lay subsidy data for the same county would suggest. The same thing can be said in reverse for Buckinghamshire, where the level of horses in the heriots was considerably lower than in the lay subsidy assessments for the same county. There were, as well, a small but significant number of manors that seem to have been almost totally horse-oriented as far as the peasantry were concerned.[66] These, however, were very scattered and did not form any definite regional trend, although the relative lack of evidence in some areas, such as East Anglia and the east midlands, makes it difficult to be certain of this.

Turning away from these general observations, the essential problem we face is this: what exactly does an animal heriot or mortuary tell us? Well, essentially only that the animal was likely to be the most valuable or second most valuable beast that the peasant owned. As a general picture of a peasant's draught stock it is patently unreliable. For instance, if a recently deceased peasant had an expensive horse and four less expensive oxen, the horse would be chosen as heriot. On this basis, we might then conjecture that the peasant had only horses for draught, but nothing would be further from the truth. If, as the Black Death data indicate, draught animal heriots at the time of the plague were split about evenly between horses and oxen, all we can say is that half of these peasants had at least one horse and half had at least one ox. When peasants surrender more than one heriot, e.g., for several holdings, we can sometimes build up a better picture – for instance, the estate of Robert atte Hurne of Coulsdon, Surrey, in 1334 rendered as heriots to the lord one horse and two oxen for a half-virgate of land and two cottages[67] – but in the main such cases are rare.

Nevertheless some valuable insights can be gained from the heriot and mortuary data. In the Robert atte Hurne example just given, the horse was the most valuable of the three animals. In fact,

---

[66] Thus, considering only manors which had a sample of at least five draught animal heriots, those with 80 per cent or more horses in these heriots were Brightwell and Harwell, Berkshire; West Wycombe, Buckinghamshire; Twyford, Crawley, Old Alresford, Beauworth and Overton, Hampshire; Hollingbourne and Meopham, Kent; Yeoveney with Staines, Middlesex; Cuxham and Adderbury, Oxfordshire; and Palgrave, Suffolk.

[67] *Chertsey Abbey Court Roll Abstracts*, ed. E. Toms, 2 pts (Surrey Rec. Soc., nos. 38 and 48, 1937 and 1954), i, p. 65. The horse was worth 10s. and the two oxen 8s. apiece.

the most normal course of events was for horses to be the least valuable of the draught stock. Part of this can be inferred from demesne livestock prices. These show that, although the purchase prices of horses at the start of their demesne careers were generally comparable with those for oxen and cows, the selling prices at the end of their careers were often far less than those for the adult cattle, because of their much greater depreciation. This was particularly the case with lower quality horses, such as affers, stotts and *jumenta*. An example will help to highlight this point. The bishop of Winchester's demesne at Bishop's Waltham (Hampshire) had a particularly abundant harvest of heriots during the account year of Michaelmas to Michaelmas, 1348–9. Altogether 5 cart-horses, 44 affers, 24 oxen, 40½ cows and various other stock were received, many of which were sold immediately upon receipt. Of the latter, 7 oxen were sold at an average price of 9s. 4d. each, 8½ cows at an average of 3s. 4½d. each, 5 cart-horses for an average of 7s. 10¾d. each, and 32 affers sold "at various prices" for an average of 2s. 6d. apiece.[68] As we can see, the average selling price for oxen was higher than that for cart-horses and considerably above that for affers. Even cows were on average priced higher than affers, as were some of the lesser beasts on occasion; in the same account, for instance, a boar was sold for 4s. and 8 other pigs for 3s. apiece. It may be that the low price of affers here was an exceptional case, but many other similar examples can be given.[69] From all this, we can state with a fairly high degree of probability that if a peasant surrendered an affer, stott or *jumentum* as a heriot, then it is highly likely that he had only horses for draught. The situation is not as clear for cart-horses taken as heriots, but it does seem that in a good number of cases the same likelihood could be stated for them as well.

Returning to Table 27, then, affers, stotts and *jumenta* comprised 44.0 per cent of the Black Death draught animal heriots. Thus, it seems that a substantial portion of the draught-animal-owning peasantry had only horses for draught, perhaps a third to a half. This, of course, does not take into account the possibility that the

[68] H.R.O. Eccles. 2 159358, fo. 32v.
[69] Thus at Brockhampton (also Hampshire) seven *equi* were taken as heriots during the plague year 1348–9. These were sold for an average 4s. 11½d. each, while a single affer taken as heriot was sold for 2s. 6d.; in comparison, three heriot oxen were sold for 12s. apiece and two cows for 4s. 6d. each. *Ibid.*, fo. 17v.

affer, stott or *jumentum* was the second or third heriot following
oxen already given, but this minority of cases would be more than
balanced by that proportion of the cart-horse heriots taken from
holdings where again horses were the only draught animals. This
body of tenants using only horses for draught would seem to equate
with the large horse-owning group of small and middling holders
noted in the lay subsidy returns. This helps to explain the haphazard
distribution of those manors with a large preponderance of horse
heriots. In this case, it would seem that the high level of horses in the
heriots of a particular manor reflects not so much a strong predisposition towards horses because of soil and terrain but rather a large
proportion of tenants with relatively little land.[70] Even where horses
were the normal draught animal heriot in an area, however, this
does not mean that they necessarily dominated. Thus a county like
Wiltshire, where fairly large all-ox plough-teams seem to have been
the norm even for the peasantry,[71] may still have had substantial
numbers of oxen even though the heriots (in Table 27) suggest a
majority of peasants owning horses only for draught. Such a situation, in fact, would be quite consistent with the growth in the
number of smallholders known to have taken place in some parts of
this region at least.[72] The evidence suggests that these smallholders
generally only had one horse each,[73] which was probably sufficient
for the small-scale hauling and harrowing that they did. On the
other hand, if a peasant did plough in medieval Wiltshire, it appears
he needed a team of at least two animals and probably many more.
Thus, a typical draught stock holding for more substantial tenants
here was something like one horse and two oxen, one horse and four

[70] The best printed example of this is Cuxham in Oxfordshire, where the nominal
holdings of customary tenants were small enough – at twelve acres or less – to
encourage the use of horses only. At the same time, economic and environmental conditions at Cuxham still favoured the use of oxen on larger farms (that
is, on the demesne and the freeholding of John Grene). Harvey, *Medieval
Oxfordshire Village*, pp. 174–5; Langdon, "Economics of Horses and Oxen",
p. 38.

[71] See p. 229 and the sixteenth-century plough-teams for the county in Table 32
below.

[72] For example, as in the Taunton group of manors in Somerset. J. Z. Titow, "Some
Differences between Manors and their Effects on the Condition of the Peasant in
the Thirteenth Century", in *Essays in Agrarian History*, i, ed. W. Minchinton
(Newton Abbot, 1968), p. 42.

[73] E.g., only 3 out of the 177 peasants having only horses in the 1225 south Wiltshire
assessment had more than one of the animals. P.R.O. E179 242/47.

oxen, or even one horse and six oxen.[74] Consequently even if these substantial tenants were outnumbered by their horse-owning, small-holding contemporaries, oxen could still dominate overall.[75] The point confirms that already noted for the demesne (pp. 170–1), that horses cannot really come to dominate as draught animals in a region until they are used for ploughing. Where this happened and did not happen for the peasantry will be discussed in the next section, but for the moment it is enough to repeat that the heriots do confirm the existence of a substantial section of the peasantry – mostly small and middling holders – using nothing but horses for draught.

Finally, the heriots help us in another way. One of the problems with the lay subsidies and also with the inventories is that we cannot easily compare one period with another. To a certain extent, we can do this with heriots. For example, Table 28 compares the draught animal heriots recorded in four of the bishopric of Winchester pipe rolls over a period of 170 years. There are some changes in the manors covered from roll to roll, but in the main they include much the same area and yield enough heriots for a valid comparison to be made.

The pipe rolls show clearly that there was a definite and continued rise in the level of horses found in the heriots. In the first three cases up to the Black Death, this is consistent with, among other things, the growth in smallholdings taking place during this period. But the rise in the percentage of horses after the Black Death is much more curious in that it indicates a rise in the number of horses as heriots despite the decline in the smallholding class known to have occurred in this period.[76] Part of this may be due to the proportional increase in cart-horses. This implies two things. First, as suggested earlier in this chapter, peasants were becoming more market-oriented and thus using more carting horses. Second, many of the cart-horses probably concealed less expensive oxen that the peasant had. When, in fact, the cart-horses are excluded and only the lowly

---

[74] Such proportions are often indicated in the 1225 south Wiltshire assessment.

[75] Thus if, say, 60 per cent of the draught-animal-owning peasants had one horse, and the remaining 40 per cent was split between those tenants owning one horse and two oxen and those owning one horse and four oxen (a reasonable proportion according to the 1225 south Wiltshire assessment), then the level of oxen overall (at 54.5 per cent) would still be higher than that for horses (45.5 per cent).

[76] E.g., Postan, *Medieval Economy and Society*, pp. 156–8.

Table 28. *Comparison of draught animal heriots over time (from Winchester pipe rolls)*

Year	No. of cart-horses[a]	No. of avers, affers or *jumenta*	No. of oxen	% horses	% horses excluding cart-horses
1210–11	2	6	30	21.1	16.7
1286–7	3	19	28	44.0	40.4
1348–9	60	494	528½	51.2	48.3
1381–2	9	15	21	53.3	41.7

[a] As before, *equi carectarii* or just *equi* (some of these latter were females, i.e., *equae*).

Notes and sources: *The Pipe Roll of the Bishopric of Winchester, 1210–1211*, ed. N. R. Holt (Manchester, 1964); H.R.O. Eccles. 2 159308, 159358, 159388.

affers, etc., are considered, the level of horses in the draught animal heriots for 1381–2 is 41.7 per cent, a fall compared to that on the eve of the Black Death. Nevertheless this decline is probably much less than the degree to which smallholdings dried up after the plague, and there is also the consideration that some of the cart-horses did not necessarily conceal less expensive oxen. The general impression is that, despite the drop in smallholders which may in turn have reduced the proportion of horses employed by the peasantry as a whole, this to a large extent was being counterbalanced by an increase in the range of uses to which horses were being subjected, particularly hauling. The employment of horses may also have been increasing among more substantial tenants, a trend we shall investigate shortly with later material.

Summarizing the evidence examined so far, the inventories, lay subsidy assessments and heriots provide a composite, but nonetheless consistent picture regarding the degree to which horses were employed as draught animals among the peasantry. The inventories show a much lower percentage of peasant draught horses than do the other sources, but much of this is due to the fact that most of the inventories are found in the more ox-oriented west and north of the country. They are also biased towards the major peasant landholders, perhaps because the lord was interested in keeping a greater degree of surveillance on these larger holdings than on smaller ones. On the other hand, small and middling land-holders figure much more prominently in the lay subsidy material, and it was this group which gave the subsidy material its relatively high level of draught horses.[77] Although this high proportion of horses may be somewhat exaggerated in the subsidies, it is to a large degree confirmed by draught animal heriots, which also show a substantial proportion of horses, again due probably to the presence of large numbers of relatively small land-holders. The overall picture one has, then, is of a peasantry where horses for draught were most popular at the low end of the social and economic scale, but much less so among more substantial tenants, a phenomenon seen even in East Anglia. It is difficult to be precise about where the dividing line was between these two groups of tenants, but a holding size of 10–15 acres would seem a likely threshold above which oxen tended to be used much more frequently.[78] In any case, the failure of the horse to penetrate the substantial tenant substratum more completely than it did indicates that, technically, the animal was valued no more by the peasantry than by the demesne and that – probably to the end of the fourteenth century at least – its popularity was based mainly upon its versatility in the hands of smallholders and the like.

What does all this mean in terms of numbers? Using the information supplied by Tables 23, 24 and 27, the percentages of horses among peasant draught animals at about the year 1300 were estimated by region, as shown in Table 29.

It must be emphasized that these figures are only estimates, relying heavily, in many cases, on assumption or even guesswork.[79] For this reason, the figures have been rounded off to the nearest 5 per

---

[77] To these should be added peasants for whom farming played a minor part in their income: that is, smiths, millers, carpenters, weavers, and the like, who would be more likely to have horses, for carrying purposes especially, than oxen.

[78] As indicated by the Cuxham case above in note 70. It is noticeable, too, that ploughing services (often expressly involving oxen) only tended to begin at the half-virgate or virgate levels.

[79] Thus, as an example, the data for East Anglia point to a strongly horse-oriented peasantry. The reasonably accurate Blackbourne Hundred subsidy assessment (see Table 24) indicates that the level of horses among the peasantry here was high – 83.3 per cent. The later and less reliable Essex assessments for Wendon and Nazeing (Table 24) suggest a similar level, as do the only inventories for the region (at Standon, Essex and Coltishall, Norfolk (Table 23)). The Black Death heriots for Suffolk (although based on only two manors) also imply a horse-oriented peasantry, but those for Cambridgeshire and Essex less so (Table 27). The overall impression is that the use of horses was very prevalent in Suffolk and probably Norfolk, but not quite so much in Cambridgeshire and Essex. On this basis, it was decided to downgrade the Suffolk lay subsidy data slightly and accept

Table 29. *Estimated levels of horses among peasant draught animals (by region), c. 1300*

Region	% horses
East Anglia	75
Home Counties	55
The South	45
South-west	20
East Midlands	50
West Midlands	30
The North	40
Overall	45

cent. Altogether they show a trend similar to that for the demesne, with the level of peasant draught horses being highest in the south and east and tailing off markedly towards the north and west, the overall figure for the country as a whole being some 15–20 per cent above that for the demesne (cf. Table 11). Indeed, if the figures in Table 29 are even roughly correct, it indicates that the proportion of horses in the draught stock of all farms – peasant and demesne together – would be of the order of 40 per cent in England at the end of the thirteenth century.[80]

This, however, still leaves the question of what happened afterwards. With the exception of a few of the inventories, none of the material looked at so far covers a period later than the end of the fourteenth century. We are left with a gap of a century or more when the available documentation fails us almost completely, due

a figure of 75 per cent horses for the draught stock of the peasantry of East Anglia as a whole.

The percentages for the other regions were arrived at by a similar process, and the overall figure was calculated by taking all the regional estimates and weighting according to the poll tax method outlined above (pp. 90–1).

[80] Assuming a 1:2 demesne to peasant draught stock ratio (more or less in line with the lay subsidies) and taking the overall level of horses for the peasantry at 45 per cent and for the demesne, 26.7 per cent (as in Table 11 under Sample A), the level of horses among all farming draught animals is:

$((2 \times 45) + (1 \times 26.7))/3 = 38.9$ per cent, or, rounding off, 40 per cent.

If a 1:3 demesne to peasant draught stock ratio is assumed instead, then the overall level is 40.4 per cent, again rounding off to 40 per cent.

to the well-known decline in the quality of manorial records as evidence that occurred from the end of the fourteenth century onward.[81] In order to determine what happened in this period regarding the growth or decline in the peasant use of horses and oxen, we are to a great extent forced to look at later material. This brings with it the danger of making late medieval farming seem more advanced than it really was; but, used with care, early modern evidence can shed much light on medieval conditions. In particular, the tremendous growth in probate material that characterizes the documentation of the sixteenth century is of great help here. Most useful in this regard are probate inventories, which list all the moveable goods of deceased persons. Inventories acted essentially as addenda to wills, their purpose being to ensure that all the goods left by the deceased made their way intact to the rightful heir or heirs. They were usually drawn up by four of the deceased person's friends and neighbours, acting as disinterested parties, and included a wide range of household and farming effects, including all the livestock. Table 30 contains the data relating to draught animals for seventy-six of these inventories, covering the period from 1534 to 1598.[82] These inventories were specially chosen because in each case we are also given some indication of farm size, or at least of its arable component, in the form of sown acres. In this regard, only inventories taken in the months of April, May, June and July could be considered; otherwise the sown acreages given in the inventories were most likely to be incomplete, either because some of the crops had already been harvested (if the inventory were taken in August or September) or had not yet been sown (if taken earlier in the farming year than April).

Altogether horses outnumbered oxen in the sample by a ratio of about 6 to 4 (the percentage of horses was actually 62.1), a considerable advance in the level of horses since the medieval period. However, this result should be qualified in several ways. First, seventy-six inventories can hardly be called a representative sample for the country as a whole. The fact that many counties are not represented at all is a difficulty, particularly as many of these missing counties, such as Worcestershire, come from traditionally ox-oriented

---

[81] E.g., see R. H. Hilton, "The Content and Sources of English Agrarian History before 1500", *Agric. Hist. Rev.*, iii (1955), pp. 5–6, 14–18.

[82] Inventories did not become a legal requirement until 21 Henry VIII and are not truly abundant until the latter part of the century.

areas.[83] Second, all the inventories in Table 30 listed at least one plough (in fact, they were chosen as such in order to give some idea as to the equipment status of the farm). This means that we are necessarily concentrating on self-sufficient farmers, that is, those not having to count on others to help them with their farming.[84] This is not an entirely satisfactory situation, because it leaves out that potentially substantial body of farmers who had part of the equipment and stock needed to cultivate their land, but not all, a deficiency they made up by borrowing, hiring, or cooperating with neighbours. But this type of farmer is very unevenly represented in the inventories, and for consistency's sake it was decided to concentrate on his self-supporting neighbour. Third, as with the medieval peasant inventories, there are some problems with heriots, which may have been excluded from some at least of the probate inventories. It is difficult to assess the effect this had, since the prevailing trend, through much of the later medieval period at least, was to commute these heriots to money payments.[85] Nevertheless, references to draught animals taken as heriots do crop up occasionally in sixteenth-century wills and inventories.[86] Fourth, although the great majority of horses in Table 30 were obviously working animals, a few may have been solely for riding.[87] Finally, not so much of a problem but still worthy of mention, is the fact that many of the inventories may have represented rundown holdings, since many, if not most, of the deceased were old men and women, not having the ability or the compulsion to carry on farming at the level of their prime. This may have affected the proportions of draught animals on the farm, possibly in the favour of horses, since riding and carrying animals would probably have been the last to go.

Although most of these qualifications would seem to indicate a

[83] Even in the sixteenth century oxen easily outnumbered horses on Worcestershire farms, as indicated by the inventories (e.g., Wo.R.O. Ref. 008:7, 1536–43, box 3b, nos. 323, 323a, 326, 327, 351, 362a, etc.).
[84] Although some co-aration may have been practised even among these largely well-to-do farmers. Most of them, however, had sufficient numbers of working stock to fill the plough-teams normally encountered in sixteenth-century England; see pp. 234–5 below.
[85] E.g., see Dyer, *Lords and Peasants in a Changing Society*, pp. 286–7.
[86] As, for example, in the *c.* 1551 inventory of William Brokeman of Wylye (Wiltshire), who had three horses "whereoff on ys taken for the lorde" (Wi.R.O. Arch. Sarum inventories, Wm Brokeman, 1551).
[87] Most likely in the case of some of the geldings.

Table 30. *Draught horses and oxen from probate inventories, 1534–98*

County	No. of inventories	No. of adult horses	No. of oxen	No. of all-horse farms	Avg. size of farm (sown acres)	Range of farm sizes (sown acres)	Range of dates for inventories
Bedfordshire	2	13	2	1	39.0	36–42	1556, 1575
Berkshire	1	3	6	0	22.0	22	1579
Cambridgeshire	1	4	0	1	17.0	17	1576
Cornwall	1	2	8	0	7.5	7½	1579
Dorset	7	22	2	6	22.6	4–50	1575–1579
Durham	3	6	36	0	44.3	20–85	1557 (*bis*), 1565
Hampshire	2	15	0	2	132.5	36–229	1559, 1563
Hertfordshire	3	10	0	3	14.6	9–20	1545, 1548 (*bis*)
Lincolnshire	11	64	55	4	30.6	6–160	1553–1598
Norfolk	7	31	0	7	20.2	9–34	1554–1595
Northamptonshire	2	8	0	2	23.3	9–37½	1573, 1598
Nottinghamshire	8	48	15	4	24.2	10–50	1542–1592
Oxfordshire	8	26	0	8	31.9	11½–55	1550–1587
Suffolk	7	39	0	7	13.9	4–32	1576–1587
Surrey	1	2	0	0	8.0	8	1559
Warwickshire	3	9	1	2	28.7	14–38	1534–1562
Wiltshire	4	15	10	2	72.9	25–142	1560–1576
Yorkshire	4	14	68	0	41.0	35–44	1559–1569
County unknown	1	5	0	1	36.0	36	1587
Total	76	336[a]	205[b]	50[c]			
Overall average					31.3		

bias towards horses in the sample, they are more than balanced by the almost complete omission of the smallholding class, which contributed so much to the high level of horses in medieval times. Even in areas using oxen, the man having only a horse with a cart and harrows is a common enough sight in the probate inventories,[88] and this class could be quite large.[89] Another striking feature of Table 30

Notes to table 30

[a] Includes some foals at Postwick, Norfolk (N.R.O. Inv./3, no. 1), but excludes an unspecified number of cart-horses at South Leigh, Oxfordshire (P.R.O. Probate 2, no. 289).

[b] Includes six "hagge" (haggard or old?) oxen at Kirklington, Yorkshire (*Wills and Inventories . . . of the Archdeaconry of Richmond*, pp. 134–6).

[c] However, two of these farms – at Haxley, Lincolnshire (Li.R.O. Inventories, Box 23, no. 94) and Walsoken, Norfolk (P.R.O. Probate 2, no. 258a) – had yokes.

Notes and sources: Bedfordshire: P.R.O. Probate 2, no. 263; *Elizabethan Inventories* ed. C. E. Freeman (Beds. Hist. Rec. Soc., xxxii, 1952), pp. 102–3; *Berkshire:* Wi.R.O. Dean of Sarum Inventories, Richard Denne, 1579; *Cambridgeshire:* W.Suff.R.O. IC 500/3/1/16; *Cornwall:* Co.R.O. Archd. Cornwall Probate, John Beale, 1579; *Dorset:* Wi.R.O. Dean of Sarum Inventories, Joan Meader, 1575; John Sherwin, 1575; John Tezer, 1575; Edward Hazard, 1576; Robert Squier, 1576; Thomas Marten, 1578; Robert Bartlett, 1579; *Durham: Wills and Inventories . . . of the Northern Counties of England*, ed. J. Raine (Surtees Soc., ii, 1835), pp. 158 (*bis*), 242–3; *Hampshire:* P.R.O. Probate 2, no. 352; Wi.R.O. Archd. Sarum, John Lannam, 1563; *Hertfordshire:* Herts.R.O. ASA 25/7, 63, 77; *Lincolnshire:* P.R.O. Probate 2, no. 277; Li.R.O. Inventories, Box 22, nos. 4, 6, 19; Box 23, nos. 78, 91, 94; Box 54, no. 228; Box 89, nos. 8, 10, 19; *Norfolk:* P.R.O. Probate 2, nos. 258a, 369; N.R.O. Inv./3, nos. 1, 27, 81; Inv./12, nos. 41, 252; *Northamptonshire: Household and Farm Inventories in Oxfordshire, 1550–1590*, ed. M. A. Havinden (Historical Manuscripts Commission, JP10, London, 1965), p. 61; No.R.O. C Wills, no. 153; *Nottinghamshire: Nottinghamshire Household Inventories*, ed. P. A. Kennedy (Thoroton Soc., Rec. Ser., xxii, 1963), pp. 33–4, 48–9, 100, 114–16, 126–8; Notts.R.O. PR SW 22/4b, 7b, 20b; *Oxfordshire:* P.R.O. Probate 2, no. 289; *Household and Farm Inventories in Oxfordshire*, pp. 42, 43–4, 89–90, 170–1, 186–7, 223–6, 228–9; *Suffolk:* N.R.O. Inv./3, nos. 24, 28, 37; E.Suff.R.O. FEI/1/59, 81, 82; W.Suff.R.O. IC 500/3/1/53; *Surrey:* G.L.R.O. DW/PA/5/1559; *Warwickshire:* L.J.R.O. Lichfield Probate Records B/C/11, William Hopkins, 1534; William Stills, 1562; Wo.R.O. Ref. 008:7, 1537–41, box 3a, no. 238; *Wiltshire:* Wi.R.O. Archd. Sarum, Thomas Hurle, 1560; John Martin, 1561; Wi.R.O. Dean of Sarum Inventories, Jerome Head, 1574; Thomas Brunsden, 1576; *Yorkshire: Wills and Inventories . . . of the Archdeaconry of Richmond*, ed. J. Raine, Jr (Surtees Soc., xxvi, 1853), pp. 132–4, 134–6, 222 (*bis*); *County unknown:* N.R.O. Inv./3, no. 11 (Carleton, in Norfolk or Suffolk).

[88] For example, Walter Payge of North Piddle, Worcestershire (1545), Wo.R.O. Ref. 008:7, 1545, box 7a, no. 49.

[89] Particularly in areas of some industrialization, as in south Staffordshire in the late sixteenth century, where two-thirds of those who left inventories owned at least one horse while only 38 per cent owned oxen. P. Frost, "Yeomen and Metalsmiths: Livestock in the Dual Economy in South Staffordshire 1560–1720", *Agric. Hist. Rev.*, xxix (1981), p. 37.

is the number of all-horse farms indicated. Altogether they comprise nearly two-thirds of the sample, and although this proportion may be inflated by the under-representation of ox-oriented areas, the number is still very significant. The geographical spread of these all-horse farms was also very wide ranging, being found as far west as Dorset and as far north as Nottinghamshire. The sheer number of these all-horse farms denotes a significant shift since medieval times. Since the average sown acreage for these sixteenth-century farms was 31.3 acres (and the median 25.4 acres), we are talking of a mean farm size probably approaching 50 acres with fallow included, somewhat in excess of the typical medieval virgate. In the lay subsidies, farms of this size (probably employing at least 3–5 draught animals; see Table 26) were – in the main – still employing significant levels of oxen, but, as we can see from the probate inventories, the majority of them were now using nothing but horses.[90] One is also aware from the inventories that there was a growing dichotomy between those areas converting solely to horses and those maintaining, and perhaps even intensifying, the use of oxen; all-horse farms were found more to the south and east, farms using oxen to the north and west.

Much of this polarization was obviously taking place during the period of the inventories,[91] but some must have occurred before. The problem again is proof. Probate inventories before the sixteenth century are a rare commodity for all but the most influential of people. Some do exist for more ordinary farmers in the late fifteenth century, though. Twenty-two of these, found in a collection of inventories from the Prerogative Court of Canterbury, are contained in Table 31, arranged in order of county.

Again, all these farms had ploughs or at least an arable acreage large enough to require ploughs. The horses may have included a number of riding animals, but none was specified as such. Overall, it appears that horses were once more in a majority (they comprised 54.9 per cent of the draught animals in the sample), even though

---

[90] Although two of these all-horse farms, while not having oxen, did admittedly have some yokes; see notes for Table 30 above.

[91] For example, while inventories for Bedfordshire in the early seventeenth century show the farmers of the county to be using only horses for draught, wills from a century earlier (that is, the 1530s) show oxen to be still in use in some parts of the county at least. *Jacobean Household Inventories*, ed. F. G. Emmison (Beds. Hist. Rec. Soc., xx, 1938), pp. 50ff.; B.R.O. ABP/R 3, esp. will nos. 115 and 195.

Table 31. *Draught horses and oxen from late fifteenth-century inventories*

Place	Name	Year of inventory	No. of adult horses	No. of oxen
1. Barton-in-the-Clay, Bedfordshire	Jacob Woodward, maltman	1497	0	4
2. Buckland, Berkshire	Wm. Sclatter	1494	4	6
3. Bassingbourn, Cambridgeshire	Ric. Hychen, yeoman	1494–5	5	0
4. Newton St James (nr Wisbech), Cambridgeshire	John Cooke	1499	4	0
5. Stalbridge, Dorset	John Davye	1496	8	6
6. Wormingford, Essex	Thomas Bowden[a]	1491	5	0
7. Kirby le Soken, Essex	John Sadler	1493	6	8
8. Chipping Campden, Gloucestershire	Wm. Bradway	1488	2	8
9. Kingsley, Hampshire	Henry at Lode	1494	15	2
10. Winchester, Hampshire	Edith Boland	1500	7	0
11. Long Marston, Hertfordshire	Wm. Puttenham	1492	5	13
12. Buntingford, Hertfordshire	Thom. Gooderyche	1500	6	0
13. East Peckham, Kent	Thom. Caysar, yeoman	1491	2	6
14. Watlington, Norfolk	Hugh Schuldham, esq.	1499	12	5
15. Alvescot, Oxfordshire	John Bonde	1499	6	0
16. Boxford, Suffolk	Walter Coopar	1495	3	0
17. Slaugham, Sussex	Wm. Covert, gent.	1494	6	7
18. Welford and Wolfhamcote, Warwickshire	Ric. Makrings	1474	7	6
19. Barton (on the Heath?), Warwickshire	Roger Eritage	1495	6	16
20. Westbury, Wiltshire	Edmund Leversage	1496	1	8
21. Southwark and Stepney, Surrey and Middlesex	John Bowell	1495	7	7
22. "Hawkyton", dioc. of Ely (Hauxton, Cambridgeshire?)	John Cosyn, husbandman	1498–9	7	0
Total			124[b]	102[c]

[a] Katherine Bowden (Thomas's wife?) left a similar inventory in the following year (P.R.O. Probate 2, no. 54).
[b] Includes some colts of Henry at Lode.
[c] Includes 10 "lean" oxen, but excludes a "fatt oxe" (belonging to Edmund Leversage).

Notes and sources: Sources in order as in table: P.R.O. Probate 2, nos. 128, 455, 86, 161, 458, 45, 64, 21, 110, 168, 52, 709, 47, 159, 151, 94, 72, 693, 457, 110, 91, 459.

most of the farms were very substantial ones[92] of the type that would have found it economical to use oxen in an earlier age.[93] Again a feature of the table is the number of farms that only used horses – eight in all – although the proportion, just over a third, was less than that noted for the sixteenth-century inventories. Some of these all-horse farms were found as far afield as Winchester in Hampshire or Alvescot in west Oxfordshire. The overall impression is of an intermediate stage, with many areas in the process of converting vigorously to horses. It should be mentioned, however, that all the inventories in Table 31 were drawn from the relatively horse-oriented south of the country, since the PCC courts did not normally prove wills in the north. This may have created a bias in favour of the level of all-horse farms and of horses overall in the sample. Nevertheless, the impression of an intermediate stage is still strong and confirms the trend already noted for the demesne that there was a growing polarization in the use of horses and oxen from region to region. It seems, in short, that the fifteenth century was a period of economic rationalization, with some farms going completely to horses and others bolstering the use of oxen through a reversion to ox-hauling. This rationalization continued into the sixteenth century, along with a gradual spread in the use of horses overall,[94] which eventually put the beast in a solidly dominant position as far as draught work was concerned.

b) THE EMPLOYMENT OF PEASANT HORSES AND OXEN, 1200–1500

We have, then, concerning the use of horses, two main periods of growth to consider in the period under discussion. The first, covering the thirteenth century and much of the fourteenth, was of a rather amorphous expansion in the employment of horses, for both peasant and demesne farmers.[95] This varied in degree from region to region but had much the same characteristic everywhere, in that the tendency to employ horses seems to have been stronger in the

---

[92] The PCC courts generally only proved wills of people with land in more than one diocese, so in the main we are dealing with very well-to-do farmers.

[93] See Langdon, "Economics of Horses and Oxen", p. 40.

[94] Generally more farms seem to have gone to all-horse farming rather than to have reverted to oxen.

[95] E.g., see pp. 87, 94–6, 202–3 above.

smallholding sector and weaker among more substantial tenants.[96] The second phase of growth – starting essentially in the fifteenth century – was of a more diverse nature – involving a much wider adoption of the horse among substantial farmers, or failing that, a reorganization based on a more intensive use of oxen. This difference in choices began to set up the regional variation between horse- and ox-using areas so notable in the sixteenth century and afterwards.

How does this picture square with what we know about practice over the period, particularly as it applies to peasant farming? Again, we are faced with problems of documentation, the key one being that there is no one source that adequately covers the whole period. Surveys and extents, for instance, are excellent for supplying details about peasant farming practice, but they stop effectively in the fourteenth century and, in fact, are really only useful for the thirteenth. Otherwise, we have to make do with a combination of court rolls, accounts and other miscellaneous records.

Nevertheless, some sort of picture can be built up. As we have just intimated, surveys and extents are the best for supplying comprehensive views as to how peasants employed their draught animals. These are revealed through the passages in the surveys relating to peasant labour services, which are often minutely detailed so that lord and peasant were under no illusion as to the amount and type of work actually owed. For example, Peter, son of Margaret, a virgate holder at Butleigh in Somerset, c. 1235–40, is recorded as having to appear at the lord's plough-boons with as many oxen as he had, and also to harrow at the same boons with his horse; he had also to carry hay to Glastonbury by pack-horse, or by cart (*carecta*; spelled here as *careta*) and horse if he had one; he had also to supply a load of hay in a *carrus* to the court at Butleigh, or with a cart and horse, or by pack-horse; and so on and so on.[97] A study of even a small number of extents and surveys with these sorts of references can yield a substantial body of evidence. However, the surveys and extents have at least one serious limitation. Because they are dealing essentially with custom, it is not always evident that the details given are actually referring to contemporary practice.

[96] See pp. 193–6 above.
[97] *Rentalia et custumaria Michaelis de Ambresbury, 1235–1252, et Rogeri de Ford, 1252–1261, abbatis monasterii beatiae Mariae Glastoniae*, ed. C. J. Elton (Somerset Rec. Soc., v, 1891), p. 7.

They may, for instance, be recalling a system of practice from an earlier survey, one which may have been long obsolete, particularly in those cases where a money payment was sought rather than the actual performance of the service itself.[98] As a result, terms used in the surveys are often more archaic than those found in other documents, such as accounts and court rolls, particularly, as we shall see, in relation to vehicle types. Nevertheless, in most cases, it does appear that the practices referred to were those currently in use. An obvious example is recorded for Pilton in Somerset in 1260, where Robert Hostarius, a half-virgate holder, was charged with carrying hay and corn for six days with a cart (*carecta*; invariably horse-hauled in the surveys – see pp. 246–7 below); the custumal, however, goes on to comment that "the jurors say that Simon, Robert's predecessor, was accustomed to find three oxen and a half *plaustrum*", indicating that Robert had changed his mode of hauling.[99] Such a reference has a very contemporary ring to it and shows that lords were interested in keeping their surveys up-to-date. This is also reinforced by the fact that surveys in the thirteenth century, in particular, usually appear in a very much more detailed and expanded form than those in the twelfth century.[100] Much of this extra detail may have been new, particularly as many lords were increasing the burden of labour services on their tenants.[101]

Altogether the surveys and extents for over 330 manors were examined. These came from 31 different sources, most of them available in print.[102] The great majority of these surveys were from the thirteenth century, although some were from the fourteenth, usually the early part. Only two were from the fifteenth century,[103]

---

[98] As for the ploughing, harrowing and carrying services listed in a fifteenth-century survey for Bilsington Priory in Kent. *The Cartulary and Terrier of the Priory of Bilsington*, ed. N. Neilson (British Academy Records of Social and Economic History, viii, London, 1928), pp. 148, 153, 154, 159, etc.

[99] *Rentalia et custumaria . . . Glastoniae*, p. 210.

[100] See, for example, the surveys and extents over time for Ramsey Abbey and the bishopric of Worcester (*Cartularium monastarii de Rameseia*; *Red Book of Worcester*).

[101] Miller and Hatcher, *Medieval England: Rural Society and Economic Change*, pp. 125–6.

[102] The majority of these sources is given in Langdon, "Horse Hauling", table 3 (pp. 56–7).

[103] That is, for Bilsington (Kent) and Ashton-under-Lyne (Lancashire): *Cartulary and Terrier of the Priory of Bilsington*; *Three Lancashire Documents of the Fourteenth and Fifteenth Century*, ed. J. Harland (Chetham Soc., lxxiv, 1868).

both supplying very little useful information. There tended to be rather more surveys for the south than the north, and those for the former were also inclined to yield the better information.

Concerning the activity of ploughing, the animals in the peasants' teams were often specified. Only in the case of three villages in central and north-west Norfolk, however, was it indicated that peasants used only horses for ploughing.[104] On the other hand, references mentioning only oxen or at least draught cattle for ploughing – as in the case of Peter of Butleigh above – are much more numerous; altogether 36 manors displayed some sign of it.[105] Most of these references came from the south-west and west of the country, although some of the more easterly counties – Berkshire, Cambridgeshire and particularly Sussex – were also represented. On five manors – two in Norfolk and one each in Cambridgeshire, Berkshire and Wiltshire – it is stated that peasants could use horses or oxen for ploughing or both,[106] and another two cases implied the

[104] Gressenhall (1282), Binham (t. Edward II) and Brancaster (1239 & 1240). N.R.O. 21187; Brit. Lib. Cott. MS Claud. D. XIII, fos. 8, 8v, 9, etc.; *Cartularium monasterii de Rameseia*, i, p. 419. I am deeply indebted to Dr J. Williamson for supplying me with transcripts of the Gressenhall and Binham material.

[105] That is, Upton, Combe and Ashbury, Berkshire; Gransden, Cambridgeshire; Sturminster Newton and Barton (Ash, in Marnhull?), Dorset; Henbury-in-Salt-Marsh and Shirehampton, Gloucestershire; Holway, Stoke sub Hamdon, Dundon, Butleigh, Street, Berrow, Wrington, Glastonbury, East Pennard, Doulting, Shapwick, Ashcot, Walton, High Ham, Baltonsborough, Meare, Pilton and Mells, Somerset; Preston, Bishopstone, Denton and Marley (in Battle), Sussex; Ogbourne St Andrew, Badbury, Winterbourne Monkton, Grittleton, Nettleton and Edmiston, Wiltshire. Sources (not in order as given above): *Accounts and Surveys of the Wiltshire Lands of Adam de Stratton*, ed. M. W. Farr (Wilts. Arch. Soc. Rec. Ser., xiv, 1959), pp. 19–20; *Red Book of Worcester*, pp. 385, 393; Brit. Lib. Cott. MS Claud. C. XI, fo. 150v; *The Medieval Customs of the Manors of Taunton and Bradford on Tone*, ed. T. J. Hunt (Somerset Rec. Soc., lxvi, 1962), p. 3; *Rentalia et Custumaria . . . Glastoniae*, pp. 7, 12, 45, 52, 58, 61, 65, 68, 72–8, 84 and 94, 96–100, 120–4 and 182–91, 125, 129 and 132, 149, 152–3, 156–8, 163, 166, 197, 204, 210–12, 220 and 225; *Thirteen Custumals of the Sussex Manors of the Bishop of Chichester and other Documents*, ed. W. D. Peckham (Sussex Rec. Soc., xxxi, 1925), pp. 79 and 81, 89, 101; *Select Documents of the English Lands of the Abbey of Bec*, ed. M. Chibnall (Camden Third Series, lxxiii, 1951), pp. 37, 41; *Two Registers Formerly Belonging to the Family of Beauchamp of Hatch*, ed. H. C. Maxwell-Lyte (Somerset Rec. Soc., xxxv, 1920), pp. 3, 50; *Custumals of Battle Abbey in the Reigns of Edward I and Edward II (1283–1312)*, ed. S. R. Scargill-Bird (Camden New Series, xli, 1887), p. 15.
 The dates for these references range from *c.* 1230 to 1299.

[106] That is, Ditton, Cambridgeshire (1251); Walpole, Norfolk (1251); Walton, Norfolk (1251); Brightwalton, Berkshire (1283–4); Bromham, Wiltshire (t.

The peasantry: 1200–1500

same in Essex and Huntingdonshire.[107] Only in one case – Ditton (Cambridgeshire) – was a mixed team virtually certain; the other six were ambiguous and could indicate either mixed teams or separate teams of horses and oxen. These cases of uncertainty as to the type of animal the peasant was likely to have for his ploughing services are reinforced by the much more frequent instances where the surveys mention the peasant's plough-team but studiously avoid specifying the type of animal in it. In this case, the survey will say something like "he [the peasant] will plough with as many animals as he has in his plough (or plough-team)".[108] This kind of reference is found in surveys all over the country, but is especially a feature of those covering the south-east.[109] Although this may have been nothing more than a convention of the area, the implication is that the peasant use of both horses and oxen for ploughing was a common sight in the region and the scribes were simply playing safe and using the more general form. That this interpretation is the correct one would seem probable in view of the fact that the scribes generally had no hesitation in specifying horses for harrowing, where the chance of contradiction was slight.[110]

To this survey material can be added a small amount of data from other sources. Thus the Wakefield court rolls show oxen or other ploughing cattle being employed in a number of Yorkshire villages in the late thirteenth and early fourteenth centuries, while oxen were also recorded for ploughing at Chalgrave (Bedfordshire) in 1293 and an ox and a cow for the same in Kent in 1259. On the other

high> Edw. I). Brit. Lib. Cott. MS Claud. C. XI, fos. 116, 193v and 194v, 200 and 201; *Custumals of Battle Abbey*, pp. 60, 78.

[107] That is, at Chingford, Essex, in 1222, where each half-virgate tenant owed harrowing services if he had a horse outside the plough-team (. . . *si equum habeat extra carucam*; *Domesday of St. Paul's of the Year 1222*, p. 87). Similarly at Broughton (Huntingdonshire) in 1252 tenants owed charity bread according to how many animals they had in their plough-teams, excepting their horses. *Cartularium monasterii de Rameseia*, i, p. 331.

[108] This could take several forms: e.g., *Et debet ii precarias ad semen hyemale ad custum proprium cum animalibus quot habuerit in caruca sua propria* (Kempsey, Worcester, 1299; *Red Book of Worcestershire*, i, p. 65), or *Arabit ter per annum, secundum quot habet averia ad carucam* (Crawley, Bedfordshire, prob. *c.* 1240; *Cartularium monasterii de Rameseia*, i, p. 441).

[109] For example, in the bishopric of Ely survey of 1251 (Brit. Lib. Cott. MS. Claud. C. XI, fos. 116–116v, 117v, 171, 172, 178, etc.); see also *Cartularium monasterii de Rameseia*, i, pp. 282, 322, 335, 343, 365, 366, 368, etc.; *Select Documents of . . . the Abbey of Bec*, pp. 69, 70, 92, 93, 95, 100, 119.

[110] See pp. 220–1 below.

hand, there are at least two references to horses being seized from peasant plough-teams at "Hussey" (Bedfordshire) and Hipper-holme (Yorkshire) in 1262 and 1297, and ploughing horses also figure in disputes at Alton, Hampshire, in 1332 and Polstead, Suffolk, in 1292, perhaps as part of mixed teams or perhaps alone. Some mixed teams at least were clearly evident. Thus, a team of two horses and four oxen was distrained from a well-to-do peasant at Thorpe Satchville (Leicestershire) in 1284, while horses and oxen together in a plough-team are indicated in a tragic case from Bretby, Derbyshire, in 1249, where a man accidently killed his son while both of them were out ploughing in the fields.[111]

All these references date from the thirteenth or early fourteenth century. It seems, then, that the peasant use of horses and oxen for ploughing at this time had some similarities with that on the demesne. It is to be noted that the only region where horses were indicated as the sole ploughing animal on peasant farms, that is, Norfolk, was also one of the earliest all-horse areas for demesnes (see Figure 23). On the other hand, the peasant use of oxen alone for ploughing would seem to be a feature of much of the south-west and west and probably the north, just as it was for the demesne. Further east, though, the situation becomes more unsettled, with peasants seemingly using horses and oxen together in mixed or as separate horse and ox plough-teams. From the surveys, it seems that this partial turnover of peasant ploughing to horses might well have had a distribution similar to that for demesne mixed teams (Figures 25 and 26). Thus, we should not be surprised when we find peasant plough-oxen and plough-horses mentioned in conjunction as far west and north as Wiltshire and Derbyshire.

However, it should be pointed out that, with the survey material in particular, we are dealing mainly with more substantial tenants, that is, half-virgaters and above, since lesser tenants were much less likely to owe ploughing services.[112] In this regard, the survey

[111] *Court Rolls of the Manor of Wakefield*, i, p. 284; ii, p. 72; iv, p. xiii; *Court Roll of Chalgrave Manor 1278–1313*, ed. M. K. Dale (Beds. Hist. Rec. Soc., xxviii, 1948), p. 31; Richardson, "The Medieval Plough-team", p. 290n; *Court Rolls of the Manor of Wakefield*, i, p. 297; Homans, *English Villagers of the Thirteenth Century*, pp. 78, 79; R. H. Hilton, "Medieval Agrarian History", in *Victoria County Histories, Leicestershire*, ii (London, 1954), p. 167; *Calendar of Inquisitions Miscellaneous*, i, p. 553.
[112] Although there were some exceptions. For example, tenants holding five acres of arable land at Wrington and High Ham, Somerset, were expected to attend

material makes the same sort of conclusion already indicated by the
lay subsidy returns, inventories, and heriots: namely that the introduction of the horse does not seem to have been any more advanced
among the substantial tenantry than it was on the demesne.[113] The
prevalence of all-horse ploughing and all-ox ploughing seems to
have been the same in both cases, as was the tendency to use a combination of horses and oxen, although in the case of the peasantry it
is difficult to say whether this was predominantly in the form of
mixed teams or not.

The situation as regards smallholders was probably very different. The difficulties in keeping two types of draught animals on
a smallholding would have encouraged their peasant owners to
plump entirely for one or the other, almost certainly horses because
of their versatility and the fact that the costs for them need not have
been substantially greater than those for oxen.[114] As a result, this
group would have used only horses for ploughing. Although some
hard evidence for this is supplied by studies such as that for
Cuxham,[115] the surveys comment very little on the ploughing
potential of this smallholding group. The fact that many of them did
plough with their horses can only be implied from the massive
superiority of horses among the peasantry in such counties as
Bedfordshire and Suffolk, where holding fragmentation was often
known to be severe.

What about the latter part of our period? Specific references to
the makeup of the peasant plough-team are meagre after the Black
Death. Ploughs surrendered complete with yokes figure among the
principalia listed for Worcestershire peasants in the late fourteenth
and early fifteenth century,[116] indicating the continued use of oxen
as ploughing animals there, a fact of little surprise since oxen were
still the dominant draught animal in the county even in the sixteenth
century.[117] An interesting case is cited in an account for Wetwang in
the Yorkshire Wolds in 1373–4, where the customary tenantry

ploughing boons with their oxen. *Rentalia et custumaria . . . Glastoniae*, pp. 78,
163; see also p. 225 below.
[113] That is, see pp. 203–4 above.
[114] Langdon, "Economics of Horses and Oxen", pp. 37–40.
[115] *Ibid.*
[116] R. K. Field, "Worcestershire Peasant Buildings, Household Goods and Farming
Equipment in the Later Middle Ages", *Medieval Archaeology*, ix (1965), pp.
141–5.
[117] See note 83 above.

showed up for a winter ploughing service with 52 horses and 13 ploughs.[118] The peasantry here were obviously accustomed to ploughing with four-horse teams, but it should also be noted that the demesne too used only horses.[119] More significant is the reference to a virgate of land being transferred in Wistow (Huntingdonshire) in 1429, complete with a plough and "apparatus" for three horses.[120] The evidence of a three-horse peasant plough here contrasts with the demesne ploughs evident at Wistow, which used oxen well into the fifteenth century.[121] This seems to indicate that the "rationalization" of going completely to horses occurred first among the peasantry here, although how recent the change was is difficult to judge. Although outnumbered by horses, oxen were amply evident among peasant goods in the 1290 lay subsidy assessment for the village, and Wistow virgate holders in 1252 needed to pay a fine to sell them.[122] It may be basing too much on one piece of evidence, but it does seem that Wistow villagers were making the changeover to all-horse farming by at least the beginning of the fifteenth century. Certainly, by the sixteenth century, Huntingdonshire was a county where horses dominated almost totally.[123]

Finally, one thing that is clear from the evidence looked at in this study is that peasants were not as choosy in their choice of plough animals as the demesne. Cows and even a heifer were mentioned as ploughing beasts,[124] while on two manors an *averium bovinum* was

[118] *Et in sustentatione .Lij. equorum custumariorum euntium ad .xiij. carucas in yemale . . .* ; P.R.O. S.C. 6 1144/10.

[119] See p. 104 above.

[120] J. A. Raftis, *Tenure and Mobility* (Toronto, 1964), pp. 73, 237. The virgate at Wistow apparently contained thirty acres (*Cartularium monasterii de Rameseia*, iii, p. 208).

[121] That is, as late as 1466. Raftis, *Ramsey Abbey*, p. 133.

[122] *Early Huntingdonshire Lay Subsidy Rolls*, ed. J. A. Raftis and M. P. Hogan (Toronto, 1976), pp. 31–4; *Cartularium monasterii de Rameseia*, i, p. 358.

[123] As indicated by wills; e.g., see Hunts.R.O. Archdeaconry Court of Huntingdonshire Reg. Copy Wills, vi, 1538–1541, fos. 95, 185v, 205, 234v, 241 (all good examples of all-horse farms).

[124] Cows as peasant plough animals were indicated at Upton and Brightwalton, Berkshire, in 1271 and 1283–4 respectively and in Kent in 1259, while a heifer was harnessed to a plough in Rastrick (Yorkshire) in 1297: *Accounts and Surveys . . . of Adam de Stratton*, pp. 19–20; *Custumals of Battle Abbey*, p. 60; Richardson, "The Medieval Plough-team", p. 290n; *Court Rolls of the Manor of Wakefield*, ii, p. 7.

specified, implying that not only oxen, but also bulls, cows, or even young steers and heifers, would be suitable.[125]

Peasants, however, do not seem to have applied this flexibility to harrowing, where horses were employed almost exclusively. Specific references to horses harrowing were found in almost every county covered by the extent and survey material.[126] References to ox harrowing were very few and far between. For example, among a series of *principalia* lists for Ombersley (Worcestershire) in the late fourteenth to early fifteenth century, 52 harrows were recorded in 85 lists. Of these 52 harrows, 39 were described as horse harrows, 12 simply as harrows, and only one as an ox harrow.[127] This last was found on the lands of a substantial tenant, holding over a virgate, who also had a horse harrow. Sixteenth-century inventories indicate a rather greater incidence of ox harrows than this,[128] but at no time do they become a serious challenge to horse harrowing.

One thing evident from the surveys is that harrowing services were demanded by the lord every bit as often as ploughing services, and in fact harrowing as a service tended to reach further down into the social order than did ploughing. Thus it was not uncommon to find tenants who did not owe ploughing services, presumably because they did not have the necessary stock and equipment, but were still expected to harrow with their horses.[129] The same is even

---

[125] That is, at Ogbourne St Andrew (Wiltshire) and Combe (Berkshire). *Select Documents . . . of the Abbey of Bec*, pp. 37, 41.

[126] E.g., *Domesday of St. Paul's of the Year 1222*, pp. 48, 51, 56; *Select Documents . . . of the Abbey of Bec*, pp. 46, 58, 69, 93, 97, 110; *Cartularium monasterii de Rameseia*, i, p. 369; ii, pp. 28, 38; Brit. Lib. Cott. MS Claud. C. XI, fos. 83v, 98v, 153v, 157, 158, 159, 159v, 161, 162v, 178, etc.; *Custumals of Battle Abbey*, pp. 19–20, 39, 53, 66, 150; *Red Book of Worcester*, ii, pp. 158, 176; iii, p. 265; iv, p. 358; *Rentalia et custumaria . . . Glastoniae*, pp. 7, 12, 13, 14, 37, 45, 81, 97, 104, 108, etc.; *Thirteen Custumals . . . of the Bishop of Chichester*, pp. 28, 35, 46, 64, 75–6, 76, 84, 101, etc.; *Bishop Hatfield's Survey*, ed. W. Greenwell (Surtees Soc., xxxii, 1856), pp. 8, 161.

[127] From unpublished work on the Ombersley court rolls in the Worcestershire Record Office (Ref. 705:56 BA 3910) by Gabriele Scardellato, to whom the author is greatly indebted for permission to quote these findings.

[128] E.g., Wo.R.O. Ref. 008:7, 1545, box 7a, nos. 25, 40, 47 (Worcestershire inventories); *Wills and Inventories . . . of the Northern Counties of England*, pp. 162, 240, 281, 341, 350, 365, 436; *Wills and Inventories . . . of the Archdeaconry of Richmond*, p. 101. See also *Fitzherbert*, p. 24, for more on ox harrowing in general.

[129] For example, David Tayle of Street (Somerset) in 1238–9, who held ten acres of arable but did not owe ploughing services, was nonetheless expected to harrow if

observed with more substantial tenants, because, if for some reason they had no ploughing stock, they were still expected to harrow with their horses.[130] The implication is that it was by no means unusual for peasants to have horses for harrowing, but no other draught animals for ploughing.[131]

Peasant hauling seems to have taken on much the same characteristic as demesne hauling. The most salient feature, up to about 1300, was a substantial increase in horse hauling. Direct references to peasant horses engaged in hauling occurred on at least forty manors in the survey and extent material, a typical example being that at Crawley (Hampshire), *c.* 1280, where among the services of Robert at Mere, a half-virgate tenant, it is stated that he ought to carry hay *cum equo et carecta*.[132] For all but one of these forty

he had a horse, for which he was quit of two handworks (*handaynis*). *Rentalia et custumaria . . . Glastoniae*, p. 14.
[130] Thus at Shapwick in Somerset (*c.* 1235–40) it was specified that virgate holders ought to harrow whether they had oxen (for the plough) or not. *Ibid.*, p. 148. For other similar examples see *ibid.*, p. 45; Brit. Lib. Cott. MS Claud. C. XI, fos. 83v, 161, 162v; *A Terrier of Fleet Lincolnshire*, ed. N. Neilson (British Academy Records of Social and Economic History, iv, London, 1920), pp. 7, 13.
[131] The surveys most commonly indicate that only one horse pulled the harrow, as at Walpole (Norfolk) in 1251, where it was specified of a number of tenants that, when performing ploughing services, each was to have his plough followed by a single horse and harrow (. . . *et unusquisque habebit equum suum cum hercia et homine ad herciandum immediate post carucam suam dum aret*; Brit. Lib. Cott. MS Claud. C. XI, fo. 193v; see also fo. 194v). Occasionally, though, it is mentioned that a peasant or peasants had to harrow with two horses, as at Rattlesden, Suffolk, in 1251 and at Appledram, Sussex, t. Edw. I (*ibid.*, fo. 279; *Custumals of Battle Abbey*, p. 53). Whether this meant a single harrow drawn by two animals or two separate harrows drawn by a single animal each is not clear, but the latter was probably more likely.
[132] Gras and Gras, p. 232. Other references to horses hauling are as follows: *Cartularium monasterii de Rameseia*, i, pp. 289–90, 324, 335, 371–2, 488; Brit. Lib. Cott. MS Claud. C. XI, fos. 32, 36v, 39v, 45v, 47v, 56, 57v, 66v, 83, 100, 112, 112v, 122, 122v–123, 146, 146v, 150, 152v, 153, 169v, 172v, 178, 193v, 195 (*bis*), 195v, 200, 201v (*ter*), 211, 211v, 215v, 229 (*bis*), 245, 256; Brit. Lib. Cott. MS Claud. D. XIII, fos. 8vff. (I am indebted to J. Williamson for this reference); *Historia et cartularium monasterii Sancti Petri Gloucestriae*, iii, pp. 116, 124, 159–60, 167; *Extents of the Prebends of York*, p. 38; *Select Documents . . . of the Abbey of Bec*, p. 47. Although the majority of manors to which these references relate are found in the south and east of the country, some are located further west and north, the counties and numbers of manors in each (given in brackets) being Cambridgeshire (11), Essex (2), Gloucestershire (4), Hampshire (2), Hertfordshire (2), Huntingdonshire (6), Norfolk (8), Somerset (3), Wiltshire (1) and Yorkshire (1).

manors,[133] the horse hauling was associated with carts (*carectae*), as indicated in the Crawley example. Some idea of the extent and spread of horse hauling can thus be indicated by the number of carts about. An analysis of vehicle terms in the survey (see Table 33 below) indicates that on just over 70 per cent of manors in the first half of the thirteenth century the peasants had *carectae* or carts, a figure rising to over 85 per cent in the second half of the century. The thirteenth century was thus clearly an important period for the continued rise of horse hauling. We have already indicated how horse hauling first became frequent in England in the twelfth century,[134] and the survey evidence shows how these initial beginnings were consolidated in the following century. It appears in fact that, as on the demesne, at least 75 per cent of peasant hauling was performed by horses by the start of the fourteenth century.[135] Nevertheless, again as on the demesne, ox hauling among the peasantry was still retained in many areas. For example, at Doulting (Somerset), *c.* 1235–40, the widow Sedburgha, holding one and three-quarter virgates, was required to find *j carrum et vj boves* to carry the lord's hay and corn,[136] and many other similar references could be cited.[137] These references, however, were very much circumscribed geographically, being limited – in the survey material – to Sussex and the western counties of Somerset, Dorset, Gloucestershire and Wiltshire.[138] As with horse hauling, ox hauling was very directly connected with certain types of vehicles, in particular the

[133] I.e., Monxton, Hampshire (*Select Documents . . . of the Abbey of Bec*, p. 47), where the vehicle indicated was a *quadriga*.
[134] Pp. 59–60 above.
[135] Langdon, "Horse Hauling", pp. 55–8. Again, the figures were corrected for uneven data distribution across regions.
[136] *Rentalia et custumaria . . . Glastoniae*, p. 129.
[137] Representing twenty-one manors in all (excluding Doulting): *Select Documents . . . of the Abbey of Bec*, p. 85; *Custumals of Battle Abbey*, pp. 4–6, 14, 20, 28–9; *Rentalia et custumaria . . . Glastoniae*, pp. 77, 82, 86, 140, 210, 216, 220–1; *Thirteen Custumals . . . of the Bishop of Chichester*, pp. 8, 16–17, 47, 57, 61, 88, 101, 107, 111; *Two Registers Formerly Belonging to the Family of Beauchamp of Hatch*, pp. 5, 8, 16; *Historia et cartularium monasterii Sancti Petri Gloucestriae*, iii, p. 143; *The Medieval Customs of the Manors of Taunton and Bradford on Tone*, pp. 4, 17–18, 22; *Custumals of the Sussex Manors of the Archbishops of Canterbury*, ed. B. C. Redwood and A. E. Wilson (Sussex Rec. Soc., lvii, 1958), p. 89.
[138] Numbers of manors by county: Sussex (11), Somerset (8), Dorset (1), Gloucestershire (1), Wiltshire (1).

plaustrum, carrus and *curtana*. Except for one ambiguous case,[139] these vehicles were always hauled by oxen in the surveys,[140] just as carts were always hauled by horses.[141] Altogether peasant *plaustra, carri* and *curtanae* were found on just over 50 per cent of manors in the first half of the thirteenth century, declining to just over 20 per cent in the second half.[142] The latter figure is again similar to that found for these vehicles in the 1250–1320 demesne account sample. Altogether it denotes a significant loss of popularity in ox hauling over the thirteenth century, which can be seen in individual cases, such as that for Robert Hostarius already cited.

On the other hand, as with the demesne, horse hauling obviously reached very high levels among the peasantry in the later thirteenth century. Whether it declined after this – as it seems to have done on the demesne (see p. 157 above) – is difficult to say given the unsatisfactory nature of the post-1350 survey material. Court rolls for the late fourteenth century show ox-hauled *plaustra* in counties such as Durham and Worcestershire, but carts still dominated even here.[143] It is likely that, as with the demesne, any major reversion to ox hauling on peasant farms did not occur until the fifteenth century, but that it did in some counties is almost certain.[144]

The size of the team indicated in the surveys for the various types

---

[139] At Sturminster Newton (Dorset), *c.* 1235–40, Robert de la Rode, holding a virgate, was to *summagiare cum equo suo et carro suo*; it is unclear here whether the horse is involved as a pack-animal (*summagiare*) or in hauling the *carrus*. *Rentalia et custumaria . . . Glastoniae*, p. 85.

[140] See also pp. 247–9 below.

[141] That is, where the original Latin is available. Some of the English translations of the surveys show "carts" as being hauled by oxen (e.g., *Custumals of the Sussex Manors of the Archbishops of Canterbury*, p. 89), but it is likely that in most cases this is a mistranslation of *carrus* or *carra*.

[142] See Langdon, "Horse Hauling", table 3 (p. 56).

[143] The Durham halmote rolls for the late fourteenth century mention carts (*carectae*) eight times and *plaustra* three times (*Halmota Prioratus Dunelmensis*, pp. 33, 87, 151 (*ter*), 165, 168 (*bis*), 174, 178, 179). Similarly Field's *principalia* lists for Worcestershire peasants in the late fourteenth to early fifteenth century mention carts fourteen times and *plaustra* nine times (Field, "Worcestershire Peasant Buildings", pp. 137–45; Field translates *plaustrum* as "wagon").

[144] As noted in Durham, where sixteenth-century probate inventories show that virtually all vehicles in the county were ox-hauled at this time. Langdon, thesis, p. 272. In other counties, however, it is likely that the proportion of hauling by horses was continuing to rise (as indicated, for example, by the rising level of cart-horses among the heriots of the bishopric of Winchester shown on pp. 202–3 above), another reflection of the polarizing effect in the employment of horses and oxen increasingly evident in the later middle ages.

of peasant ox-hauled vehicles – *carri, plaustra*, etc. – ranged from two to eight oxen, the mean being about four.[145] For comparison, Gervase Markham in the early seventeenth century indicated that a wain required a hauling team of no less than six oxen, except perhaps at the harvest when four might do.[146] Large ox-hauling teams are also indicated from records other than surveys. Thus, among forest pleas held at Carlisle in 12 Edward I (1283–4), a man from Penrith and his son were charged with cutting down an oak and attempting to carry it away with a *plaustrum* and eight oxen. Similar offences involving *plaustra* drawn by six oxen were also heard in the same pleas; and teams of six oxen (three times) and of four oxen (once), drawing the same type of vehicle, were involved in cases from the Forest of Pickering (Yorkshire) in 1334.[147]

On the other hand, peasant horse-hauling teams were very much smaller. Teams of two, three and four horses are all encountered in the surveys, but the most common by far was that of only a single animal.[148] The size of the hauling team depended very much upon the job in hand. Small teams of one or two horses were used for

---

[145] *Select Documents . . . of the Abbey of Bec*, p. 85; *Custumals of Battle Abbey*, pp. 4–6, 20, 28; *Thirteen Custumals . . . of the Bishop of Chichester*, pp. 17, 46–7, 57, 61, 88, 101, 107; *Two Registers . . . Belonging to the Family of Beauchamp of Hatch*, pp. 5, 8; *Rentalia et custumaria . . . Glastoniae*, pp. 82, 129, 146, 216; *Historia et cartularium monasterii Sancti Petri Gloucestriae*, iii, p. 143. With one exception (*Thirteen Custumals . . . of the Bishop of Chichester*, p. 107; late fourteenth century), all these references date from the thirteenth or early fourteenth century. Mixed hauling teams of horses and oxen together were noted at Denton, Sussex, in 1274 and at "Prinkehamme" in Limpsfield, Surrey, in 1312 (*Thirteen Custumals . . . of the Bishop of Chichester*, p. 101; *Custumals of Battle Abbey*, p. 156).

[146] *Farewell to Husbandry*, p. 147. Markham also cited teams of four or five oxen for hauling "carts" (*loc. cit*).

[147] P.R.O. E. 32/5, fo. 25; *The Honour and Forest of Pickering*, iii, ed. R. B. Turton (North Riding Rec. Soc., new series, iii, 1896), pp. 36–8. I am indebted to Jean Birrell for supplying me with these references.

[148] Altogether the surveys yielded references to at least 43 one-horse cart teams, 11 two-horse cart teams, 2 three-horse cart teams, and 2 four-horse cart teams. *Cartularium monasterii de Rameseia*, i, pp. 289, 290, 335, 372; Brit. Lib. Cott. MS Claud. C. XI, fos. 32, 36v, 39v, 45v, 47v, 56, 57v, 66v, 82v, 83, 100, 106, 112v, 122, 122v–123, 146, 146v, 150, 152v, 169v, 172, 172v, 173v, 178, 184, 184v, 193v (*bis*), 195, 195v, 200, 201v (*ter*), 211, 211v, 229 (*bis*), 229v, 245, 256; *Rentalia et custumaria . . . Glastoniae*, pp. 7, 64, 140, 148, 225; Brit. Lib. Cott. MS Claud. B. XIII, fos. 8v, 9 (other references on following folios, but not listed here); *Historia et cartularium monasterii Sancti Petri Gloucestriae*, iii, pp. 116, 124, 159, 167; *Extents of the Prebends of York*, p. 38; Beaumont, "Manor of Borley", p. 264.

short hauling around the farm, while larger teams were used for road transport. A good example of both types is observed at East Dereham (Norfolk) in 1251, where Ralph de Humbeltoft and other virgate holders were required not only to carry dung and corn about the lord's demesne with a cart and two horses, but also to undertake an *averagium longum* with a cart and four horses to Norwich and other places.[149] Finally, some of the carrying services performed by horse and cart were, in fact, carried out by smallholders. Thus each of the cottagers at Colne in Somersham (Huntingdonshire), holding five acres apiece, were to perform carrying services *si habeat carectam et equum*. It should be noted that, in addition, these tenants did a small amount of ploughing (three acres per year), although they were of such lowly status as tenants that they also owed carrying services on foot (*averagium pedile*).[150]

Carrying service by pack-horse (*summagium* or *averagium cum equo et sacco*) was something that a great number of peasants had to perform. It is prevalent in virtually all the surveys, although less in some than in others.[151] As with carting, the chores performed by pack-horse varied from those discharged on the manor itself to those involving long-distance trips. As examples of the first type, tenants at Berkhamsted (Hertfordshire) in 1356 were each required to take seed from the barn to the fields *cum equo suo proprio et sacco*, and the same was also required of the reeve at Pegsdon (Bedfordshire) in 1255.[152] But more often it was carrying outside the manor that was performed, and long trips "inside and outside" the hundred and county were often specified. As one example out of many, tenants at Longbridge Deverill (Wiltshire), c. 1235–40, were required to supply pack-horse service when needed to any place within fifteen leagues (*leucas*) of the manor and even to Glastonbury on occasion.[153] Much of this pack-carrying involved taking the

[149] Brit. Lib. Cott. MS Claud. C. XI, fos. 229–229v.
[150] *Ibid.*, fo. 100; see also fo. 106.
[151] For example, pack-horse services seem to occur much less frequently in the 1222 survey of the manors of St Paul's in London than, say, in the c. 1235–40 Glastonbury extents, where they are included among the services for virtually every major tenant. *Domesday of St. Paul's of the Year 1222*, pp. 1–107; *Rentalia et custumaria . . . Glastoniae*, pp. 1–167.
[152] P.R.O. S.C.11, roll 271; *Cartularium monasterii de Rameseia*, i, p. 467.
[153] *Rentalia et custumaria . . . Glastoniae*, p. 136.

lord's corn to market, and here the amount to be carried was often specified, as at Chisenbury (Wiltshire), *c.* 1230, where virgate holders were to carry to market one quarter of wheat or an equivalent load of other grains.[154] At modern conversions, the wheat would have weighed 504 lbs.[155] This is rather a lot for one horse,[156] so more than one animal may have been involved. More realistic pack-horse loads for single animals are evident at other places, such as at Borley (Essex) in 1308, where the loads for horses carrying up to twelve leagues from the manor were limited to two bushels of salt, three bushels of wheat, rye, peas or beans, or four bushels of oats.[157] These loads were obviously much less than those which could be carried by a cart or other type of vehicle, although this may have been compensated for to some degree by the greater speed of the pack-horses. In the end, the transportation of goods by pack-horse was thought, at best, to be only half as effective as, say, hauling by cart. At Longbridge Deverill, for instance, a labour service hauling wood by cart was credited with two days' work compared to only one if the same was performed by pack-horse.[158]

The equipment for pack-horses was, in the main, very primitive. Most references simply refer to a "horse and sack",[159] and a similar arrangement appears in a Broughton (Huntingdonshire) court roll for 1258, where a substantial free tenant, holding one and a half hides, had to supply a horse, sumpter saddle, sack and fastening pin for military service.[160] The more sophisticated crooks, pots and panniers of a later period[161] are noticeably missing. As indicated by

---

[154] *Item averare debet et summagium portare ad vicina mercata blada domini . . . scilicet unum quarterium frumenti*, etc. *Select Documents . . . of the Abbey of Bec*, p. 54.

[155] See Chapter 3, note 68.

[156] See p. 116 above.

[157] Beaumont, "Manor of Borley", p. 265. See also *Thirteen Custumals . . . of the Bishop of Chichester*, pp. 96, 111; *Rentalia et custumaria . . . Glastoniae*, p. 62; *Select Documents . . . of the Abbey of Bec*, p. 30, for references to pack-horse services involving loads of corn ranging from three to seven bushels.

[158] *Rentalia et custumaria . . . Glastoniae*, pp. 145–6 (*c.* 1235–40). Similarly, the cost of transportation by wagon in the eighteenth century was thought to be about half that for pack-horses; Hey, *Packmen, Carriers and Packhorse Roads*, p. 98.

[159] E.g., Brit. Lib. Cott. MS Claud. C. XI, fos. 143v, 149v, 195, 201v, etc.; *Red Book of Worcester*, iii, p. 309; *Thirteen Custumals . . . of the Bishop of Chichester*, p. 96.

[160] *Select Pleas in Manorial and other Seigneurial Courts, Hen III–Edw I*, ed. F. W. Maitland (Selden Soc., ii, 1889), p. 62.

[161] *Devon Inventories of the Sixteenth and Seventeenth Centuries*, ed. M. Cash (Devon and Cornwall Rec. Soc., new series, xi, 1966), esp. p. 43.

medieval and early modern illustrations, the normal method of packing may have been simply to tie the filled sack at the neck and throw it across the back of the animal, perhaps tying it down with ropes if necessary.[162]

It is not possible to say with any certainty whether the use of pack animals among the peasantry was increasing or decreasing in the middle ages or even at what level it was carried out. It would appear, though, that – in the absence of horse hauling – carrying by pack-horse was of considerable importance at Domesday.[163] If so, then the general trend in the usage of pack-horses over the middle ages, especially on farms, was presumably one of decline, since sixteenth- and seventeenth-century evidence indicates that vehicle hauling was by far the most dominant form of transport by this time, although pack-horses were still very prevalent in some areas.[164] At the intervening time of the surveys, however, the pack-horse was clearly still an important element of peasant transport, not only for the peasants themselves but also for the demesne, since, from the lack of pack-horses that they commanded (see p. 117), demesne officials were very dependent upon peasants for this quick, if less effective, form of carrying.

Finally, as with harrowing, there were some peasants who did not plough, but who were expected to do pack-horse services. In none of the surveys do they comprise a substantial body of tenants, but they are often found here and there.[165]

Horses were also useful to peasants in other ways. The possibility of peasant horse mills has already been indicated (p. 118). Another obvious use was that of riding. The multi-purpose nature of peasant horses in this regard can be seen at Burton (in Marnhull), Dorset, c. 1235–40, where Robert Tac, a virgate holder, was required to ride

---

[162] E.g., see *English Rural Life in the Later Middle Ages*, Bodleian Picture Book no. 14 (Oxford, 1975), plates 2b and 6b.

[163] See p. 49 above; also Langdon, "Horse Hauling", p. 59.

[164] A preliminary survey of sixteenth- and early seventeenth-century inventories indicates that the main concentration of pack-horses and pack-horse equipment on farms was found in the south-west (e.g., *Devon Inventories of the Sixteenth and Seventeenth Centuries*), with occasional references in the north and East Anglia; elsewhere, vehicle hauling dominated almost totally.

[165] As, for example, William Comes de Poteria and other cotsetlanders in Long-bridge Deverill (Wiltshire), c. 1235–40, who were expected to do both *summagium* and harrowing, but not ploughing. *Rentalia et custumaria . . . Glastoniae*, p. 142.

to a hay-making service at Sturminster Newton on his affer (for which the animal was given fodder), as well as using it as a pack-horse and for harrowing at other times.[166] Pasture or stubble in the fields was also supplied to horses ridden by peasants of the tithing of Woodland in Taunton (Somerset), *c.* 1245–52, when they attended harvest and hay-making services on the lord's demesne, presumably some distance away.[167] For freemen, services due to the lord that required riding horses might include message-carrying or accompanying the lord's officials in some capacity.[168]

We shall conclude this section with a few general points. The most obvious one is that the horse was a very versatile animal for the peasant. It was extremely handy for harrowing, hauling, pack-work, riding and perhaps even milling. Only in the instance of ploughing were oxen likely to be better, and even here horses often took a part. In any case, ploughing animals were probably the last a peasant would have, since the surveys indicate that he was more likely to have animals for harrowing and pack-work or even riding and hauling first, mainly because one animal – that is, a horse – could do all these jobs, while ploughing required several. Thus it was entirely feasible to find a group of tenants on a manor who had horses for all the subsidiary tasks but stopped short of owning plough animals. This group would be comprised not only of small-holders but also of more substantial tenants who for one reason or another found themselves short of plough beasts. It is difficult to say how large this group with its limited draught capacity was. The lay subsidy and heriot material we have already examined indicates that it was quite sizeable, and thus it had a marked effect on the number of horses found in villages. On the other hand, the survey material, while at times indicating the group's presence, nonetheless tended to minimize it considerably. Much of this is due to the nature of the surveys themselves, which often adopted an "all or nothing" policy: that is, tenants were listed as performing the full battery of plough-ing, harrowing, hauling and pack-horse services, or not at all. The fact that a smallholder might have a horse to do some of these tasks

[166] *Ibid.*, pp. 96–7.
[167] *The Medieval Customs of the Manors of Taunton and Bradford on Tone*, pp. 7–8 (*c.* 1245–52).
[168] As indicated for the freemen of Bishop's Cleeve (Gloucestershire) in 1299. *Red Book of Worcester*, iv, pp. 329–30.

was simply not catered for.[169] As a result, the surveys are ambiguous about this "limited draught capacity" group and can tell us little about its size except the fact that it existed in some areas at least. What *is* clear from the surveys is that, in the use of horses versus oxen, substantial tenants were to a large degree removed from this group and employed draught animals in ways very much closer to those used on the demesne.

c) THE SIZE OF THE PEASANT PLOUGH-TEAM, 1200–1500

Direct evidence about the size of the peasant plough-team is unfortunately very scarce, and much must be derived from inference. Dealing with the early evidence first, that is, that before the Black Death, peasant plough-teams were often shown as being quite large. We have already mentioned the mixed team of two horses and four oxen found at Thorpe Satchville (Leicestershire) in 1284, and the "horses and oxen" found in the plough-team of the Bretby peasant above indicate that the team was of some size, probably at least four animals. Large peasant plough-teams are also indicated in the surveys. For instance, it is specified in a 1299 extent for Henbury-in-Salt-Marsh (Gloucestershire) that virgate tenants should perform ploughing services with teams of six oxen, although these teams were still very much smaller than those of ten oxen apiece found on the demesne at Henbury ten or so years earlier. At nearby Shirehampton in the same extent half-virgate tenants were similarly instructed to plough with six oxen in winter and eight in summer, while at Sturminster Newton (Dorset), *c.* 1235–40, every tenant holding two virgates was supposedly to plough with six, eight, or even ten oxen in a team, the acreage of the ploughing service required being proportional to the number of oxen he supplied.[170] Eight-ox teams were also requested of tenants at Ashbury (Berkshire), Nettleton (Wiltshire) and Pilton (Somerset), and a six-ox team of tenants at Walpole (Norfolk), although in all

---

[169] E.g., the bishopric of Worcester surveys, where the labour services for the customary tenants followed this rigid policy; labour services for freemen were much more flexible. *Ibid.*, i–iv.

[170] *Ibid.*, iv, pp. 384–5, 393; *Rentalia et custumaria . . . Glastoniae*, p. 84. For the Henbury demesne teams, see *Red Book of Worcester*, iv, p. 403.

these cases, except Pilton, it was acknowledged that the tenant might have ploughed with less.[171]

It should be noted here that the generally large size of the plough-team given in the surveys may not have reflected actual team sizes, but a notion in the minds of manorial officials as to what the size should be. Other more indirect references tend to indicate smaller teams. For example, jurors at Gransden (Cambridgeshire) in 1251 stated that Andrew le Wodeward, holding a virgate of eighteen acres in customary tenure, was allowed to have four oxen of his plough "at most" pastured along with the oxen of the bishop of Ely, his lord. However, the jurors go on to say that "if he yokes with fewer [oxen], then he will have less [oxen] in the aforesaid pasture".[172] The passage strongly implies that a plough-team of four oxen was the normal occurrence, although it could vary according to circumstances. Similarly at Stoke sub Hamdon (Somerset) in 1287, Walter Vox and others holding a half-virgate apiece in villeinage, were each to plough and harrow an acre in winter, called a "lesacre", for which each was allowed pasture for two oxen and a horse (*affrus*).[173] Since co-aration was not indicated for this particular boon (although it was for another one later in the year), the passage might imply that pasture was being allowed for a two-ox plough-team and a harrowing horse. On the other hand, at Warboys (Huntingdonshire) in 1251, it is stated that each person in the community was allowed pasture for six oxen and two horses in the woods, marshes and other places in the manor "along with the plough-teams of the Abbot", which might imply very large plough-teams for the tenants of this particular village.[174]

The evidence after 1350, though scarcer, is more definite. Thus the three- and four-horse plough-teams already cited for Wistow and Wetwang above seem fairly certain. The smaller nature of the all-horse teams here is hardly surprising after our study of such teams on the demesne, which could be as small as two horses in such

---

[171] *Rentalia et custumaria . . . Glastoniae*, pp. 52, 68 (*c.* 1235–40); *ibid.*, p. 210 (1260); Brit. Lib. Cott. MS Claud. C. XI, fos. 193–193v (1251).

[172] *Et iuratores dicunt quod quatuor boues caruce sue ad plus ibunt cum bobus domini in pastura episcopi. Et si de paucioribus iungat, tunc pauciores habeat in predicta pastura.* Brit. Lib. Cott. MS Claud. C. XI, fo. 150v.

[173] *Two Registers Formerly Belonging to the Family of Beauchamp of Hatch*, p. 15.

[174] *Cartularium monasterii de Rameseia*, i, p. 306. Many more pasture arrangements of this type could be cited to support contentions of both large and small teams.

areas as north-west Norfolk.[175] Presumably the same applied for the
peasantry in these areas, and certainly two-horse peasant plough-
teams can be implied for such places as Cuxham in Oxfordshire.[176]
All-ox plough-teams in the post-Black Death period might have
been smaller for the peasantry as well. There is no definite evidence
for this, but it is notable that the ploughs in R. K. Field's *principalia*
lists for Worcestershire in the late fourteenth and early fifteenth
century have only one yoke apiece, implying that the ploughs were
each drawn by only two oxen.[177]

Altogether we have a bewildering array of possibilities as to the
size of the peasant plough-team. We have also to consider various
items of literary evidence, such as the four-animal plough-teams
indicated by the Piers Plowman legends,[178] not to mention the evidence from medieval illustrations, which also indicate small plough-
teams, some of them probably representing peasant ploughs.[179] Is it
possible, then, to make some sense out of this often conflicting
material? A useful point of comparison may be to consider
sixteenth-century material when evidence about plough-team size is
at least a little more forthcoming. From an examination of a large
body of probate wills and inventories, forty-five cases were found,
covering the period from 1506 to 1590, where the size of the team
was given or could be inferred with a reasonable degree of probability.[180] These are summarized by county in Table 32.

[175] See Chapter 3, note 85 above.
[176] Langdon, "Economics of Horses and Oxen", p. 38.
[177] See especially the lists of Thomas Mody, John Ondrow, John atte Wall, John
More and Nicholas atte Wall: Field, "Worcestershire Peasant Buildings", pp.
140–5.
[178] *The Vision of William concerning Piers the Plowman*, ed. W. W. Skeat (London,
1869), pp. 355–6; *Pierce the Ploughmans Crede*, pp. 16–17.
[179] For example, an illustration from a fourteenth-century copy of Langland's *Piers
the Plowman* showing a two-ox team pulling a heavy mould-board plough is
almost certainly a peasant plough, because the team is being driven by a woman,
a thing virtually unheard-of for a demesne plough. Steensberg, "North West
European Plough-types", fig. 14 (p. 271).
[180] The following are a few examples, listed from strongest to weakest likelihood:
    1. "Item one plowe and gere for viij oxen" (St Nicholas, nr Richmond,
    Yorkshire, 1562; *Wills and Inventories . . . of the Archdeaconry of Richmond*,
    p. 164).
    2. "a plough with 3 horses and all gear" (Houghton Regis, Bedfordshire,
    1521; B.R.O., ABP/R 2, no. 92, from a modern English transcription at the
    B.R.O., p. 97).
    3. "a plowe ij yowkes ij chaynes and all thynge to the plowe aperteynyng"

Table 32. *Distribution of sixteenth-century plough-team sizes*

1. *All-ox teams*

County	No. of oxen in team							
	2		4		6		8	
	a	b	a	b	a	b	a	b
Berkshire	—	—	1	2	—	—	—	—
Buckinghamshire	—	—	—	—	1	1	—	—
Cornwall	—	—	1	2	—	—	—	—
Devon	—	—	1	1	—	—	—	—
Dorset	—	—	—	—	1	1	—	—
Gloucestershire	—	—	—	—	1	2	—	—
Hampshire	—	—	2	3	—	—	1	1
Kent	—	—	1	1	—	—	—	—
Lincolnshire	—	—	1	1	—	—	—	—
Oxfordshire	—	—	1	2	—	—	—	—
Staffordshire	—	—	—	—	1	1	—	—
Sussex	—	—	1	1	1	1	—	—
Warwickshire	1	1	—	—	—	—	—	—
Westmorland	—	—	—	—	—	—	1	3
Wiltshire	—	—	—	—	1	2	—	—
Yorkshire	—	—	1	1	1	1	1	1
Total	1	1	10	14	7	9	3	5
% (cases)	4.8		47.6		33.3		14.3	
% (teams)		3.4		48.3		31.0		17.2

Key to column headings
a – Number of cases
b – Number of teams

Notes and sources: Bedfordshire: B.R.O. ABP/R 2, no. 93; 3, no. 146; *Berkshire:* Wi.R.O. Dean of Sarum Inventories, William Keylling, 1579; Thomas Lawrence, 1574; *Buckinghamshire:* Bu.R.O. D/A/We/4/79, Wf/4/329; *Cornwall:* Co.R.O. Archd. Cornwall Probate, John Beale, 1579; *Devon:* P.R.O. Probate 2, no. 405; *Dorset:* Wi.R.O. Dean of Sarum Inventories, Edith Southaye, 1579; Thomas Marten, 1578; *Essex:* E.R.O. D/A MR 2, fo. 55; *Gloucestershire:* P.R.O. Probate 2, no. 498; *Hampshire:* H.R.O. Bishopric Wills, 1545, no. 91; 1549, no. 136; 1550, no. 30; *Huntingdonshire:* Hunts.R.O. Archd. of Huntingdon Wills, 1538–1541, fo. 241; *Kent:* K.A.O. PRC 10/1, fos. 17v–18v, 26–7, 103–4; *Lincolnshire:* Li.R.O. Box 22, no. 21; *Norfolk:* N.R.O. Inv./3, nos. 33, 68, 77, 107; *Northamptonshire:* No.R.O. Archd. Northampton Wills, E, fos. 181, 200v; *Oxfordshire: Household and Farm Inventories in Oxfordshire, 1550–1590,* ed. M. A. Havinden (Historical Manuscripts Commission, JP10, London, 1965), p. 48; *Staffordshire:* L.J.R.O. Lichfield Probate

Table 32 (cont.)

2. All-horse teams

	No. of horses in team									
	2		3		4		5		6	
County	a	b	a	b	a	b	a	b	a	b
Bedfordshire	—	—	1	1	—	—	—	—	1	1
Berkshire	—	—	1	1	—	—	—	—	—	—
Buckinghamshire	—	—	—	—	—	—	—	—	1	1
Dorset	—	—	—	—	—	—	1	1	—	—
Essex	—	—	—	—	—	—	—	—	1	1
Huntingdonshire	—	—	1	1*	—	—	—	—	—	—
Kent	2	2	—	—	—	—	—	—	—	—
Norfolk	4	5	—	—	—	—	—	—	—	—
Northamptonshire	—	—	1	1	1	1	—	—	—	—
Suffolk	—	—	1	1	4	5	—	—	1	1
Warwickshire	—	—	—	—	1	1	—	—	—	—
Worcestershire	—	—	—	—	1	1	—	—	—	—
County unknown	—	—	—	—	1	1	—	—	—	—
Total	6	7	5	5	8	9	1	1	4	4
% (cases)	25.0		20.8		33.3		4.2		16.7	
% (teams)		26.9		19.2		34.6		3.8		15.4

Records B/C/11, Thomas Hylman, 1535; *Suffolk:* P.R.O. Probate 2, no. 180; N.R.O. Inv./3, no. 37; E.Suff.R.O. FEI/1/8, 29, 79; W.Suff.R.O. IC 500/3/1/80; *Sussex:* W.Suss.R.O. Archd. Chichester Wills, v, 1544–7, fos. 62v–63v; E.Suss.R.O. Archd. Lewes Wills W/A/3, 1550–9, fo. 48; *Warwickshire:* Wo.R.O. ref. 008:7, 1551, box 11a, no. 19; L.J.R.O. Lichfield Probate Records B/C/11, Richard Coke, 1538; *Westmorland: Wills and Inventories . . . of the Archdeaconry of Richmond*, ed. J. Raine, Jr (Surtees Soc., xxvi, 1853), p. 218; *Wiltshire:* Wi.R.O. Archd. Sarum, Thomas Hulberd, 1561; *Worcestershire:* Wo.R.O. Ref. 008:7, 1590, box 94b, no. 26; *Yorkshire: Wills and Inventories . . . of the Archdeaconry of Richmond*, pp. 164, 247; B.I. Preb. Court of Fenton Wills, Miles Rawling, 1559; *County unknown:* N.R.O. Inv./3, no. 11 (Carleton, in Norfolk or Suffolk).

*This may have been a four-horse plough: "Item to my said wiff a gelding and iij marys to her plowgh" (from the will of Thomas Smyth of Fenton, in Somersham, Huntingdonshire, 1541; Hunts.R.O. Archd. Huntingdon Wills, vi, 1538–41, fo. 241). As the gelding was probably a riding animal, only the mares were considered as plough beasts.

As might be expected, the table displays a great variety in plough-team size, from two horses to eight oxen. The mode team size for both the all-ox and all-horse plough-teams was four animals per plough, although the mean all-ox team size, at 5.2 animals per plough, was significantly larger than that for the all-horse teams (3.6 animals per plough). In both cases, these were over two animals per plough shorter than the average all-ox and all-horse plough-teams on the medieval demesne (see p. 119 above). Definite references to mixed plough-teams were entirely absent, but it would be surprising if there were none at all at this time, since documentary and icono-graphic evidence from the seventeenth century clearly indicates that they were fairly common in some parts of the country at least.[181] Nevertheless the absence of verifiable references to mixed plough-teams in the sixteenth-century material would seem to suggest a falling-off of popularity in the use of such teams since the middle ages, as they were gradually replaced by all-horse teams.

The generally smaller teams noted in the sixteenth-century material also suggest the possibility that such small teams already existed to a considerable degree in medieval times. Moreover, there seems to have been more than just a passing connection between farm size and the size of the plough-team. Thus the eight-ox plough-teams in Table 32 were only found on the very largest of farms, equivalent in size to medieval demesnes.[182] Lesser farms in the table clearly made do with lesser teams.[183] We should also remember that

(indicating a four-ox team; Birdham, Sussex, 1544; W.Suss.R.O., Archd. of Chichester Wills, v, 1544–7, fos. 62v–63v).

4. "Item a shod Cartte iiij payer of Cartt trayes one plough iiij peyer of plough trayes iiij Collers & all other thinges belonging to the plough & Cartte" (indicating a four-horse plough-team; Sutton, Suffolk, 1583; E.Suff.R.O. FEI/1/8).

5. "a plowe . . . iiij payer of plowe trayse" (indicating a four-horse team; Sibton, Suffolk, 1583; *ibid.*, FEI/1/29).

[181] R. Lennard, "English Agriculture under Charles II: The Evidence of the Royal Society 'Enquiries'", in *Essays in Agrarian History*, i, ed. W. E. Minchinton (Newton Abbot, 1968), p. 170; Orwin and Orwin, *The Open Fields*, plate 22 (opp. p. 140).

[182] Judging from the amounts of stock involved. Even the smallest of them – Walter Carter's farm at Romsey (Hampshire) in 1550 – had 8 oxen (for his plough), 11 adult horses, 3 colts, 1 bull, 20 cows, 40 younger cattle, 80 sheep and 24 pigs. H.R.O. Bishopric Wills, 1550, no. 30; see also the farms of Johanna Wycliffe and Walter Strickland: *Wills and inventories . . . of the Archdeaconry of Richmond*, pp. 164, 218.

[183] For example, the two-ox team noted in Table 32 was found on the farm of Richard Coke of Stretton-on-Dunsmore (Warwickshire) in 1538 and was part of

the wills and inventories in Table 32 would tend to deal mainly with prosperous farms.[184] Thus, if the smallholding group had been better represented in the table we might have had a larger proportion of smaller teams.

The concept of a plough-team varying with holding size is an attractive one for explaining some of the paradoxes associated with the medieval plough-team. But does it have much basis in fact? We have seen from the patchy medieval evidence that there was some variety in the size of the peasant plough-team, and this variety in team size is also reflected in the sixteenth-century evidence. Unfortunately there are not enough data, even for the sixteenth century, to allow a detailed breakdown of plough-team versus holding size, and other more indirect methods must be employed. One way may be to consider co-aration again. It has long been maintained that the necessity of a large plough-team required the co-operation of peasant farmers. Thus, two, three, four or even more peasants would need to club together to make up, say, an eight-ox team. If, however, peasants in the main managed to avoid having to participate in co-aration, then it would indicate a more flexible approach to ploughing, involving – presumably – smaller teams. We have already reviewed the twelfth-century evidence, which does indicate that peasants tended to plough separately with the resulting probability of smaller plough-teams.[185] Does the post-1200 documentation tell us the same thing?

First, it must be said that references to co-aration occur with some frequency in the agrarian records of the thirteenth and fourteenth centuries, particularly in the extents and surveys.[186] This does not

a total stock of 2 oxen, 2 colts, 2 cows, 4 calves, 7 sheep and 9 pigs. Thus Richard's farm would seem to have been no larger than a good-sized peasant holding a few centuries earlier, even considering the fact that some of his stock may already have been removed as heriots (cf. the average peasant livestock levels given in Postan, "Village Livestock", Tables 1–3).

[184] Probably approaching fifty acres in size on average, if the data in Table 30 are any guide (see also p. 210).

[185] See pp. 69–72 above.

[186] Thus references to co-aration in surveys and extents, including those given in the text below, occur in *Cartularium monasterii de Rameseia*, i, pp. 310, 317, 346, 461, 463, 493; ii, p. 23; *Custumals of Battle Abbey*, pp. 74, 76; Brit. Lib. Cott. MS Claud. C. XI, fos. 30–30v, 36, 44v, 58, 116–116v, 121v–122, 146, 154, 164, 176v–177, 178; *Rentalia et custumaria . . . Glastoniae*, p. 136; *Domesday of St. Paul's of the Year 1222*, p. 86; *Extent of Monk Friston, 1320*, ed. T. A. M. Bishop

mean that the practice was predominant at the time, since, as we shall see, there are also numerous indications of peasants ploughing alone; but certainly the references to co-aration in the thirteenth century in particular represent a marked increase over those evident in the preceding century.[187] This is only what we should expect given the population growth of the period, as declining levels of land and livestock per person forced peasants to pool their resources. In a few cases, the surveys indicate that this degree of cooperation could be quite intense. Thus at Barton in the Clay (Bedfordshire) an inquest dated 39 Hen III (1254–5) stated that four or even eight men may have contributed to a plough, if circumstances made it necessary.[188] Arrangements of such complexity as these begin to resemble the ploughing clauses of the Welsh Laws, allegedly from the tenth century, where up to twelve farmers could be involved,[189] but to suggest that this was the normal case in England would be grossly misleading. In fact, the vast majority of references to co-aration indicates that it was very much a function of individual circumstances and by no means a ruling condition for the peasantry as a whole. One of the best examples of this is provided in the services recorded for William le Neweman, holding a virgate of twenty-four acres in villeinage on the Ramsey Abbey manor of Ellington (Huntingdonshire), *c.* 1250:

> Item if he [William] has ploughed alone [i.e. has been accustomed to ploughing alone], he will plough one-half acre each Friday during the year at ploughing time; and if he has ploughed with another, or with others, all will perform together the same that he would have ploughed if alone.[190]

(Miscellanea, iv, Yorkshire Arch. Soc. Rec. Ser., xciv, 1936), pp. 44, 54, 60, 63; *The Crondal Records*, ed. F. J. Baigent (Hampshire Rec. Soc., 1890), p. 102; *Extents of the Prebends of York*, p. 11; N.R.O. 21187 (Gressenhall Extent; per J. Williamson); Brit. Lib. Cott. MS Claud. D. XIII, fo. 8 (Binham Priory Register; per J. Williamson).

[187] Compare, for instance, the thirteenth-century extents of Ramsey Abbey, where at least seven references to co-aration exist (see note 186) as against none in the twelfth-century extents (*Cartularium monasterii de Rameseia*, iii, pp. 241–314).

[188] *Licet vero bene quatuor hominibus vel octo si cogat necessitas inuicem associari ad carucam si sue facultates vlterius non extendant* . . . Brit. Lib. Add. Roll 24333; also quoted in Homans, *English Villagers*, pp. 77, 424.

[189] E.g., for a summary of the Welsh Laws as they pertain to co-aration, see *Agrarian History of England and Wales*, i, pt 2, pp. 352–3; H. D. Emanuel (*The Latin Texts of the Welsh Laws* (Cardiff, 1967), p. 15) supplies the pertinent passage from one of the Latin texts of the Laws.

[190] *Item si araverit solus, arabit dimidiam acram quolibet die Veneris tempore arurae*

The clerks or monastic officials making up the extent have clearly recognized what is evidently a shifting situation. William may have had his own plough-team; equally he may not have, in which case he would have to cooperate with at least one other tenant to fulfil his ploughing services. Most other references to co-aration are similarly stated and suggest that the land-holding threshold below which peasants generally had to practise co-aration was something less than a virgate. This "threshold" can be seen among the tenants of Swandrop in the large manor of Crondal (Hampshire) in 1287. John Chapellayne, for instance, holding a virgate containing twenty-four acres, was to plough three acres at the winter seeding and three at the Lenten seeding. Co-aration was not indicated in any way.[191] However, when we consider the half-virgate holding of Elvitha Sterclesdene, containing sixteen and a half acres (*sic*; the size of the virgate varied enormously on this manor, even within hamlets), the record changes slightly. Here it is stated that if Elvitha has her own plough or plough-team she will fulfil the same services as John Chapellayne.[192] The conditional clause, however, indicates that she might not have her own plough-team. The situation becomes even more doubtful when we descend to the holding of Henry de la Lynch, containing a quarter-virgate of twelve acres. Now the record states: "if he [Henry] has his own full plough-team or half [of a team], then he will plough, as his neighbours, three acres in winter and three acres in Lent."[193] Altogether it appears that of these three tenants only John Chapellayne was virtually certain to have his own plough-team. There is a good chance that the other two tenants did as well, but a certain level of doubt has crept in, particularly in the case of Henry de la Lynch, for whom co-aration was thought likely enough to add the qualifying "half plough". We might say, then, that co-aration in this community was only likely with holdings of less than twenty acres; indeed it was probably only common for those holdings of twelve acres or less.

per annum; et si cum alio, vel cum aliis araverit idem facient omnes simul quod ipse solus si solus araverit. Cartularium monasterii de Rameseia, ii, p. 23; for the number of acres to a virgate at Ellington, see *ibid.*, iii, p. 210.

[191] *Et ad semen hiemale arabit iij acras . . . Et similiter in quadragesimale arabit iij acras.* Crondal Records, p. 87.

[192] *Et si habet carucam suam propriam, tunc arabit sicut Johannes Chappellayn.* Ibid., p. 88.

[193] *Et si habet carucam propriam integram vel dimidiam, tunc arabit sicut alii vicini sui tres acras hiemales et tres acras quadragesimales.* Ibid., p. 89.

Is it possible to dismiss the case of Swandrop as exceptional in its low level of co-aration? It would appear not. References in other surveys indicate even lower levels, with tenants having less than ten acres of land ploughing alone.[194] In fact, references to co-aration in general in the surveys are greatly outnumbered for almost all sectors of peasant society by those references which indicate individual ploughing or at least fail to mention co-aration altogether. As has already been suggested,[195] this may only mean that the people drawing up the surveys and extents simply considered co-aration as such a commonplace event that they failed to see the need to mention it. Nonetheless, many of the references are clear enough to indicate that individual ploughing by peasants was very common. Thus at Street in Somerset, *c.* 1235–1240, Jordan de Legha, a customary virgate holder, was to come to the lord's plough-boons "with all his oxen joined to his plough".[196] Again at Gorton (Lancashire) in 1320, Henry le Reve, holding a bovate in villeinage, ploughed for the lord "with his own plough [or plough-team]."[197] A reference of a different kind is evident at Frome Episcopi, Herefordshire, in the second half of the thirteenth century, where it is stated that five virgates of land ought to find five ploughs or plough-teams on two occasions during the year, the implication being that each virgate ploughed individually.[198]

We have up till now been considering only the evidence from extents and surveys. These are generally statements of intent rather than a record of actual events, and thus they depict co-aration as the clerks conceived it to be, not necessarily as it was in day-to-day practice. It rests on other types of documents to show it in working operation. The main impression gained from this alternative material, however, is how few times co-aration is actually mentioned. Refer-

---

[194] For example, no co-aration was indicated for the cottagers of Colne in Somersham (Huntingdonshire) above. Similarly Roger, son of Walter, of Bridgham (Norfolk), holding six acres in 1251, was expected to plough with "a whole plough (or plough-team)" for three days: Brit. Lib. Cott. MS Claud. C. XI, fo. 249.

[195] See pp. 71–2 above.

[196] . . . *cum omnibus bobus suis caruce sue junctis*. The same was requested of three other virgate holders: *Rentalia et custumaria . . . Glastoniae*, pp. 12–13.

[197] *Mamecestre*, ii, ed. J. Harland (Chetham Soc., lvi, 1861), pp. 229, 311.

[198] *A Transcript of "The Red Book"*, ed. A. T. Bannister (Miscellany xv, Camden Third Series, xli, 1929), p. 15.

ences to ploughing services in accounts very occasionally indicate co-aration,[199] but equally often a total lack of cooperative ploughing is suggested.[200] The most revealing references to co-aration emanate from those few disputes over the practice that come to light in the manorial court records. These generally emphasize the small-scale and transitory nature of cooperative ploughing. Thus, from a court case in Thorner (Yorkshire) in 1365, one man accused another of defaulting on a ploughing partnership called a *marrow*, where each man was required to supply an equal number of animals to the plough each year. Another case in Yorkshire from nearly a century earlier (1286), states that "Richard de Tothill was the companion of Roger de Bosco to plough jointly with his plough, and at the time of ploughing cast him off, so that his lands lie untilled."[201]

Co-aration is also indicated in a lengthy court entry for Chalgrave (Bedfordshire), where in 1313 John Gildulf, Robert le Reve and William ate hall were allowed to be quit of ploughing services simply by contributing their animals to other tenants' plough-teams. The case is interesting because Gildulf and Robert le Reve already had a history of non-fulfilment of ploughing services.[202] It seems here that the lord had finally acknowledged that these men were no longer capable of performing their ploughing services by themselves and thus allowed them to perform these services in league with others. A similar case in reverse is indicated at Rastrick (Yorkshire) in 1309, when Henry Steven of Fixby was charged with concealing "a certain custom of ploughing". This "custom" required Henry to

---

[199] Thus in the works section of an account for Tickhill (Yorkshire) in 1315–16 it is stated that each tenant residing in socage and "having a whole plough or joining with a friend" owed two ploughing services per year. The most extensive case of actual co-aration encountered in this study occurred in an account for Bourton-on-the-Hill (Gloucestershire) in 1370–1, where it is recorded that twenty-four out of ninety-four potential ploughing works were excused to twelve tenants who joined together because they did not have whole plough-teams. P.R.O. S.C. 6 1088/1; W.A.M. 8299. I am indebted to Dr C. Dyer for drawing my attention to the latter entry.

[200] For example, at Wisbech Barton (Cambridgeshire) in 1419 eighteen customary tenants with eighteen ploughs or plough-teams (*carucae*) came to a winter plough-boon called a "benerth", which would seem to indicate fairly conclusively that each tenant ploughed individually. C.U.L. Ely Diocesan Records D8/3/29; for a similar case at Cuxham (Oxfordshire) in 1288–9, see Langdon, "Economics of Horses and Oxen", p. 38.

[201] Bennett, *Life on the English Manor*, p. 45; *Court Rolls of the Manor of Wakefield*, iii, pp. 161–2.

[202] *Court Roll of Chalgrave Manor*, pp. 65–6, 62.

pay 4d. for a whole plough and 2d. for half a plough yearly in return for a holding of twelve acres; Henry, however, had "withheld the service for 10 years, namely as to ½ a plough for 8 years, and to a whole plough for 2 years, which amounts to 2s."[203] The passage clearly relates to a commuted ploughing service which has not been paid for some years. The court, however, still took note of Henry's ploughing situation; and, although co-aration is not specifically mentioned, it is implied from the record that Henry, with his half-plough, joined with another for eight years and ploughed on his own for two, perhaps in that order.

More examples of definite or implied co-aration could be given,[204] but enough have been indicated to make some rough conclusions. First, from the evidence gathered, co-aration would seem to be a casual affair, with tenants dropping into and out of the practice virtually at will. In this case, it may have been no more significant than the cases of borrowing or hiring of ploughing facilities that also occur in the documents.[205] Nowhere does co-aration appear to have been a highly organized affair. Although the survey and extent material sometimes indicates the possibility of four or more tenants cooperating to do their ploughing, only two ever seem to be involved in court cases. It can again be suggested that this was because peasants cooperated to make up the large teams demanded by the lord for his ploughing services, but did so to a much lesser extent on their own lands.[206] This may have been so in some cases,[207] but that it happened everywhere is belied by the account evidence given above and the fact that there is so little evidence of co-aration in ploughing service violations (see below). In fact, the predominant practice, particularly among major tenants, was probably to plough individually. Cases of bad ploughing during plough-boons, default of ploughing services, or trespasses while ploughing, were normally made against single defendants.[208] This may not signify

[203] *Court Rolls of the Manor of Wakefield*, ii, p. 208.
[204] For example, Ault, *Open-Field Farming in Medieval England*, p. 21.
[205] Homans, *English Villagers*, pp. 79–80; E. Clark, "Debt Litigation in a Late Medieval English Vill", in *Pathways to Medieval Peasants*, ed. J. A. Raftis (Toronto, 1981), pp. 261–2.
[206] See pp. 70–1 above.
[207] As at Barton in the Clay above, or on other manors where large plough-teams were required of tenants for their ploughing services (pp. 229–30 above).
[208] As indicated by numerous court roll entries: e.g., *Select Pleas in Manorial and other Seigneurial Courts*, pp. 12, 90, 93, 94; *Court Rolls of the Manor of Hales,*

much in the case of trespasses, since charges would probably only be brought against the man whose land was being ploughed, whether he was being helped by another tenant or not. But it is harder to explain in cases involving the default or poor performance of ploughing services, where it would seem to be in the lord's interest to charge all the peasants involved. Other evidence from the court rolls strongly indicating a lack of cooperation in ploughing is that supplied by the Worcestershire *principalia* lists already referred to. Of those published by R. K. Field, the interesting feature is that, excepting cottagers having less than a half-virgate of land, 90 per cent of the remaining tenants, that is, half-virgaters and above, had full sets of ploughing equipment.[209] If co-aration was being practised to any great degree in this area, there would seem to have been a remarkable excess of ploughs. It would appear from this that Worcestershire virgate and half-virgate tenants at this time (the late fourteenth and early fifteenth century) were all accustomed to individual ploughing, and we must presume from the other evidence given that such a situation was by no means uncommon in the rest of England as well.

What does all this tell us about the size of the peasant plough-team? Generally, the relative lack of co-aration indicated above supports the thesis of smaller peasant plough-teams. If eight-animal teams were the norm, as they were on the demesne, it would seem inconceivable that there should have been so little cooperative ploughing, before or after the plague. From the evidence of the medieval peasant inventories and the lay subsidies, only a very few tenants had the draught capacity to cope with demesne-sized teams. In short, plough-teams of the size shown for the sixteenth century in Table 32 were much more likely to have been the case for the medieval peasantry. This would then suggest a range of plough-team sizes for the peasantry from two to six animals, excluding the eight-ox teams as a preserve of only the largest of peasant farms.

1272–1307, ed. J. Amphlett, S. G. Hamilton and R. A. Wilson, 3 pts (Worcs. Hist. Soc., 1910, 1912, 1933), i, pp. 36, 152, 250; ii, pp. 515–16; iii, p. 156; *Halmota Prioratus Dunelmensis*, p. 5; *Court Rolls of the Manor of Wakefield*, iii, pp. 149–50; v, p. 149.

[209] Field, "Worcestershire Peasant Buildings", pp. 139–45. The "miscellaneous" tenants have been counted as major peasant land-holders, making twenty altogether. Of these, only two did not have full sets of ploughing equipment.

Some at least of the evidence we have as to peasant plough-teams, especially that outside the surveys, also indicates teams grouped around the four-animal mark. But this and the sixteenth-century evidence are strongly biased towards more substantial tenants, and thus the proportion of very small plough-teams among the medieval peasantry may have been much higher than that indicated in, say, Table 32, especially as co-aration was not absolutely certain even among smallholders having less than ten acres.[210] Certainly there are signs that two-animal teams may have been very common among the peasantry, as at Cuxham.[211] Altogether the evidence points to a gradation of plough-team size, with demesnes and perhaps the very largest of peasant farms ploughing with teams centred around the eight-animal mark; middle- or largeholding peasant farmers, that is, those having, say, a half-virgate to two virgates, employing middle-sized teams of up to four or even six animals; and smallholders ploughing with the smallest teams of all, possibly consisting of only two animals. The continual recurrence in the surveys of the statement that a peasant will plough "with as many animals as he has in his plough [or plough-team]" shows the uncertainty over the size of peasant plough-teams and the fact that it may have varied considerably even within the same manor.[212] The small plough-teams pictured in medieval illustrations thus become much more plausible when looked at in this light, and many of them may well have represented true peasant teams. The picture, of course, is complicated by the factor of regional variations in soil and terrain, which would have made small plough-teams more unlikely in some areas, such as on heavy clay lands, than in others, although even in these regions of difficult land some difference in plough-team size found on large versus small farms was seemingly evident, as at Henbury-in-Salt-Marsh above.[213]

As for the large demesne plough-team, far from being essential to all levels of farming, the evidence suggests that it was only needed for the largest of farms; here long ploughing seasons required substantial plough-teams to prevent the over-taxing of individual

---

[210] See note 194 above.
[211] Langdon, "The Economics of Horses and Oxen", p. 38; see also the two-ox teams implied by the Worcestershire *principalia* lists (p. 231 above).
[212] See p. 216 above.
[213] Cf. the peasant and demesne plough-teams found there in the late thirteenth century (p. 229 above).

animals. In this regard, the large plough-teams are very unlikely to have been the forerunners of smaller teams, as Seebohm suggested,[214] but in fact may have been relatively recent creations to accommodate the cultivation of large estates in the particular farming conditions of north-west Europe. From the numbers of oxen in some of the French *polyptyques* and Anglo-Saxon stock-and-land leases, often neatly divisible by eight, these large plough-teams were apparently common by the ninth and tenth centuries at least.[215]

This interpretation of a large plough-team for large estates does contradict the Welsh Laws, which do apparently show a very complex system of co-aration between Welsh smallholders, involving an eight-ox team.[216] Here, though, even if we are inclined to accept such a large team as being the rule in this case – and the question is in some doubt[217] – it may simply have been a feature peculiar to a highly pastoral economy. An element of Welsh agriculture at this time was the extensive cultivation of temporary outfield.[218] Perhaps the potentially large acreage of this outfield and its ruggedness encouraged the Welsh peasants to cooperate in farming it in demesne-like fashion (that is, with a larger plough-team over longer ploughing seasons). This, however, is well outside the scope of this study and can only be offered as a possibility here.

What seems clear is that the large plough-team was never an essential part of *English* peasant farming. Thus the role of communal ploughing in the open-field system was apt to be a rather minor one. Most peasants, in fact, opted for a much more individualistic mode of cultivation, preferring to avoid the complications and inevitable frictions that accompanied co-aration. There is little reason to believe that the situation had changed markedly from the past. If we can believe ancient and medieval illustrations at all, they indicate that small plough-teams of no greater than four animals had a continuous history stretching back to Roman times and before, regardless of the type of plough in operation. It would

[214] *English Village Community*, pp. 74–5.
[215] Slicher van Bath, *Agrarian History of Western Europe*, p. 67; see also Table 1 above.
[216] See note 189 above.
[217] Giraldus Cambrensis, for instance, indicates that plough-teams of four or even two oxen were the norm in twelfth-century Wales; this, though, may have been as much as two centuries after the Laws were formulated. See pp. 72, 236 above.
[218] *Agrarian History of England and Wales*, i, pt 2, p. 351.

seem pointless to discount this source entirely to accommodate the large demesne plough-team, when that team itself can be accounted for simply as an accessory for large-scale farming that in no way excludes the possibility of smaller teams for the peasantry.

d) PLOUGHS, HARROWS AND VEHICLES ON PEASANT FARMS, 1200–1500

To a large extent, the preceding discussion on peasant plough-teams is related to the type of plough the peasant used. Unfortunately specific documentary evidence about peasant ploughs is virtually non-existent, and much of what we can discover about them must necessarily be inferred from other indicators, such as plough-team size.

The item of most crucial importance is whether peasants in medieval England used ards (or scratch ploughs) that generally only scored the surface of the ground, or the heavy mould-board ploughs that could turn a substantial furrow. The argument relating the heavy mould-board plough with the long, narrow strip is well-known from the writings of Marc Bloch,[219] and the lack of cross-ploughing in medieval England of the type normally associated with scratch ploughs[220] is a strong point in favour of the view that peasants in both Europe and England used only mould-board ploughs. But arguments of this type often depend on the view that the normal peasant plough-team was one of about eight animals.[221] As we have seen, the evidence indicates that this was by no means the case; for the majority of peasants much smaller plough-teams were the normal occurrence. The question is: were these smaller teams also linked with smaller and lighter ploughs, possibly of the ard type? Unfortunately it is very difficult to tell. According to F. G. Payne, the asymetric shares and coulters found as early as

---

[219] Esp. *Les Caractères Originaux de L'Histoire Rurale Française*, 2nd edn (Paris, 1955), pp. 49–57.

[220] E.g., see Steensberg, "North West European Plough-types", pp. 256, 279; Haudricourt and Delamarre, *L'Homme et la Charrue*, p. 330; also as in Ireland in the eighteenth century (A. H. R. Baker and R. A. Butlin (eds.), *Studies of Field Systems in the British Isles* (Cambridge, 1973), p. 591).

[221] E. C. Curwen, "Prehistoric Agriculture in Britain", *Antiquity*, i (1927), pp. 280–2, 287–8; also for the role of the large plough-team in creating the curving reverse-S strip, see S. R. Eyre, "The Curving Plough-Strip and its Historical Implications", pp. 92–3.

Romano-British times and before point to a long history for the mould-board plough in England.[222] On the other hand, coulters in particular could also be found on ards.[223] Linguistic evidence is equally ambivalent. The term *carruca* is used almost exclusively in the surveys when describing peasant ploughs or plough-teams. This may indicate the mould-board plough, although, as we have already observed,[224] the distinction between the terms *carruca* and *aratrum* in the documents seems to bear little relationship to the type of ploughs in actual operation. Medieval illustrations offer a little more help. What looks to be a peasant plough, because a woman is shown driving on the team with a goad while her husband (apparently) held the plough, appears in a late fourteenth-century copy of Langland's *Piers the Plowman*.[225] The plough, drawn by two oxen, has a large and pronounced mould-board. If other English medieval illustrations showing small plough-teams can also be considered as likely peasant ploughs, then some of these have mould-boards as well.[226] Finally, Fitzherbert, writing virtually at the end of the medieval period, lists mould-boards as an essential part of ploughs at the time, although here he is probably concerned more with large farms than small ones.[227]

It would seem, on balance, that the English peasantry of the last three centuries of the middle ages used mould-board ploughs rather than ards, although substantial differences in the quality of these ploughs undoubtedly existed. In any case, if used sparingly, small plough-teams could probably have pulled mould-board ploughs with comfort, as indicated in the *Piers the Plowman* illustration just mentioned. It was only for extended ploughing over long periods of time that larger teams would be needed.[228]

It is equally difficult to tell much about the other features of peasant plough design, such as whether they were wheeled, foot, or swing ploughs. The post-1200 illustrations – if we assume that some of them at least portray peasant ploughs – show mainly swing

---

[222] Payne, "The British Plough: Some Stages", pp. 77–9; see also *Agrarian History of England and Wales*, i, pt 2, pp. 83–7.
[223] E.g., see Steensberg's illustrations of fifteenth- and sixteenth-century Danish ards, all with coulters ("North West European Plough-types", figs. 15–19 (pp. 272–5)).
[224] See pp. 75, 128 above.
[225] See note 179 above.
[226] See Figure 11; also Singer et al., *History of Technology*, ii, fig. 55 (p. 90).
[227] See p. 128 above.   [228] As discussed above, pp. 73–4.

ploughs.[229] This seems to be a trend away from the wheeled ploughs of earlier illustrations.[230] There is, however, a reference to a peasant having to make plough wheels for the lord as a labour service at Limpsfield (Surrey) in 1321, and it is possible that this man also made plough wheels for his peasant neighbours.[231]

If the evidence about peasant ploughs in medieval England is scanty, even less is known about peasant harrows. That peasants did harrow has already been discussed, and since they seem in general to have employed the same one-horse harrowing teams as on the demesne (see pp. 113, 221n above), we can perhaps surmise that peasant and demesne harrows were therefore similar and probably looked something like the Luttrell Psalter harrow or that described by Fitzherbert.[232] Some peasants at least had ox-harrows (see p. 220 above), but again we have no real idea as to what they looked like, beyond presuming that they may have been similar to those on the demesne.[233]

Rather more information exists for peasant vehicles, mostly from the surveys and extents, where altogether seven different vehicle types or terms were specified – *carecta* (or cart), *carrus* (also *carra* or *currus*), *plaustrum*, *curtana*, *quadriga*, *biga* and *tumberellus* (or tumbrel) – all in relation to hauling services (for example, see pp. 221–5 above). These terms have all been encountered in previous chapters, but the survey material does add considerably to our knowledge about the vehicles that these terms represented, particularly for the thirteenth century. As an aid to analysis, all the manors for which peasant vehicle terms were given in the surveys have been arranged by county and vehicle for the two halves of the thirteenth century, as shown in Table 33.

As with the account material examined for the demesne, the most common peasant vehicle indicated in the surveys was the cart (*carecta*). In the 1201–1250 period it was found on 70.7 per cent of manors for which peasant vehicle terms were given, rising to 87.2

[229] Singer et al., *History of Technology*, ii, figs. 54, 55 (pp. 89–90); Steensberg, "North West European Plough-types", fig. 14 (p. 271).
[230] E.g., see Figures 12, 13, and 15 above.
[231] *Custumals of Battle Abbey*, p. 146.
[232] Millar, *Luttrell Psalter*, fo. 171; *Fitzherbert*, p. 24.
[233] See pp. 141–2 above.

per cent in the 1251–1300 period. As has already been indicated (pp. 221–2, 224–5), it was always horse-hauled and fairly light, since a single animal most normally drew it. The next two most popular vehicles in the surveys were the *carrus* (sometimes *carra* or *currus*) and the *plaustrum*. Their presence in the surveys declined markedly over the thirteenth century. In fact, the surveys indicate that the *carrus* and the *plaustrum* were virtually the same vehicle. Both were ox-hauled,[234] and both had double the capacity of carts.[235] In some cases the terms are used so interchangeably that it is almost certain that they signified the same vehicle. Thus at Thorpe-le-Soken (Essex) in 1222, tenants called *hidarii* had to find "one *carrus* with two men to carry hard corn and another to carry soft corn, and each *plaustrum* will have one sheaf".[236] It may be, as suggested in Chapter 3,[237] that the term *carrus* is the older of the two signifying the same vehicle; in this case, the more backward-looking surveys seem to have kept it in currency longer than more contemporary-minded documents, such as accounts. Whether the same vehicles or not, *carri* and *plaustra* must have been very heavy, as six- and eight-ox teams were often needed to haul them.[238] Nowhere in the peasant material was there a reference to the covered, four-wheeled *carrus* found in seigneurial households.[239]

The other certifiable ox-hauled peasant vehicle was the *curtana*

---

[234] Thus, references to *carri* or *carri*-loads being ox-hauled are as follows: *Select Documents of . . . the Abbey of Bec*, p. 85; *Custumals of Battle Abbey*, pp. 4–5; *Rentalia et custumaria . . . Glastoniae*, pp. 82, 86, 129, 140; *Two Registers Formerly Belonging to the Family of Beauchamp of Hatch*, pp. 5, 8; also for *carri* or *curri* being hauled by mixed teams, see *Custumals of Battle Abbey*, p. 156. For *plaustra* or *plaustra*-loads being ox-hauled, see *Rentalia et custumaria . . . Glastoniae*, pp. 210, 216, 220, 221; *Historia et cartularium monasterii Sancti Petri Gloucestriae*, ed. W. H. Hart, 3 vols. (Rolls Series, 1863–7), iii, p. 143; also *Court Rolls of the Manor of Hales 1272–1307*, ed. J. Amphlett, S. G. Hamilton and R. A. Wilson (Worcs. Hist. Soc., 1910, 1912, 1933) ii, p. 551.

[235] For a *carrus* or *carrus*-load being equal to two carts or cart-loads, see *Red Book of Worcester*, i, p. 14; ii, p. 194; *Rentalia et Custumaria . . . Glastoniae*, pp. 65, 140; *Historia et cartularium monasterii Sancti Petri Gloucestriae*, iii, p. 62. For a *plaustrum* or *plaustrum*-load being equal to two carts or cart-loads, see *Domesday of St. Paul's of the Year 1222*, pp. 62, 94; *Rentalia et custumaria . . . Glastoniae*, pp. 67, 68.

[236] . . . *j carrum cum duobus hominibus ad portandum durum bladum & aliud ad portandum molle bladum & utrumque plaustrum habebit j garbam. Domesday of St. Paul's of the Year 1222*, pp. 42–3. For similar references, see *Rentalia et custumaria . . . Glastoniae*, pp. 72, 82, 125–6.

[237] See p. 153 above.
[238] See pp. 222–4 above.
[239] See p. 152 above.

Table 33. *Peasant vehicle type distribution*

County	No. of manors having a particular peasant vehicle						
	C	Ca	P	Cu	Q	B	T
(a) *1201–50*							
Bedfordshire	2	—	—	—	—	—	—
Berkshire	1	—	—	—	—	—	—
Cambridgeshire	2	—	—	—	1	1	—
Dorset	—	2	2	—	—	—	—
Essex	1	3	5	—	—	—	—
Hampshire	1	—	—	—	2	—	—
Hertfordshire	—	—	1	—	—	—	—
Huntingdonshire	6	—	—	—	—	—	—
Middlesex	3	—	2	—	—	—	—
Norfolk	2	1	1	—	1	—	—
Nottinghamshire	6	1	—	—	—	—	—
Somerset	7	13	3	—	—	—	—
Surrey	1	—	—	—	—	—	—
Sussex	—	1	—	—	—	—	—
Wiltshire	9	2	2	—	2	—	—
Total	41	22	16	—	6	1	—
% (from a total of 58 manors)	70.7	37.9	27.6	—	10.3	1.7	—
(b) *1251–1300*							
Bedfordshire	1	—	—	—	—	—	—
Cambridgeshire	12	—	—	—	—	—	—
Essex	3	—	—	—	—	—	—
Gloucestershire	9	4	2	—	—	—	—
Hampshire	7	—	—	—	—	—	—
Hertfordshire	4	—	—	—	—	—	—
Huntingdonshire	8	—	—	—	—	—	—
Norfolk	10	—	—	—	—	—	2
Oxfordshire	1	—	—	—	—	—	—
Somerset	5	2	2	—	—	—	—
Suffolk	6	—	—	—	—	—	2
Sussex	1	3	2	1	—	—	—
Warwickshire	2	—	—	—	—	—	—
Wiltshire	1	1	—	1	—	—	—
Worcestershire	4	2	—	—	—	—	—
Yorkshire	1	—	—	—	—	—	—
Total	75	12	6	2	—	—	4
% (from a total of 85 manors)	87.2	14.0	7.0	2.3	—	—	4.7

found on certain of the manors of Battle Abbey.[240] These may have been shorter versions of the *carrus*, as the normal hauling teams for these peasant *curtanae* were quite small, being no more than four oxen, and often only two, or even one.[241] On the Battle Abbey estates at least, they seem to have been reserved solely for hauling dung. Perhaps they had some form of tipping action, although to require teams of up to four oxen they still must have been of a fair size.

Quadrigae were found as peasant vehicles in a few cases in the early thirteenth-century extents, but the vehicle tends to fade out after that, confirming the impression gained from studying the demesne records that, as a term at least, it was becoming antiquated.[242]

The vehicle called the *biga* only occurred once as a peasant vehicle in the surveys and extents examined in this study, so it is difficult to add much to what has already been said.[243] Presumably it was similar to a cart.

Tumbrels were mentioned as peasant vehicles on four manors. They were clearly distinct from carts, but similar in capacity. Thus

Notes to Table 33
Key
C – cart (*carecta*)
Ca – *carrus, carra,* or *currus*
P – *plaustrum*
Cu – *curtana*
Q – *quadriga*
B – *biga*
T – tumbrel (*tumberellus*)
– – No vehicles of this type found

Notes and sources: For sources, see J. Langdon, "Horse Hauling: A Revolution in Vehicle Transport in Twelfth- and Thirteenth-Century England?", *Past and Present*, no. 103 (1984), table 3. In some cases the vehicles were indicated by their vehicle-load equivalents (*carectata, plaustratum, cariatus,* etc.).

[240] That is, Marley and Barnhorn (Sussex), Bromham (Wiltshire) and Limpsfield (Surrey); *Custumals of Battle Abbey,* pp. 5, 6, 14, 20, 74, 150. The Barnhorn and Limpsfield cases were post-1300.
[241] *Ibid.,* pp. 5, 6, 20.
[242] The term did survive for some time in the north, however; see *Bishop Hatfield's Survey,* ed. W. Greenwell (Surtees Soc., xxxii, Durham, 1856), pp. 4, 7, 9, 10, 11, 14, 20, 23, etc. Information regarding the vehicle itself is contradictory, since both ox-hauled and horse-hauled *quadrigae* are indicated in the records (e.g., *ibid.,* pp. 9, 10, 29, 30, etc.; *Select Documents of . . . the Abbey of Bec,* p. 47; see also Langdon, thesis, p. 308).
[243] See pp. 78, 153 above.

tenants at Walpole and Walton (Norfolk) in 1251 had to find carts or tumbrels (*carectas vel tumberellos*) to carry dung, for which the lord was to supply them with horses.[244]

e) THE ROLE OF HORSES AND OXEN IN PEASANT FARM MANAGEMENT, 1200–1500

It is difficult to discuss with any accuracy the various policies and decisions that were involved in the running of medieval peasant farms. We have no accounts for peasant farms that allow us the sort of glimpse into the decision-making process that we have for the demesne. As a result, any conclusions here regarding peasant attitudes as to the use of draught animals must be inferred rather indirectly and as a consequence are somewhat conjectural.

First of all, it is to be presumed that the same arguments concerning the speed and stamina of the horse already considered in Chapter 3 (pp. 160–4) must also have applied to peasant horses. It may be said, though, that being of inferior stock – the lay subsidies, for instance, supply ample evidence of lame, blind and generally decrepit horses among the peasantry[245] – peasant horses were of such poor quality that questions of increased speed and stamina were largely superfluous. The low values that these horses often had would tend to support this view.[246] However, the fact that peasant horses were seldom worth much does not necessarily mean that they were vastly inferior draught animals. In a number of cases, they were simply old horses without many years of life remaining (although these last few years could be very useful indeed to the peasant). Part of the confusion over how useful horses were for peasants rests with their relatively low value in relation to oxen. It might be assumed that this price difference reflected the superior draught qualities of oxen, but this was not so. Much of the value of an ox was made up by its meat, a consideration that did not apply to horses, because of the medieval taboo against the eating of horse flesh.[247] Thus the price of an ox in medieval times consisted of three

[244] Brit. Lib. Cott. MS CLaud. C. XI, fos. 195v, 201v.
[245] For example, as in the lay subsidy assessment for south Wiltshire in 1225, where peasant horses ("avers" or *jumenta*) are indicated as being lame (*claudus*), blind (*cecus*), or weak (*debilis*) with some frequency. P.R.O. E179 242/47.
[246] E.g., see the heriot prices for peasant affers above (p. 200).
[247] For the effect of the taboo on the eating of horseflesh, see pp. 263–4 below.

value components: that is, meat + hide + draught potential; the price of a horse was made up of only two components: hide + draught potential. The meat and hide components were relatively stable in value, but that for draught depreciated rapidly over time, not only because the animal gradually lost power as it got older,[248] but also because of the decrease in the expectation of useful work. If the meat and hide values were subtracted from both horses and oxen, then – judged solely from the point of view of draught – the value of each at the same age would have been much more alike; indeed, horses, having the greater speed and stamina, might well have been more valuable.

The main objection to peasants using horses would seem to have been that of day-to-day costs. Our analysis of demesne accounts shows that horses were at least 40 per cent more expensive to keep than oxen, even considering things like hay and straw which demesne officials tended to ignore.[249] These figures, however, were based on demesne working conditions. It has been a familiar refrain in this study that these conditions were difficult. Demesne ploughing was a day in, day out activity for most of the year; and, judging from the oats rations in the accounts, demesne carting animals were under an even heavier work load. As a result, higher energy feeds, such as oats, were in particular demand. This was especially the case for horses, which did not perform as well as oxen on a diet of hay and grass.

Because of the smaller size of peasant farms, however, the work load on draught animals was usually much less severe. Although a virgate holding with heavy ploughing services might have had up to 100 days' work or more for its draught animals, most holdings needed considerably less than this.[250] We must presume that for much of the time peasant draught were standing idle. As a result, most peasants could get by with feeding their horses and oxen on a non-working diet of hay and grass, reserving high energy foods, such as oats or even vetches, for the relatively short periods

---

[248] It has been estimated that a horse aged 15–20 years has only half the working capacity of one in its prime (5–11 years). E. J. T. Collins, "The Farm Horse Economy of England and Wales in the Early Tractor Age 1900–40", in *Horses in European Economic History: A Preliminary Canter*, ed. F. M. L. Thompson (Reading, 1983), pp. 89–90.

[249] Pp. 158–9 above; Langdon, "Economics of Horses and Oxen", pp. 36–7.

[250] See pp. 73–4 above.

of peak activity. Because of this the oats or legume consumption by peasant animals was presumably very low, and thus the cost difference between horses and oxen inevitably narrowed. There is little doubt that horses would still have cost a little more to keep than oxen, but now the other advantages held by horses over oxen became much more important.

One of these advantages was versatility. Whereas oxen were only employed for ploughing and perhaps a little hauling and harrowing, horses were used for all three, plus riding and pack-animal work, and generally they were quicker at them all. Horses were versatile economically as well as functionally. They had a much greater price range and, not having value as meat, could often be bought at very low prices. This meant that, despite its relatively higher operating costs, the horse was a low-capital investment ideal for peasants. Furthermore, as we have seen in the demesne case, it was often possible to replace a given number of oxen with a smaller number of horses.[251] It is interesting to note that those lay subsidies where horses dominated as draught animals among the peasantry had significantly lower levels of draught animals per taxpayer than those where oxen were dominant.[252] Such potential reductions in the total numbers of draught animals needed on a holding would have quickly compensated for any cost disadvantage that still attached to horses. It also gave smallholders a much greater opportunity of participating in full-scale, self-sufficient farming, by providing them with an effective technology based on all-horse traction. The smaller plough-teams that the use of horses allowed played a special part in this.

Nevertheless their more substantial peasant neighbours – that is, those holding virgates or even half-virgates – continued to use some oxen at least, preferring – it seems – to follow the lead of the demesne, probably for the same economic reasons. Some of this may have been due to the presence of labour services which kept the animal work level on these more substantial holdings at such a pitch that it still made sense to use oxen. Once these labour services were commuted or dropped into disuse, the decline in animal work

---

[251] Pp. 167–9 above.

[252] Thus, for example, there were only 0.9 draught animals per peasant taxpayer in the horse-oriented lay subsidy assessment for Blackbourne Hundred (Suffolk) in 1283, compared to 1.7 working animals per taxpayer for the ox-oriented 1225 south Wiltshire assessment (as calculated from Table 24).

required may have had a part in encouraging the "rationalization" observed in the fifteenth century of either going completely to all-horse farming or reverting to an increased use of oxen, both for the same reason of making more efficient use of animals now more lightly employed than before.

We have shown in this chapter that the peasantry used horses to a much greater degree than the demesne. By the end of the thirteenth century, peasants across England were employing almost as many horses as oxen, and the trend towards horses continued afterwards, although it probably did not gain real momentum until well into the fifteenth century. Despite this, peasant and demesne experience was still very similar in many essentials. The timing for the large-scale introduction of the horse to farm hauling over the late twelfth and early thirteenth century seems to have been the same for both peasant and demesne, as it was for the period of "rationalization" in the fifteenth century. In any case, the distinction between demesne and peasant farms was largely an irrelevant one as far as this study is concerned. What seemed to matter far more was farm size, no matter who held it. In this regard, the most interesting economic group was that of smallholders. The advantages that the horse held as a cheaply bought, all-purpose beast meant a disproportionate interest in the animal by this particular group, which in turn gave villages with a large smallholding population a very horse-oriented appearance. But even in these villages more substantial tenants continued to use oxen. It was only in the fifteenth century and later that the technical argument for using only horses began to conquer all levels of farming society over substantial areas of England. Even then, the transformation was only partial, since many areas elected to stick with oxen and, indeed, often intensified their use of them. Why this movement should have taken on such a complex pattern is a subject for the next chapter.

5. *Conclusions*

It has been the purpose of the previous three chapters to provide, as far as possible, a statistical base for assessing the significance of the introduction of the work-horse to English farming between 1066 and 1500. The difficulties in obtaining this base in the face of often inadequate data have already been outlined. Nevertheless some basic conclusions can be drawn. First of all, it is clear that the horse's influence in medieval agriculture steadily increased right through the period. Figure 42 shows this in graphical form for the country as a whole. Much of the figure is necessarily impressionistic,[1] since only the solid curve for the demesne in the three centuries after Domesday is based on abundant and reliable evidence. Nevertheless it does highlight the fact that there were two key periods for the increase in the use of horses during the middle ages, the first covering the twelfth and thirteenth centuries and the second beginning sometime in the fifteenth century[2] and continuing – it would appear – into the sixteenth, with a stagnant period during the fourteenth century, when the proportion of horses tended to level off (see especially pp. 94–6 and Table 28 above). Of the two ascendant phases for the use of horses, the second covering the fifteenth century and later was the more complex, resulting in the polarizing effect noted in the previous chapter. Here animals were introduced, or – in the case of oxen – reintroduced, to certain jobs, with an eye

---

[1] The figure is made up from the data from Tables 2, 7, 11, 28, 29, 30 and as on pp. 30, 38, 48. A detailed explanation of how the curves were arrived at and of the various assumptions made is given in Langdon, thesis, ch. 5, n. 1 (pp. 384–5). The end-point for the three curves (1574) is the median year of the sample of probate inventories given in Table 30. The bottom solid line represents the fairly precise demesne experience up to the median point for the Sample B accounts (i.e. 1381); the dashed lines represent the much less certain experience for the peasantry, the demesne after the fourteenth century, and the peasantry and the demesne averaged together.
[2] See pp. 205–12 above.

254

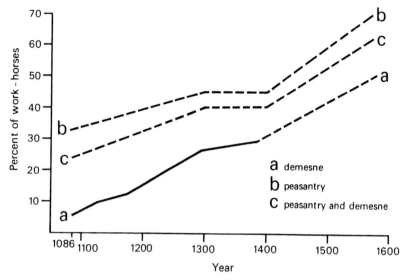

Fig. 42: Percentage of work-horses in demesne and peasant draught stock from 1086 to 1574.

to the total farm economy.[3] The end result, as is so evident in the sixteenth-century wills and inventories, was a patchwork of areas using horses only and others using mainly oxen. Indeed, as we have shown in the previous three chapters, the use of horses varied considerably from region to region right through our period. This regional variation, however, should not be regarded as arising strictly out of economic needs, since there were many other factors that led to one animal or the other being favoured in a particular area.

One of the more important of these factors was soil, which often directly determined whether horses or oxen were employed. Horses, for instance, had difficulties in ploughing or hauling through heavy clay lands and were much better on light, easily worked soils; on the other hand, oxen tended to slip or suffer hoof damage on stony land.[4] We should then expect the distribution of

---

[3] E.g., see pp. 212 and 252–3 above.
[4] *Walter of Henley*, p. 319, c. 36; *Fitzherbert*, pp. 15–16; J. Crofts, *Packhorse, Waggon and Post*, p. 113.

horses and oxen in medieval England and afterwards to follow the distribution of the various soils in the country, and to some degree this was the case. Thus the thin, stony chalk-lands of the Chilterns or the Yorkshire Wolds and the light soils of Norfolk were areas where horses were employed on their own from a very early period indeed. On the other hand, the much more predominantly clay lands of the midlands tended to keep using oxen right to the end of the sixteenth century.[5] At the same time, however, there were often contradictions to this general rule of oxen for heavy soils, horses for light ones. For example, the use of horses in medieval Essex was surprisingly popular, given that it is a county which has its share of heavy soils.[6] On the other hand, areas like the west midlands, also with a reputation for heavy soils, nonetheless had a variety of lighter ones as well, particularly where gravels and sands were intermixed with belts of heavier clays and marls;[7] yet oxen seem to have been used in almost all cases here. Clearly other factors were at work. Only in a few counties, such as Kent, was the distribution of horses and oxen variable enough to suggest that it may have been following existing soil patterns.[8]

Terrain also seems to have had a variable effect on the use of horses and oxen. Thus upland areas with their predisposition to thin, often stony soils were more favourable to horses than lowland areas, where heavier clays and loams were liable to be found.[9] In addition, it appears that oxen were suspect when cultivating slopes, where there was presumably a tendency for ploughs to slip at slow speeds.[10] Again, this pattern did not apply everywhere. The demesnes on the Cotswold Hills, for instance, continued to use oxen in great numbers, and presumably the same applied to the

[5] According to probate inventories: e.g., Wo.R.O. Ref. 008:7, 1590, box 94b, nos. 39, 43, 47f; box 95a, no. 55; L.J.R.O. Lichfield Probate Records B/C/11 Alice Lees, 1590; Thomas Litlehales, 1590; Robert Laken, 1592; Thomas Lythall, 1592; *Probate Inventories of Lichfield and District 1568–1680*, ed. D. G. Vaisey (Staffs. Rec. Soc., 4th series, v, 1969), pp. 41–3, 44–5.
[6] Darby (ed.), *The Domesday Geography of Eastern England*, 3rd edn (Cambridge, 1971), fig. 55 (p. 217); Kerridge, *Agricultural Revolution*, p. 89.
[7] As at Yardley, Warwickshire (Victor Skipp, *Medieval Yardley* (Chichester, 1970), pp. 5–8); see also Dyer, *Lords and Peasants*, p. 23.
[8] E.g., see p. 101 above.
[9] E.g., see pp. 100–1 above.
[10] Kerridge, *Agricultural Revolution*, p. 49; Edward Little, "Farming in Wiltshire", *Journal Royal Agric. Soc.*, v (1844), p. 170.

peasantry.[11] Other areas of extremely broken country, such as Devon, also used oxen to a great degree.[12]

Rainfall appears to have been an important factor as well. The concentration of horses in the south and east of England in medieval times shows a marked correlation with the drier areas of the country shown on modern-day precipitation maps. That rainfall was an important factor has a certain logic. Modern experiments show that excessive moisture increases the adhesion between plough and soil,[13] and very muddy soils certainly seem to have suited oxen better than horses.[14] Even here there are anomalies, however. The particularly ox-oriented region of the Weald, for instance, falls into the drier part of the country, and the relatively dry northern districts on the east coast, such as Durham, also remained strongly committed to using oxen.[15]

Turning to more ecological factors, the distribution of meadow and pasture also seems to have been an important factor in determining the use of horses and oxen, as stressed by Fitzherbert.[16] In general terms, pasture and meadow were more abundant towards the north and west, where oxen were more likely to be employed. Significantly, seemingly isolated ox-oriented areas, such as the Weald, were also areas where woodland pasture and meadow were abundant. Again, of course, there are anomalies. Regions such as south-east Worcestershire and the Feldon in Warwickshire, where arable land clearly dominated at the expense of meadow and pasture as early as Domesday, still continued to use oxen in considerable number. In these cases, though, the importing of hay or the transhumance of stock to nearby pastoral parishes may have been easier than in the south-east.

[11] E.g., see under Gloucestershire in Table 11, where many of the demesnes represented were from the Cotswolds. We have little evidence for the peasantry, but it seems that in the sixteenth century the Cotswold farmers were still employing oxen to a significant degree. Kerridge, *Agricultural Revolution*, p. 68.

[12] They were still using them in the late sixteenth and early seventeenth centuries. *Devon Inventories of the Sixteenth and Seventeenth Centuries*, pp. 4–38.

[13] B. F. Willetts, "The Performance of Footings on, and Cultivation Implements in, Soils" (Univ. of Durham Ph.D. thesis, 1954), ii, p. 20. As a result, the draining of fields often allowed the use of smaller plough-teams: W. Palin, "The Farming of Cheshire", *Journal Royal Agric. Soc.*, v (1844), p. 82.

[14] That is, for hauling conditions at least (Crofts, *Packhorse, Waggon and Post*, p. 6).

[15] See Table 11 under Durham and Sussex; also the Durham inventories in Table 23.

[16] *Fitzherbert*, p. 15.

As we have already seen, the character of land-holding also seems to have played a key role in determining whether horses or oxen were preferred in a particular area. Thus, in parts of eastern England, where the fragmentation of holdings had reached such a pitch that few tenants had more than ten acres, the use of the horse was almost universal.[17] Admittedly it is often hard to distinguish between what may have been a *bona fide* preference for the horse in technological terms rather than just as a result of being a small-holder, but there does seem to have been a definite relationship between holding size and the use of horses for draught. In this case, the use of horses must be seen as being more probable in areas of partible rather than impartible inheritance, since the fragmentation of holdings was often connected with the former,[18] although the question of Kent, with its partial allegiance to oxen while still being an area of partible inheritance (or gavelkind), complicates this somewhat.

The type of landlord may have had an effect on the use of horses as well. We have seen that in the early centuries after the Conquest there may have been a greater tendency for ecclesiastic landlords to use horses than for lay landlords, and part of this trend may have been passed on to their tenants, although we have little proof of it. It has been suggested, too, that lords often exerted considerable control in the matter of field systems, particularly in the creation of systemized grazing arrangements, such as harvest and winter shack (the grazing periods between the end of the harvest and the sowing of the crops for the following year), full-year fallow grazing, and fold-course.[19] This careful husbanding of grazing resources may have encouraged the use of oxen instead of horses. Since the most systemized grazing arrangements occurred in the Midland system,[20] where more oxen often predominated, a connection between the two may exist. There are, however, some grave inconsistencies.

---

[17] E.g., as in Blackbourne Hundred (Table 24); for the fragmentation of holdings in this area, see H. E. Hallam, *Rural England, 1066–1348* (London, 1981), p. 72.

[18] E.g., Miller and Hatcher, *Medieval England: Rural Society and Economic Change*, p. 129.

[19] B. M. S. Campbell, "Commonfield Origins – the Regional Dimension", in *The Origins of Open-Field Agriculture*, ed. T. Rowley (London, 1981), pp. 112–29; idem, "The Regional Uniqueness of English Field Systems? Some Evidence from Eastern Norfolk", *Agric. Hist. Rev.*, xxix (1981), pp. 16–28.

[20] As outlined by Gray, *English Field Systems*, frontispiece map; see also *A New Historical Geography of England before 1600*, ed. Darby, fig. 23 (p. 82).

Oxen, for instance, were also employed extensively in the far less regularized field systems of the south-west and north-west, while counties like Bedfordshire and Northamptonshire, which generally had regular commonfield systems, nevertheless displayed a very horse-oriented peasantry. We have also in the matter of lordship to consider the effect that certain feudal bans had in encouraging or discouraging the use of horses versus oxen, particularly the manorial restrictions in the selling of draught livestock. In the main these would appear to have made no difference since the fines or licences involved usually applied equally to horses and oxen, although occasionally one beast was discriminated against more than the other.[21]

The control that lords and indeed the village community as a whole had over the organization of field systems was reflected not only in grazing arrangements but also in those for cropping. In particular, it has been claimed that the transition from a two-course to a three-course rotation allowed farmers to obtain a much greater harvest of oats, which in turn encouraged the use of horses for agricultural work.[22] We should then expect a greater concentration of work-horses in areas of three-course or even more intensive rotations than in those following only two-course rotations. Since, in the very broadest of terms, three-course and more intensive rotations were found further south and especially east,[23] this might be seen as conveniently coinciding with the intensification in the use of horses towards the south-east. But the distribution of two- versus three-course rotations – let alone more intensive ones – across England in the middle ages was in fact a very complicated affair.

---

[21] As at Ashcot in Somerset, *c.* 1235–40, and at Rackham (Sussex) in the latter half of the thirteenth century, where the licences only applied to male foals, which may have discouraged horse breeding. *Rentalia et custumaria . . . Glastoniae*, p. 153; *Thirteen Custumals . . . of the Bishop of Chichester*, p. 66.

[22] White, *Medieval Technology and Social Change*, pp. 72–4; B. H. Slicher van Bath, *Agrarian History of Western Europe*, pp. 63–4; idem, "Yield Ratios, 810–1820", *Afdeling Agrarische Geschiedenis Bijdragen*, 10 (1963), p. 14.

[23] Hallam, *Rural England*, p. 249; Miller and Hatcher, *Medieval England: Rural Society and Economic Change*, pp. 89–90; Dyer, *Lords and Peasants*, pp. 68–9, 322 (two-course rotations on the west midland estates of the bishop of Worcester); P. F. Brandon, "Demesne Arable Farming in Coastal Sussex during the Later Middle Ages", *Agric. Hist. Rev.*, xix (1971), pp. 126–9 (intensive rotations in coastal Sussex); B. M. S. Campbell, "Agricultural Progress in Medieval England: Some Evidence from Eastern Norfolk", *Econ. Hist. Rev.*, 2nd series, xxxvi (1983), pp. 28–9 (intensive rotations in eastern Norfolk).

Three-field systems, for instance, presumably with similar degrees of rotation, were found in considerable number as far west and north as Somerset, Staffordshire and Yorkshire, often intermingled with two-field systems.[24] As a result, it is impossible at the moment to establish with any accuracy a correlation between the distribution of two- versus three-course rotations and the relative use of horses and oxen. In any case, despite assertions by some writers to the contrary,[25] it was perfectly possible to grow considerable quantities of oats and other spring crops on two-course rotations, especially where soil and climate favoured their cultivation, thus undermining the whole theoretical basis for the connection.[26]

It is possible that enclosure encouraged the use of horses, in that the smaller teams in which horses were employed allowed them to plough more easily in the relatively confined and awkward areas of closes. Such a theory is attractive when taking stock of comparatively enclosed counties, such as Essex, Hertfordshire and Kent, where horses generally outnumbered oxen,[27] but it fails when taking into account similar areas elsewhere, such as the Arden in Warwickshire, where significant levels of enclosure in the middle ages nonetheless went hand in hand with the continued use of oxen.[28] To a certain extent we have the same problem when considering scattered versus nucleated settlement. Lynn White, Jr, has made the claim that when peasants lived far away from their fields, as they were apt to do in nucleated villages, then the use of horses for ploughing became very handy, as they also acted as a quick means of getting these peasant farmers to and from their places of work.[29] Conversely, where hamlet settlement was the prevailing pattern, as in much of the west and south-west, the proximity of the fields in these instances would theoretically have made the use of horses for

---

[24] E.g., *A New Historical Geography of England before 1600*, fig. 23 (p. 82).

[25] Esp. White, *Medieval Technology and Social Change*, pp. 70–4.

[26] Hilton and Sawyer, "Technical Determinism", pp. 98–9; Titow, *English Rural Society*, p. 39.

[27] See Tables 11, 24 and 27.

[28] Oxen were still employed in the Arden in the sixteenth century: e.g., L.J.R.O. Lichfield Probate Records B/C/11 William Coke, 1536–7; Richard Coke, 1538; Robert Dagull, 1547; John Undertre, 1537; P.R.O. Probate 2, nos. 223, 294, 295, 390, 499 (Warwickshire inventories for Sutton Coldfield, Stretton on Dunsmore, Bedworth, Weddington, Berkswell, Kingshurst, Ward End, Little Bromwich and Maxstoke).

[29] White, *Medieval Technology and Social Change*, pp. 67–8, makes this point as a possible explanation for the desertion of hamlets.

the pre- and post-cultivation transport much less crucial. This factor was obviously not a dominating one, otherwise oxen would have been restricted to a much smaller area than they were, but it may have had a contributing effect in some instances.

A much more profound influence upon the distribution of horses and oxen may have been the increasing sophistication of market transactions, coupled with the growing influence of urban communities. One of the problems with having only horses for draught is that you now have no use for that body of male cattle formerly employed as work animals. This problem must have been particularly acute for the peasantry, since, even in areas where these peasants used horses almost exclusively for draught, there is still ample evidence that they raised cattle. Cows and their followers, for instance, figure prominently among the goods of these peasants in the lay subsidy returns.[30] Presuming that they kept young females as breeding and milking stock, we are forced to wonder what they did with the majority of the young males. They may have been slaughtered as meat for the peasants themselves, but from what we know of peasant diet, with its generally low emphasis on meat, especially before the Black Death,[31] this seems unlikely. They may well have been sold to wealthier tenants or demesnes still using oxen in the area. Demesne accounts, in particular, almost always show demesnes buying more oxen than they raised themselves.[32] Another likely outlet for these unwanted bullocks would have been in supplying the meat demands of urban populations. This was of particular importance in the case of London, which had a voracious demand for meat that in the later middle ages drew cattle from as far away as the west midlands and Wales.[33] This pull was undoubtedly

---

[30] E.g., see the Blackbourne Hundred (Suffolk) and Bedfordshire lay subsidies. *A Suffolk Hundred in the Year 1283*; *The Taxation of 1297*.
[31] Miller and Hatcher, *Medieval England: Rural Society and Economic Change*, pp. 159–61; C. C. Dyer, "English Diet in the Later Middle Ages", in *Social Relations and Ideas: Essays in Honour of R. H. Hilton*, ed. T. H. Aston, P. R. Coss, C. Dyer and J. Thirsk (Cambridge, 1983), p. 216.
[32] E.g., see Harvey, *Medieval Oxfordshire Village*, pp. 60–1; also N. S. B. and E. C. Gras, *The Economic and Social History of an English Village* (Cambridge, Mass., 1930), pp. 382–5. The same applied to horses.
[33] C. C. Dyer, "Warwickshire Farming 1349–c. 1520: Preparations for Agricultural Revolution", *Dugdale Society Occasional Papers*, no. 27 (1981), p. 20; C. Skeel, "The Cattle Trade between Wales and England from the Fifteenth to the Nineteenth Century", *Trans. of the Royal Hist. Soc.*, 4th series, ix (1926), pp. 137–8.

strongest in the immediate vicinity of the city and may have encouraged farmers in the Home Counties and East Anglia to sell their ploughing and hauling oxen as meat cattle and to replace them with horses instead. This works best for Essex, which, on soil grounds, should probably have been employing much more in the way of oxen in the middle ages (see p. 256 above). On the other hand, the pull of London as a meat consuming centre had a much smaller effect on the counties immediately south, notably Surrey and Sussex, which on this basis should have been using many more horses for draught than they in fact were.[34] Proximity to the Continent was also a likely factor, since the more progressive attitude to farming found in Norfolk and coastal Sussex indicates a susceptibility to ideas from mainland Europe.[35] We have already commented upon this in relation to the use of the mixed plough-team in East Anglia during the twelfth century (p. 53), and this would seem to have had a continuing influence.

Finally we come to some of the more psychological reasons for choosing either horses or oxen for draught. Prime among these was resistance to change. The conservative and unadventurous nature of medieval farmers, rich and poor alike, has often been commented upon as being a barrier to agricultural improvement.[36] It has been claimed that such advances as there were arose not so much out of a spirit of technological enquiry as from a "slowly forming local tradition",[37] perhaps in the same way as dialect or other features of regional custom were formed. R. H. Britnell has commented on this in relation to crop rotations in Essex,[38] and it might

---

[34] Surrey, for instance, of all the counties surrounding London, had the lowest proportion of horses in both demesne and peasant stock and certainly much lower than in many more distant counties, such as Suffolk and Norfolk (see Tables 11 and 27).

[35] Campbell, "Agricultural Progress", esp. pp. 26–7; Brandon, "Demesne Arable Farming in Coastal Sussex", pp. 113–34; E. Searle, *Lordship and Community: Battle Abbey and its Banlieu* (Toronto, 1974), pp. 272–86.

[36] Gray, *English Field Systems*, pp. 8–9; Homans, *English Villagers*, pp. 24, 303; R. H. Hilton, "Rent and Capital Formation in Feudal Society", *Second International Conference of Economic History, 1962* (Paris, 1965), pp. 36–7; Campbell, "Commonfield Origins", p. 120; Dyer, "Warwickshire Farming", p. 35.

[37] R. H. Britnell, "Agricultural Technology and the Margin of Cultivation in the Fourteenth Century", *Econ. Hist. Rev.*, 2nd series, xxx (1977), p. 55.

[38] Britnell, "Agricultural Technology", pp. 55–6. It has recently been argued that this very traditional approach to farming was further reinforced by the various agricultural treatises in circulation, which tended to guide demesne farmers in

also explain the demesne loyalty to mixed plough-teams in this same county, which seemingly cut across a great variety of soils.[39] We have already indicated, too, that the decision of the demesne managers at West Wycombe to go completely to horses for draught was probably based on local experience, as much as anything else. Similarly the refusal of such areas as the Cotswolds to go more to horses, as other upland areas had, may have been due to a desire to remain in line with the traditions of the surrounding lowlands. Local plough and vehicle type must often have reinforced this attitude. We have already indicated the close connection that the use of the horse had with carts, and, to a certain extent at least, wheeled ploughs were also much more likely with horses.[40] On the other hand, ox-oriented areas tended to be those with foot and swing ploughs and – particularly – wains or *plaustra*. Later experience suggests that wheeled ploughs were generally more expensive than foot or swing ploughs,[41] and, as we have seen, wains were too large to be hauled by horses. Thus a peasant or demesne farmer in the west or north of the country might well hedge at introducing all-horse draught if it meant not only the extra cost of employing horses but also that of changing over his ploughs and making his larger vehicles redundant.

Such conservatism at least had a rational basis. In some cases, though, the resistance to change might have arisen out of sheer obstinacy or even perversity, as indicated by Walter of Henley's complaint that the "malice" of the ploughman would not allow the horse-plough to go any faster than if it were drawn by oxen.[42] Also, the taboo on the eating of horseflesh, which was followed with remarkable consistency in England,[43] seriously weakened the

particular into very conservative and uniform farming practices. M. Mate, "Medieval Agrarian Practices: The Determining Factors", pp. 22–31.
[39] See Figures 25 and 26; also Darby, *Domesday Geography of Eastern England*, p. 217, fig. 55 (for the Essex soil experience). Essex seemingly only departed from the mixed plough-team pattern when all-horse farms began to appear after the Black Death in the south-eastern part of the county (see Figure 24).
[40] As at West Wycombe (see p. 169 above).
[41] Arthur Young, *A Six Months Tour through the North of England*, 2nd edn (London, 1771), i, pp. 23–4.
[42] *Walter of Henley*, p. 319, c. 37.
[43] The taboo was only broken in times of emergency, as during the 1315–17 famine, when it was reported that even horseflesh fetched a good price on the market (Kershaw, "Agrarian Crisis", p. 91). Otherwise, no references to horseflesh being sold or consumed were found in any of the accounts or other medieval records examined in this study.

economic case for horses. There is also the question of fashion, which could have worked in both directions. It may have been that, initially, horses were considered too grand to indulge in menial work,[44] which would have favoured the continued use of oxen; on the other hand, once they caught on, it may have been a point of pride among some farmers to have a team of horses rather than oxen, a consideration which seems to have become important in later times.[45]

In summary, we are faced with a bewildering array of possible causes for the introduction and distribution of work-horses in medieval English farming. Some of these were obviously very important. Thus, for the demesne, as we have already indicated in Chapter 3, the economic consideration that horses cost significantly more than oxen to keep patently played a crucial role in keeping oxen in work on these farms. For the peasantry, however, such a factor was of much less importance or at least could be countered by other considerations, such as the versatility of the horse. In this case, soils may have formed the deciding factor. Horses, no matter how useful they were to peasants in other ways, were just unable to perform on some types of ground, especially when ploughing. But we should not see this as the only reason for peasants using oxen, any more than we would say the same for the demesne. Rather, in any one particular area, there would be a combination of factors working in concert. Thus, in areas where the ox continued to hold sway we would tend to find the complementary equipment of swing or foot ploughs and wains, the relative availability of pasture and meadow, large holdings and impartible inheritance, lowland terrain, wetter climate, heavy soils, highly regulated field systems, two-course rotation, and location away from both London and the influence of the Continent. On the other hand, horses were more often found with wheeled ploughs and carts, scarcity of meadow and pasture, small fragmented holdings and partible inheritance, upland terrain, drier climate, light soils, less regulated field systems or even enclosure, three-course or better rotation, and location close to London and the Continent. Not all these factors applied in

---

[44] Trow-Smith, *History of British Livestock*, pp. 62–3, indicates this may have been the case in Celtic and Anglo-Saxon times.

[45] E.g., see Slicher van Bath, *Agrarian History of Western Europe*, p. 290; Haudricourt and Delamarre, *L'Homme et la Charrue*, p. 180; D. Warriner, *The Economics of Peasant Farming* (Oxford, 1939), p. 158n.

every instance, and in any case the situation was often complicated by more irrational reasons such as the strength of local tradition and the tendency to resist change. Nonetheless, all these considerations taken together generally meant that oxen were found more to the north and west (with the notable exception of the Weald) and horses to the south and particularly the east. We should point out, however, that even in those areas where oxen survived as draught animals, horses were still used for harrowing and pack-animal work, not to mention the possibility of hauling. There is also, in the first three centuries after Domesday, the phenomenon of the demesnes and more substantial peasants tending to use oxen much more than their smallholding colleagues, who used mainly horses. This makes it difficult to mark off with total precision "horse" areas from "ox" areas. However, as the concentration of tasks upon one animal or the other became more common, resulting in the polarizing effect already noted, the boundaries between areas that used mainly oxen and those that used only horses, although complex, became much clearer, particularly in the sixteenth century.[46]

Having discussed the various factors that governed the adoption of the horse as a work animal in medieval England, we can now turn to the other side of the question: what effect did the horse have on the country's agriculture, society and economy?

Dealing with agriculture first, the most important point to consider concerns the productivity of land. The dilemma facing medieval society as a whole, especially in the period leading up to the Black Death, was one of simply growing enough food to satisfy the hunger of the population at large. Did the introduction of the work-horse to English agriculture have any impact upon this at all? There are theoretical reasons for supposing that it could, particularly in relation to increasing crop yields. For instance, the faster ploughing and harrowing that the horse allowed – at least in theory

---

[46] To a certain extent some idea of these boundaries can be gained by looking at the distribution of mixed versus all-ox plough-teams in Figures 25–28, which seems to have had a strong similarity to the distribution of all-horse farms versus those with oxen in the sixteenth century (based upon a preliminary mapping of the data from over 870 sixteenth- and early seventeenth-century inventories carried out by the author). It seems that when the time came farms with mixed plough-teams, both peasant and demesne, generally converted to all-horse farming (as at West Wycombe, pp. 167–8 above; see also pp. 106, 234).

– meant that these cultivating techniques could be used more often. This was particularly important for fallow ploughing, which killed off the weeds that would otherwise appear in the crop of the following year. In general, the more fallow ploughings the better. In medieval times, twice over was thought to be sufficient;[47] in comparison, at the time of the Agricultural Revolution, when yields were some two or three times better than in the medieval period,[48] there could be as many as eight fallow ploughings.[49] Second, shorter ploughing, harrowing and hauling times would free more labour for other activities, such as weeding, breaking down the clods still left after harrowing, digging in marl, lime, seaweed or other additives, carting and spreading manure, beat-burning (the practice of paring off and burning the turf in order to kill off weeds and rejuvenate the soil), and so on. Weeds, in particular, are claimed to have played a very prominent role in keeping down medieval yields,[50] and certainly more weeding would have helped. Also if extra land had been available, then quicker ploughing and harrowing would also have freed more time to deal with it. It is perhaps no accident that the first significant upsurge in the use of horses during the twelfth and thirteenth centuries occurred during a period of known assarting (although the areas where the horses were introduced in greatest number did not always coincide with those where assarting was most extensive). Quicker ploughing may also have been useful in the post-Black Death period, when holding sizes became larger and presumably more prone to suffer from the labour shortages that were increasingly a feature of the time.[51] Finally, the efficiencies of traction, especially as regards ploughing, may have been improved by horses. Horses were generally able to plough a much neater furrow than oxen,[52] and, with the animals' greater stamina, perhaps ploughing depth was improved as well in some cases.

---

[47] E.g., see *Walter of Henley*, p. 321, c. 42.
[48] D. B. Grigg, *Population Growth and Agrarian Change* (Cambridge, 1980), p. 36.
[49] Robert Baker, "On the Farming of Essex", *Journal Royal Agric. Soc.*, v (1844), p. 34.
[50] W. Harwood Long, "The Low Yields of Corn in Medieval England", *Econ. Hist. Rev.*, 2nd series, xxxii (1979), pp. 459–69.
[51] E.g., see Postan, *Medieval Economy and Society*, pp. 156–7; Dyer, *Lords and Peasants*, pp. 299–301, 314–15; Hatcher, *Plague, Population and the English Economy*, pp. 47–54.
[52] Personal communication with Mr Philip Brooks, retired farmer from Churt in Surrey, who worked with both horses and oxen in Argentina and England.

Most of these hypothetical aids to land productivity depend upon an assumed increase in speed when using horses instead of oxen. We have some indications that when mixed plough-teams were employed in place of all-ox plough-teams there was an increase in ploughing speed. However, when all-horse plough-teams were introduced the trend was to cut down on team size rather than capitalize on an increase in speed by using only horses.[53] Even if we assume that there was some improvement in speed during the eventual transition from all-ox to mixed or even all-horse plough-teams, was this reflected in, say, an increase in the number of fallow ploughings given to the land? The answer is probably not, especially in the long run, since the reduction of fallow ploughings was a common phenomenon on demesnes after 1350, where shortage of labour seems to have been more of a problem than draught.[54]

It is equally difficult to prove that time saved by using horses was invested in weeding or other yield-improving activities. For the demesne, the thirteenth-century treatise, *Fleta*, calculated that out of a total cost of 25½d. per acre, exclusive of seed, needed to prepare and harvest a crop, only ½d. was spent on weeding, less than 2 per cent of the total cost,[55] and it was unlikely to have been much greater in practice.[56] There was definitely some room for improvement, but without a detailed analysis of individual cases it is difficult to assess whether the degree of weeding did increase. Presumably, being labour intensive, it came under the same sort of pressure as fallow ploughing and probably decreased after 1350,[57] a situation that may have applied to peasant farms as well.[58]

It is equally difficult to assess whether the use of horses improved the efficiency of cultivation, perhaps most crucially ploughing depth. To a large extent, this would have depended on the type of plough employed. If a conversion to horses occasioned a change to a different type of plough, then some influence on ploughing

---

[53] See pp. 163–4, 167–8 above.
[54] Dyer, "Warwickshire Farming", p. 15; *idem, Lords and Peasants*, pp. 126–7.
[55] *Fleta*, ii, ed. H. G. Richardson and W. O. Sayles (Seldon Soc., lxxii, 1953), p. 256.
[56] An analysis of costs in accounts indicates the same low level of expenditure on weeding: e.g., Langdon, thesis, p. 390, n. 63.
[57] E.g., see Dyer, "Warwickshire Farming", p. 15.
[58] Thus, estimated yields from two Warwickshire peasant holdings in 1377 and 1481 were very low, implying that such things as weeding were not performed very efficiently. *Ibid.*, pp. 29–30.

efficiency may have resulted, either for better or for worse. We have seen in the West Wycombe case that the conversion from mixed plough-teams to all-horse teams was accompanied, it appears, by a change from swing to foot and wheeled ploughs.[59] We have no reason to believe, however, that ploughing depth was affected; indeed the most likely result of the change, with wheeled ploughs in particular, would have been to improve the regulation of depth, which may have had a beneficial effect. On the peasant side, we have indicated that smaller plough-teams were the norm and that these teams were probably reduced further in size when horses were used. On the surface, this might seem to imply a significant reduction in the efficiency of cultivation, with peasants ploughing less deep than they did before, but, as we have seen, a small number of horses could do the work of a larger number of oxen.[60] Indeed, small two-horse peasant plough-teams may have been as effective as the eight-animal monsters on the demesne, which, in any case, do not seem to have been created so much for ploughing efficiency as to preserve the strength and well-being of animals worked over very long ploughing seasons. In this regard, we should not be looking so much at the plough-team permutations in which demesne and peasant farmers indulged as at the ploughs themselves. The evidence, such as it is, indicates that heavy mould-board ploughs were used on both demesne and peasant land. Furthermore, as the analysis of demesne plough types suggests (pp. 128–41), plough construction and design were somewhat static and unlikely to have changed significantly over our period. On balance, if we are to blame traction for poor medieval yields, it should be levelled at the lack of it – for instance, in the number of fallow ploughings – than at its quality or efficiency.

The general conclusion here is that there is little to indicate that the introduction of the work-horse improved crop yields directly or indirectly. Indeed, judging from both demesne and peasant experience, the main concern was not to increase production, but rather to save on costs through a reduction in labour or plough-team size. Even when a strictly speed-increasing change was made, for example, to mixed teams, it is likely that the increase in speed was transformed into a reduction of teams rather than into more yield-

[59] P. 169 above.   [60] Pp. 163–4 above.

efficient practices.[61] Thus, although the level of work-horses might increase on a farm, yields were as likely to go down as up, as on the estates of the bishop of Winchester.[62] Also, it is not totally clear whether medieval farmers were always successful in their cost-saving attempts, since the case of West Wycombe shows how difficult it was to be certain that cash was actually saved. In some cases, however, as in the Norfolk demesnes, saving would seem to have been unavoidable, and the same probably applies to peasants who replaced, say, four oxen with two horses. As a result of this reduction in cultivation costs the peasant or demesne owner was left with a greater cash surplus. If this extra cash were used as a capital investment, say for purchasing marl, lime, additional manure or other additives for the fields, then it would have some direct benefit for productivity. In the case of demesnes, however, given their owners' poor record in agricultural investment,[63] most of this extra cash would seem to have been channelled into other forms of lordly expenditure, such as high living and conspicuous display. In any case, the amount of extra cash involved was generally very marginal compared to the total operational costs on the demesne. On the other hand, even a small input of extra cash may have made a considerable difference to the productivity of a peasant's farm, although this small input may have been soon eroded by the adjustment of grain prices to the new technical circumstances, or – even more probably – by an increase in the expropriation of his surplus by the lord in the shape of higher rents, entry fines, and so on. The peasant may even have used it to improve his own standard of living, particularly his diet.

* * *

[61] No individual manor was studied in sufficient depth to determine conclusively if this in fact were true, but it is to be noted that the transition to mixed plough-teams at Elton (Huntingdonshire) in the twelfth century was accompanied by a reduction in teams from five to four. The same may also have been true of the twelfth-century manors of "Adulvesnasa" (Essex) and Hardley (Norfolk), where significant reductions of draught stock were effected upon the introduction of mixed plough-teams (or, in the case of "Adulvesnasa", what looks to have been mixed teams from the proportion of horses in the stock). *Cartularium monasterii de Rameseia*, iii, pp. 257, 259–60; *Domesday of St. Paul's of the Year 1222*, pp. 129–32; *Register of the Abbey of St. Benet of Holme*, pp. 129, 112.

[62] Thus, although there was a modest increase in the proportion of work-horses on the bishop's estates during the thirteenth and fourteenth centuries (see p. 95 above), yields in general showed a slow decline, especially before the Black Death (J. Z. Titow, *Winchester Yields* (Cambridge, 1972), pp. 12–29).

[63] See especially Hilton, "Rent and Capital Formation", pp. 33–68.

Although attempts to establish a significant connection between the introduction of the work-horse and improvements in agricultural production have proved fruitless, this is not to say that the use of horses did not have substantial effects in other ways. Perhaps the most crucial of these was in relation to hauling. As we have seen, the horse worked a remarkable transformation in carrying by vehicle in the two centuries following Domesday. From a position at the end of the eleventh century, where virtually only oxen were employed for carrying goods by vehicle, horses dominated by the end of the thirteenth, accounting for a good 75 per cent of farm hauling and possibly more.[64] Indeed, horse-hauled carts were found on nearly 90 per cent of manors at this time for both demesne and peasant farms,[65] and it would appear that there was hardly a region that did not have some familiarity with them. Assessing the impact of this transition to horse hauling, however, is somewhat difficult. This is especially the case on the farm itself, where the exact benefits of horse over ox hauling are not always easy to discern.[66] In some cases, though, they seem clear enough. We have already indicated that having horses as plough animals also had the desired effect of getting the farmer and his equipment to and from his fields more quickly at ploughing time. Similarly, the ability to haul a load of corn or hay swiftly from the fields or meadow may have been a factor of some importance, particularly at harvest, when time was usually short. This may have mattered more to the peasant than the lord, particularly in those cases, as at Cuxham, where the peasants' lands were not intermingled with the lord's land but lay outside it at some distance from the village.[67]

But the key to the substantial rise of horse hauling in the twelfth and thirteenth centuries would seem to lie in the concurrent growth of the market economy with which both peasant and demesne farmers were becoming increasingly involved. The nature of this

---

[64] Langdon, "Horse Hauling", pp. 46–58.

[65] See Tables 21 and 33.

[66] In some cases the greater speed of horse-hauled vehicles could be balanced out in terms of carrying efficiency by the larger capacity of the ox-hauled variety. Langdon, "Horse Hauling", pp. 60–2.

[67] Harvey, *Medieval Oxfordshire Village*, pp. 20–2. The Cuxham peasants lived on average a half-mile from their strips in the fields (*ibid.*, map II, facing p. 30).

involvement has yet to be fully understood,[68] but it would seem highly unlikely that such a sudden shift in the mode of vehicular transport was not in some way connected with the performance of the economy. As I have discussed elsewhere,[69] horse hauling tended to increase the speed and range of market transactions. Significantly, too, with its emphasis on light haulage, it was particularly geared towards the small-scale producer. It was just this social group – that is, smallholding peasants and the like – which was the fastest growing in terms of numbers and which, on the basis of this study at least, was showing the greatest inclination to use horses. But the growing employment of horses for hauling was hardly restricted to smallholders. Demesne farmers were also using horses to a much greater degree and, perhaps even more significantly, horse-hauled vehicles were also to be found increasingly among urban vehicles.[70] This contribution of horse hauling across virtually all sectors of urban and rural society could hardly have failed to have some effect upon the movement of goods, and indeed the rapid transformation from ox to horse haulage suggests that the former had been a notable restriction on the flow of goods at the time. It is difficult, of course, to put a figure on all this, but an improvement of up to double the previous hauling speed (see p. 162 above), with a resultant increase in range of travel of up to quadruple (in proportion to the increase in area which was now accessible to a day or two's journey), would seem capable of producing a marked effect upon the economy of the time. Explanations for the expansion of the English economy in the twelfth and thirteenth centuries have

---

[68] For example, how much of the delivery of grain and other produce from farm to market was performed by the farmers themselves as against urban or local middlemen (e.g., see N. S. B. Gras, *The Evolution of the English Corn Market* (Cambridge, Mass., 1915), ch. VI)?

[69] Langdon, "Horse Hauling", p. 62.

[70] *Carectae* (or *carretae*), presumably horse-hauled, were being used to haul various goods from town to town as early as the twelfth century and were seemingly commonplace in urban situations by the early thirteenth century, as at Bristol. In the fifteenth century the Southampton brokage books indicate that the ratio of horse-hauled to ox-hauled vehicles leaving or entering the city gates was four to one or more. *Pipe Roll 30 Henry II*, p. 85; *Pipe Roll 31 Henry II*, pp. 78, 127; *Pipe Roll 6 Richard I*, p. 211; *Accounts of the Constables of Bristol Castle in the Thirteenth and Early Fourteenth Centuries*, ed. M. Sharp (Bristol Rec. Soc., xxxiv, Gloucester, 1982), pp. 6–7; *The Brokage Book of Southampton, 1443–1444*, ed. O. Coleman, 2 vols. (Southampton Rec. Ser., iv, vi, 1960–1). See also Langdon, "Horse Hauling", p. 64, for the Southampton reference; the pipe roll references are to the volumes published by the Pipe Roll Society.

generally concentrated upon the amount of money in circulation, especially in silver, or upon the demands of a rapidly increasing population.[71] Relatively little attention has been paid to the velocity of circulation, either of money or commodities.[72] If, as I have suggested, however, the rise of horse hauling significantly raised the velocity of goods transportation and hence, in the opposite direction, money circulation, then this, too, would have directly stimulated the economy. Just how big a part this played alongside the other factors such as population growth and a possible increase in the money supply is open to debate and requires a much closer scrutiny than was possible in this study, in particular among the records of urban communities, where the rise of horse hauling may have been even more crucial than on the farm. In both cases, however, the market economy was the most obvious beneficiary.

Besides improving the medieval farmer's contact with the market, the horse also increased the complexity of his involvement in it. The horse trade in pre-industrial England has been compared to the car trade of today, where huge price differentials allow rich and poor alike to participate in the market. As Thirsk commented of the latter trade: " . . . there is a car within the price of everyone; you can pay £20 or you can pay £10,000".[73] Thirsk felt that wide discrepancies of price created a similar situation in the horse trade of early modern England. In fact, this flexibility of the horse market was amply evident by the thirteenth century at least,[74] and accordingly it made cheap draught animals as available to the peasantry as the "banger" trade in cars does in supplying private transport to less

[71] P. D. A. Harvey, "The English Inflation of 1180–1220", in R. H. Hilton (ed.), *Peasants, Knights and Heretics: Studies in Medieval English Social History* (Past and Present Publications, Cambridge, 1976), esp. pp. 79–84; M. M. Postan, "The Economic Foundations of Medieval Society" and "The Rise of a Money Economy" in his *Essays on Medieval Agriculture and General Problems of the Medieval Economy* (Cambridge, 1973), esp. pp. 7–16 and 28–40.

[72] Although Postan does cite the development of new credit and payment arrangements, which also quickened commercial transactions: Postan, "Economic Foundations of Medieval Society", p. 10; see also Postan, "Rise of a Money Economy", p. 34.

[73] J. Thirsk, *Horses in Early Modern England: for Service, for Pleasure, for Power* (the Stenton Lecture for 1977; published Reading, 1978), p. 24.

[74] *Vide* the variety of selling prices for horses at this time. Farmer, "Some Livestock Price Movements in Thirteenth-Century England", *Econ. Hist. Rev.*, 2nd series, xxii (1969), p. 6; Langdon, "Economics of Horses and Oxen", p. 40.

8tpe="

well-off people today. The importance of this in the medieval period should not be underestimated, as it must have had a tremendously liberating effect on smallholders in particular. We have already indicated how horses allowed them to participate more actively in cultivation,[75] and it must also have given them a much greater degree of freedom in the matter of transport. The incidence of horse hauling among these smallholders must be seen as one reflection of this.[76]

Horse trading also added another dimension to peasant economics. It must now have been possible for some peasant entrepreneurs actually to make a modest amount of money out of it, as petty car traders do today.[77] Just how active this trade was is difficult to say. In areas such as East Anglia, where horses were very prevalent even in the thirteenth century, the trade must have been well developed, stimulated no doubt by the proximity of London and the horse markets there, particularly at Smithfield.[78] On the other hand, in areas removed from the chief centres of trade, the market for horses was considerably weaker. In this regard, a series of tolls collected for the sale of horses and oxen on the estates of the bishop of Worcester in 1302–3 are instructive. Out of 36 cases where the animal involved was specified, 31 were oxen and only 5 horses.[79] Although the sample is too small to enable us to draw definite conclusions, the horse trade here would seem to have been substantially inferior to that for cattle, hardly surprising given the fact that the ox was the dominant draught animal in the area.[80]

Finally, the introduction of the work-horse also played an important part in establishing regional variations in agriculture. Regionalism, of course, exists in many forms, many of which were already evident in medieval times. These included variations in field systems,

[75] P. 252 above.
[76] E.g., see p. 225.
[77] For example, "corsours" or horse dealers were a craft in London in 1422 (G. Unwin, *The Gilds and Companies of London* (London, 1908), p. 370). There are, however, no instances of peasants being specified solely as horse dealers, so at best it would seem to have been a secondary occupation for them, if at all.
[78] Where a market for horses was held every Friday; e.g., see *The Peasants' Revolt of 1381*, ed. R. B. Dobson (London, 1970), p. 193.
[79] *Red Book of Worcester*, iv, pp. 499, 502, 510, 513, 515, 524 (for six Gloucestershire and Worcestershire manors).
[80] For example, see Tables 12 and 29 under "West Midlands".

inheritance customs, arable versus pastoral economies, and so on.[81] Most people in the middle ages were clearly aware of these regional differences;[82] nonetheless they were, in many cases, not as distinct in medieval times as they later came to be. One of these was in regard to traction. Compared to the "monochrome" nature of draught work evident at Domesday, with ploughing and hauling being performed only by oxen and harrowing and pack-animal work by horses, the degree of regional variation of a few centuries later is quite marked. Even so, until the fifteenth and sixteenth centuries, differences in practice as regards traction were often more evident between the various economic sectors of medieval society than between regions. This was particularly true of the contrast between horse-using smallholders and the much more ox-oriented substantial tenants and demesnes. There were, of course, some geographical variations: for example, areas of mixed plough-teams versus those of all-ox teams, the use of more horses in the south and east than in the north and west, and so on. But the really dramatic ones, such as the complete transformation of the farm to all-horse draught, occurred only in a few rather circumscribed areas, such as Norfolk and the Chilterns. Demesne agriculture in particular was very uniform, with its loyalty to, among other things, the large plough-team, the continued use of oxen, and a long ploughing season. Much of this, of course, was a function of the common ideas circulating through the aristocratic community of the time, as typified by such agricultural works as those written by Bishop Grosseteste and Walter of Henley.[83] But this consistency in the basic outlines of practice is also evident in the ranks of the more substantial tenants, where the use of horses, or the lack of it, seems to have had strong similarities to that on the demesne. It was only in the fifteenth century that this relative uniformity in draught animal practice among the more substantial sector of peasant and demesne farmers began to break up, resulting in the polarization between horse- and ox-using areas so evident in the sixteenth century.

---

[81] For some thoughts on early forms of regionalism, see G. C. Homans, "The Explanation of English Regional Differences", pp. 18–34; W. G. Hoskins, "Regional Farming in England", *Agric. Hist. Rev.*, ii (1954), pp. 3–11.

[82] As, indeed, Walter of Henley indicates in several instances. *Walter of Henley*, pp. 313, 315, 323, 325 (cc. 23–4, 49–50, 60).

[83] E.g., see Mate, "Medieval Agrarian Practices", pp. 22–31.

The overall conclusion, then, is that regional variation in traction formed slowly over the medieval period and in general remained somewhat shapeless until the fifteenth century, when it finally began to attain the complexity it would show a century later. What importance does this new aspect of regional variation have then? It may be said that it has a mild curiosity value only. But there is more to it than that. The development of regional variation, whether in agriculture, industry or commerce, reflects an increasing sophistication in the economy as a whole, and the same may be said of the narrower question of traction. Thus, regardless of its virtues and performance *vis-à-vis* the ox, the horse provided a new set of agricultural circumstances with which problems of farming traction could be attacked. Consequently some areas, such as the Chilterns, Norfolk and the Yorkshire Wolds, were quick to use horses at both the demesne and peasant levels, because use of the animals was ideally suited to the conditions there. Equally there were areas which, for technical, economic or other reasons, remained with oxen and tended to reinforce that decision through the use of specifically ox-drawn equipment, such as wains. The contrast which this eventually established between regions soon attracted to them other attributes besides the merely technical. Thus areas using horses have been characterized as being regions of progressive and intelligent farming, while farmers and farm-labourers in areas employing mainly oxen have been represented as dull and slow-witted, the attitudes to change and farming in general being supposedly reflected in the pace of the animals which they used.[84] Much of this was undoubtedly less than fair to regions using oxen; the employment of the animals did not necessarily reflect a backward technology but simply an alternative one in which oxen could be used in a particular area more efficiently or economically than horses. Furthermore, the two systems, ox-traction and horse-traction, could in fact be highly complementary, and variations mixing the two are evident in the sixteenth century. Thus we have areas where oxen were used for ploughing and horses for carting,[85] much as was the pattern for many medieval demesnes or

[84] J. D. Chambers and G. E. Mingay, *The Agricultural Revolution 1750–1880* (London, 1966), p. 172; W. Marshall, *The Rural Economy of the Southern Counties* (London, 1798), i, pp. 56–7.
[85] Particularly for Hampshire: e.g., "Item ij iron bownde cartes & vij horsse bestes with ther apparrell, x li . . . Item viij oxen for the plough with ther apparrell

substantial peasants, while there were even some localities where the situation seems to have been reversed, with horses being used for ploughing and oxen for hauling.[86] In short, regional variation in traction came to be both flexible and versatile and provided a valuable range of experience with which to approach the often widely differing problems of ploughing and hauling that faced medieval and early modern farmers.

As we have seen, the impact of the horse was felt in a variety of ways. Some of these influences were seemingly weak, as in the case of agricultural production, and some were strong, as in the case of the market economy and the involvement of farmers in it. What does all this tell us about the role of technology in general in medieval society? To answer this, we are here going to consider five major theories concerning the role of technology in society, particularly as it relates to the middle ages.

The first of these is the neo-Malthusian argument developed by M. M. Postan and others.[87] The theory here suggests that by the end of the thirteenth century Europe had virtually reached a state of overpopulation, to the point where medieval society was beginning to outrun its food supply, a situation which was exacerbated by declining crop yields as land fertility became exhausted through the excessive demands made upon it. This in turn led to an increase in mortality and a stagnation and perhaps even a decline in population in the first half of the fourteenth century prior to the advent of the

---

belonginge to the same, viij li" (1550 inventory for Walter Carter of Romsey; H.R.O. Bishopric Wills, 1550, no. 30).

[86] For example, James Nightgale of North Leverton (Nottinghamshire) in 1545 is listed as having "3 cartes & a wayne with yokes & temes / Horce harnes carte ropes halters carte harnes plow harnes & collers" (*Nottinghamshire Household Inventories*, ed. P. A. Kennedy (Thoroton Soc. Rec. Ser., xxii, 1963), p. 46), the order here indicating that oxen were employed for hauling wains and horses for ploughing and hauling carts. A similar arrangement of oxen hauling and horses ploughing also seems to have occurred on the South Downs: Kerridge, *Agricultural Revolution*, pp. 52–3.

[87] Postan, *Medieval Economy and Society*, esp. chapters 3 and 4; *Cambridge Economic History of Europe*, i, pp. 552–70; Titow, *English Rural Society*, esp. pp. 64–96; Miller and Hatcher, *Medieval England: Rural Society and Economic Change*, esp. p. xv; see also D. B. Grigg, *Population Growth and Agrarian Change: An Historical Perspective* (Cambridge, 1980), pp. 65–6, for a general review of the argument and its supporters.

plague.[88] Historians following the precepts of Malthus do not claim that there was no technological advancement during the middle ages (although they come dangerously close to implying it at times[89]), but they do claim that the rate of this advance was not enough to prevent subsistence crises and left virtually unaltered the vital relationship between food production and population.

In certain respects, our study must endorse this view, since the introduction of the horse to English farming seemingly failed to make any impression on such things as crop yields, particularly in the crucial period *c*. 1250–1348. The prime reason for this is that any advantages gained by changes in traction were channelled into cost-saving rather than increasing production. Again, individual cases may supply exceptions to this rule, but in broad terms it would seem valid. Furthermore, any capital released by these cost-savings was not redirected back into attempts to improve production but rather, it seems, into satisfying consumer wants or "the general increase in the expenses of the political superstructure".[90] This was probably aggravated by the concurrent expansion of the market economy (aided, as we have suggested, by horse hauling), which must have greatly increased the opportunities and temptations for non-agricultural spending. On the other hand, the effect of this growing economy in raising grain prices should also have been an incentive to increase production, but this does not seem to have happened. Part of this may have been due to the uncertainties of the grain market, particularly towards the end of the thirteenth century and the beginning of the fourteenth,[91] but it would also seem that when a straight choice between agricultural investment versus consumer

[88] M. M. Postan, "Some Economic Evidence of Declining Population in the Later Middle Ages", *Econ. Hist. Rev.*, 2nd series, ii (1950), pp. 221–46.

[89] Postan in 1950, for example, characterized medieval technical development as being "remarkably static for the whole of the middle ages": "Economic Foundations of Medieval Society", p. 17; see also M. M. Postan, "Why was Science Backward in the Middle Ages?", in his *Essays on Medieval Agriculture and General Problems of the Medieval Economy*, p. 84. For similar views concerning agricultural technology specifically, see Postan, *Medieval Economy and Society*, p. 49; J. Z. Titow, *English Rural Society*, pp. 37, 50; G. E. Fussell, "Social Change but Static Technology: Rural England in the Fourteenth Century", *Hist. Studies*, i (1968), pp. 23–32.

[90] R. H. Hilton, "A Crisis of Feudalism", *Past and Present*, no. 80 (1978), p. 13.

[91] Miller and Hatcher, *Medieval England: Rural Society and Economic Change*, p. 59.

and other spending was presented to demesne owners and peasants the latter course usually won out.

This was not necessarily the story for the whole of our period, however. It would seem that this pattern of increased non-agricultural spending in the thirteenth century was preceded by a legitimate and massive effort to improve crop production through land clearance in the twelfth. Here the extra power and speed of horses may have had a genuine effect. Nevertheless, the fact that such changes towards the use of horses as are evident in the twelfth century – such as the conversion to mixed plough-teams – occurred in areas already well-populated at Domesday rather than in areas of woodland and marsh, where most of the assarting was carried on,[92] indicates that the connection between land clearance and the increased use of horses was weak.

For the second period of substantial increase in the employment of horses, that is, the fifteenth and sixteenth centuries, connections with agricultural production may be more direct. The rise in the use of horses at this time does coincide with what appears to be a modest increase in crop yields.[93] There are, of course, a multitude of other factors that could equally have led to these increases in crop yields, and indeed were probably more likely to have done so, such as a better balance between arable and pasture, as in convertible husbandry.[94] The horse, however, may have played its part, although there is little in the way of suitable material, in the fifteenth century at least, with which to judge the matter. The point to be made here is that the relative lack of effect that the introduction of the workhorse seemingly had in late thirteenth- and early fourteenth-century agricultural production may not necessarily have applied to the whole medieval period. Indeed, in the more flexible agricultural conditions of the fifteenth and sixteenth centuries the horse might have contributed some positive advantages. Nevertheless, insofar as this one technological innovation is concerned, there is not much in this study to refute the basic neo-Malthusian position that improvements in technology did little to alleviate subsistence crises

---

[92] *Ibid.*, pp. 33–41.

[93] Grigg, *Population Growth and Agrarian Change*, pp. 91–2; D. M. Palliser, "Tawney's Century: Brave New World or Malthusian Trap?", *Econ. Hist. Rev.*, 2nd series, xxxv (1982), p. 348.

[94] Palliser, "Tawney's Century", p. 348; Kerridge, *Agricultural Revolution*, ch. III; Dyer, "Warwickshire Farming", pp. 9–14.

in the middle ages. Indeed, it might be argued that the work-horse actually aggravated these crises by supplying a technological solution to such problems as ploughing (that is, by allowing smaller plough-teams) which actively encouraged the fragmentation of holdings or at least made it easier for these smallholdings to exist as self-sufficient farming units.

Where historians holding to the neo-Malthusian line can be criticized, though, is for their tendency to underestimate the capacity that medieval society had for technological change, especially in the two or three centuries leading up to the Black Death.[95] This study indicates that innovations in traction at least were clearly taking place during this period, some of them, like horse hauling, at a considerable pace, and one could name other innovations not related to traction, such as windmills and higher levels of legume-growing, that were also adopted in the interval between Domesday and the beginning of the fourteenth century.[96] That these innovations in most cases did not seem to have a sizeable effect on agricultural production must not blind us to the fact that they were occurring and often had important effects in other ways, or were pointers to the future. In this regard, it is interesting to note that even in the pre-Black Death period there were some signs that the Malthusian stranglehold was being broken, as in eastern Norfolk or Holderness, where high yields were recorded, along with the progressive techniques of fallow reduction, thick sowing rates, the growing of a high proportion of legumes, and intensive manuring.[97]

In direct opposition to the neo-Malthusian view is the model proposed by Ester Boserup.[98] This theory contends that, rather than limitations in agricultural production being the factor determining population growth, it is population growth itself that provides the motor for economic and social development. In relation to technology, Boserup claims that as societies begin to experience food

[95] See note 89 above; also Postan, *Medieval Economy and Society*, pp. 46–9.
[96] Singer et al., *History of Technology*, ii, p. 623; Miller and Hatcher, *Medieval England: Rural Society and Economic Change*, p. 215; Hallam, *Rural England*, pp. 13–14.
[97] Campbell, "Agricultural Progress", pp. 28–36; *idem*, thesis, pp. 338–55; Mate, "Profit and Productivity on the Estates of Isabella de Forz", pp. 332–3; see also Hallam, *Rural England*, pp. 13–14, 248.
[98] First in *The Conditions of Agricultural Growth* (London, 1965) and later in *Population and Technology* (London, 1981).

shortage due to population pressure they actively seek to relieve that pressure by intensifying agricultural production; in other words, they raise their agriculture to a new technological level. Much of this is based upon the premise that there is a readily available pool of information about agricultural techniques, which either lies dormant in the social knowledge until circumstances bring it to the fore, or is easily borrowed from neighbouring cultures.[99] These techniques are considered adequate to deal with the new population pressure. Thus, as an example, a region where two-course rotation was the rule will adopt a more intensive rotation, say a three-course, in order to improve food production to meet the needs of an expanding population. Conversely when population declines the tendency is to return to the less intensive form of agriculture, where labour requirements (in ploughing, weeding, etc.) per unit of food grown, are not so great. In recent years support for some elements at least of the Boserup theory has grown, particularly from medieval studies of such regions as eastern Norfolk or, further afield, Flanders and Artois, where population growth and progressive methods of agriculture seemingly went hand in hand.[100] Similarly there are some instances at least of villages in England converting from two- to three-field systems (with, presumably, a similar change in the crop rotation) during the thirteenth century.[101] On the other hand, some of this intensification was also occurring in the late fourteenth century, well after the population had collapsed.[102]

What evidence for or against Boserup's theory does this study contribute? First of all, it should be said that Boserup generally limits her consideration of technological improvements only to those developments which intensified agriculture.[103] Thus certain technological developments lie outside her frame of reference. In this regard, she makes a distinction between, as she puts it, the "kind of tool" and the "make of tool".[104] Changes in the kind of

---

[99] *Conditions of Agricultural Growth*, pp. 38–9; *Population and Technology*, pp. 3–4.

[100] Campbell, "Agricultural Progress", pp. 26–46; Slicher van Bath, *Agrarian History of Western Europe*, pp. 175–80, 240–3.

[101] Miller and Hatcher, *Medieval England: Rural Society and Economic Change*, p. 90; Hallam, *Rural England*, pp. 14, 116, 137, 249.

[102] Brandon, "Demesne Arable Farming in Coastal Sussex", p. 129.

[103] At least in *Conditions of Agricultural Growth*. *Population and Technology* is more wide-ranging.

[104] *Conditions of Agricultural Growth*, pp. 26–7.

tool, such as from the hoe to the plough, which had direct relevance to the intensification of agriculture, are far more important in Boserup's scheme than changes in the make of tool, for instance, from wooden spade to metal one, both varieties of which could occur within the same system of cultivation. In this sense, the replacement of oxen by horses would probably count as a change in the make of tool, since it did not necessarily result in the intensification of agriculture. Nonetheless, as we have already indicated (p. 259), there may well have been some connection between the use of the horse and the intensification of agriculture, since the animal could be fed more effectively on field crops than could oxen. On the other hand, where agriculture was less intensive and pasture more available, the ox became the favoured animal. We should then expect – following Boserup's hypothesis – that the horse would become increasingly popular as population rose and as agriculture, theoretically at least, became more intense. This would characterize the period leading up to the beginning of the fourteenth century. Conversely, when population declined after the onset of the plague, or perhaps even before if one accepts the neo-Malthusian chronology, oxen would regain their popularity as reserves of pasture became free again upon the disintensification of farming systems.

As we have seen, however, such a pattern only resulted in part. The rise in popularity of the horse did occur much as predicted in the early period up to about 1300. After this, the rate of rise in the level of horses tapered off considerably, again as might be expected. But there was no fall back to previous levels, even after the Black Death. Indeed, the proportion of horses began to rise again, quite steeply it seems, in the fifteenth century, when population was still very much lower. In other words, for much of the period covered by this study, the introduction of the horse to farming seemed to carry on regardless of the population trend. This may have been because the introduction of the horse was, after all, a "make of tool" and was not really suitable for testing the theory. But it would seem equally plausible that, after the Black Death, the connection between the introduction of the work-horse and population increase (and perhaps the intensity of farming systems) was somehow severed, probably because of some other factor at work, which was much stronger than pure population rise or fall. We shall consider such a factor shortly. In general, because of the confusion as to how the introduction of the horse should be considered as a technological innovation, it is difficult to pass judgment on the Boserupian model, but there is little in this study to indicate that population rise or fall by itself was a dominant influence on technological fluctuations in the middle ages.

Another view of technology is that voiced by Marxist historians, who see technological advance as being firmly dependent upon the ruling mode of production, whether slave, feudal, capitalist or otherwise, which shaped the economic and social framework beyond which a technological innovation could not function.[105] For example, a slave mode of production, because of its resources of captive labour, finds it unnecessary to indulge in the technological improvements that a capitalist society in particular finds essential.[106] Here the relationship between classes, or at least between the exploiters and the exploited, is of prime importance. Thus, in the feudal system, slaves were gradually replaced by a mass of peasantry, who had a certain degree of social and economic freedom. In technological terms this transformation had two potential directions. It meant first of all that, in order to feed their families and also possibly to accumulate surpluses with which to improve their social and economic position, peasants now had more incentive to farm efficiently than had their slave predecessors. As a result, they were more likely to be attracted to and to adopt technological innovations. At the same time, however, they were nonetheless subject to very high levels of surplus extraction, through rents and other demands, by their feudal lords. Some historians feel that this extraction was so severe that peasants had virtually no excess production, beyond that needed for subsistence, with which to invest in new technologies.[107] As a result, technological advances among the peasantry are considered to have been very limited and those innovations that did occur, particularly during the

---

[105] E.g., see Perry Anderson, *Passages from Antiquity to Feudalism* (London, 1974), p. 183.

[106] *Ibid.*, pp. 25–8, 79–80.

[107] As most recently stated by R. Brenner, "The Agrarian Roots of European Capitalism", *Past and Present*, no. 97 (1982), pp. 35–6. Brenner also comments that the "patriarchal" nature of the feudal system shielded both peasant and lord from the market and the "economic compulsion to produce competitively" (p. 34).

early medieval period, were those which first and foremost benefited lords, such as the mill.[108]

The latter interpretation would seem very out of place in our study, since we have shown that technological advances in regard to traction at least were definitely taking place among the peasantry during the medieval period. In any case, as even Marx himself admitted,[109] there was enough flexibility in the relationship between lord and peasant, if only through the inefficiencies of surplus extraction in the more primitive conditions of feudalism, to allow peasants to set aside some of their surplus for their own use, whether for acquiring new land or improving techniques. In this regard, it should also be noted that pronouncements on the low capacity of medieval peasant agriculture for technical improvement are often based on the assumption that technological developments necessarily needed large inputs of capital. Some innovations, such as – again – the mill, certainly rank in this category, but, as we have seen, others, such as the introduction of the work-horse, often needed less capital than the technologies they replaced, although day-to-day operational costs may have been more. A more promising line of thought with some connection to the Marxist theme would seem to be that of the non-Marxist historian, Georges Duby, who suggests that heavy seigneurial demands, far from discouraging improvements in agricultural production, actually encouraged peasants to look even harder at technological innovations and other methods of improving production as a way of meeting the pressure of these seigneurial exactions.[110] In this regard, the peasantry can be seen as the most technologically active sector in medieval society.[111] On the surface, this fits in quite well with our study, which shows horses being adopted more readily on peasant farms than on demesnes. However, as we have seen, this picture of a horse-oriented peasantry applied mostly to smallholders. More substantial tenants, significantly the most exploited in terms of the absolute amount of rents and labour services owed, tended to use draught animals in much the same way as the demesne, including having substantial levels of oxen. The division here between farmers tend-

[108] E.g., P. Dockès, *Medieval Slavery and Liberation* (Chicago, 1982), pp. 22–4.
[109] *Capital*, iii, Lawrence and Wishart edition (London, 1959), pp. 793–4 (ch. XLVII).
[110] Duby, *Early Growth of the European Economy*, esp. pp. 181, 211, 269–70.
[111] See also Anderson, *Passages from Antiquity to Feudalism*, pp. 185–6.

ing to use oxen and those tending to use horses, in other words, seems to have been an economic one, depending mainly on the size of farm rather than on a distinction between classes. As regards whether the increase in the use of horses was initiated by demesnes or by the peasantry, there is no certain way of telling. The somewhat more precipitous rise in the level of horses in the Winchester heriots than in the demesne stock levels for the same estate (cf. Table 28 and pp. 94–5) might indicate that the peasantry were a little slower in adopting horses than the demesne and were in the process of catching up, although this might also be explained by increases in the number of smallholders. Certainly, whoever introduced the work-horse, the peasantry as a whole took it much further. It seems likely, though, that this was because of a combination of economic and technological factors, involving such things as the versatility of the horse, rather than because the feudal system of exploitation made peasants more innovatory.

Towards the end of our period, English agriculture began to move towards a new mode of production. Marx saw this as first happening in the transition from an arable to a sheep or cattle economy, which began to divide English peasant society into a class of capitalist farmers and a rural proletariat.[112] Although this may put too much emphasis on the pastoral element of the rural economy,[113] this gradual drift to agrarian capitalism is often cited as a feature of English society of the time, apparently beginning, according to most accounts, sometime towards the end of the fifteenth century and gathering momentum in the sixteenth.[114] Marx himself does not mention specific innovations, beyond a quoted reference to enclosure,[115] but many other innovations, such as convertible husbandry and floated meadows, have been claimed as occurring from the second half of the sixteenth century and perhaps even earlier.[116] The relationship between the rise of

---

[112] *Capital*, i (Penguin edition, Harmondsworth, Middlesex, 1976), pp. 877–83, 905–7; also iii (Lawrence and Wishart edition), p. 801.

[113] More recent Marxist interpretations take a broader line by emphasizing, among other things, the continuation of the demesne (in both its arable and pastoral components) as a feature of early modern English agriculture: Brenner, "The Agrarian Roots of European Capitalism", pp. 84–5.

[114] Marx, *Capital*, i (Penguin edition), p. 878; Brenner, "Agrarian Roots of European Capitalism", pp. 83–9; R. H. Hilton, *The Decline of Serfdom in Medieval England* (London, 1969), esp. pp. 58–9.

[115] Marx, *Capital*, i (Penguin edition), pp. 879–80.

[116] Kerridge, *Agricultural Revolution*; Dyer, "Warwickshire Farming".

capitalistic tendencies in agriculture, which included the trend towards larger farm sizes,[117] and a quickening in the pace of farming innovations may thus be significant. Does our study support this contention? To some extent it does. The number of work-horses employed on English farms does seem to have increased substantially during the fifteenth and sixteenth centuries. The beginning of this surge occurred a little in advance of most Marxists' timetables for the advent of English agrarian capitalism, but the agreement may be considered close enough in the circumstances. It is notable, too, that the rationalization process of going completely to horses or mainly to oxen, to make as much use of the chosen animal as possible, indicates a sophistication perhaps characteristic of a new type of social and economic relationship. On the other hand, it is clear that it was not just wealthy farmers who were participating in this phase of rationalization but the whole of farming society; indeed, in the case of those areas going to all-horse draught, the movement may have been led by relatively humble farmers (e.g., the virgate holder at Wistow; see p. 219 above). It is unlikely that capitalism in its very tentative beginnings could account for changes of this order;[118] other mechanisms were almost certainly involved.

One of these mechanisms was the market, allied with the rise of trade and industry. As Pirenne stated, when discussing economic expansion in the twelfth century:

> Commerce and industry did not merely find a place alongside of agriculture; they reacted upon it. Its products no longer served solely for the consumption of the landed proprietors and the tillers of the soil; they were brought into general circulation, as objects of barter or as raw material. The rigid confines of the demesnial system, which had up to now hemmed in all economic activity, were broken down and the whole social order was patterned along more flexible, more active and more varied lines.[119]

---

[117] E.g., see J. P. Cooper, "In Search of Agrarian Capitalism", *Past and Present*, no. 80 (1978), pp. 33–4; Brenner, "Agrarian Roots of European Capitalism", p. 95.

[118] Indeed, it has been doubted whether capitalist tendencies could ever have accounted for the agrarian changes that were eventually to set English agriculture apart from that on the Continent. Cooper, "In Search of Agrarian Capitalism", pp. 20–65.

[119] Henri Pirenne, *Medieval Cities* (Princeton, New Jersey, 1925), p. 72.

This "commercialization theory", which saw the growth of trade, the market, and the money economy as the key determinants in the revival of the medieval European economy and society, has been criticized on several points, primarily in that it ignores such factors as population growth and the constrictive relationship between lord and tenant.[120] Nevertheless, our study does show that the influence of the market was felt on the technological side of agriculture. In particular, there seems to have been a connection between the quickening of market forces in the twelfth and thirteenth centuries and the adoption of horse hauling on farms. It is difficult to know which came first. As we have seen, the introduction of mixed plough-teams dated from the early part of the twelfth century[121] and horse hauling was evident from at least the middle of the century.[122] Markets and trade, of course, had very ancient roots in England,[123] but the substantial expansion of market activity in the twelfth and thirteenth centuries is unlikely to have predated the year 1150. For example, the impact of this activity was not felt in grain and live-stock prices until the last two decades of the twelfth century, and the creation of new markets did not peak until the third quarter of the thirteenth century.[124] Both these indicators are unlikely to have followed immediately upon the first stirrings of economic expansion, but for prices in particular it is improbable that they were delayed by more than a generation or two; therefore, the rate of increase in market activity probably did not take off in any substantial way until at least the middle of the twelfth century. In this instance, the rise of horse hauling and the renewed growth of the market in England occur so closely together as to be almost simultaneous. In any case, it appears they were mutually reinforcing, particularly as horse hauling was specifically geared to a more active and fast-paced economy. It is significant, too, that as the economy

---

[120] Postan, "Rise of a Money Economy", pp. 28–40; *idem*, "Economic Foundation of Medieval Society", esp. pp. 13–16; R. Brenner, "Agrarian Class Structure and Economic Development in Pre-Industrial Europe", *Past and Present*, no. 70 (1976), esp. pp. 42–6. The term "commercialization theory" is essentially Brenner's, who calls it the "Commercialization Model" (*ibid.*, p. 42).
[121] See Figure 17 and pp. 50–3 above.
[122] See pp. 59–60 above.
[123] E.g., Postan, "Rise of a Money Economy", pp. 29–32.
[124] Farmer, "Some Price Fluctuations in Angevin England", pp. 34–43; Harvey, "English Inflation", pp. 57–8; R. H. Britnell, "The Proliferation of Markets in England, 1200–1349", *Econ. Hist. Rev.*, 2nd series, xxxiv (1981), pp. 209–10.

showed signs of contraction in the fourteenth century, so did the rate of adoption of the horse.

The second phase of the rapid rise in the use of the horse, that is, the period of "rationalization" in the fifteenth century, is harder to explain in terms of market activity. Although some authorities have argued vigorously that the economy was still expanding in the fifteenth century,[125] the general consensus is that the period was one of contraction or even depression for the economy.[126] Yet we have shown that a significant restructuring of draught animal use along with a renewed rise in the employment of horses overall began again in the same century, well before the age of economic expansion in the Tudor era.[127] What may have occurred here, though, was not a change in the activity of the market, but in its degree of complexity. For example, it has been suggested that there was a growing tendency for specialization in agriculture during the fifteenth century. Instead of following a system that tried to suit both animal husbandry and arable farming, communities now tended to concentrate much more on one or the other. Allegedly this was a result of the growing influence of market forces, which meant that a community no longer had to be self-sufficient in both grain and livestock.[128] Certainly the development of heavily pastoral economies was a marked feature of the period,[129] and specialization of this order was also occurring in the use of draught animals, as we have seen. The latter, in fact, was probably reflected in the marketing and trading patterns of the age. P. R. Edwards has noted how, during the seventeenth century, the nature of the horse trade varied from region to region, with some areas specializing in riding, pack, or pit animals

[125] E.g., A. R. Bridbury, *Economic Growth: England in the Later Middle Ages* (London, 1962).
[126] M. M. Postan, "The Fifteenth Century", in *Essays on Medieval Agriculture, etc.*, pp. 41–8; *idem*, "The Economic Foundations of Medieval Society", pp. 22–7; Hatcher, *Plague, Population and the English Economy*, pp. 35–54. A. R. H. Baker (in *A New Historical Geography of England before 1600*, ed. Darby, pp. 192–5) suggests an economic decline in the first half of the century followed by a modest period of recovery in the second half.
[127] Agricultural prices, for instance, only began to rise significantly again after 1500. Grigg, *Population Growth and Agrarian Change*, p. 85; Hatcher, *Plague, Population and the English Economy*, pp. 50–1.
[128] C. J. Dahlman, *The Open Field System and Beyond* (Cambridge, 1980), ch. 5.
[129] E.g., Dyer, "Warwickshire Farming", pp. 16–21; *idem*, "A Small Landowner in the Fifteenth Century", *Midland History*, i (1972), esp. pp. 6–8.

and others in heavy draught horses.[130] The same would also seem to
have occurred, in rudimentary form at least, in the medieval period,
with some market areas – notably in the east – concentrating more
on horses than other regions (see p. 273 above). This differentiation
in the nature of horse-trading areas must have sharpened considerably during the fifteenth century as the polarization between areas
using horses and those using oxen became more marked. In short,
it seems highly probable that there was a connection between the
growth of market complexity and the polarization in the use of
horses and oxen. The general drift in favour of horses within this
polarization is somewhat more difficult to explain in market terms,
but it may have had something to do with the growing demand for
beef during the period,[131] which would have encouraged the
tendency to replace oxen with horses.[132]

Finally, we come to the concept of technical determinism, which –
in its purest form – views technological development as the main
factor behind social and economic change. Here it is the fortuitous
technological idea or inspiration that matters most. Social and
economic progress must often wait until such ideas come to fruition
or, as was most usual for medieval Europe, are imported from areas
that have already developed them. Thus, dealing with the medieval
period, it has been claimed, *inter alia*, that the development of the
modern horse harness led to the abolition of slavery;[133] the advent
of the stirrup to the development of heavy cavalry and the eventual
creation of the feudal system;[134] and a whole series of agricultural
improvements – the heavy plough, equine power, the replacement
of two-course by three-course rotations, the dissemination of the
corn mill, the reintroduction of legumes and the use of iron in farming implements – to what is claimed to have been an agricultural
revolution in the early medieval period, which in turn provided the
impetus for a new wave of urbanization and commerce.[135]

[130] "The Horse Trade of the Midlands in the Seventeenth Century", *Agric. Hist. Rev.*, xxvii (1979), pp. 91–6.
[131] E.g., Dyer, "Warwickshire Farming", p. 20; *idem*, "English Diet", pp. 213–14.
[132] According to the mechanism already discussed on pp. 261–2.
[133] Lefebvre des Noëttes, *L'Attelage*, pp. 184–8.
[134] White, *Medieval Technology and Social Change*, pp. 1–38.
[135] *Ibid.*, pp. 39–78; J. Gimpel, *The Medieval Machine* (London, 1977), pp. 29–58. In a Weber-like fashion, Lynn White links these developments to the peculiarly activist brand of Christianity that emerged in western Europe during the early

Not surprisingly this view of technology as the prime motor behind the development of medieval society has met with considerable opposition.[136] But what is the view of this study? Did any of the innovations we have examined have consequences substantial enough to justify the technical determinist view? At best, only partly. Only horse hauling as a technological development was seemingly of a sufficient magnitude to have had an immediate and pronounced effect upon affairs at the time, particularly in the economic expansion of the twelfth and thirteenth centuries.[137] But even here it was only one of a triad of possible factors, population growth and an increase in the money supply being two other likely candidates. It would be very difficult – at the moment at least – to make a case that horse hauling was the *sole* factor behind this economic expansion.

In other spheres the introduction of the work-horse was patently less successful in bringing about important change. For example, since the introduction of the horse has been claimed as one of the cornerstones of the "agricultural revolution" of the middle ages, we should perhaps expect to see this reflected in significant improvements in agricultural production. As we have seen, however, there is no positive indication that these occurred; rather, any improvements in cultivating efficiency seem only to have added to the consumption by landlords or peasants. More outlandish claims, such as that the introduction of horse-power led to the wholesale desertion of hamlets, seem equally unlikely.[138]

The problems for the technical determinist view continue when considering the fifteenth century. Here it would seem obvious that specializations in the market economy were leading to specializ-

medieval period. See his "What Accelerated Technological Progress in the Western Middle Ages?" in *Scientific Change*, ed. A. C. Crombie (London, 1963), pp. 272–91, and also his essays, "Cultural Climates and Technological Advance in the Middle Ages" and "The Iconography of *Temperantia* and the Virtuousness of Technology", in his *Medieval Religion and Technology* (Berkeley, 1978), pp. 217–53 and 181–204.

[136] Mainly on the grounds that none of the supposed innovations can be proven to have been sufficiently revolutionary to have had much effect upon the material well-being of the society of the time or that they were secondary to other factors, such as the development of the feudal mode of production: Hilton and Sawyer, "Technical Determinism", pp. 90–100; Titow, *English Rural Society*, pp. 37–42; Anderson, *Passages from Antiquity to Feudalism*, p. 183.

[137] See pp. 270–2 above.

[138] White, *Medieval Technology and Social Change*, pp. 67–8.

ations in the use of draught animals instead of vice versa, since draught animals comprised only a small part of this economy. It may be suggested that possible breeding improvements noted in the later middle ages (see pp. 17–19 above) might account for the more intensified use of either one animal or the other in a particular district and that this in turn added to the degree of regionalism noted; but, at best, this development would seem to be reinforcing market specialization rather than in any way causing it.

It appears, then, that technological changes were seldom as free-wheeling as the technical determinist argument would indicate, but as often as not were held back or controlled by other mechanisms, such as the market, or perhaps simply conservatism on the part of medieval society in preferring cost-saving methods to those that improved production. Nevertheless technological change often seems to have had a certain inexorability that transcended these other controlling mechanisms. It is interesting to note, for instance, how often the work-horse was adopted in medieval England despite the often powerful economic arguments against it, a situation reminiscent of the adoption of the tractor in the first half of this century.[139] In some cases, too, the lack of a specific invention was clearly crucial. Thus the fact that four-wheeled vehicles in medieval Europe did not have moveable forecarriages meant that oxen were still needed to haul the heavy, two-wheeled wain.[140] However, when four-wheeled wagons with moveable forecarriages, capable of being hauled by horses, began to replace those wains in some districts in the seventeenth century it is notable that the use of oxen died away, possibly because they could no longer be justified for ploughing alone.[141] If such a change had occurred, say, in the fifteenth century, it might have dramatically altered the appearance of English traction at the time.

*   *   *

[139] Where difficulties in the supply of horses seem eventually to have allowed the dissemination of the much more expensive tractors in the late 1930s. E. J. T. Collins, "The Farm Horse Economy of England and Wales in the Early Tractor Age 1900–40", in *Horses in European Economic History: A Preliminary Canter*, pp. 73–100.

[140] See p. 155 above.

[141] This seems to occur in the Lichfield and district inventories, where oxen and wains disappear over the seventeenth century, to be replaced – occasionally at least – by wagons. *Probate Inventories of Lichfield*, pp. 199, 280.

In summary, at least three things stand out from this study. The first is that many alterations in traction were clearly taking place over the period under consideration. These included not only the introduction of horses to vehicular transport but also the employment of the animals in all-horse or mixed plough-teams, as well as possible changes in plough and vehicle type. Many of these innovations were a long time coming to fruition. Thus the use of horses for ploughing was a slow process that only really gathered momentum with the more rapid propagation of all-horse teams in the fifteenth century and afterwards.[142] Others were transitory, such as the development of mixed plough-teams, which grew in popularity in the twelfth and thirteenth centuries but seemingly died out towards the end of our period.[143] Altogether these developments suggest not only a degree of technological activity and competence of a significantly higher order than previously thought[144] but also a great variety in technological response, from the rapid (the rise in horse hauling) to the nearly stagnant (the dissemination of the various plough types[145]). The second point is that the introduction of the work-horse to farming in general seems to have interacted most strongly with changes in the market economy, whether it was a simple expansion of that economy or a change in the degree of its sophistication or complexity. In this regard, the so-called "commercialization theory" would seem to provide the best theoretical model to explain the development of this particular innovation during the middle ages. If one were to take a technical determinist stance, it could be argued that it was in relation to the market that the horse had its greatest effect in medieval England, contributing to much closer ties between town and country, which probably had much to do with the renewed vitality of the former. The third and final point to be emphasized is the strength of the role played by peasants, especially smallholders, in promoting the use of horses overall. In this instance, it was the peasantry – and, again, especially smallholders – who seem to have been the most technologically progressive sector in medieval society. This is the very antithesis of the widely held belief that only large farms could satisfactorily fulfil this innovatory

---

[142] See pp. 212, 219 above.   [143] See pp. 112, 234 above.
[144] Particularly when compared to the neo-Malthusian view above.
[145] See pp. 132–41 above.

role;[146] but it may well have been the guiding principle behind many, if not most, of the improvements to agriculture during the medieval period.[147]

[146] E.g., Brenner, "Agrarian Class Structure", pp. 63–4; *idem*, "Agrarian Roots of European Capitalism ", pp. 96–100; see also Cooper, "In Search of Agrarian Capitalism", pp. 24–5.

[147] Another peasant-oriented innovation may have been the growing of legumes; see, for example, the high level of legumes grown on peasant holdings at Cuxham compared to the demesne there (Harvey, *Medieval Oxfordshire Village*, pp. 130–1).

Appendix. Problems of translation

One of the difficulties faced in this study involves the translation of the various Latin and Anglo–Latin terms applied to demesne and peasant livestock, especially horses and cattle. Some of these are fairly straightforward: for instance, the word *bos* has been translated as "ox" throughout this study,[1] *vacca* as "cow", *taurus* as "bull", *equus* as "horse", and so on, as in any Latin–English dictionary. Others, however, are far less clear. The terms covering horses alone – *averus, avrus, affrus, carectarius, hercatorius, jumentum, runcinus, stottus*, etc. – can be very confusing. In many of these cases it has been the policy of scholars, particularly those compiling Latin word-lists, to play safe and simply refer to them as "draught animals".[2] While this satisfies the purists and adds a useful note of caution for the beginner, it is unnecessarily fastidious from the point of view of this study, since in the majority of cases the internal evidence from the sources and its consistency of application make it clear which species of animal is being referred to by a particular term. Fortunately enough documents of a varied nature have been examined in this study such that it is possible to lay down some general rules about the more confusing of these terms, and a short glossary relating primarily to work animals has been constructed below.[3]

* * *

[1] By "oxen" we mean non-breeding adult male cattle. Presumably they were castrated, although we cannot be sure of this in every case, since the accounts in particular curiously omit the costs of this castration (as against, say, castration costs for pigs, which are often recorded in the accounts). Occasional references do exist, however, to indicate that some oxen at least were castrated animals, as, for example, at Wrabness (Essex), where a *taurus castratus* was added to the demesne oxen in 1353–4 (W.A.M. 3229).

[2] For example, see the translation of *affrus, avrus*, etc., in the *Revised Medieval Latin Word-list* (ed. Latham), p. 40 (under 2 *averium*).

[3] Terms relating to young animals, such as *bovettus* (steer or young ox) have not been included. Where they occur in our study, the Latin is usually given.

293

Affrus, affra, afrus, afra, etc., anglicized as "affer" – this is the most common term for the demesne or peasant work-horse, especially during the period from 1250 to 1400. "Affers" referred to as horses or with foals occur frequently in the accounts.[4] They could be either male or female and were virtually always adult animals.[5] More often than not they were plough-beasts, particularly in the south and east.[6] As price data indicate, they tended to be less valuable beasts than oxen or cart-horses.[7] Although some historians consider "affer" as a term applicable to both horses and oxen and even donkeys,[8] there is no evidence in this study to indicate that they were anything other than horses.[9]

Animal (pl. *animalia*) – usually a term designating livestock in general, although occasionally, as in Domesday, it had a more specialized meaning as non-working or even young cattle.[10]

Averium (pl. *averia*) – again a term for livestock in general, as is best seen in a brief glossary contained in a late thirteenth- or early fourteenth-century legal textbook: *Differencia inter affrum et averium: scilicet affrus est equus carretivus, averium est nomen*

---

[4] E.g., *In j equo affro empto, xiijs. iiijd.* (Lawshall, Suffolk, 1374–5; P.R.O. S.C. 6 1002/1); *Idem de .viij. Afris anno preterito remanentibus . . . De quibus In adiunctione cum equis carectariis .j. (Wellingborough Manorial Accounts*, p. 39); see under *averium* below.

[5] Although a confusing case does occur in the account-book for Beaulieu Abbey, c. 1270, where in listing the various stages in an animal's life for accounting purposes it is stated for horses that *Pullani equorum primo compoto postquam nati sunt pullani vocantur, secundo compoto vocantur superannales, tercio compoto vocantur affri. Quarto compoto coniunguntur masculi cum masculis, femelle cum femellis et efficientur equi vel eque.* (*Account-Book of Beaulieu Abbey*, ed. S. F. Hockey (Camden Fourth Series, xvi, 1975), p. 51). Here it seems that affers were young animals, perhaps being broken in for work. However, nowhere is this interpretation supported by the accounts themselves, even for Beaulieu Abbey, where horses designated as "affers" invariably retain that appellation all through their adult lives.

[6] E.g., *In j affro empto ad carucam . . .* (Billingbear, Berkshire, 1286–7; H.R.O. Eccles. 2 159308, fo. 17v).

[7] Cf. the price for plough-horses (*afers* and *stots*) versus oxen and cart-horses in D. L. Farmer, "Some Livestock Price Movements in Thirteenth-Century England", pp. 2–5.

[8] *Early Taxation Returns*, pp. 1–2; Searle, *Lordship and Community*, p. 292.

[9] At least in the medieval period. Two "affers" seemingly appear as cattle in a 1528 Bedfordshire will, but this seems to be a corruption for heifers. B.R.O. ABP/R2, fo. 187v.

[10] Darby, *Domesday England*, p. 163; R. Trow-Smith, *A History of British Livestock Husbandry to 1700* (London, 1957), pp. 70–3. For *animalia* as young cattle, see *Yorkshire Lay Subsidy*, esp. pp. 9–13.

generale ad equos, boves, oves, porcos, etc.[11] Perhaps the most
common usage in this sense occurred in regard to heriot and
mortuary payments: e.g., *dominus habebit melius averium suum
nomine dominii, et aliud melius averium nomine rectoris.*[12]

Averus, avera, averius, averia, avrus, avra, etc., anglicized as "aver"
– when used in the second declension masculine or first declension feminine forms, terms with the base *aver-* or *avr-* refer only
to horses,[13] and in this regard it seems likely that they were forerunners of the term *affrus* (or *affra*). As such, they occur frequently in the documents before 1250, especially in accounts and
surveys, but become increasingly infrequent afterwards, as the
term "affer" gradually takes over. Much confusion, however, can
arise from the scribes' habit of abbreviating the pertinent word to
aver' or even *av'*, so that it is impossible to determine if it is the
averus or *averium* form that is meant. In such cases one can only
go by the order or context in which the words occur. In the lay
subsidy assessments, for instance, horses are generally listed first,
cattle next, so that an *aver'* appearing at the head of a list is almost
certainly a horse, especially if followed by a foal (*pullus* or
pullanus) or other horses.[14]

Caballus – a term which, in classical Latin, represents an inferior
class of riding or pack-horse,[15] although in the medieval period it
seems to have had the more general meaning of work-horse.[16]
Altogether it was found only on a few occasions, primarily in
twelfth- and early thirteenth-century documents.

---

[11] C.U.L. MS Dd. VII. 14, fo. 19, as quoted in *Walter of Henley*, p. 27n.

[12] From a 1266–7 extent of Frocester in Gloucestershire. *Historia et cartularium monasterii Sancti Petri Gloucestriae*, iii, p. 88.

[13] E.g., *In stabulum . . . remanent . . . iij avers equorum* (Jarrow, Durham, 1416–17; *Inventories and Account Rolls . . . of Jarrow and Monk-Wearmouth*, p. 91); *Idem reddunt compotum de x averiis Remanentibus anno preterito et de j equo de testamento ywonis coc. Summa xj. Et omnes Remanent* (Crawley, Hampshire, 1232–3; Gras and Gras, *Economic and Social History of an English Village*, p. 211); *Idem reddunt compotum de 3 avris et 1 pullo* (foal) *remanentibus anno preterito. Et de 1 pullo Roberti conbustoris. In mortuo, 1. Et remanent 2 avri, et 2 pulli 2 annorum* (Bitterne, Hampshire, 1210–11; *Pipe Roll of the Bishopric of Winchester, 1210–1211*, pp. 7–8); *Centum equos, quorum alii erunt manni, alii vero runcini, alii summarii, alii veredarii, alii vero averii* (*Vitae Abbat. S. Albani 76*, as quoted in *Oxford English Dictionary* (1933 edn), i, p. 582).

[14] As, for example, the *j aver' cum pullo* found among the stock listed for Roger de Nueva of Semley (Wiltshire) in the 1225 lay subsidy (P.R.O. E179 242/47, m. 14).

[15] *Chambers–Murray Latin–English Dictionary* (London, 1976), p. 87.

[16] E.g., the *caballus hercerius* at Middleton (Norfolk) in 1185 (*Rotuli de Dominabus*, p. 51).

Carectarius, carretarius, etc. – a cart-horse; often given less ambiguously as *equus carectarius.*

Hercatorius, hercarius, hercharius, etc. – a harrowing horse, again often less ambiguously given as *equus hercatorius.*[17]

Jumentum (pl. *jumenta*) – usually mares serving as combination breeding–working stock.[18]

Occatorius, occator – a harrowing horse, often given as *equus occarius.*[19]

Runcinus – a rouncey, the most common term for horses found in the Domesday survey. It is felt by some that the rouncey was primarily a riding or pack-horse at this time,[20] although, as we have seen in Chapter 2 (p. 34), its proportions in the demesne stock would seem to point to its use as a harrowing animal. After Domesday, *runcini* are infrequently found among demesne or peasant stock listings,[21] and gradually they seem to have come to represent a class of riding animals only.[22]

Summarius – as far as can be seen from this study, this always represented a pack-horse and was found most often among the stock servicing a noble or ecclesiastic household.

Stottus – an alternative term for "affer", used especially in the southeast and particularly East Anglia. Like "affers", "stotts" seem to have been mostly plough-horses and were presumably male, since very few instances of female "stotts" are recorded. In the north, especially towards the end of the medieval period, "stotts" came to represent young oxen or steers rather than horses, a meaning that eventually became widespread.[23] Similarly, in the south and east, although the term *stottus* continued to be applied

---

[17] E.g., *Domesday of St. Paul's of the Year 1222*, pp. 52–3, 69.

[18] As at Chalvington (Sussex) in 1366–7, where it is stated that the *jumenta* had no foals during the year *propter magnum laborem.* E.Suss.R.O. SAS CH 257.

[19] Or some form of it. See *Cartularium monasterii de Rameseia*, iii, pp. 257, 261, 266, 274, 278, 279, 307, 310, 311, 313 (*bis*).

[20] Darby, *Domesday England*, p. 165; H. C. Round in *Victoria County Histories, Somerset*, i, p. 424; Ryder, "Livestock", pp. 350, 400.

[21] Some are listed for the Crowland Abbey demesnes in 1258–9: Page, *Estates of Crowland Abbey*, pp. 182ff.

[22] Thus at Finchale (Durham) in 1307 were found *duo runcini pro armigeris* (*Priory of Finchale*, p. ii).

[23] "Stotts" as young oxen or steers appear frequently in sixteenth-century probate inventories. E.g., see *Yorkshire Probate Inventories 1542–1689*, ed. P. C. D. Brears (Yorks. Arch. Soc. Rec. Ser., cxxxiv, 1972), p. 17.

to work-horses right to the end of the direct demesne farming
period, it gradually lost ground to the term *affrus*.[24]

In general, the risk of confusing cattle with horses is greatest in the
pre-1250 documents, mainly because of the conflicting meanings of
the words with the base *aver-*. Indeed, the development of the word
"affer" during the thirteenth century may have been a device to
eliminate some of this confusion, in order that a more consistent
terminology for describing work animals could be established;
thereafter it was much easier to discern the species of animal – horse
or ox – involved.

[24] See, for example, J. A. Raftis, *The Estates of Ramsey Abbey* (Toronto, 1957).
p. 130.

Bibliography

MANUSCRIPT SOURCES

a) ACCOUNTS

Altogether over 1800 accounts were examined for this study from a variety of repositories (for some of the record offices involved, see the list of abbreviations at the beginning of this book). There are too many to list individually here, but the sources for those found in Samples A and B are included in Langdon, thesis, Appendix C, along with abbreviated summaries of the data taken from them. Many are also referred to in the footnotes of this book, especially those for Chapter 3.

b) COURT ROLLS

E.R.O. D/DP (per C. Dyer); Wo.R.O. Ref. 009:1 BA 2636/167 (per C. Dyer); Wo.R.O. Ref. 705 BA 54 (per C. Dyer); Wo.R.O. Ref. 009:1 BA 2636/175 (per C. Dyer); B.R.L. 346320–2; W.A.M. 27744.

c) LAY SUBSIDY ASSESSMENTS

P.R.O. S.C. 11, Roll 531 (per R. H. Hilton); P.R.O. E179 123/5, 238/119a, 242/12, 13, 47, 127.

d) SURVEYS AND EXTENTS

T.C.L. MS R.5.33, fos. 115–116A; P.R.O. S.C. 11, Roll 271; Brit. Lib. Cott. MS Claud. C. XI; Brit. Lib. Cott. Claud. D. XIII (per J. Williamson); N.R.O. 21187 (per J. Williamson).

e) WILLS AND INVENTORIES

The fifteenth- and sixteenth-century probate wills and inventories used in this study come from a much larger body of wills and inventories collected by the author for future work. For those employed in this study, see especially Tables 30–32.

PRINTED SOURCES

The Account-Book of Beaulieu Abbey, ed. S. F. Hockey (Camden Fourth Series, xvi, 1975)

Account Roll of the Manor of Clapham Bayeux, ed. F. G. Emmison (Beds. Hist. Rec. Soc., xiv, 1931)

Accounts and Surveys of the Wiltshire Lands of Adam de Stratton, ed. M. W. Farr (Wilts. Arch. Soc. Rec. Ser., xiv, 1959)

Accounts of the Constables of Bristol Castle in the Thirteenth and Early Fourteenth Centuries, ed. M. Sharp (Bristol Rec. Soc., xxxiv, Gloucester, 1982)

Accounts of the Executors of Richard Bishop of London 1303 and of the Executors of Thomas Bishop of Exeter 1310, ed. W. H. Hale and H. T. Ellacombe (Camden New Series, x, 1874)

Accounts of the Obedientaries of Abingdon Abbey, ed. R. H. G. Kirk (Camden New Series, li, 1892)

Anglo-Saxon Charters, ed. A. J. Robertson (Cambridge, 1939)

Anglo-Saxon Wills, ed. D. Whitelock (Cambridge, 1930)

Bishop Hatfield's Survey, ed. W. Greenwell (Surtees Soc., xxxii, 1856)

Boldon Buke: a survey of the possessions of the see of Durham, 1183, ed. W. Greenwell (Surtees Soc., xxv, 1852)

Book of Fees, 3 vols. (London, 1920–31)

The Book of Husbandry by Master Fitzherbert, 1534 edn, ed. W. W. Skeat (London, 1882)

The Burton Abbey Twelfth Century Surveys, ed. C. G. O. Bridgeman (William Salt Arch. Soc., 1916)

Calendar of Close Rolls (London, 1892–1963)

Calendar of Inquisitions Miscellaneous, 7 vols. (London, 1916–68)

Calendar of Patent Rolls (London, 1891–in progress)

Giraldus Cambrensis, *Descriptio Kambriae*, in *Opera*, vi, ed. J. F. Dimock (Rolls Series, 1868)

Cartularium monasterii de Rameseia, ed. W. W. Hart and P. A. Lyons, 3 vols. (Rolls Series, 1884–93)

The Cartulary and Terrier of the Priory of Bilsington, ed. N. Neilson (British Academy Records of Social and Economic History, viii, London, 1928)

Cartulary of Oseney Abbey, vi, ed. H. E. Salter (Oxford Hist. Soc., ci, 1936)

Chancellor's Roll (8 Ric. I) (Pipe Roll Soc., new series, vii, 1930)

Charters and Custumals of the Abbey of Holy Trinity Caen, ed. M. Chibnall (British Academy Records of Social and Economic History, new series, v, London, 1982)

Chertsey Abbey Court Roll Abstracts, ed. E. Toms, 2 pts (Surrey Rec. Soc., nos. 38 and 48, 1937 and 1954)

Columella, *De Re Rustica*, i and ii, trans. H. B. Ash, E. S. Forster, and E. H. Heffner (London, 1941 and 1954)

Court Roll of Chalgrave Manor 1278–1313, ed. M. K. Dale (Beds. Hist. Rec. Soc., xxvii, 1948)

Court Rolls of the Abbey of Ramsey and of the Honor of Clare, ed. W. O. Ault (Yale, 1928)

Court Rolls of the Manor of Hales, 1272–1307, ed. J. Amphlett, S. G. Hamilton and R. A. Wilson, 3 pts (Worcs. Hist. Soc., 1910, 1912, 1933)

Court Rolls of the Manor of Wakefield, 1274–1331, ed. W. P. Baildon, J. Lister and J. W. Walker, 5 vols. (Yorks. Arch. Soc. Rec. Ser., xxix, 1901; xxxvi, 1906; lvii, 1917; lxxviii, 1930; cix, 1945)

Court Rolls of the Wiltshire Manors of Adam de Stratton, ed. R. B. Pugh (Wilts. Arch. Soc. Rec. Ser., xxiv, 1970)

The Crondal Records, ed. F. J. Baigent (Hampshire Rec. Soc., 1890)

Custumals of Battle Abbey in the Reigns of Edward I and Edward II (1283–1312), ed. S. R. Scargill-Bird (Camden New Series, xli, 1887)

Custumals of the Sussex Manors of the Archbishops of Canterbury, ed. B. C. Redwood and A. E. Wilson (Sussex Rec. Soc., lvii, 1958)

Devon Inventories of the Sixteenth and Seventeenth Centuries, ed. M. Cash (Devon and Cornwall Rec. Soc., new series, xi, 1966)

Documents Illustrating the Rule of Walter de Wenlock, Abbot of Westminster, 1283–1307, ed. B. F. Harvey (Camden Fourth Series, ii, 1965)

Documents in Economic History, ed. H. E. S. Fisher and A. R. J. Juřica (London, 1977)

Documents Relating to the Manor and Soke of Newark-on-Trent, ed. M. W. Barley (Thoroton Soc. Rec. Ser., xvi, 1955)

Domesday Book, 4 vols. (Record Commission, 1783–1814)

Domesday of St. Paul's of the Year 1222, ed. W. H. Hale (Camden Soc., lxix, 1858)

Early Compotus Rolls of the Priory of Worcester, ed. J. M. Wilson and C. Gordon (Worcs. Hist. Soc., 1908)

Early Huntingdonshire Lay Subsidy Rolls, ed. J. A. Raftis and M. P. Hogan (Toronto, 1976)

Early Taxation Returns, ed. A. C. Chibnall (Bucks. Rec. Soc., xiv, 1966)

Early Yorkshire Charters, ed. W. Farrer and C. T. Clay, 12 vols. (Yorks. Arch. Soc. Rec. Ser., extra series, 1914–65)

The Ecclesiastical History of Ordericus Vitalis, ed. M. Chibnall, 5 vols. (Oxford, 1968–75)

Elizabethan Inventories, ed. C. E. Freeman (Beds. Hist. Rec. Soc., xxxii, 1952)

English Historical Documents, i, c. 500–1042, 2nd edn, ed. D. Whitelock (Oxford, 1972)

English Historical Documents, ii, 1042–1189, 2nd edn, ed. D. C. Douglas (London, 1961)

Extent of Monk Friston, 1320, ed. T. A. M. Bishop (Miscellanea, iv, Yorks. Arch. Soc. Rec. Ser., xciv, 1937)

Extents of the Prebends of York, ed. T. A. M. Bishop (Yorks, Arch. Soc. Rec. Ser., xciv, 1937)

Extracts from the Account Rolls of the Abbey of Durham, i, ed. J. T. Fowler (Surtees Soc., xcix, 1898)

Feudal Aids, 6 vols. (London, 1899–1920)

Fleta, ii, ed. H. G. Richardson and W. O. Sayles (Selden Soc., lxxii, 1953)

Halmota Prioratus Dunelmensis, ed. W. H. D. Longstaffe and J. Booth (Surtees Soc., lxxxii, 1886)

Herefordshire Domesday, ed. V. H. Galbraith and J. Tait (Pipe Roll Soc., new series, xxv, 1947 and 1948)

Historia et cartularium monasterii Sancti Petri Gloucestriae, ed. W. H. Hart, 3 vols. (Rolls Series, 1863–7)

The Honour and Forest of Pickering, iii, ed. R. B. Turton (North Riding Rec. Soc., new series, iii, 1896)

Household and Farm Inventories in Oxfordshire, 1550–90, ed. M. A. Havinden (Historical Manuscripts Commission, JP10, London, 1965)

Inquisitio Comitatus Cantabrigiensis . . . subjicitur Inquisitio Eliensis, ed. N. E. S. A. Hamilton (London, 1876)

The Inventories and Account Rolls of the Benedictine Houses or Cells of Jarrow and Monk-Wearmouth, ed. J. Raine (Surtees Soc., xxix, 1854)

Jacobean Household Inventories, ed. F. G. Emmison (Beds. Hist. Rec. Soc., xx, 1938)

The Kalendar of Abbot Samson of Bury St. Edmunds and Related Documents, ed. R. H. C. Davis (Camden Third Series, lxxxiv, 1954)

King Alfred's Orosius, ed. H. Sweet (London, 1883)

Lancashire and Cheshire Wills and Inventories, ed. G. J. Piccope and J. P. Earwaker, 5 vols. (Chetham Soc., xxxiii, 1857; li, 1860; New Series, iii, 1885; xxviii, 1893; xxxvii, 1897)

Liber Henrici de Soliaco abbatis Glastoniae, ed. J. E. Jackson (Roxburghe Club, 1882)

"Liber Niger monasterii S. Petri de Burgo", in *Chronicon Petroburgense*, ed. T. Stapledon (Camden Soc., xlvii, 1849)

William of Malmesbury, *De gestis rerum Anglorum*, 2 vols. (Rolls Series, 1887–9)

Mamecestre, ii, ed. J. Harland (Chetham Soc., lvi, 1861)

The Manor of Manydown, Hampshire, ed. G. W. Kitchen (Hampshire Rec. Soc., 1895)

Manorial Records of Cuxham, Oxfordshire, ed. P. D. A. Harvey (Oxfordshire Rec. Soc., 1, 1976)

The Medieval Customs of the Manors of Taunton and Bradford on Tone, ed. T. J. Hunt (Somerset Rec. Soc., lxvi, 1962)

Ministers' Accounts of the Earldom of Cornwall, 1296–1297, ed. L. M. Midgley, 2 vols. (Camden Third Series, lxvi, 1942; lxviii, 1945)

Ministers' Accounts of the Warwickshire Estates of the Duke of Clarence, 1479–80, ed. R. H. Hilton (Dugdale Soc., xxi, 1952)

Alexander Neckam, *De Naturis Rerum*, ed. T. Wright (Rolls Series, 1863)

Nottinghamshire Household Inventories, ed. P. A. Kennedy (Thoroton Soc., Rec. Ser., xxii, 1963)

Percy Bailiff's Rolls of the Fifteenth Century, ed. J. C. Hodgson (Surtees Soc., cxxxiv, 1921)

Pierce the Ploughmans Crede, ed. W. W. Skeat (London, 1867)

The Pipe Roll of the Bishopric of Winchester, 1210–1211, ed. N. R. Holt (Manchester, 1964)

Pipe Rolls 5 Henry II–I John (Pipe Roll Soc., i, 1884 – new series, x, 1933)

The Priory of Coldingham, ed. J. Raine (Surtees Soc., xii, 1841)

The Priory of Finchale, ed. J. Raine (Surtees Soc., vi, 1837)

Probate Inventories and Manorial Excepts of Chetnole, Leigh and Yetminster, ed. R. Machin (Bristol, 1976)

Probate Inventories of Lichfield and District 1568–1680, ed. D. G. Vaisey (Staffs. Rec. Soc., 4th series, v, 1969)

Records of the Templars in England in the Twelfth Century, ed. B. A. Lees

(British Academy Records of Social and Economic History, ix, London, 1935)

Red Book of Worcester, ed. M. Hollings, 4 pts (Worcs. Hist. Soc., 1934–50)

The Register of the Abbey of St. Benet of Holme, 1020–1210, ed. J. R. West, 2 vols. (Norfolk Rec. Soc., ii and iii, 1932)

Rentalia et custumaria Michaelis de Ambresbury, 1235–1252, et Rogeri de Ford, 1252–1261, abbatis monasterii beatiae Mariae Glastoniae, ed. C. J. Elton (Somerset Rec. Soc., v, 1891)

Rolls of the King's Court (Pipe Roll Soc., xiv, 1891)

Rotuli de Dominabus et Pueris et Puellis (Pipe Roll Soc., xxxv, 1913)

Select Documents of the English Lands of the Abbey of Bec, ed. M. Chibnall (Camden Third Series, lxxiii, 1951)

Select Pleas in Manorial and other Seigneurial Courts, Hen III–Edw I, ed. F. W. Maitland (Selden Soc., ii, 1889)

A Suffolk Hundred in the Year 1283, ed. E. Powell (Cambridge, 1910)

Surrey Manorial Accounts, ed. H. M. Briggs (Surrey Rec. Soc., no. 37, 1935)

Surrey Taxation Returns, ed. H. Jenkinson, with an introduction by J. F. Willard (Surrey Rec. Soc., no. 18, 1922)

The Taxation of 1297, ed. A. T. Gaydon (Beds. Hist. Rec. Soc., xxxix, 1959)

The Terfinnas and Beormas of Ohthere, ed. A. S. C. Ross (Leeds, 1940)

A Terrier of Fleet Lincolnshire, ed. N. Neilson (British Academy Records of Social and Economic History, iv, London, 1920)

Testamenta Eboracensia, ed. J. Raine, Jr (Surtees Soc., xlv, 1864)

Thirteen Custumals of the Sussex Manors of the Bishop of Chichester and other Documents, ed. W. D. Peckham (Sussex Rec. Soc., xxxi, 1925)

Three Lancashire Documents of the Fourteenth and Fifteenth Century, ed. J. Harland (Chetham Soc., lxxiv, 1868)

Three Records of the Alien Priory of Grove and the Manor of Leighton, ed. R. Richmond (Beds. Hist. Rec. Soc., viii, 1923)

A Transcript of "The Red Book", ed. A. T. Bannister (Miscellany xv, Camden Third Series, xli, 1929)

Thomas Tusser, *Five Hundred Points of Good Husbandry*, ed. W. Payne and S. J. Herrtage (London, 1878)

Two "Compoti" of the Lancashire and Cheshire Manors of Henry de Lacy, Earl of Lincoln, xxiv and xxxiii Edward I, ed. P. A. Lyons (Chetham Soc., cxii, 1884)

Two Registers Formerly Belonging to the Family of Beauchamp of Hatch, ed. H. C. Maxwell-Lyte (Somerset Rec. Soc., xxxv, 1920)

The Vision of William concerning Piers the Plowman, ed. W. W. Skeat (London, 1869)

Walter of Henley, ed. D. Oschinsky (Oxford, 1971)

Wellingborough Manorial Accounts, ed. F. M. Page (Northants. Rec. Soc., viii, 1936)

Wills and Inventories . . . of the Northern Counties of England, ed. J. Raine (Surtees Soc., ii, 1835)

Wills and Inventories . . . of the Archdeaconry of Richmond, ed. J. Raine, Jr (Surtees Soc., xxvi, 1853)

Wills and Inventories from the Registry at Durham, ed. J. C. Hodgson
(Surtees Soc., cxii, 1906)
The Yorkshire Lay Subsidy, 25 Edward I, ed. W. Brown (Yorks. Arch.
Soc. Rec. Ser., xvi, 1894)
Yorkshire Probate Inventories 1542–1689, ed. P. C. D. Brears (Yorks.
Arch. Soc. Rec. Ser., cxxxiv, 1972)

SECONDARY WORKS (INCLUDING UNPUBLISHED THESES AND PAPERS)

B. Almack, "On the Agriculture of Norfolk", *Journal Royal Agric. Soc.*, v
(1844)
A. L. Anderson, *Introductory Animal Husbandry* (New York, 1943)
P. Anderson, *Passages from Antiquity to Feudalism* (London, 1974)
P. L. Armitage, "A Preliminary Description of British Cattle from the Late
Twelfth to the Early Sixteenth Century", *Ark* (Journal for the Rare
Breeds Survival Trust), vii, pt 12 (1980)
J. Arnold, *Farm Waggons and Carts* (Newton Abbot, 1977)
J. Arnold, "Waggons of Mystery", *Countryman*, lxxxiv (1979)
W. O. Ault, "Open-Field Husbandry and the Village Community", *Trans.
of the American Philosophical Society*, lv, pt 7 (1965)
W. O. Ault, *Open-Field Farming in Medieval England* (London, 1972)
A. R. H. Baker and R. A. Butlin (eds.), *Studies of Field Systems in the
British Isles* (Cambridge, 1973)
R. Baker, "On the Farming of Essex", *Journal Royal Agric. Soc.*, v (1844)
R.-B. and A.-M. Bautier, "Contribution à l'Histoire du Cheval au Moyen
Âge", *Bulletin Philologique et Historique* (1976 and 1978)
G. F. Beaumont, "The Manor of Borley, A.D. 1308", *Trans. of the Essex
Arch. Soc.*, new series, xviii (1928)
H. S. Bennett, *Life on the English Manor* (Cambridge, 1937)
J. R. Birrell, "Medieval Agriculture", *Victoria County Histories, Stafford-
shire*, vi (London, 1979)
T. A. M. Bishop, "The Distribution of Manorial Demesne in the Vale of
Yorkshire", *Eng. Hist. Rev.*, xlix (1934)
M. Bloch, *Les Caractères Originaux de l'Histoire Rurale Française aux xv^e
et xvie Siècles*, 2nd edn (Paris, 1955)
M. Bloch, "The Advent and Triumph of the Watermill", in *Land and Work
in Medieval Europe* (London, 1967)
E. Blum and P. Laver, *La Miniature Française aux xve et xvie siècles* (Paris
and Brussels, 1930)
J. L. Bolton, *The Medieval English Economy 1150–1500* (London, 1980)
E. Boserup, *The Conditions of Agricultural Growth* (London, 1965)
E. Boserup, *Population and Technology* (London, 1981)
M. N. Boyer, "Medieval Pivoted Axles", *Technology and Culture*, i (1959–
60)
P. F. Brandon, "Demesne Arable Farming in Coastal Sussex during the
Later Middle Ages", *Agric. Hist. Rev.*, xix (1971)
R. Brenner, "Agrarian Class Structure and Economic Development in Pre-
Industrial Europe", *Past and Present*, no. 70 (1976)

R. Brenner, "The Agrarian Roots of European Capitalism", *Past and Present*, no. 97 (1982)

A. R. Bridbury, *Economic Growth: England in the Later Middle Ages* (London, 1962)

R. H. Britnell, "Agricultural Technology and the Margin of Cultivation in the Fourteenth Century", *Econ. Hist. Rev.*, 2nd series, xxx (1977)

R. H. Britnell, "Minor Landlords in England and Medieval Agrarian Capitalism", *Past and Present*, no. 89 (1980)

R. H. Britnell, "The Proliferation of Markets in England, 1200–1349", *Econ. Hist. Rev.*, 2nd series, xxxiv (1981)

A. Burford, "Heavy Transport in Classical Antiquity", *Econ. Hist. Rev.*, 2nd series, xiii (1960)

James Caird, *English Agriculture in 1850–1* (London, 1852)

Cambridge Economic History of Europe, i, 2nd edn, ed. M. M. Postan (Cambridge, 1966)

B. M. S. Campbell, "Field Systems in Eastern Norfolk during the Middle Ages: A Study with Particular Reference to the Demographic and Agrarian Changes of the Fourteenth Century" (Univ. of Cambridge Ph.D. thesis, 1975)

B. M. S. Campbell, "Population Change and the Genesis of Commonfields on a Norfolk Manor", *Econ. Hist. Rev.*, 2nd series, xxxiii (1980)

B. M. S. Campbell, "Commonfield Origins – the Regional Dimensions", in *The Origins of Open-Field Agriculture*, ed. T. Rowley (London, 1981)

B. M. S. Campbell, "Agricultural Progress in Medieval England: Some Evidence from Eastern Norfolk", *Econ. Hist. Rev.*, 2nd series, xxxvi (1983)

B. M. S. Campbell, "Agricultural Productivity in Medieval England: Some Evidence from Norfolk", *Journal of Economic History*, xlviii (1983)

E. M. Carus-Wilson, "An Industrial Revolution in the Thirteenth Century", *Econ. Hist. Rev.*, xi (1941)

Cassell's Gazetteer of Great Britain and Ireland, 6 vols. (London, 1894–8)

J. D. Chambers and G. E. Mingay, *The Agricultural Revolution 1750–1880* (London, 1966)

J. A. Chartres, "Road Carrying in England in the Seventeenth Century: Myth and Reality", *Econ. Hist. Rev.*, 2nd series, xxx (1977)

A. V. Chayanov, *The Theory of Peasant Economy*, ed. D. Thorner, B. Kerblay, and R. E. F. Smith (Illinois, 1966)

A. V. Chernetsov, "On the Origin and Early Development of the East-European Plough and the Russian Sokha", *Tools and Tillage*, ii, pt 1 (1972)

K. Chivers, *The Shire Horse* (London, 1976)

C. M. Cipolla, *The Fontana Economic History of Europe*, i (London, 1972)

H. M. Clark, "Selion Size and Soil Type", *Agric. Hist. Rev.*, viii (1960)

E. Clark, "Debt Litigation in a Late Medieval Vill", in *Pathways to Medieval Peasants*, ed. J. A. Raftis (Toronto, 1981)

E. M. Clifford, "Working Oxen at Cirencester", *Trans. of the Bristol and Glos. Arch. Soc.*, lxiii (1942)

E. J. T. Collins, "The Farm Horse Economy of England and Wales in the

Early Tractor Age", in *Horses in European Economic History: A Preliminary Canter*, ed. F. M. L. Thompson (Reading, 1983)

H. M. Colvin, "A Medieval Drawing of a Plough", *Antiquity*, xxvii (1953)

J. P. Cooper, "In Search of Agrarian Capitalism", *Past and Present*, no. 80 (1978)

J. Cowie, "An Essay in the Comparative Advantages in the Employment of Horses and Oxen in Farm Work", *Journal Royal Agric. Soc.*, v (1844)

J. Crofts, *Packhorse, Waggon and Post* (London, 1967)

W. Cunningham, *The Growth of English Industry and Commerce*, 4th edn (Cambridge, 1905)

E. C. Curwen, "Prehistoric Agriculture in Britain", *Antiquity*, i (1927)

C. J. Dahlman, *The Open Field System and Beyond* (Cambridge, 1980)

H. C. Darby (ed.), *The Domesday Geography of Eastern England*, 3rd edn (Cambridge, 1971)

H. C. Darby (ed.), *A New Historical Geography of England before 1600* (Cambridge, 1976)

H. C. Darby, *Domesday England* (Cambridge, 1977)

H. C. Darby, "Some Early Ideas on the Agricultural Regions of England", *Agric. Hist. Rev.*, ii (1954)

H. C. Darby and E. M. J. Campbell (eds.), *The Domesday Geography of South-east England* (Cambridge, 1962)

H. C. Darby and R. W. Finn (eds.), *The Domesday Geography of South-west England* (Cambridge, 1967)

H. C. Darby and I. S. Maxwell (eds.), *The Domesday Geography of Northern England* (Cambridge, 1962)

H. C. Darby and I. C. Terrett (eds.), *The Domesday Geography of Midland England* (Cambridge, 1954)

H. C. Darby and G. R. Versey, *Domesday Gazetteer* (Cambridge, 1975)

M. Daumas (ed.), *A History of Technology and Invention*, 2 vols. (New York, 1962 and 1964)

M. Daumas, "The History of Technology: its Aims, its Limits, its Methods", *History of Technology*, i (1976)

F. G. Davenport, *The Economic Development of a Norfolk Manor, 1086–1565* (London, 1906)

R. H. C. Davis, "The Medieval Warhorse", in *Horses in European Economic History: A Preliminary Canter*, ed. F. M. L. Thompson (Reading, 1983)

P. Deffontaines, "Sur la Répartition géographique des Voitures à deux Roues et à quatre Roues", *Travaux du Ier Congrès International de Folklore, Paris, 1937* (Tours, 1938)

L. Delisle, *Études sur la Condition de la Classe Agricole et l'État de l'Agriculture en Normandie au Moyen-Âge* (Paris, 1903)

A. Dent, *The Horse through Fifty Centuries of Civilization* (London, 1974)

E. B. Dewindt, *Land and People in Holywell-cum-Needingworth* (Toronto, 1972)

Dictionary of Medieval Latin from British Sources, fascicules I and II, ed. R. E. Latham (London, 1975 and 1981)

R. B. Dobson (ed.), *The Peasants' Revolt of 1381* (London, 1970)

P. Dockès, *Medieval Slavery and Liberation* (Chicago, 1982)
R. A. Dodgshon, *The Origin of British Field Systems: An Interpretation* (London, 1980)
J. S. Drew, unpublished notes in the care of the committee for the *Dictionary of Medieval Latin from British Sources*, Bodleian Library (Oxford)
F. R. H. Du Boulay, "Who were Farming the English Demesnes at the End of the Middle Ages?", *Econ. Hist. Rev.*, 2nd series, xvii (1965)
F. R. H. Du Boulay, *The Lordship of Canterbury* (London, 1966)
G. Duby , *Rural Economy and Country Life in the Medieval West* (London, 1968)
G. Duby, *The Early Growth of the European Economy* (London, 1974)
G. Duby and A. Wallon (eds.), *Histoire de la France Rurale*, 2 vols. (Paris, 1975)
C. C. Dyer, "Population and Agriculture on a Warwickshire manor in the Later Middle Ages", *Univ. of Birmingham Hist. Journal*, xi (1967–8)
C. C. Dyer, "A Small Landowner in the Fifteenth Century", *Midland History*, i, no. 3 (1972)
C. C. Dyer, "A Redistribution of Incomes in Fifteenth-Century England?", in *Peasants, Knights and Heretics*, ed. R. H. Hilton (Cambridge, 1976)
C. C. Dyer, *Lords and Peasants in a Changing Society: The Estates of the Bishopric of Worcester, 680–1540* (Cambridge, 1980)
C. C. Dyer, "Warwickshire Farming 1349–c. 1520: Preparations for Agricultural Revolution", *Dugdale Society Occasional Papers*, no. 27 (1981)
C. C. Dyer, "English Diet in the Later Middle Ages", in *Social Relations and Ideas: Essays in Honour of R. H. Hilton*, ed. T. H. Aston, P. R. Coss, C. Dyer, and J. Thirsk (Cambridge, 1983)
P. R. Edwards, "The Horse Trade of the Midlands in the Seventeenth Century", *Agric. Hist. Rev.*, xxvii (1979)
H. D. Emanuel, *The Latin Texts of the Welsh Laws* (Cardiff, 1967)
English Rural Life in the Middle Ages, Bodleian Picture Book no. 14 (Oxford, 1975)
Lord Ernle, *English Farming: Past and Present*, 6th edn (London, 1961)
G. E. Evans, *The Horse in the Furrow* (London, 1960)
S. A. Eyre, "The Curving Plough-strip and its Historical Implications", *Agric. Hist. Rev.*, iii (1955)
R. J. Faith, "Peasant Families and Inheritance Customs in Medieval England", *Agric. Hist. Rev.*, xiv (1966)
D. L. Farmer, "Some Price Fluctuations in Angevin England", *Econ. Hist. Rev.*, 2nd series, ix (1956)
D. L. Farmer, "Some Livestock Price Movements in Thirteenth-Century England", *Econ. Hist. Rev.*, 2nd series, xxii (1969)
D. L. Farmer, "Grain Yields on the Winchester Manors in the Later Middle Ages", *Econ. Hist. Rev.*, 2nd series, xxx (1977)
S. Fenoaltea, "Authority, Efficiency and Agricultural Organization in Medieval England and Beyond: A Hypothesis", *Journal of Economic History*, xxxv (1975)

R. K. Field, "Worcestershire Peasant Buildings, Household Goods and Farming Equipment in the Later Middle Ages", *Medieval Archaeology*, ix (1965)

H. P. R. Finberg, *Tavistock Abbey* (Cambridge, 1951)

H. P. R. Finberg, "The Domesday Plough-Team", *Eng. Hist. Rev.*, lxvi (1951)

H. P. R. Finberg (ed.), *The Agrarian History of England and Wales*, i, pt 2 (Cambridge, 1972)

J. L. Fisher, *A Medieval Farming Glossary of Latin and English Words* (London, 1968)

R. Floud, *An Introduction to Quantitative Methods for Historians* (London, 1975)

R. J. Forbes, *Studies in Ancient Technology*, ii (Leiden, 1955)

C. Fox, "Sleds, Carts and Waggons", *Antiquity*, v (1931)

W. Fream, *The Complete Grazier*, 13th edn (London, 1893)

P. Frost, "Yeomen and Metalsmiths: Livestock in the Dual Economy in South Staffordshire 1560–1720", *Agric. Hist. Rev.*, xxix (1981)

R. A. Fuller, "The Tallage of 6 Edward II (Dec. 16, 1312) and the Bristol Rebellion", *Trans. of the Bristol and Glos. Arch. Soc.*, xix (1894–5)

G. E. Fussell, *The Farmer's Tools: A.D. 1500–1900* (London, 1952)

G. E. Fussell, *The Classical Tradition in West European Farming* (Newton Abbot, 1972)

G. E. Fussell, *Farms, Farmers and Society* (Lawrence, Kansas, 1976)

J. Gimpel, *The Medieval Machine* (London, 1977)

P. V. Glob, *Ard og Plov i Nordens Oldtid* (Ard and Plough in Prehistoric Scandinavia) (Aarhus, 1951)

D. M. Goodall, *A History of Horse Breeding* (London, 1977)

R. Grand and R. Delatouche, *L'Agriculture au Moyen Âge de la Fin de l'Empire Romain au XIVᵉ Siècle* (Paris, 1950)

N. S. B. Gras, *The Evolution of the English Corn Market* (Harvard, 1915)

N. S. B. and E. C. Gras, *The Economic and Social History of an English Village* (Cambridge, Mass., 1930)

H. L. Gray, *English Field Systems* (Cambridge, Mass., 1915)

C. Green, "The Purpose of the Early Horseshoe", *Antiquity*, xl (1966)

D. B. Grigg, *Population Growth and Agrarian Change: An Historical Perspective* (Cambridge, 1980)

L. F. Hadwin, "The Medieval Lay Subsidies and Economic History", *Econ. Hist. Rev.*, 2nd series, xxxvi (1983)

E. M. Halcrow, "The Decline of Demesne Farming on the Estates of Durham Cathedral Priory", *Econ. Hist. Rev.*, 2nd series, vii (1955)

A. R. Hall, "More on Medieval Pivoted Axles", *Technology and Culture*, ii (1961)

H. E. Hallam, *Rural England 1066–1348* (London, 1981)

H. Handley, "On Wheel and Swing Ploughs", *Journal Royal Agric. Soc.*, i (1840)

J. N. Hare, "The Demesne Lessees of Fifteenth-Century Wiltshire", *Agric. Hist. Rev.*, xxix (1981)

B. F. Harvey, "The Leasing of the Abbot of Westminster's Demesnes in the Later Middle Ages", *Econ. Hist. Rev.*, 2nd series, xxii (1969)

B. F. Harvey, *Westminster Abbey and its Estates in the Middle Ages* (Oxford, 1977)
N. Harvey, "Walter of Henley and the Old Farming", *Agriculture*, lix (1953)
P. D. A. Harvey, *A Medieval Oxfordshire Village: Cuxham 1240–1400* (Oxford, 1965)
P. D. A. Harvey, "Agricultural Treatises and Manorial Accounting in Medieval England", *Agric. Hist. Rev.*, xx (1972)
P. D. A. Harvey, "The English Inflation of 1180–1220", in *Peasants, Knights and Heretics*, ed. R. H. Hilton (Cambridge, 1976)
J. Hatcher, *Rural Economy and Society in the Duchy of Cornwall, 1300–1500* (Cambridge, 1970)
J. Hatcher, *Plague, Population and the English Economy 1348–1530* (London, 1977)
J. Hatcher, "English Serfdom and Villeinage: Towards a Reassessment", *Past and Present*, no. 90 (1981)
A. G. Haudricourt and M. J.-B. Delamarre, *L'Homme et la Charrue à travers le monde* (Paris, 1955)
M. A. Havinden, "Agricultural Progress in Open-field Oxfordshire", in *Essays in Agrarian History*, i, ed. W. E. Minchinton (Newton Abbot, 1968)
C. F. C. Hawkes and M. R. Hull, *Camulodunum* (Oxford, 1947)
H. J. Hewitt, *The Horse in Medieval England* (London, 1983)
D. Hey, *Packmen, Carriers and Packhorse Roads* (Leicester, 1980)
R. H. Hilton, *The Economic Development of some Leicestershire Estates in the Fourteenth and Fifteenth Centuries* (Oxford, 1947)
R. H. Hilton, "Kibworth Harcourt: A Merton College Manor in the Thirteenth and Fourteenth Centuries", in *Studies in Leicestershire Agrarian History*, ed. W. G. Hoskins (Leicester, 1949)
R. H. Hilton, "Medieval Agrarian History", *Victoria County Histories, Leicestershire*, ii (London, 1954)
R. H. Hilton, "The Content and Sources of English Agrarian History before 1500", *Agric. Hist. Rev.*, iii (1955)
R. H. Hilton, "Rent and Capital Formation in Feudal Society", *Second International Conference of Economic History, 1962* (Paris, 1965)
R. H. Hilton, *A Medieval Society* (London, 1966)
R. H. Hilton, *The Decline of Serfdom in Medieval England* (London, 1969)
R. H. Hilton, *The English Peasantry in the Later Middle Ages* (Oxford, 1975)
R. H. Hilton, "A Crisis in Feudalism", *Past and Present*, no. 80 (1978)
R. H. Hilton and P. A. Rahtz, "Upton, Gloucestershire, 1959–1964", *Trans. of the Bristol and Glos. Arch. Soc.*, lxxxv (1966)
R. H. Hilton and P. H. Sawyer, "Technical Determinism: The Stirrup and the Plough", *Past and Present*, no. 24 (1963)
G. C. Homans, *English Villagers of the Thirteenth Century* (Cambridge, Mass., 1942)
G. C. Homans, "The Explanation of English Regional Differences", *Past and Present*, no. 42 (1969)

W. G. Hoskins, "Regional Farming in England", *Agric. Hist. Rev.*, ii (1954)

W. G. Hoskins, *The Midland Peasant* (London, 1957)

W. G. Hoskins, *The Age of Plunder: the England of Henry VIII 1500–1547* (London, 1976)

G. W. B. Huntingford, "Prehistoric Ox-Yoking", *Antiquity*, viii (1934)

R. H. Inman, *Domesday and Feudal Statistics* (London, 1900)

J. G. Jenkins, *The English Farm Wagon* (Reading, 1961)

J. G. Jenkins, "Sledges and Wheeled Vehicles in Wales", in *Land Transport in Europe*, ed. A. Fenton, J. Podolak and H. Rasmussen (Copenhagen, 1973)

A. Jones, "Caddington, Kenworth, and Dunstable in 1287", *Econ. Hist. Rev.*, 2nd series, xxxii (1979)

A. Jones, "Land Measurement in England, 1150–1350", *Agric. Hist. Rev.*, xxvii (1979)

W. F. Karkeek, "On the Farming of Cornwall", *Journal Royal Agric. Soc.*, vi (1845)

E. Kerridge, "Ridge and Furrow and Agrarian History", *Econ. Hist. Rev.*, 2nd series, iv (1951)

E. Kerridge, *The Agricultural Revolution* (New York, 1968)

I. Kershaw, *Bolton Priory* (Oxford, 1973)

I. Kershaw, "The Great Famine and Agrarian Crisis in England 1315–1322", in *Peasants, Knights and Heretics*, ed. R. H. Hilton (Cambridge, 1976)

E. King, *Peterborough Abbey, 1086–1310* (Cambridge, 1973)

E. A. Kosminsky, *Studies in the Agrarian History of England in the Thirteenth Century* (Oxford, 1956)

W. Kula, *An Economic Theory of the Feudal System* (London, 1976)

R. H. Lane, "Waggons and their Ancestors", *Antiquity*, ix (1935)

J. Langdon, "The Economics of Horses and Oxen in Medieval England", *Agric. Hist. Rev.*, xxx (1982)

J. Langdon, "Horses, Oxen and Technological Innovation: The Use of Draught Animals in English Farming from 1066 to 1500" (Univ. of Birmingham Ph.D. thesis, 1983)

J. Langdon, "Horse Hauling: A Revolution in Vehicle Transport in Twelfth- and Thirteenth-Century England?", *Past and Present*, no. 103 (1984)

N. E. Lee, *Travel and Transport through the Ages* (Cambridge, 1955)

R. Lefebvre des Noëttes, *L'Attelage et le Cheval de Selle à Travers les Âges* (Paris, 1931)

A. C. Leighton, *Transport and Communication in Early Medieval Europe AD 500–1100* (Newton Abbot, 1972)

A. C. Leighton, "A Technological Consideration of Early Medieval Vehicles", *Fifth International Conference of Economic History, Leningrad, 1970* (Paris, 1977)

R. Lennard, "An Unidentified Twelfth-Century Custumal of Lawshall (Suffolk)", *Eng. Hist. Rev.*, li (1936)

R. Lennard, "Domesday Plough-teams: the South-Western Evidence", *Eng. Hist. Rev.*, lx (1945)

R. Lennard, "The Economic Position of the Domesday Villani", *Economic Journal*, lvi (1946)

R. Lennard, "The Economic Position of the Domesday Sokemen", *Economic Journal*, lvii (1947)

R. Lennard, *Rural England 1086–1135* (Oxford, 1959)

R. Lennard, "The Composition of Demesne Plough-Teams in Twelfth-Century England", *Eng. Hist. Rev.*, lxxv (1960)

R. Lennard, "English Agriculture under Charles II: The Evidence of the Royal Society's 'Enquiries' ", in *Essays in Agrarian History*, i, ed. W. E. Minchinton (Newton Abbot, 1968)

E. Le Roy Ladurie, *The Peasants of Languedoc* (Urbana, Illinois, 1974)

A. E. Levett, *Studies in Manorial History* (Oxford, 1938)

E. Lipson, *The Economic History of England*, 11th edn, i (London, 1956)

E. Little, "Farming in Wiltshire", *Journal Royal Agric. Soc.*, v (1844)

T. H. Lloyd, "Ploughing Services on the Demesnes of the Bishop of Worcester in the Thirteenth Century", *Univ. of Birmingham Hist. Journal*, viii (1961)

R. A. Lomas, "The Priory of Durham and its Demesnes in the Fourteenth and Fifteenth Centuries", *Econ. Hist. Rev.*, 2nd series, xxxi (1978)

W. H. Long, "The Low Yields of Corn in Medieval England", *Econ. Hist. Rev.*, 2nd series, xxxii (1979)

R. S. Lopez, "The Evolution of Land Transport in the Middle Ages", *Past and Present*, no. 9 (1956)

R. S. Lopez and J. W. Raymond, *Medieval Trade in the Mediterranean World: Illustrative Documents* (London, 1955)

E. C. Lowry, "The Administration of the Estates of Merton College in the Fourteenth Century" (Univ. of Oxford D.Phil. thesis, 1934)

H. R. Loyn, *Anglo-Saxon England and the Norman Conquest* (London, 1962)

A. T. Lucas, "Irish Ploughing Practices", 4 pts, *Tools and Tillage*, ii, pts 1–4 (1972–5)

D. N. McCloskey, "English Open Fields as Behavior towards Risk", *Research in Economic History*, i, ed. P. Uselding (Greenwich, Connecticut, 1976)

M. K. McIntosh, "Land, Tenure, and Population in the Royal Manor of Havering, Essex, 1251–1352/3", *Econ. Hist. Rev.*, 2nd series, xxxiii (1980)

C. A. McNeill, "Technological Developments in Wheeled Vehicles in Europe, from Prehistory to the Sixteenth Century" (Univ. of Edinburgh Ph.D. thesis, 1979)

F. W. Maitland, *Domesday Book and Beyond* (Cambridge, 1921 edn)

Gervase Markham, *Farewell to Husbandry* (London, 1631 edn)

William Marshall, *The Rural Economy of Norfolk*, 2nd edn, 2 vols. (London, 1795)

William Marshall, *The Rural Economy of Gloucestershire*, 2nd edn, 2 vols. (London, 1796)

William Marshall, *The Rural Economy of the Midland Counties*, 2nd edn, 2 vols. (London, 1796)

William Marshall, *The Rural Economy of Yorkshire*, 2nd edn, 2 vols. (London, 1796)

William Marshall, *The Rural Economy of the Southern Counties*, 2 vols. (London, 1798)

William Marshall, *The Rural Economy of the West of England*, 2nd edn, 2 vols. (London, 1805)

Karl Marx, *Capital*, i and ii (Penguin edn, Harmondsworth, Middlesex, 1976 and 1978); iii (Lawrence and Wishart edn, London, 1959)

Leonard Mascall, *The Government of Cattel* (London, 1662 edn)

M. Mate, "Profit and Productivity on the Estates of Isabella de Forz (1260–92)", *Econ. Hist. Rev.*, 2nd series, xxxiii (1980)

M. Mate, "Medieval Agrarian Practices: The Determining Factors", *Agric. Hist. Rev.*, xxxiii (1985)

E. G. Millar, *The Luttrell Psalter* (London, 1932)

E. Miller, *The Abbey and Bishopric of Ely* (Cambridge, 1951)

E. Miller, "The English Economy in the Thirteenth Century", *Past and Present*, no. 28 (1964)

E. Miller, "England in the Twelfth and Thirteenth Century: An Economic Contrast", *Econ. Hist. Rev.*, 2nd series, xxiv (1971)

E. Miller, "Farming in Northern England", *Northern History*, xi (1975)

E. Miller and J. Hatcher, *Medieval England: Rural Society and Economic Change 1086–1348* (London, 1978)

W. C. Miller and E. D. S. Robertson, *Practical Animal Husbandry*, 4th edn (Edinburgh, 1945)

G. E. Mingay, *The Agricultural Revolution* (London, 1977)

S. K. Mitchell, *Taxation in Medieval England* (New Haven, Connecticut, 1951)

J. H. Moore, "The Ox in the Middle Ages", *Agricultural History*, xxxv (1961)

M. Morgan, *The English Lands of the Abbey of Bec* (Oxford, 1946)

R. Morgan, *Dissertations in British Agricultural History* (Reading, 1981)

L. Mumford, *Technics and Civilization* (New York, 1934)

J. Needham, *Science and Civilisation in China*, 7 vols. (Cambridge, 1954–in progress), iv, pt 2 (1965)

J. U. Nef, *The Rise of the British Coal Industry*, 2 vols. (London, 1932)

K. C. Newton, *The Manor of Writtle* (London and Chichester, 1970)

I. Niall, *To Speed the Plough* (London, 1977)

M. Nightingale, "Ploughing and Field Shape", *Antiquity*, xxvii (1953)

C. S. and C. S. Orwin, *The Open Fields*, 3rd edn (Oxford, 1967)

Oxford English Dictionary

F. M. Page, *The Estates of Crowland Abbey* (Cambridge, 1934)

W. Palin, "The Farming of Cheshire", *Journal Royal Agric. Soc.*, v (1844)

D. M. Palliser, "Tawney's Century: Brave New World or Malthusian Trap?", *Econ. Hist. Rev.*, 2nd series, xxxv (1982)

C. Parain, "The Evolution of Agricultural Technique", in *Cambridge Economic History of Europe*, 2nd edn, i, ed. M. M. Postan (Cambridge, 1966)

M. Partridge, *Farm Tools through the Ages* (Reading, 1973)

J. B. Passmore, "The English Plough" (Univ. of Reading M.Sc. thesis, 1929)

J. B. Passmore, *The English Plough* (Oxford, 1930)

F. G. Payne, "The Plough in Ancient Britain", *Archaeological Journal*, civ (1947)

F. G. Payne, "The British Plough: Some Stages in its Development", *Agric. Hist. Rev.*, v (1957)

J. A. Perkins, "The Ox, the Horse, and English Farming, 1750–1850" (unpublished working paper in economic history, Univ. of New South Wales, 1975)

S. Piggott, " 'The First Wagons and Carts': twenty-five years later", *Bulletin of the Institute of Archaeology*, xvi (1979)

S. Piggott (ed.), *The Agrarian History of England and Wales*, i, pt 1 (Cambridge, 1981)

H. Pirenne, *Medieval Cities* (Princeton, New Jersey, 1925)

C. Platt, *The Monastic Grange in Medieval England* (London, 1969)

S. Porter, "Farm Transport in Huntingdonshire, 1610–1749", *Journal of Transport History*, iii (1983)

M. M. Postan, "Some Economic Evidence of Declining Population in the Later Middle Ages", *Econ. Hist. Rev.*, 2nd series, ii (1950)

M. M. Postan, "Glastonbury Estates in the Twelfth Century", *Econ. Hist. Rev.*, 2nd series, v (1953)

M. M. Postan, "The Famulus: The Estate Labourer in the Twelfth and Thirteenth Century", *Econ. Hist. Rev. Supplement No. 2* (1954)

M. M. Postan, "Village Livestock in the Thirteenth Century", *Econ. Hist. Rev.*, 2nd series, xv (1962)

M. M. Postan, *Essays on Medieval Agriculture and General Problems of the Medieval Economy* (Cambridge, 1973)

M. M. Postan, *The Medieval Economy and Society* (Harmondsworth, Middlesex, 1975)

D. Postles, "Problems in the Administration of Small Manors: Three Oxfordshire Glebe-demesnes, 1278–1345", *Midland History*, iv (1977)

R. B. Pugh, "Ministers' Accounts of Norhamshire and Islandshire, 1261–2", *Northern History*, xi (1975)

P. Pusey, "Experimental Inquiry on Draught in Ploughing", *Journal Royal Agric. Soc.*, i (1840)

J. A. Raftis, *The Estates of Ramsey Abbey* (Toronto, 1957)

J. A. Raftis, *Tenure and Mobility* (Toronto, 1964)

Rankine's Useful Rules and Tables, 6th edn (London, 1883)

Z. Razi, *Life, Marriage and Death in a Medieval Parish: Economy, Society and Demography in Halesowen 1270–1400* (Cambridge, 1980)

Z. Razi, "Family, Land and the Village Community in Later Medieval England", *Past and Present*, no. 93 (1981)

Revised Medieval Latin Word-list, ed. R. E. Latham (London, 1965)

H. G. Richardson, "The Medieval Plough-team", *History*, xxvi (1942)

D. Roden, "Demesne Farming in the Chiltern Hills", *Agric. Hist. Rev.*, xvii (1969)

J. E. T. Rogers, *A History of Agriculture and Prices in England, 1259–1793*, 7 vols. (Oxford, 1866–1902)

J. C. Russell, *British Medieval Population* (Albuquerque, 1948)

M. L. Ryder, "The Animal Remains found at Kirkstall Abbey", *Agric. Hist. Rev.*, vii (1959)

M. L. Ryder, "Livestock Remains from Four Medieval Sites in Yorkshire", *Agric. Hist. Rev.*, ix (1961)

M. L. Ryder, "Livestock", in *The Agrarian History of England and Wales*, i, pt 1, ed. S. Piggott (Cambridge, 1981)

L. F. Salzman, "Social and Economic History: Medieval Cambridgeshire", *Victoria County Histories, Cambridgeshire*, ii (Oxford, 1948)

L. F. Salzman, "The Property of the Earl of Arundel, 1397", *Sussex Arch. Coll.*, xci (1953)

L. F. Salzman, "Early Taxation in Sussex, Parts I and II", *Sussex Arch. Coll.*, xcviii (1960) and xcix (1961)

H. W. Saunders, *An Introduction to the Obedientary and Manor Rolls of Norwich Cathedral Priory* (Norwich, 1930)

E. Searle, *Lordship and Community: Battle Abbey and its Banlieu* (Toronto, 1974)

F. Seebohm, *The English Village Community*, 4th edn (London, 1905)

M. E. Seebohm, *The Evolution of the English Farm* (London, 1927)

T. Shanin (ed.), *Peasants and Peasant Societies* (Harmondsworth, Middlesex, 1971)

C. Singer, E. J. Holmyard, A. R. Hall and T. I. Williams (eds.), *A History of Technology*, 7 vols. (Oxford, 1954–78)

C. Skeel, "The Cattle Trade between Wales and England from the Fifteenth to the Nineteenth Century", *Trans. of the Royal Hist. Soc.*, 4th series, ix (1926)

V. Skipp, *Medieval Yardley* (Chichester, 1970)

B. H. Slicher van Bath, *The Agrarian History of Western Europe A.D. 500–1850* (London, 1963)

B. H. Slicher van Bath, "Yield Ratios, 810–1820", *Afdeling Agrarische Geschiedenis Bijdragen*, 10 (1963)

A. Smith, "Regional Differences in Crop Production in Medieval Kent", *Archaeologia Cantiana*, lxxviii (1963)

R. A. L. Smith, *Canterbury Cathedral Priory* (Cambridge, 1943)

R. A. L. Smith, *Collected Papers* (London, 1947)

I. G. Sparkes, *Old Horseshoes* (Aylesbury, 1976)

J. Spruytte, *Études Expérimentales sur l'Attelage* (Paris, 1977) (now published in English as *Early Harness Systems: Experimental Studies*, London, 1983)

A. Steensberg, "North West European Plough-types of Prehistoric Times and the Middle Ages", *Acta Archaeologica*, vii (1936)

A. Steensberg, "The Vebbestrup Plough", *Acta Archaeologica*, xvi (1945)

F. M. Stenton, "The Road System of Medieval England", *Econ. Hist. Rev.*, vii (1936)

F. M. Stenton (ed.), *The Bayeux Tapestry* (London, 1957)

F. M. Stenton, *Anglo-Saxon England*, 3rd edn (Oxford, 1971)

E. Stone, "The Estates of Norwich Cathedral Priory during the Twelfth and Thirteenth Centuries" (Univ. of Oxford D.Phil. thesis, 1956)

E. Stone, "Profit-and-Loss Accountancy at Norwich Cathedral Priory", *Trans. of the Royal Hist. Soc.*, 5th series, xii (1962)

G. Stretton, "Some Aspects of Medieval Transport", *Trans. of the Royal Hist. Soc.*, 4th series, vii (1924)

R. H. Tawney, *The Agrarian Problem in the Sixteenth Century* (London, 1912)

J. Thirsk, *English Peasant Farming* (London, 1957)

J. Thirsk (ed.), *The Agrarian History of England and Wales*, iv (Cambridge, 1967)

J. Thirsk, "The Common Fields", in *Peasants, Knights and Heretics*, ed. R. H. Hilton (Cambridge, 1976)

J. Thirsk, *Horses in Early Modern England: for Service, for Pleasure, for Power* (Stenton Lecture, 1977) (Reading, 1978)

J. Z. Titow, "Some Differences between Manors and their Effects on the Condition of the Peasant in the Thirteenth Century", in *Essays in Agrarian History*, i, ed. W. E. Minchinton (Newton Abbot, 1968)

J. Z. Titow, *English Rural Society 1200–1350* (London, 1969)

J. Z. Titow, *Winchester Yields* (Cambridge, 1972)

R. Trow-Smith, *A History of British Livestock Husbandry to 1700* (London, 1957)

K. Ugawa, *Lay Estates in Medieval England* (Tokyo, 1966)

G. Unwin, *The Gilds and Companies of London* (London, 1908)

A. P. Usher, *A History of Mechanical Invention*, 2nd edn (Cambridge, Mass., 1954)

B. Vesey-Fitzgerald, *The Book of the Horse* (London, 1946)

Victoria County Histories

J. Vince, *Discovering Carts and Wagons* (Aylesbury, 1978)

P. Vinogradoff, *Villainage in England* (Oxford, 1892)

A. W. Wade-Evans, *Welsh Medieval Law* (Oxford, 1909)

B. Waites, *Moorland and Vale-land Farming in North-east Yorkshire*, Borthwich Papers, no. 32 (York, 1967)

D. Warriner, *The Economics of Peasant Farming* (Oxford, 1939)

R. E. M. Wheeler, *Maiden Castle, Dorset* (Oxford, 1943)

R. E. M. and T. V. Wheeler, *Verulamium: a Belgic and two Roman Cities* (Oxford, 1936)

Lynn White, Jr, *Medieval Technology and Social Change* (Oxford, 1962)

Lynn White Jr, "What Accelerated Technological Progress in the Western Middle Ages?", in *Scientific Change*, ed. A. C. Crombie (London, 1963)

Lynn White, Jr, *Medieval Religion and Technology* (Berkeley, 1978)

J. F. Willard, "Inland Transportation in England during the Fourteenth Century", *Speculum*, i (1926)

J. F. Willard, "The Use of Carts in the Fourteenth Century", *History*, xvii (1932)

J. F. Willard, *Parliamentary Taxes on Personal Property 1290 to 1334* (Cambridge, Mass., 1934)

B. F. Willetts, "The Performance of Footings on, and Cultivation Implements in, Soils" (Univ. of Durham Ph.D. thesis, 1954)

J. Williamson, "Peasant Holdings in Medieval Norfolk: A Detailed Investigation into Holdings of the Peasantry in Three Norfolk Villages in the Thirteenth Century" (Univ. of Reading Ph.D. thesis, 1976)

D. M. Wilson, "Anglo-Saxon Rural Economy", *Agric. Hist. Rev.* x (1962)

D. M. Wilson (ed.), *The Archaeology of Anglo-Saxon England* (London, 1976)

D. M. Wilson, *The Anglo-Saxons*, 3rd edn (Harmondsworth, Middlesex, 1981)

J. Wilson, *The Evolution of British Cattle* (London, 1909)

M. Wretts-Smith, "Organization of Farming at Croyland Abbey, 1257–1321", *Journal of Economic and Business History*, iv (1931–2)

Arthur Young, *The Farmer's Tour through the East of England*, 4 vols. (London, 1771)

Arthur Young, *A Six Months Tour through the North of England*, 2nd edn, 4 vols. (London, 1771)

Arthur Young, *Rural Oeconomy: Or, Essays on the Practical Parts of Husbandry*, 2nd edn (London, 1773)

Arthur Young, *Tours of England and Wales*, London School of Economics and Political Science, Reprint No. 14 (London, 1932)

Index

breeding: of horses, 4, 17–19, 290; of oxen, 17–18, 290; programmes in Italy in the fourteenth century, 19
Bretby (Derbyshire), 217
Bretforton (Worcestershire), 49
bridles, 16
Bristol, 117
Bristol Channel, 133
Britnell, R. H., 262
Broughton (Huntingdonshire), 226
Buckland Abbas (Dorset), 71
Bulbulcus, John, 70
Bulkere, John, 176, 179
bulls: as working stock, 86, 220; castration of, 293n
"bulls" of wood (for harrows), 141
"Bulney" (Suffolk), 71
Burstwick (Yorkshire), 115
Burton Abbey, 26, 38, 50
Burton, abbot of, 60
Burton (in Marnhull, Dorset), 227
Burton upon Trent (Staffordshire), 42, 50, 60
Butleigh (Somerset), 213

caballus, definition of, 295
Caddington (Bedfordshire), 185
Canterbury Cathedral Priory, 101
Canterbury (Kent), 76
carectarius, definition of, 296
Carlisle (Cumberland), 224
carra, *carrus*, etc.: as a two-wheeled vehicle hauled by oxen, 77, 152, 154, 222–4, 247; as a four-wheeled wagon hauled by horses, 152, 247; distribution of, 152, 248; having twice the carrying capacity of carts, 77, 152–3, 162, 247; in the twelfth century, 77; on demesnes, 114, 152–3; on peasant farms, 152, 213, 222–4, 247; size of hauling team for, 77, 152, 222, 223–4, 247; similar to the *plaustrum*, 79, 247
carrying services, *see* services
cart (*carecta*), 14, 49; as a two-wheeled vehicle hauled by horses, 60, 77, 143, 154, 156, 213, 214, 221–2, 225, 246–7; axle costs for, 150–1; "cart" hauled by oxen at Domesday, 49; construction of wheels for, 143; cost of wheels for, 151; distribution of, 142–3, 248; important for road transport, 76, 79, 114, 225; on demesnes, 114–15, 142–3, 150–1, 156–7; on peasant

farms, 213, 214, 221–2, 225, 246–7; partly replaced by ox-hauled vehicles after the Black Death, 115, 157; size of hauling team for, 221, 224–5, 247
cart-horses, 296; doubling as harrowing animals, 113–14; on demesnes, 60, 86, 95–6, 112n, 113–14, 115, 143, 156; on peasant farms, 174, 197–8, 200, 202–3
cart-saddles, 16
castration, of bulls to produce oxen, 293n
Cawood (Yorkshire), 151
Chalgrave (Bedfordshire), 216, 239
Chapellayne, John, 237
chariots, 8, 26
Chayanov, A. V., 74
Checkendon (Oxfordshire), 101
Cheriton (Hampshire), 105
Chiltern Hills, 100, 104, 168, 195, 256, 274, 275
Chisenbury (Wiltshire), 226
Clermont, Council of (1095), 20
climate: and the use of various plough types, 140; effect on the use of horses and oxen, 159, 160, 257
Clopton (Cambridgeshire), 49
coaches, Anglo-Saxon, 26
coach-loads, of 6,000 to 9,000 kilograms hauled by horses in the nineteenth century, 8
coal-mining, and the use of *plaustra*, 156
co-aration, 62–3, 69–72, 235–41
Cockfield, Adam of, 39
Colne (in Somersham, Huntingdonshire), 225
"commercialization theory", 285–8, 291
Continent, the: borrowing of techniques from, 53; effect upon the regional distribution of horses and oxen, 262, 264; influencing the use of demesne horses, 171
convertible husbandry, 278, 284
"corsours" (horse dealers), 273n
Cotswold Hills, 256
Cottingham (Nottinghamshire), 66
"Couhous" (Yorkshire), 151
Coulsdon (Surrey), 199
coulters, 244–5
"coup", 154
"coupwane", 154
"courtpot", 154
court rolls, 3, 81, 176, 196, 216, 223; as

324   *Index*

mules, 5, 8, 26, 27, 29, 42, 67, 86–7, 187

Nantwich (Cheshire), 49
Neckam, Alexander, 60, 78
neo-Malthusian argument, 276–9, 281
Nettleton (Wiltshire), 61, 70, 77, 229
Neweman, William le, 236
North Downs, 133
Northwich (Cheshire), 49
Northwick (Worcestershire), 71, 152
Norwich Cathedral Priory: profit-and-loss accountancy at, 170; switch to all-horse farming on demesnes of, 168–70

Oakham (Rutland), 104
occatorius, occator, definition of, 296
Offenham (Worcestershire), 49
Ohthere, 19
Old Weston (Huntingdonshire), 78
Ombersley (Worcestershire), 220
Ongar (Essex), 26
open fields, 175; various theories concerning the origins of, 62–3
Orwin, C. S. and C. S., 63
Ospringe (Kent), 60
ox-bows, 5
oxen: as recorded in accounts, heriots, etc., *see under* demesnes, peasant farms; black Welsh, 18; breeding of, 17–19, 290; cost of compared to horses, 96, 158–60, 251–2, 264; definition of, 293n; first harnessed, 4; for harrowing on demesnes (1200–1500), 114; for harrowing on peasant farms (1200–1500), 220; for harrows in the sixteenth century, 220; for hauling (general), 10, 20, 61, 162, 212, 270–1, 274, 276, 290; for hauling at Domesday, 49; for hauling in ancient times, 8; for hauling in Anglo-Saxon times, 22, 26–7, 49; for hauling in the twelfth century, 50, 59, 60–1, 77–9; for hauling on demesnes (1200–1500), 115, 151, 152–7, 171; for hauling on peasant farms, 222–5, 247–9; for ploughing (general), 38, 62, 63, 67, 68–9, 72, 75, 115, 158, 252, 266, 268, 274, 275; for ploughing at Domesday, 28, 31–3, 49; for ploughing in ancient times, 8; for ploughing in Anglo-Saxon times, 22, 26–7, 49; for ploughing in the twelfth century,

50–8, 61, 65–6, 70–1; for ploughing on demesnes (1200–1500), 105–12, 115, 119–23, 127, 155–6, 160–1, 167, 169, 170, 219; for ploughing on peasant farms (1200–1500), 213, 215–20, 228, 229–30, 231–4, 236, 238, 241; harrows for, 141–2, 220; in very large hauling teams, 10; numbers of versus horses at Domesday, 27–38; numbers of versus horses in Anglo-Saxon times, 22–4, 27; numbers of versus horses in the twelfth century, 38–48; numbers of versus horses on demesnes (1200–1500), 86–100; numbers of versus horses on peasant farms (1200–1500), 176–212; polarization in the use of in the fifteenth century, 97–9, 157, 210–12, 253, 274, 288; prices of, 200, 250–1; pulling power of versus horses, 21; red Devon, 18; regional variation in the use of (overall), 273–6; shoeing of, 17; speed, stamina and strength of (relative to horses), 2, 21, 160–4, 266–7; yokes for, 5, 6; yoked to carts and ploughs, 22; yoking by the horns, 5; yoking in file, 17; yoking as a relatively unchanged practice for oxen in the medieval period, 16–17

pack-horses, 86, 175, 265, 274, 287, 295, 296; as mentioned in peasant carrying services, 24, 56n, 60–1, 117, 213, 225–6, 228; at Domesday, 49, 227; distances covered, 225–6; equipment for, 226–7; in Anglo-Saxon times, 24, 26, 27; in the sixteenth and seventeenth centuries, 227; in the twelfth century, 50, 60, 61, 79; maximum load for, 116; methods of carrying by, 226–7; on demesnes (1200–1500), 116–17; on peasant farms (1200–1500), 213, 225–7, 228, 252; types of goods carried by, 117, 226; weights carried by, 226
pasture: and the distribution of horses and oxen, 257; importance of for oxen, 159, 171
Payne, F. G., 244
peasant farms: all-horse (in probate inventories), 210–12; all-horse plough-teams on, 195, 215, 216, 217, 219, 230–1, 231–4; all-ox plough-teams on, 58, 70–2, 213, 215, 216, 217, 218, 229–30, 231–4, 235–6, 238,

251; wine-hauling, 77
settlement type, and the distribution of
horses and oxen, 260–1
shares, asymetric, 244
Sherburn (Yorkshire), 157
Shirehampton (Gloucestershire), 229
Skidby (Yorkshire), 151
sled (*traha*), 78
smallholders, 175, 176–7, 193, 194–5,
196, 201–3, 203–4, 209, 213, 220, 227,
264, 271, 273, 291; and co-aration, 66,
237, 242, 243; carrying services by
vehicle among, 225; horses for hauling and harrowing among, 201; using
only horses for ploughing, 218; using
small plough-teams, 234–5, 242;
versatility of horses for, 218, 228–9;
versus substantial tenants in the use
of horses, 228–9, 252–3, 274, 283; *see
also* largeholders; middling holders
Smithfield (London), 273
soils: affecting the use of horses, 34–5,
159–60, 171; and plough-team size,
66, 242; and plough-team type, 53,
100–1; and plough type (wheeled,
foot or swing), 129; and the distribution of horses and oxen, 255–6;
effect upon the use of horses and oxen
according to Walter of Henley and
Fitzherbert, 100–1, 158; in Romney
Marsh, 101; lack of correlation with
levels of horses in heriots, 201; "pan"
(or subsoil) of Norfolk, 133
Solent, the, 107
Somerden Hundred (Kent), 107
Somersham (Huntingdonshire), 112
Sotterley (Suffolk), 32
Southampton brokage books, for horse
versus ox hauling, 271n
South Burton (Yorkshire), 151
South Kirby (Yorkshire), 187
Southwell (Nottinghamshire), 152
Spec, William, 38
speed, stamina and strength of horses
versus oxen: *see under horses; oxen*
steers, 220
Sterclesdene, Elvitha, 237
stirrup, as a technological innovation,
288
stock-and-land lease: at Domesday,
36n; in Anglo-Saxon times, 23, 38,
243; in the twelfth century, 39
Stogursey (Somerset), 152

Stoke sub Hamdon (Somerset), 230
stottus (or "stott"), definition of, 296–7
Street (Somerset), 238
stud farms (for horses), 26, 29, 40, 86
Sturminster Newton (Dorset), 228, 229
summarius, definition of, 296
Surlingham (Norfolk), 32
surveys and extents, 3, 38, 40–2, 46, 50,
64, 81–2, 118, 173–4, 213–14, 217–18,
223, 225, 227, 228, 230, 235–8, 240,
246–50
Swandrop (in Crondal, Hampshire),
237, 238

Tac, Robert, 227
Tana (Azov), 162
technical determinism, 288–90, 291
technological innovation: and
feudalism, 282; east to west spread of
on demesnes, 171; importance of in
early societies, 1; lack of early references to, 1; phases of, 4; variable
nature of, 171, 291; *see also* views of
technological innovation
Temple Ewell (Kent), 58, 60, 76
tentor, tenator (plough holder), 123,
164n
terrain: affecting the use of horses,
34–5, 160; and plough-team size, 66,
242; and plough-team type, 53; and
plough type (wheeled, foot or swing),
129; and the distribution of horses
and oxen, 256–7; lack of correlation
with levels of horses in heriots, 201
Theodosian Code, 8
Thirsk, J., 63
Thorner (Yorkshire), 239
Thorpe-le-Soken (Essex), 247
Thorpe Satchville (Leicestershire), 217,
229
three-field system; *see* two- and three-
field systems
Tinwell (Rutland), 66
Tothill, Richard de, 239
traces, 13–14
tradition, *see* local tradition
transport, road, 3, 20, 76, 79, 114, 225
Tredington (Worcestershire), 60
Troston (Suffolk), 26
tumbrel (*tumberellus*), 153–4, 249–50
two- and three-field systems, 280, 288;
and the distribution of horses and
oxen, 259–60

Past and Present Publications

General Editor: PAUL SLACK, *Exeter College, Oxford*

Family and Inheritance: Rural Society in Western Europe, 1200–1800, edited by Jack Goody, Joan Thirsk and E. P. Thompson*
French Society and the Revolution, edited by Douglas Johnson
Peasants, Knights and Heretics: Studies in Medieval English Social History, edited by R. H. Hilton*
Towns in Societies: Essays in Economic History and Historical Sociology, edited by Philip Abrams and E. A. Wrigley*
Desolation of a City: Coventry and the Urban Crisis of the Late Middle Ages, Charles Phythian-Adams
Puritanism and Theatre: Thomas Middleton and Opposition Drama under the Early Stuarts, Margot Heinemann*
Lords and Peasants in a Changing Society: The Estates of the Bishopric of Worcester 680–1540, Christopher Dyer
Life, Marriage and Death in a Medieval Parish: Economy, Society and Demography in Halesowen 1270–1400, Zvi Razi
Biology, Medicine and Society 1840–1940, edited by Charles Webster
The Invention of Tradition, edited by Eric Hobsbawm and Terence Ranger*
Industrialization before Industrialization: Rural Industry and the Genesis of Capitalism, Peter Kriedte, Hans Medick and Jürgen Schlumbohm†*
The Republic in the Village: The People of the Var from the French Revolution to the Second Republic, Maurice Agulhon†
Social Relations and Ideas: Essays in Honour of R. H. Hilton, edited by T. H. Aston, P. R. Coss, Christopher Dyer and Joan Thirsk
A Medieval Society: The West Midlands at the End of the Thirteenth Century, R. H. Hilton
Winstanley: 'The Law of Freedom' and Other Writings, edited by Christopher Hill
Crime in Seventeenth-Century England: A County Study, J. A. Sharpe†
The Crisis of Feudalism: Economy and Society in Eastern Normandy c. 1300–1550, Guy Bois†
The Development of the Family and Marriage in Europe, Jack Goody
Disputes and Settlements: Law and Human Relations in the West, edited by John Bossy
Rebellion, Popular Protest and the Social Order in Early Modern England, edited by Paul Slack
Studies on Byzantine Literature of the Eleventh and Twelfth Centuries, Alexander Kazhdan in collaboration with Simon Franklin†
The English Rising of 1381, edited by R. H. Hilton and T. H. Aston

Praise and Paradox: Merchants and Craftsmen in Elizabethan Popular Literature, Laura Caroline Stevenson
The Brenner Debate: Agrarian Class Structure and Economic Development in Pre-Industrial Europe, edited by T. H. Aston and C. H. E. Philpin
Eternal Victory: Triumphal Rulership in Late Antiquity, Byzantium, and the Early Medieval West, Michael McCormick†
East-Central Europe in Transition: From the Fourteenth to the Seventeenth Century, edited by Antoni Mączak, Henryk Samsonowicz and Peter Burke†
Small Books and Pleasant Histories: Popular Fiction and its Readership in Seventeenth-Century England, Margaret Spufford**
Society, Politics and Culture: Studies in Early Modern England, Mervyn James
Horses, Oxen and Technological Innovation: The Use of Draught Animals in English Farming 1066–1500, John Langdon

* Published also as a paperback
** Published only as a paperback
† Co-published with the Maison des Sciences de l'Homme, Paris

Printed in the United Kingdom
by Lightning Source UK Ltd.
115171UKS00001B/55